C000130113

WHO'S WHO
of
LINCOLN CITY
1892-1994

By
Donald & Ian
Nannestad

Published by:
Yore Publications
12 The Furrows, Harefield,
Middx. UB9 6AT.

© Donald & Ian Nannestad 1994

....

All rights reserved. No part of this publication may be reproduced or copied in any manner without the prior permission in writing of the copyright holder.

British Library Cataloguing-in-Publication Data.
A catalogue record for this book
is available from the British Library.

ISBN 1 874427 90 9

Yore Publications specialise in football books, normally of an historic theme.
Newsletters (which detail all current and new titles) are posted free, three times per year.
Please send a S.A.E. for your initial copy of the latest Newsletter.

Printed by 'The Book Factory'

THE AUTHORS

Donald Nannestad is a 36 year old journalist who has worked for the last nine years for *Raymonds Press Agency* in Lincoln. He previously worked for the *Lincolnshire Chronicle* and the *Sheffield Morning Telegraph*. He is a Lincoln City Councillor for Castle Ward and has followed Lincoln City since 1966.

His brother **Ian** was born at North Hykeham, near Lincoln, in 1957 and now works as a teacher at Tindal JI School in Balsall Heath, Birmingham, having previously been employed for 11 years by the Inland Revenue. He has followed the Imps since attending his first match at Sincil Bank in April 1966.

ACKNOWLEDGEMENTS

The authors wish to express their sincere gratitude to Doug Lamming who provided a first draft covering 80 per cent of the players and whose assistance throughout has been of great value. Many others have helped provide leads and details including Jim Creasy and Mike Davage (who both provided early assistance to Doug), Kathryn Anderson (granddaughter of James Livingstone), Harry Berry, Denis Clarebrough, Bill Cooke, B.W. Day, David Downs, Terry Frost, Seamus Heath, Trefor Jones, Dawn Maidment (granddaughter of Tom Maidment), Alan & Hazel Moore (re Isaac Moore), Ray Simpson, Bryan Stainton, Ken Trushell, Keith Warsop and Lars-Olof Wendler. The staff at the Local Studies Collection, Lincoln Central Library, the British Newspaper Library, Colindale, and Manchester Central Library all provided valuable help as did the staff at the Football League.

PHOTOGRAPHIC ACKNOWLEDGEMENTS

Photographs supplied from the Doug Lamming Collection, from the Lincolnshire Local Studies Collection, by courtesy of Lincolnshire County Council Recreational Services, Libraries, and the Lincolnshire Echo.

Donald Nannestad
Ian Nannestad

October 1994

Publisher's note: Many of the players' photographs have been taken either from very old team groups (of variable quality) or have required considerable enlargement from original modern squad or team groups. Consequently, in some cases, the quality of reproduction has suffered to a certain degree.

CONTENTS

*T*he modern game of football in Lincoln dates back to the early 1860's when the first local club was established. The Lincoln Football Club was one of the strongest English provincial sides in the late 1860's competing on equal terms with the Nottingham and Sheffield clubs. They had strong links with the Lindum Cricket Club and from 1871 the two were merged under the official title 'The Lincoln Cricket and Football Club', although the footballers soon became known as 'Lincoln Lindum' or just 'Lindum'. This team drew most of its members from amongst the upper classes - many of its players had been to public schools such as Marlborough, Eton and Rugby and several were employed in the legal profession. Ordinary working people found it difficult to participate in organised leisure activities and it was only when the local engineering works brought forward their Saturday half-holiday from 2.30pm to 12.30pm in 1872 that football began to involve a wider section of the population. One of the first and most prominent of the new clubs to emerge was the Recreation club, formed by clerks from several local engineering works who played on the Cowpaddle, adjacent to Robey's foundry.

In 1881 the Lincolnshire Football Association was formed but its strongest teams were found away from the county town and Spilsby won the first three Challenge Cup competitions. Civic pride and memories of the Lindum club's former pre-eminence seem to have inspired the Lincolnshire Chronicle's football writer ('Goalkeeper') to raise an important question in October 1883 : *"Is it not possible to form a Lincoln F.A. (similar to Sheffield and other towns) and to play a collective Lincoln team against all comers?"* The idea was taken up during the season and on a couple of occasions the Lindum and Rovers (the name adopted by Recreation in 1879) played a combined team against better class opposition. The matter was taken a step further in the summer of 1884 when two local football enthusiasts, Cllr Sharpley Bainbridge and William Mortimer, organised a series of public meetings at the Monsons Arms Hotel, then situated at the top of High Street. At the second of these, held on 5 July, the Lincoln City Football Club was established. Its objectives were threefold: to improve football in the City, to win the Lincolnshire Cup and to do well in the F.A. Cup. An enclosed ground at the rear of John O'Gaunts stables had already been hired and the club made its headquarters at the Blue Anchor public house, adopting the old Rovers' colours of red and white striped shirts.

The very first match was played at home to Sleaford on 4 October 1884 resulting in a 9-1 victory and the inaugural season was moderately successful - 14 of the 26 games played were won and the team progressed to the third round of both the Lincolnshire and F.A. Cup competitions. Perhaps more importantly the new club attracted large numbers of spectators with often up to 1,000 attending ordinary home games. The circumstances in which the club had been formed led to some ambiguity as to the actual nature of the new organisation. Those connected with the Rovers had disbanded their own club and concentrated all their efforts into building Lincoln City, perhaps due to the fact that two of their number - Jack Strawson (secretary) and William Mortimer (treasurer) had gained important positions.

Another body of feeling, generally represented by those with Lindum connections, believed the City club should merely serve as a representative team for Lincoln and in the summer of 1885 Lindum approached City with a view to fielding a combined team in the Lincolnshire Cup. They were rejected and for a short while the two contested local supremacy. Lindum cut their links with the cricket club and hired a field on the opposite side of the Sincil Drain to John O'Gaunts - probably a little to the north of the present Sincil Bank ground. Both arranged quality fixtures and Lindum actually reached the county cup final in 1885/86, losing to Grimsby Town. However, this was to prove the peak of their achievements for they were unable to compete against City's greater resources and soon declined, moving back uphill and continuing in various guises as a 'pure' amateur team until 1939.

The City club meanwhile went from strength to strength. In September 1885 they recruited Joe Duckworth from Blackburn Olympic as a professional player-coach and after strengthening their team with more players from Lancashire they reached the last 16 of the F.A. Cup in 1886/87 before losing 3-0 away to Glasgow Rangers. They also reached the final of the Lincolnshire Cup where they met Grimsby Town on the neutral venue of the Northolme, Gainsborough. The 1,700 visitors from Lincoln were outnumbered in a crowd of 7,500, but City drew the first match 2-2 and went on to take the trophy three weeks later with a 2-0 victory. A large crowd gathered at the railway station to meet the heroes on their return and there were great celebrations.

This early success was not developed and after early exits from the F.A. Cup in the following two seasons there was mounting criticism of the club committee. After a public meeting in November 1888 two major policy changes were agreed. A revised constitution would be introduced allowing a greater involvement of the working men who formed the bulk of the club's support and the committee would follow the example of near neighbours Grimsby Town and strengthen the team with 'imported' professionals from Scotland. The F.A. rules on the eligibility of professional players were quite stringent at the time and the club had to maintain that the four men signed - Quinten Neill (Queens Park), Harry Millar (Airdrieonians), Humphrey Barbour (Third Lanark) and Hugh McPhee (Hibernian) - had arrived in Lincoln by chance to seek employment.

Fundamental changes were taking place in the wider football world at this time with the formation of the Football League by 12 of the country's leading clubs and in response a group of 20 lesser clubs, including City, set up the Football Combination. The competition proved to have very little organisation and folded after just one season with the Imps moving on to the newly formed Midland League in 1889/90. The opposition did not really extend City's team which was now made up almost entirely of imported professionals, and they finished champions with ease losing just two of the 20 games played. The professional players of this time were part-time only and most worked in the local foundries during the day, training in the evenings. Committee member William Flatters later recalled how they kept the players in shape for important matches : *"... we used to take great precautions to keep the players from the temptations of going to dances or public houses and keeping late hours. We used to have the players at Mr Strawson's house* [Strawson's Dining Rooms at St. Marks] *in the evening, keeping them interested with card games, and finishing by giving them a plate of porridge each. Then several of us were appointed to take them home"*.

There followed a further season in the Midland League and one in the much stiffer Football Alliance before the club was accepted as a founder-member of the newly formed Second Division of the Football League in May 1892. The committee took steps to strengthen the side signing new men and increasing the wages paid from 15 shillings (75p) to 30 shillings (£1.50) a week, but despite this the team were bottom of the table by October. Veteran Welsh international defender Bob Roberts was recruited as player-coach and performances began to improve, the final position of fourth from bottom meant they had to apply for re-election but this proved a formality.

The club suffered a major blow in the autumn of 1894 with the death of Robert Dawber who owned the John O'Gaunts field and the subsequent decision of his executors to sell the land for building purposes.

It was decided to take over the Stamp End Cricket Club ground on Sincil Bank and in anticipation of the heavy expenditure required to develop the surroundings which were little more than an open field it was agreed to form a limited company. The Lincoln City Football Club Limited was incorporated in October 1895 and shortly afterwards a paid secretary, the sports journalist Alf Martin, was appointed.

Martin was a very able man who produced many innovative ideas, including the setting up of a Working Men's Committee which was to serve the club as a volunteer workforce and supporters organisation for over 30 years. However, his year as secretary-manager was mostly a disaster both on and off the field and the club was near to collapse by the time he left. In the reorganisation that followed James West took over as secretary on an honorary basis with Jack Strawson, now a director, assisting him. Together they slowly worked to improve the financial situation and eventually the playing strength too. They followed a policy of signing quality players who were a little past their prime - men such as Will Gibson, once of Sunderland's Team of All the Talents, and Welsh international winger David Pugh, and by the turn of the century the club was returned to a sound footing.

West departed for Newton Heath and was replaced by Notts County's David Calderhead who became secretary-manager. The next few seasons were probably the best in the club's history. The team were almost invincible at home and in 1901/02 achieved their best ever performances in both the League (5th in Division Two) and F.A. Cup (last 16 of the competition). More importantly gates were up - receipts from the F.A. Cup visit of Derby County in February 1902 topped £400, and the City Council even discussed the need to build an extra bridge over the Sincil Drain to cater for the volume of spectators using the ground on match days.

In 1902/03 the team mounted a strong challenge for promotion, leading the Division Two table for a brief time, but a string of injuries to key players eventually saw them drift back to a mid-table position. However, over the next few seasons it increasingly became the case that the best players had to be sold to ensure financial stability. The club slipped into the bottom two at the end of 1906/07 and although they were successfully re-elected Calderhead moved on to take the secretary-manager's job at Chelsea, a club with almost limitless financial resources. Jack Strawson took over again, but the team suffered from a bad run of injuries and loss of form, not helped by the decision of star winger Norrie Fairgray to follow his old boss to Stamford Bridge. Attendances fell and the board were forced to cut wages and play amateurs to keep costs down. They finished bottom of the table and failed to secure re-election against strong competition from several Southern League clubs.

The Imps returned to the Midland League for the 1908/09 campaign, winning the competition with ease, although there was little public interest and gates were so low that admission prices were dropped mid-way through the season. Unlike in the 1890's, many of the players were now full-time or at least training every day and a typical week's routine from February 1909 makes interesting reading:

Monday -   day off; injuries from Saturday's match treated.
Tuesday -   morning - a brisk walk with sweaters on covering a distance of nine or ten miles, perhaps to Hykeham or Waddington.
               afternoon - ball practice, shooting, kicking, dribbling, corners.
Wednesday -   morning as Tuesday morning.
               afternoon sprinting; if wet indoor work including ball punching and Indian clubs followed by cold showers.
Thursday -   morning as Tuesday morning.
               afternoon indoor work as Wednesday afternoon.
Friday -   easy day checking boots and equipment.

The competition for League places was not so stiff at the League's 1909 AGM and City were successful in the ballot, replacing Chesterfield. However, two mediocre seasons followed with the performances particularly dismal in 1910/11 when the Imps finished bottom of the League for the second time in four years and were once again voted out. Exploratory moves to form a new Third Division in the summer of 1911 did not come to anything so the team were entered in the newly formed Central League which was mostly made up of the reserve teams of Football League clubs.

It proved a wise move for attendances remained steady and after a slow start the team went on to win the championship, well clear of their nearest challengers Burslem Port Vale. The competition was so popular that the Working Men's Committee held a ballot of the supporters to decide whether the club should seek re-admittance to the Second Division. The vote confirmed that higher grade status should be sought and the campaign leading up to the League AGM was well planned with an appeal circulated to all clubs beforehand and the introduction of a new face - John Foster Fraser, the prospective Unionist (Conservative) Candidate for the Lincoln Parliamentary seat - as spokesman in place of Strawson. The moves proved highly successful and League membership was regained at the expense of county rivals Gainsborough Trinity.

The team was not greatly strengthened on their return but even so the board had to pay out £900 to 'sign' existing players whose Football League registrations were held by their former clubs. They had a fine start and briefly led the table in October only to drift away to finish 10th. Gates were up to an average of around 10,000 and the grandstands were enlarged to cater for the extra interest. However, the following season was much more in line with City's performances of the mid-1900's. The best two players - centre forward Donald Slade and goalkeeper Tommy Fern - were sold for large fees, performances suffered and the team finished up in the re-election zone. This time the influential Athletic News mounted a strong campaign against Lincoln and in favour of Stoke, but City made great play of the fact that they had only been required to seek re-election because of goal average and successfully fought off the challenge. War broke out in August 1914 and although football continued for one more season it did so in an unreal atmosphere.

When the players travelled to Leicester for the opening fixture they had to make their way through a large crowd which had gathered to meet wounded soldiers returning from the continent. Attendances were down everywhere and the presence of khaki clad soldiers, wounded or on leave, was noted at most games. Considerable pressure was applied to the football authorities and it was no surprise when they agreed to suspend the League competition in July 1915.

When peacetime football returned in 1919/20 the Imps were ill-prepared, administrative affairs having been left to the directors over the close season following Jack Strawson's retirement. The team struggled early on and fortunes did not improve, while the board tested the supporters' loyalty by switching the home F.A. Cup tie with Middlesbrough to Ayresome Park for a cash payment of £800. They failed to avoid re-election after losing a vital match against fellow contenders Coventry City and although the local Conservative MP, Alfred Davies, was engaged to speak on the club's behalf at the League AGM, City lost their membership for the third time in 13 years. Later, in 1923, the directors of Bury and Coventry were found to have fixed the result of a match between the two teams which had an important bearing on the final table but it was too late for further action.

A season of Midland League football followed before it was confirmed in March 1921 that a northern section of the Third Division was to be formed, with Lincoln one of 14 clubs accepted as a group, the remaining four places being filled by ballot. The launch of the Northern Section coincided with the start of an economic slump and a growth in unemployment which together created severe problems for a number of clubs. Costs were high, partly because the widespread location of the teams meant long and expensive journeys to away games and often overnight stops. City were better off than some but despite selling two of their best players for large fees they still made a loss of £1500 on the 1921/22 campaign. Although steps were taken to try and reduce the deficit, matters reached crisis point in February 1923 following a run of costly away trips separated by a single home fixture. Chairman Cornelius Taylor reported debts of more than £3000 and the club was only kept alive after an agreement was reached with the players to cut wages. Those unwilling to accept this were given the option of a £10 payment in lieu of two weeks' money. Several players left the following week and three more were sold - McGrahan and 'Yaffer' Ward to Wigan Borough and Bob Fenwick to Notts County - leaving just 15 professionals.

Further trouble loomed when the team lost 7-1 at Durham and the supporters boycotted the next Saturday's return encounter, reducing the attendance to less than 2,000. The Football League offered assistance and two senior Management Committee figures - John Lewis and Charles Sutcliffe - visited the city for a public meeting in March out of which came a new supporters' club and plans to raise £1000 to cover the summer wages bill. The financial position dominated club policy over the next few seasons with the better players sold to raise money to the detriment of the team's performances and it was not until 1926 that the balance sheet was returned to credit.

The purse strings were eased in the summer of 1926 and several new players, including veteran 'keeper Albert Iremonger and bustling centre-forward Billy Dinsdale, were signed. League performances were poor however, and although the team made it to the third round of the F.A. Cup a decision by the directors to raise admission prices for the visit of Second Division Preston North End kept the attendance down to just 6,700. A record loss of £2583 was made prompting a further sale of players so that summer wages could be paid. Harry Parkes was appointed secretary-manager for the 1927/28 season and he led the team to runners-up position, their best performance since the Great War.

There was a real belief that promotion back to the Second Division was now possible and there were record season ticket sales in the following close season but the only success came in the F.A. Cup where the first two rounds were negotiated for the third year in succession. A record attendance of 16,849 was attracted for the visit of Leicester City, but the Imps went down 1-0 to a goal four minutes from time and there was a tragic aftermath when Bosbury, who had risen from his sick bed to play, fell ill again never to recover health. He passed away on 14 July that year.

In September of 1929 a serious fire gutted the South Park stand destroying the offices and all the club records. This was quickly overcome and in a matter of weeks a new structure seating 1,500 was opened.

At the same time the board purchased their Sincil Bank home for £4875 from the club's landlords thus removing the main obstacle to the modernisation of the ground. Despite these off the field troubles the Imps had finished fifth in 1929/30, and after losing the opening game of the following campaign proceeded to establish a glorious run of 10 consecutive victories which took them to the top of the table. A strong challenge was mounted for the championship with the decider coming at Saltergate on 22 April against close rivals Chesterfield. In front of a 20,000 crowd City missed a late penalty and went down 3-2 and so finished runners-up for the second time in four years.

After failing by the narrowest of margins Parkes made several changes to his playing staff during the summer of 1931, his most significant venture in the transfer market being a decision to sign Bradford City's reserve strike force of Allan Hall and Frank Keetley. The team began the new season almost exactly the same as they had done 12 months previously, winning nine of the first ten games. They led the table for much of the campaign and although pushed closely by Gateshead on the run-in, the title was clinched with a 0-0 draw against Wrexham in the penultimate match. The game was filmed and shown at a local cinema, The Exchange, throughout the following week. The team's success owed a great deal to Hall's goalscoring feats and his totals of 42 in League games and 52 in all competitions were both club records.

The club was optimistic on their return to Division Two. The sound financial position enabled them to make several new signings and further improvements were made to the ground when the old St. Andrews stand was demolished and replaced with a modern construction. Despite this the team soon slipped down the table and it was only when the defence was strengthened early in the new year with the purchase of Bill Dodgin and George Mathison that they began to move towards safety. The cost of this first season back in higher grade football was a loss of £2,560, forcing the sale of Hall to Tottenham for a club record fee of £3,000. The team was weakened by his loss and struggled badly during the 1933/34 campaign with relegation being confirmed following a 3-0 defeat at Oldham at the beginning of April.

Training methods had changed from those of the Edwardian period and appear quite modern in some respects. The day began shortly before 10 o'clock when the players had to sign the attendance book. Individual attention was given by trainer Ted Wynter and his assistant Dan Ludkin and the men might be sprinting, doing gym work - such as ball punching or skipping, or engaging in ball practise during the mornings. Afternoon training began at 2 o'clock but was only done in the early part of the week when it consisted of sprints followed by massages.

Soda baths and massages were given regularly but hot baths were avoided because it was felt they weakened the players. Friday was a light day with only a few sprints in the morning. Attention was now being paid to diet and a pre-match meal of dry toast, tea and a small portion of boiled mutton or boiled fish was eaten two hours before kick off. The players were also expected to keep themselves in shape, refrain from smoking and to be in bed by 11 o'clock in midweek.

Relegation back to the Northern Section only made the deteriorating financial situation worse, the income falling as average attendances dropped by 2,000. The annual deficit continued to run into four figures and sensational press reports appeared suggesting the club might fold. The immediate crisis was eased somewhat by September 1936 with the sale of the Watson brothers to Chesterfield and Eire international Con Moulson to Notts County which together raised well over £2000. Joe McClelland replaced Harry Parkes as secretary-manager, and he succeeded in mounting a serious challenge for the championship in 1936/37. The decider came at Edgeley Park in the final match of the season with City needing both points for the title. The defence held out for an hour but then Stockport scored two controversial goals and the 2-0 victory earned them the single promotion place available. It was around this time that the Imps played their first games abroad, both in the Netherlands. In January 1936 they were beaten 4-2 in Rotterdam by the Dutch 'B' team and two years later they played the full national side losing 5-0 in what was a warm-up match for their opponents in preparation for the 1938 World Cup finals.

War had threatened for some time however, and was finally declared with the 1939/40 season just three matches old. There was no repeat of the events of 1914 as the League reacted immediately to suspend the competition and the football world did not return to normal for another seven years. The players' contracts were scrapped for the duration of the hostilities and they appeared for a standard match fee, initially 30 shillings (£1.50), with no bonuses. In 1941/42, City's team made up of guests, former players and a few remaining pre-war men did remarkably well in the season's first championship of the emergency War League North. Eight of the opening nine games were won and they finished runners-up to Blackpool on goal average, being well clear of many of the region's bigger clubs including Manchester United, Everton and Liverpool.

Although football returned to a peacetime format in 1946 the game took a while to return to normal in the austere conditions of post-war Britain. The club had to collect sufficient clothing coupons to obtain new playing kit and there were no season tickets available in 1946/47. A lengthy period of bad weather and restrictions on midweek fixtures left City playing their final match at Bradford City on 14 June.

During the summer Bill Anderson was appointed as the club's first manager and although new players were signed the board continued their policy of operating only with part-time professionals, the players working during the day and training in the evenings. Despite losing to non-League opposition in the F.A. Cup the team rose to head the table by December. They stayed there more or less until Easter Monday when Rotherham took over. The two met at Millmoor in the season's penultimate fixture which City won 2-0 and the scenes of celebration which followed at the Stonebow were said to have been reminiscent of those on VE Day. The following week the title was clinched with a 5-0 victory over Hartlepools, and City were back in Division Two.

The club prepared for higher grade football by laying down concrete terracing on the Sincil Bank side but there were no moves to strengthen the team and the majority of players were still part-timers. It was soon clear that they were not strong enough and although Jock Dodds was purchased for a hefty fee of £6,000 the team continued to struggle badly. Off the field there was dissent amongst the shareholders and opposition to the policy of using part-timers led to the resignation of both the chair and vice-chair by Christmas. In the new year a sum of £25,000, a huge amount for the time, was made available to buy new players but to no avail as the team never rose off the bottom of the table.

New chairman Charles Applewhite promised the Imps would be back within three years and Anderson set out to build a team to achieve this. After early setbacks - former England international inside-forward Jackie Robinson had his career ended by a broken leg shortly after signing and then Dodds was banned from League football because of his involvement with a scheme to recruit players for South America - the forward line was re-shaped at the start of 1950/51 with the signing of Preston's Johnny Garvie and 23 year-old Andy Graver from Newcastle. Their partnership was an instant success, yielding 40 goals in its first season.

The 1951/52 campaign began with some spectacular scoring feats including successive home victories over Darlington (7-2) and Crewe Alexandra (11-1, a new club record) and by December the team were top of the table. The board showed their full commitment to promotion by acting quickly to sign full-back Doug Graham, after Varney suffered a bad injury at Wrexham on Christmas Day. Although top for five months they never pulled clear and the title was not clinched until the last but one fixture when Stockport County were defeated 2-1 at Sincil Bank, with 'keeper Jimmy Jones brilliantly saving a penalty kick in the closing minutes. It had been a season of club records and both the number of points gained (69) and goals scored (121) were the highest in the Imps' history.

Promotion paved the way for an uninterrupted period of nine seasons in Division Two, the club's second longest unbroken spell in higher grade football since entering the League. The fact that they survived so long is testimony to the quality of the players who won the Northern Section title, to Anderson's ability to make the best use of limited resources and at times to a degree of good fortune. Attendances rose sharply - the average for 1952/53 was 16,774 - even though the team were usually in the lower reaches of the table and there were few changes from the championship side.

Graver was sold to Leicester in December 1954 but the side was not significantly weakened and he returned the following summer as part of a string of transfer deals made by Anderson. The 1955/56 season began with three consecutive victories, defeat at Hull followed, but a 7-1 thrashing of Leicester City took the Imps to the top of the Second Division for the first time in 40 years. Their stay lasted less then a week but they remained in a healthy position, finishing the season in eighth place, the club's best performance since 1912/13.

The run of good form continued at the start of 1956/57 but a series of defeats soon pulled the team back to the more familiar reaches of the lower half of the table. A shock 5-4 defeat by Midland League Peterborough United in the F.A. Cup was followed by a serious loss of form in League matches. Gates dropped below 10,000 on a regular basis for the first time since 1946/47 and the club were forced to sell their England under-23 international Dick Neal to Birmingham. The Peterborough defeat and the sale of Neal were to mark a dividing point after which the Imps were rarely free from relegation worries. Anderson signed the skilful George Hannah the following September but the team rapidly slipped towards the foot of the table, suffering a series of heavy defeats and producing some very poor displays.

Although new men were brought in, relegation appeared inevitable after a home defeat by Barnsley on Easter Monday left the side five points adrift at the bottom with only six games to play. Victory at Oakwell the next day provided the first win since early December. Further wins over Doncaster, Rotherham, Bristol City and Huddersfield followed and they went into the final match at home to Cardiff City needing a point for safety. An 18,000 crowd saw the visitors take a lead early in the second half but City came back to win 3-1 and achieve what had seemed impossible three weeks earlier. The narrow escape had cost the club £27,000 in transfer fees, contributing to a loss on the season of £14,000, which prompted the board to announce that a tighter watch would be kept on finances in the coming year.

The team rarely rose above the bottom two positions in 1958/59 and again went into the last match needing points to ensure safety. They lost, but so did the

three teams below them and they therefore escaped the drop. The lack of cash available for transfer fees led Anderson to try and develop some of the teenagers on the club's books and players such as Roger Holmes and Brian Drysdale were given a chance, but although they survived comfortably in 1959/60 they were bottom for most of the following season and in May 1961 were finally relegated to the Third Division.

There was little money available for Anderson to rebuild the team and the deteriorating financial situation demanded that two of the better players - Roy Chapman and John McClelland - must be sold. The lifting of the maximum wage led to the board introducing a new pay structure whereby the players received a lower basic sum of £18 a week, which could be increased with bonuses paid for results (£4 win; £2 draw), position in the table (£2 for top 6; an extra £4 for top 2) and the size of the attendance (£2 if the gate topped 9,000). The team got off to a poor start, winning just one of their eight League games and despite a number of changes to personnel there was no recovery. They went into the final two matches needing maximum points to have a chance of escaping relegation but a disastrous 5-0 home defeat by Queens Park Rangers saw them drop into the Fourth Division for the first time ever. The 1961/62 season also saw the introduction of floodlights to Sincil Bank, the bulk of the money being raised by the supporters' club which had launched an appeal back in August 1960.

The Imps began their Fourth Division career relatively brightly, winning seven of their first eight home games. However, a prolonged period of bad weather meant that the team did not play at Sincil Bank at all during January and February and the subsequent disruption to cash flow provoked a serious financial crisis. The club were already heavily in debt and with no reserves of money to draw upon the board were forced to put two club houses up for sale. The situation was exacerbated because the secretary was off sick and, as it was later discovered, the administrative affairs - including financial records - were drifting into chaos with at least one court case outstanding for unpaid debts.

When football resumed in March attendances plummeted to below 3,500 and a poor run of results left the team in a bottom four position, thus necessitating the first re-election bid since 1920. The League AGM proved no problem with City gaining 47 of a maximum 48 votes, but later in the summer there were major changes to the board with local builder Cllr. Frank Eccleshare taking over as chairman. He did so on his own terms which gave him full authority over the running of the club and allowed him to bring in his accountant Roy Chapman (no relation to the player of the same name) as a financial director. A thorough investigation of the books revealed the seriousness of the situation and immediate steps were taken to reduce the number of creditors and set matters on a more businesslike footing. The team had a brief revival in 1963/64, finishing in 8th position and reaching the third round of the F.A. Cup. A crowd of 18,734 was attracted for the visit of First Division Sheffield United who ended up 4-0 winners, but the day nearly ended in tragedy after a bridge over the Sincil Drain collapsed when crowded with fans leaving the match. Although over 70 people fell into the mud below there were fortunately no serious injuries.

Anderson was effectively removed as manager in September 1964 when team selection was taken from him, but he remained with the club as 'general manager' until his contract expired in October 1966. The next two seasons were particularly dispiriting with gates at their lowest level since 1925 when official records began and the club needing to seek re-election on both occasions.

One of the many changes introduced by Eccleshare was the establishment of a Youth Development Committee in January 1964. The club had been seeking to develop young players from the late 1950's and although Roger Holmes and one or two fringe first team players had emerged there was no formal structure to promote talent. The 'A' team was withdrawn from the Lincolnshire League at a saving of £3,500 and entered with a colts team (the Pilgrims) in a local league. An organised apprenticeship scheme was begun and this soon produced Tom Brooks and Phil Hubbard. The committee existed until May 1967 when the club management again took over the running of the youth team.

Ron Gray had become manager in October 1966 and although he commenced the slow task of rebuilding the side there was no quick change of fortunes and the Imps finished the 1966/67 season bottom of the table, making a grim sequence of six years out of seven when they had either been relegated or required to seek re-election. Eccleshare stepped down in the summer of 1967 due to pressure of work and the club was effectively re-launched for the start of the new campaign with new team colours, a revamped programme, new players - only a handful of those on the books 12 months earlier remained - and a new nickname - the "Red Imps".

For the first time in almost a decade, pride was restored to City's colours with the team having a fine run in the League Cup, disposing of First Division Newcastle United 2-1 - only the second time since the war that top flight opposition had been defeated in a major cup competition. They eventually went out to Derby County in a fourth round replay which attracted a new ground record attendance of 23,196 to Sincil Bank. The Imps finished 13th in the Fourth Division table and followed this with a top 10 position in each of the following two seasons, by which time the troubles of the early '60's were firmly

behind them. However, boardroom changes in the spring of 1970 saw Collingham farmer Heneage Dove installed as chairman and soon afterwards Gray was sacked. There was talk in the press of either Pat Crerand or David Herd, both former Manchester United stars, coming to Sincil Bank, but Gray's replacement was the club trainer Bert Loxley. The Imps started brightly but then dropped back towards a bottom four position and Loxley was eased aside to be replaced by Herd.

There was no dramatic improvement in results despite the introduction of new tactics, including the use of a sweeper, and the club were forced to seek re-election yet again in the summer of 1971. Herd brought in a number of new faces and the reshaped team mounted a strong challenge for promotion in 1971/72. Gates were up too and a crowd of 16,498 saw the Imps beat Scunthorpe 1-0 in the local 'derby' encounter - the highest League attendance at Sincil Bank for 13 years. Unfortunately the team faltered in the final weeks of the campaign, winning just two of their final nine games and so failing to go up by a margin of two points. Their prospects also looked promising in 1972/73 until the team suffered a loss of form in October. Herd seemed unable to reverse the trend and with growing talk of a crisis developing he was sacked in December.

The new manager was 28 year-old Graham Taylor who was destined for a great future in the game. However, his early days proved difficult and it was not until 28 February, three months after he had taken over, that the Imps won again. The team was slowly reshaped with several senior players eased out and new men brought in. A comfortable mid-table position was achieved in the next two seasons before a strong challenge for promotion was mounted in 1974/75. Prospects look excellent until March but after this the side struggled to win - only four victories were recorded in the final 15 matches - and they approached the final match at Southport needing to win to go up. They lost 3-2 and stayed down on goal average. The setback proved to be only temporary, and the following season saw the Imps play some superb football, destroying opponents with ease.

At one point 11 consecutive League and Cup games were won, and this time there was no faltering in the closing matches, with the title clinched in style after a 5-0 victory over Doncaster Rovers. In addition to the Fourth Division championship the team also reached the third round of the League Cup and the fourth round of the F.A. Cup. It had been a memorable season with several new records set including the highest ever points total (74) in League history and the most wins (32) and fewest defeats (4) by a Division Four club. Five of the players - Peter Grotier, Ian Branfoot, Sam Ellis, Terry Cooper and John Ward - were selected for the PFA's Fourth Division team. Taylor stayed another season before moving on to a lucrative £25,000 a year contract at

Watford. His spell as manager had also encompassed off the field achievements, notably with the development of a solid youth policy and the building of links with the community and local businesses.

The Sheffield-based nursery outfit he established was to produce a number of players for Colin Murphy's teams of the late 1970's and early 1980's. The links with local industry were part of a wider trend in the game to find income from alternative sources to supplement dwindling gate receipts. Although the actual amount raised was quite small, it was possible by the mid-1970's to sponsor the players' kit, the match ball and travel to away games as well as the long standing practices of advertising in the programme and around the ground. Donations from the Red Imps Association and the supporters' club were also important sources of income, although money from the latter ceased briefly from June 1973 after a dispute with the board.

George Kerr, Taylor's former assistant, was promoted to manager but there was little money available for new signings and the squad was further depleted when key players Dennis Booth and Sam Ellis joined their former boss at Vicarage Road. Kerr introduced several youngsters to League football but results were poor and he was sacked just before Christmas. His successor Willie Bell steered the team to safety in 1977/78 but then started the following season in particularly dismal fashion and after a run of 13 games without a win he too departed.

A brief interim period followed before the directors appointed Colin Murphy, a 34 year-old Londoner who had spent several years working with Dave Mackay at Nottingham Forest and Derby. It was already too late to save the team from relegation and the poor sequence of results continued with gates dropping to below 2,000. Murphy rebuilt the side and despite selling top striker Mick Harford for a record £180,000 fee they returned to Division Three two years later. Promotion was gained with ease and the team established a new Fourth Division record by conceding only 25 goals. After a short period of adjustment, the team put together a superb run of results in the early part of 1982 and in the final match of the season they needed to defeat Fulham at Craven Cottage to regain the Second Division place they had lost 21 years earlier. In front of a 20,000 crowd, including 5,000 from Lincoln, City were reduced to 10 men after Steve Thompson was sent off for a second bookable offence and despite plenty of pressure they could only draw 1-1. Any mathematical possibility of going up disappeared the following evening when Carlisle won at Chester to take the remaining promotion slot. A number of factors including increased bonus payments, a deficit in the transfer market and a substantial loss incurred by a Country and Western Music festival combined to produce a record loss of £259,000 on the 1981/82 season. The board reacted immediately by selling the ground to the City Council for £225,000, with a lease back arrangement ensuring the club remained at their Sincil Bank home.

They also proposed a cut in bonus payments of around 45%, but the PFA and Football League intervened to ensure the existing agreement remained in force until the players accepted an 8% cut in October. With several other clubs involved in similar disputes the case attracted widespread media coverage and City's troubles provided a focus for a programme by ITV's 'TV Eye'. Meanwhile the playing staff was reduced to the absolute minimum, with only 13 men available at the start of the season, and in September striker Tony Cunningham was sold to Barnsley for £80,000. Despite all this the team performed remarkably well, shooting to the top of the table and sweeping all before them. They peaked just before Christmas, thrashing Bournemouth 9-0, but when they returned from a short New Year's break in Majorca the pressure of injuries and suspensions began to tell on the small squad. Murphy publicly announced that he wished to strengthen the team with two players costing around £30,00 in all. Chairman Gilbert Blades refused, and the dispute blew up again with the story reaching the front page of several of the tabloid newspapers. The supporters demonstrated their backing for Murphy and the team in the home match with Plymouth and the board quickly resigned. The events clearly affected results and the Imps dropped back to finish in sixth place. Murphy stayed two more seasons, ensuring the club retained Third Division status. His final match at Bradford City on 11 May 1985 ended in tragedy when fire destroyed the main stand just before half time and 56 fans died.

There was no clearer evidence of Murphy's ability as a manager than the events which followed his departure. The club were relegated to the Fourth Division in 1985/86 and at the end of the following season they became the first to face automatic relegation out of the Football League. Ironically City only fell to the bottom of the table after completing their final match and their financial position, boosted by a record profit of £101,000 in the year to June 1986, was one of the healthiest in the lower divisions. Murphy returned and led the Imps to the Vauxhall Conference championship at the first time of asking. In the six seasons since their return to Division Four the side has rarely threatened to win promotion despite a number of managerial changes and different tactical styles. The period since 1987 has seen the Sincil Bank ground transformed with the first major alterations since the 1930's. A new St. Andrews stand was opened in November 1987, the north side was developed in August 1990 with the Stacey-West stand - named after two long standing City fans who died in the Bradford fire - and in the summer of 1992 a new South Park stand came into use. During 1994 a family stand was opened on the St. Andrews side and proposals were announced to complete the redevelopment programme by building a new 5,000 seat stand on the Sincil Bank side. Financially there have been several heavy losses since the return to League status but the club are approaching the millennium with the prospects of a brand new stadium and hopefully, in the near future, a team worthy of the surroundings.

KEY TO TEXT

General

The main text includes details of every player who has made a minimum of one appearance as a used substitute for Lincoln City in peacetime League matches, up to the end of the 1993/94 season. This includes the 1914/15 season, when a full programme was completed, and the three matches played before the 1939/40 season was abandoned. Appearance totals relate to FL matches only and are taken from the authors' own records which have been compiled from the official FL registers and contemporary newspapers. Appearances as a substitute are listed separately, eg. 27 app. + 2 sub. There are no official records of goalscorers and the figures which appear have been taken from newspaper reports, principally those appearing in the Lincolnshire Echo. Appearance totals for other clubs which are given in the text have been taken from the various AFS publications and Barry Hugman's 'Football League Players' Records 1946-1988' (see bibliography). The years following each player's name are those when he was on City's books.

Height and weight

These appear in the text as, for example, '1970: 5-9, 12-7' indicating that a 1970 source stated the player's height was 5'-9" and that he weighed 12st. 7lbs. These details are included as an aid to the reader and should not be taken as having medical accuracy.

Clubs

Clubs are given the title in use when the transfer or other event took place. Leicester Fosse, for instance, became Leicester City after World War One. 'Bradford' denotes the defunct Park Avenue club.

Transfer Fees

Many of the fees quoted are known to be authentic. The rest have been taken from press reports.

Honours

Those recorded include international appearances at all levels and inter-League matches. Also, at club level, appearances in domestic finals and qualifications for divisional championship medals (ie where the player has appeared in one third or more matches). For the sake of continuity, sponsors' names have been ignored (eg the League/Milk/Littlewoods/Coca Cola Cup is referred to as the Football League Cup throughout).

Abbreviations

The following abbreviations appear:

app.	appearances
sub.	appearances as a substitute
amat.	signed amateur forms
appr.	signed apprenticeship forms
prof.	signed professional forms
WW1	World War One
WW2	World War Two
FL	Football League
cs	close season
c.	about (eg circa 1950 - about 1950)

In writing a book such as this it would be foolish to think that errors cannot creep in and the authors offer their sincere apologies for any which appear. Anyone with accredited evidence for corrections or new information about the players (particularly transfers and dates of birth and death) should write to the authors c/o Yore Publications.

ADDINALL, Percy ("Trainer")
(1914-20)
Left-half: 15 app.
1919: 5-7, 11-4.
Born: Hull, 1888
Died: 1932
Career: West End F.C. (Lincoln); CITY Oct.1914 (amat.), June 1919 (prof.); Grantham Nov.1920.

A regular in the reserves in 1914-15 he went on to make over 100 first team appearances during the Great War. Summed up as *"alert, alive, absolutely enjoys the game and has a fine record of service with the club"*.

ALEXANDER, Keith
(1990-93)
Forward: 26 app. + 19 sub., 4 goals.
1993: 6-4, 12-7
Born: Nottingham 14 Nov 1958
Career: Notts County; Worksop Town: Clifton Sep.1975; Ilkeston Town 1976-77; Kimberley Town Sep.1978; Alfreton; Stamford Mar.1979; Boston Utd. Aug.1980; Kings Lynn; Spalding 1982-83; Kings Lynn 1983-84; Grantham Aug.1984; Kettering Town (Wisbech on loan); Barnet July 1986; Grimsby Town July 1988; Stockport County Sep.1990; CITY Dec.1990 (£7,000); Youth team coach Mar. 1992; Manager May 1993 to May 1994; Mansfield Town youth coach Aug. 1994.

Honours: (Stamford) F.A.Vase winners medal 1980. St.Lucia International.

His spell as a Notts County junior was terminated by injury and he drifted into the east midlands non-League scene. Entered League football at a late age, joining City after an unsuccessful spell at Edgeley Park. A tall and awkward player who could hold the ball up well and was popular with the fans. His managerial appointment came after success with the youth team.

ALFORD, Francis James
(1925-26)
Outside-left: 20 app. 3 goals
1925: 5-5½, 10-6
Born Swindon, 14 May 1901
Died: 16 Oct.1982
Career: Swindon junior football; Swindon Town 1917; Darwen cs 1920; Barrow late 1920; Everton Jan.1921 (£450 plus proceeds from a match); Barrow June 1923; CITY May 1925; Scunthorpe Utd. June 1926.

In the summer of 1925 Lincoln signed two seasoned left-wingers in Alford and Merritt, who shared the first team spot the following term. Alford had two years Northern Section experience at Barrow but only made a couple of First Division appearances for Everton. He was a neat little forward, though no great scorer.

ALLEN, Percy William
(1924-25)
Right-half: 59 app., 4 goals
1925: 5-8, 11-0

Born: West Ham 2 July 1895
Died: 21 Oct. 1969
Career: East London junior football; West Ham United Oct. 1919; CITY Jan.1924; Northampton Town Aug. 1925; Peterborough & Fletton United 1927; Stamford Town Aug. 1928; later with Weymouth before retiring.

A class performer who appeared at outside-right and centre-forward for the Hammers before finding his true role. His arrival at Sincil Bank immediately strengthened the Imps. Very much a sports all-rounder, Percy - a commissioned officer during WWI - played three-quarters for the Rhine Army RU XV, skippered his brigade's hockey XI, distinguished himself at athletics, played cricket for Essex clubs and was a horseman. On leaving football he worked on the London buses prior to buying an East Ham newsagents.

ALLEN, Ronald L.
(1958-62)
Right back: 60 app., 1 goal
1959: 5-9, 10-11
Born: Birmingham, 22 Apr. 1935
Career: Ladywood Juniors; Birmingham City amateur during 1952-53, turning professional May 1953; CITY July 1958 to May 1962.

No League appearances at Birmingham. Became a regular first team player during 1959-60 and remained so until suffering a double fracture of his right leg in the home game with Leeds in Dec. 1960. Out of football for 14 months he never appeared in the League again and was released on a free transfer at the end of the 1961-62 season.

ALLISON, Arthur
(1897)
Outside Right: 1 app.
Career: Wisbech Town; CITY (on trial) Feb. 1897 to cs 1897.

His solitary appearance came in a 2-0 home defeat against Gainsborough Trinity in what was a troubled season for the Imps who had lost 15 of the previous 16 League fixtures despite a performance which was described as *"promising"* he was given no further chances.

ALLISON, Kenneth
(1966-67)
Centre/inside-forward: 41 app + 1 Sub, 13 goals
1966: 5-11, 12-0
Born: Edinburgh, 6 Jan. 1937
Career: Dumbarton; Cowdenbeath 1960; Darlington July 1963; CITY Feb. 1966 (in part exchange for Barry Hutchinson); Rochester (New York) Aug. 1967.

Inside forward from Scotland, who arrived with excellent figures from his near-three season stay at Darlington - 39 goals in 75 League outings. In and out of the first team at Sincil Bank until released on a free transfer in May 1967. An early member of the great migration to the States in the 'Sixties'.

ALSTON, William
(1907-1908)
Half-back: 18 app., 2 goals
1907: 5-8, 11-7
Born: c.1886, probably in Scotland
Career: Maxwelltown Volunteers; CITY May 1907, Rochdale cs 1908.

Joined along with another Maxwelltown Volunteer, Andrew Aitken who did not appear in the League side. The bustling Alston's appearances were for the most part confined to the first half of 1907-08. Pretty versatile, he once appeared at centre-forward and - for Rochdale - his 17 Lancashire Combination outings were mostly at right-back.

ANDERSEN, Nicholas J.
(1989)
Midfield: 1 app
1990: 5-10, 10-10
Born: Lincoln, 29 Mar. 1969
Career: Mansfield Town (YTS) 1985 (prof) Jan 1987; CITY July 1989 (on trial); Nuneaton Borough Oct. 1989; Grantham Oct. 1991, Leek Town Oct. 1991; Bedworth United Dec. 1991; Tamworth cs 1993, Bedworth United Mar. 1994.

Made several appearances in pre-season matches but his only League outing was in the opening fixture of the 1989-90 season at home to Scunthorpe. A total of 9 appearances plus 11 as substitute whilst at Field Mill.

ANDERSON, Geoffrey T.
(1966-1967)
Outside-right: 44 app., 6 goals
1965: 5-9, 10-7
Born: Sheerness, Kent 26 Nov. 1944
Career: Kent schools football to Birmingham City as an apprentice Aug. 1961 (prof) Dec. 1962; Mansfield Town May 1964, CITY July 1966; Brentford on 2 months trial July 1967; Hastings United in Sep. 1967.

Enjoyed regular first-team soccer in his Imps' season following more spasmodic treatment at Mansfield (44 appearances spread over two years). He had made a solitary appearance - his FL debut - for Brum. Before his apprentice days Geoff had associations with Sheerness FC and the Kent League club, Ramsgate.

ANDERSON, Robert
(1930-1932)
Right-back: 27 app.
1931: 5-7½, 11-0
Born: Ardrossan, Ayrshire, c.1902
Career: Ardrossan Winton Rovers; Luton Town June 1923, Newport County June 1926; CITY July 1930 to cs 1932.

First choice for almost the whole of his Southern Section career. Anderson had little chance to show his capabil-

ities at Lincoln because of an entrenched Albert Worthy. When he did, this short and sturdy defender's reliability and style shone through. Consistent too - he once had a run of 100 consecutive appearances at Newport. Later in the 1930's was working in Luton.

ANDREWS, Charles
(1904-1908)
Defender: 5 app.
Career: Lincoln Liberal Club; CITY cs 1904; Rotherham Town cs 1908.

Andrews was one of a number of recruits from the successful Liberal Club side of that era. He appeared regularly in the Midland League line-up during his four seasons at Sincil Bank, mostly at left-back or left-half, but his first-team outings were well spaced and in four different positions.

ANDREWS, Harold
(1925-1928)
Centre-/inside-forward: 75 app., 41 goals
1927: 5-10, 11-0
Born: Lincoln, 13 Aug. 1903
Died: Aug. 1988
Career: St Botolph's OB (Lincoln); CITY 1924-25 (amat.), (prof.) Aug. 1925; Notts County Mar. 1928; Barnsley July 1932; Luton Town May 1935; Accrington Stanley May 1936 to June 1938; Players F.C (Nottingham) in 1939-40.

Honours: (Notts County) FL Div.3 South Champions 1931; (Barnsley) FL Div.3 North Champions 1934

Among City's finest local inter-war discoveries, clever with his head and packing a left foot drive that contributed greatly to an impressive goals tally. His career record reads 136 in 384 League outings. Harold played much of his overall career at inside-left, latterly figuring at left-half also. Subsequently worked in the tobacco industry.

ARMITAGE, Harold
(1926-1927)
Right-back: 9 app.
1926: 5-9, 12-0
Born: Sheffield, 16 Aug. 1901
Died: 1973
Career: Hathersage FC; Sheffield Wednesday May 1920; Bristol Rovers Aug. 1922, CITY May 1926 (part exchange for Josiah Barrett); Scarborough cs 1927.

On his signing, a commentator wrote that Harry was *"strong, quick in decision and a fearless tackler"*, but his Lincoln season was spent as deputy to Bissett. His reputation had been earned through four years regular service at Eastville (122 FL matches) when he had shared defensive duties with Jim Haydon and that great goalkeeper, Jesse Whatley.

ASHURST, William
(1919-1920)

Right-back: 24 app.
1920: 5-9½, 12-7
Born: Willington, Co.Durham, 4 May 1894
Died: 26 Jan. 1947
Career: Willington schools; Durham City, Leeds City cs 1919; CITY Oct. 1919 (£500); Notts County June 1920 (£1,000); West Bromwich Albion Nov. 1926 (£3,100); Newark Town Aug. 1928, retired cs 1929.

Honours: England International (5 apps)
Football League (1 app vs Irish League, 1922)
(Notts County) FL Div 2 Champions 1923

A purchase at the famous Leeds City auction that brought Lincoln a tidy profit 8 months later. Billy also proved a fine investment for Notts with whom he spent his best years. Relentless in the tackle - though scrupulously fair - placing the ball precisely with either foot, fearless and excellent at heading. In short one of the best backs of his day.

ASKEW, William
(1939)

Centre-half: 3 app.
1939: 6-1, 12-4
Born: Coundon, nr. Bishop Auckland, 1914
Career: West Auckland; Chesterfield Jan. 1933; Walsall June 1937; CITY June 1939.

Ideally built pivot. Served a useful apprenticeship at Chesterfield understudying the outstanding Alan Sliman and polished heading and distribution gifts. The Imps were reported to have paid less than the £300 Walsall were asking, although Hull City were competing for his services. Askew did not resume in the first-class game when peace returned.

ASNIP, John
(1901-1902)

Inside-right: 1 app.
Career: Lincoln junior football; CITY Aug. 1901 to cs 1902, CITY again Jan. 1903 to cs 1903.

A local lad who appeared regularly in the reserves in both his spells on the club's books. His sole FL appearance came at Blackpool in Feb. 1902 when he deputised for 'flu victim Jimmy Hartley.

ASNIP, Thomas
(1904-1905)

Outside-left: 1 app.
Career: St. Catherines FC (Lincoln); CITY Aug. 1904; Adelaide (Lincoln) cs 1905.

Thomas was one of the many Lincoln League players recruited by the Working Mens Committee to fill the ranks of City's Midland League side. His first-team opportunity came in a 2-0 defeat at Manchester United in Oct. 1904.

ATKIN, Arthur
(1913-1924)

Defender: 96 app., 2 goals
1922: 5-10½, 10-7
Born: Skegness 1893
Died: 23 July 1952
Career: Skegness FC; CITY Feb. 1913, Boston Town Aug. 1924.

Came to Sincil Bank as a centre-half, although he appeared for City at full-back and in all three half-back positions. Towards the end of his stay it was written he was *"spry, resourceful, fearless of any opposition and the best man of his age to whom the term veteran could apply"*. On joining Boston it was reported he was to captain the side. Served with the Territorials pre-war, being called up on the outbreak. In the early 1930's he was working as a foreshore attendant for the council in Skegness.

ATKINSON, G(eorge) Arthur
(1930-1933)
Outside-right: 9 app., 5 goals
1934: 5-9, 11-0
Born: Goole, 30 Sep. 1909
Died: 14 July 1983
Career: Goole Town; CITY (amat.) Dec. 1930, (prof.) one month later; Hull City June 1933; Mansfield Town June 1934; Southport May 1937; Thorne Colliery cs 1938.

A reserve for most of his time with City, all his first team appearances coming in 1932/33. He had more success at Field Mill where he made 120 League appearances, mostly in the inside berth, and scored 31 goals. He was reckoned by a 1935 critic to be one of the best inside-forwards seen at Mansfield with his ball control, constructive ideas and right-foot shooting.

BACON, Arthur Parnell
(1906-07)
Centre-forward: 4 app.
1906: 5-10, 10-0
Born: Basford, Notts, 1884
Career: Sutton Junction; CITY Nov. 1906 to cs 1907.

Bacon was one of a number of men tried at centre-forward following the departure of McLeod to Leeds City. His four first-team appearances came consecutively in Dec. 1906 and he returned to the Midland League side thereafter.

BAILEY, Thomas
(1908)
Centre-forward: 1 app.
Career: Overseal Swifts (Burton & District League); Burton United 1907; (CITY trial Apr. 1908); Walsall cs 1908 to cs 1909.

Centre-forward who received a brief trial at Sincil Bank, his sole appearance coming in a 3-0 defeat at Stoke on Apr. 11 as City struggled to avoid re-election. His other senior football was played in the Birmingham League.

BAINBRIDGE, Robert
(1920-1923)
Goalkeeper: 35 app.
1921: 6-0, 11-0
Career: Jarrow; CITY Aug. 1920, Sittingbourne Mar. 1923; Gateshead Town Sep. 1923; Leadgate Park July 1924.

Bainbridge was City's first choice 'keeper for two seasons - he appeared 37 times for the Midland League championship side of 1920/21 - before losing his place to the teenaged Jack Kendall. One of several men who left Sincil Bank at the time of the financial crisis of Feb. 1923 when faced with the choice of a cut in wages or a free transfer. He had earned the following praise after season 1921-22: *"... with his wonderful reach, marvellous anticipation and quickness of judgement won high favour. Played some memorable games, especially away from home"*.

BALL, Alfred
(1913-21)
Outside-left: 97 app., 13 goals
1914: 5-7, 11-0
Born: Clowne, Derbys, 1890
Died: 3 Oct. 1952
Career: Creswell Athletic; Clowne Rising Star; CITY June 1913; Mansfield Town June 1921; Ilkeston United 1922/23.

A rare crowd-pleaser with his exceptional speed and power shooting. At the time of his departure he was the Imps' captain, a fairly unusual circumstance for an outside-left. Alf's army service in the Great War was with the South Staffs. Regiment, although he still found time to make over 100 appearances for City between 1915 and 1919.

BALL, S(tephen) Gary
(1979-80)
Outside-left: 3 app.
1980: 5-7, 9-6
Born: St. Austell, Cornwall, 15 Dec. 1959
Career: Plymouth Argyle as an apprentice, (prof.) Dec. 1977; CITY Oct. 1979, contract cancelled Mar. 1980.

Lightweight wingman signed after his release from Plymouth as cover for Gordon Hobson. The deal involved a fee being paid after 20 first team appearances.

BANNAN, Thomas N.
(1955-57)
Inside-forward: 67 app., 19 goals
1955: 5-7½, 10-12½
Born: Darngavel, Lanark, 13 Apr. 1930
Career: Airdrieonians; Wrexham June 1951; CITY June 1955 (exchange for Eric Littler and a fee); Wrexham Sep. 1957 (c.£3,000); Barrow Aug. 1959 (£1,500) to 1961.

Bannan was a consistent goalscorer during his spell at Sincil Bank, despite the absence of physical advantages. His career record in the Football League shows 112 goals from 338 matches. He later returned to Scotland and became a licensee in Airdrie.

BANNISTER, Charles
(1897-1902)
Centre-half: 106 app., 1 goal
1902: 5-7½, 11-7
Born: Burton-on-Trent, 1879
Died: Aug. 1952
Career: Burton junior football; Old Stanley FC (Liverpool); Old Town (Everton amat.); Manchester City cs 1896; Oldham County 1896-97; CITY Dec. 1897; Swindon Town Aug. 1902; Reading May 1904; Swindon T. May 1906 to cs 1912. Perth YMCA (Australia) Sep. 1912.

Honours: (Swindon Town) Southern League Champions 1911.

Bannister himself said *"I may not be able to play football myself but I can stop those who can!"*. He was, though, being somewhat modest for other commentators wrote of him as *"... one of the tireless brand. He does the work of three men in the course of a game"*, and *"one of Lincoln's strongest players, his methods are perhaps more robust than scientific"*. Charlie did yeoman service for Swindon besides City. In his two spells there he made 236 Southern League appearances, scoring 10 goals and enjoyed a benefit during season 1911/12. He later emigrated to Australia where he remained until his death.

BANNISTER, Neville
(1961-1964)

Outside-right: 68 app., 16 goals
1963: 5-7, 10-3
Born: Brierfield, Lancs., 21 July 1937
Career: Bolton junior football; Bolton Wanderers July 1954; CITY Mar. 1961 (£4,000); Hartlepools United Aug. 1964; Rochdale July 1965 to 1966.

Signed on the transfer deadline when the Imps were rooted at the bottom of the Second Division (City finished nine points below Portsmouth, who were also relegated). Gave useful service during the following three campaigns and hit a hat-trick against Torquay at Sincil Bank in Dec. 1962.

BARACLOUGH, Ian
(1992-1994)

Defender/Midfield: 68 app. + 5 sub., 10 goals.
1992: 6-1, 11-10
Born: Leicester, 4 Dec. 1970
Career: Leicester City YTS, (prof.) Dec. 1988 (Wigan Athletic on loan Mar. 1990); Grimsby Town Aug. 1991; CITY on loan Aug. 1992, made permanent Oct. 1992 (£10,000); Mansfield Town June 1994.

Honours: England Youth International

Tall utility player who was signed by Steve Thompson following a successful loan spell. A first team regular in his two seasons at Sincil Bank, although regularly switched between defence and midfield.

BARBER, William Arthur
Joseph
(1933-1935)

Right-/centre-half: 13 app.
Born: Lincoln, 20 Dec. 1908
Died: 3 July 1954
Career: Army football; Luton Town cs 1933; CITY Sep. 1933; Crewe Alexandra Sep. 1935; Peterborough United Oct. 1935; Truro City; Lincoln Claytons in 1936/37.

Although Lincoln-born he arrived at Sincil Bank via army football and a brief trial at Luton. Barber was to prove a dependable reserve in both wing-half and centre-half berths. Served in the Army again in WW2, rising to the rank of Company Sgt. Major.

BARLOW, Philip D.
(1967)

Right-half: 5 app.
Born: Shipley, Yorks., 19 Dec. 1946
Career: Guiseley; Bradford City (amat.) May 1965, (prof.) July 1966; CITY Aug. 1967 to Sep. 1967; Guiseley, as a permit player, 1968.

Barlow came to Sincil Bank on a short trial after being released by Bradford City and was a member of the team which knocked First Division Newcastle United out of the League Cup in a famous 2-1 victory. He later resumed as an amateur at the age of 21.

BARNARD, Raymond Scholey
(1960-1963)

Full-back/centre-half: 43 app.
1961: 5-9, 11-6
Born: Middlesbrough, 6 Apr. 1933
Career: Middlesbrough Schools; Middlesbrough FC (Amat.) c.1949, (prof.) Apr. 1950; CITY June 1960 (£2,500); Grantham Aug. 1963; Lincoln Claytons Aug. 1966.

Honours: England Schools International (4 apps. 1948)

Ray received an early baptism, at 18, in Middlesbrough's First Division side and went on to make 118 League and FA Cup appearances at Ayresome Park. A neat, effective player who performed usefully in several defensive positions for City. He went straight in the first team on signing but his appearances were restricted in later seasons.

BARRATT, Josiah
(1924-1926)

Outside-right: 74 app., 8 goals
1925: 5-8, 10-10
Born: Bulkington, Warks., 21 Feb. 1895
Died: Apr. 1968
Career: Nuneaton Town; Leicester Fosse Dec. 1916; Birmingham Feb. 1917; Southampton May 1919; Birmingham Mar. 1922; Pontypridd May 1923; CITY June 1924 (less than £1,500); Bristol Rovers Aug. 1926 (for Harry Armitage and a fee); retired 1927.

Honours: (Southampton) FL Div. 3 (South) Champions 1922.

An example of the prototype old-time winger - fast, and demonstrating skill in crossing the ball to his inside-forwards. Served in the Great War with the 3rd Royal Berkshire Regiment. After WW2 Jos coached Coventry City's junior players. A useful cricketer, promising enough to have a trial for Warwickshire during the 1922 season.

BARRELL, George ("Tosh")
(1908-1917)

Half-back/centre- and inside-forward: 141 app., 26 goals
1912: 5-9, 11-6

Born: Lincoln 1888
Died: 18 May 1960
Career: Rustons Engineers (Lincoln); CITY cs 1908; Rustons 1917; Boston 1921.

Hugely popular local man at home in several positions. The following extracts from press comment sum him up nicely. 1911: *"... can play in any forward position. Angled after by prominent First League clubs - a clever shot and good combination player"*. 1913: *"Enterprising, a steady shot and gets the best out of his partner ... never let the team down"*. 1914: *"Does useful service wherever placed. Has appeared in most positions except goal and would probably do well there also"*. On leaving the game he was a licensee in Boston for many years.

BARRETT, Kenneth B.
(1959-1963)
Winger: 17 app., 4 goals
1961: 5-5, 9-10
Born: Bromsgrove, Worcs, 5 May 1938
Career: Bromsgrove Schools; Stoke Works (Bromsgrove); Aston Villa Feb. 1957; CITY June 1959 (Weymouth on loan Sep. 1960); Stourbridge cs 1963; retired Feb. 1968.

A small wingman with attacking ideas his best season was 1961/62 when he made 14 appearances. Barrett served as a soldier throughout his time at Sincil Bank - the loan period at Weymouth coming when he was posted to Blandford Camp - and represented the British Army on a number of occasions. He left Stourbridge after 4½ years when he became manager of a bookmaker's shop.

BARRICK, Harry
(1907)
Centre-forward: 5 app., 2 goals
1907: 5-10, 11-0
Born: Spilsby, Lincs, 1883
Career: Scunthorpe; CITY Jan. 1907 to cs 1907; Scunthorpe & Lindsey United 1910/11.

Like Arthur Bacon before him, Barrick was offered the chance of replacing McLeod as first choice centre-forward. He scored in his first two outings but was only picked on three further occasions.

BARTON, D(avid) Roger
(1964-1966)
Outside-right: 28 app., 1 goal
1967: 5-8, 9-7
Born: Jump, Barnsley, 25 Sep. 1946
Career: Wolverhampton Wanderers as an apprentice, (prof.) Oct. 1963; CITY July 1964; Barnsley July 1966 to cs 1969.

A slimly built winger who came to Sincil Bank on a free transfer from Wolves and was in and out of the first team during his two seasons with the club. Moved on to Barnsley on another 'free' where he was a regular in 1966/67 but afterwards appeared rarely.

BARTON, William ("Kenny")
(1898-1899; 1900-1901)
Half-back: 2 app.
Career: Adelaide FC (Lincoln); CITY Sep. 1898 to cs 1899; Grantham 1899 - 1900; CITY Sep. 1900 to cs 1901; Adelaide FC in 1902/03.

A local lad who was recruited by the Working Mens Committee for City's Midland League side, with whom he was a regular in both his seasons. His two Football League outings were both against Woolwich Arsenal coming in Apr. 1898 and Mar. 1901.

BASSNETT, Alfred
(1926-1929)

Right-half: 89 app., 6 goals
1928: 5-8, 11-2
Born: St. Helens, 10 Apr. 1893
Died: 24 June 1966
Career: Star Rovers (St. Helens); St. Helens Town; Eccles Borough 1914; Burnley June 1919; CITY Nov. 1926; Ballymena as player/manager July 1929; Hereford United as player/manager June 1930; Nelson Aug. 1931.

Honours: (Ballymena) Irish Cup Finalist 1930

Early in his Burnley days this wholehearted player was described as *"a stubborn breaker-up"*. He served the Turf Moor club particularly ably, not least for utility value in being competent in all the half-back positions. Earlier he had seen much action in WW1 with the Royal Engineers. After leaving the game he was employed as a licensee. Settled in Burnley where he died.

BATES, Sydney
(1935)

Inside-right: 6 app.

1935: 5-9, 11-0

Born: Wardley Colliery, Northumberland, 17 May 1912

Died: Feb. 1984

Career: Sheriff Hill (Gateshead); Eighton Banks cs 1934; CITY Feb. 1935; Millwall Aug. 1935; Stockport County May 1936 to 1937.

Six of his eight Football League appearances were with City in Feb. and Mar. of 1935. A contemporary wrote of him "... *showed good touches but needed to be a bit quicker*".

BAUCHOP, James Rae
(1923-1924)

Inside-left: 28 app., 11 goals

1921: 5-9½, 11-6

Born: Sauchie, Stirlings, 22 May 1886

Died: 12 June 1948

Career: Alloa Athletic 1904; Celtic Jan. 1906; Norwich City May 1907; Crystal Palace Mar. 1908; Derby County May 1909; Tottenham Hotspur May 1913; Bradford Dec. 1913; Doncaster Rovers June 1922; CITY Sep. 1923 to cs 1924.

Honours: (Derby County) FL Div. 2 Champions 1912

Bauchop came to Sincil Bank after a season at Doncaster who were then members of the Midland League, but as his record shows he had not lost his scoring touch. A fine player in his younger days, a 1909 commentator wrote "... *has prolific scoring powers. A big bustling forward, a fine dribbler and a splendid worker*". He was the youngest of three sons of a fireman - an elder brother was William Bauchop who assisted Stockport County and Plymouth Argyle in pre-WW1 days. When with City he also ran a newsagents and sports shop in Bradford where he lived until his death.

BAVIN, Arthur
(1907-1910, 1914-1915)

Right-half: 5 app.

Born: Nottingham, 5 Feb. 1887

Died: 2 Jan 1961

Career: Liberal Club (Lincoln); CITY Oct. 1907; Worksop Town cs 1910; Grantham Avenue cs 1911; Mansfield Mechanics later in 1911/12 season; Grantham 1912; CITY September 1914; Ruston Aircraftmen (Lincoln) in 1915/16.

A local lad who made all his FL appearances in the 1907/08 season, otherwise appearing in Midland League football only. He settled in the Lincoln area and made a brief re-appearance as a guest player in 1916/17. Arthur was also a good cricketer appearing with the Grantham and Lindum clubs, and represented Lincolnshire in the Minor Counties competition.

BEAN, Alfred Samuel ("Billy")
(1934-1949)

Full-back/wing-half: 174 app., 10 goals

1938: 5-9, 11-0

Born: Lincoln, 25 Aug. 1915

Died: 25 Nov. 1993

Career: Corinthians FC (Lincoln); CITY (amat.) Nov. 1934 (prof.) May 1935; retired cs 1949.

Honour: (City) FL Div.3 (North) Champions 1948

Very much a man of Lincoln, "Billy" (the nickname apparently derives from his father's name and not the contemporary comic character) played virtually all his senior football for City, the exception being a few appearances for Nottingham Forest as a guest in WW2. He signed as an amateur from crack local side Corinthians and made his debut at outside-left at Chester in Apr. 1935 but was to establish himself as a wing-half by 1938-39, switching to left-back after the war when he became a regular penalty taker. He also played 208 wartime games for the Imps and had a reputation as being one of the Northern Section's finest backs - consistent and resolute in the tackle. A draughtsman by trade he continued to live in Lincoln and was employed by Robeys for many years.

BEAUMONT, Sidney
(1904-1905)

Forward: 5 app.

1910: 5-7½, 11-0

Born: Wrestlingworth, Beds, 8 Oct. 1889

Died: 12 May 1939

Career: Colchester Town; CITY (amat.) Nov. 1904, (prof. soon after), to cs 1905; returned to junior football until signed by Watford Oct. 1909 following a months trial; Preston North End July 1911 (£25); Merthyr Town cs 1912; Troedyrhiw cs 1913; Barry manager for 8 years; Llanelly secretary before briefly acting as manager 1924; Aberdare Athletic manager 1924-27; Blackpool manager 1927-28; assistant trainer for Chester 1936-39.

Recruited from Junior football, and his five appearances

came in three different positions. He was considered a half-back on joining Preston with a secondary role at outside-left. Later a prominent figure in the Welsh soccer scene for many years.

BEAVON, David G.
(1981-82)

Midfield/defender: 7 app. + 1 sub.
1982: 5-9, 10-9
Born: Nottingham, 8 Dec. 1961
Career: Notts County (appr.) June 1978, (prof.) Dec. 1979; CITY Nov. 1981 (£25,000); Tsuen Wan (Hong Kong) Nov. 1982; Northampton Town Mar. 1983; Kettering Town cs 1983; Buxton; Shepshed; Boston United; Kings Lynn Oct. 1985; Boston United July 1986; Priory Nov. 1988.

Winger, who also appeared as a full-back after signing from Notts County. He was rarely selected for the first team and after brief spells in Hong Kong and at North-ampton he drifted into the east midlands non-League scene.

BEEL, George William
(1919-1920; 1932)

Centre-/inside-forward: 32 app., 12 goals
1930: 5-9; 11-7
Born: Bracebridge, Lincoln, 26 Feb. 1900
Died: 30 Dec. 1980
Career: Army football (RAMC) during WW1, and a guest player for Blackpool; Lincoln junior football (trial with Manchester United 1919); CITY Oct. 1919; Merthyr Town June 1920; Chesterfield May 1922; Burnley Apr. 1923 (in exchange for Jackie Fisher); CITY Feb. 1932; Rochdale Sep. 1932; Tunbridge Wells Rangers as player/manager May 1933.

A prolific goalscorer remembered at Burnley as their record seasonal scorer (35 in 1927/28) and aggregate scorer (178 League goals). In all he netted 187 in 337 League and FA Cup games for the Turf Moor club. Often described as forceful and wholehearted, George's play had improved by the late 1920's through an increase of resourcefulness.

BELL, Derek Martin
(1979-1983)

Striker: 69 app. plus 14 sub., 33 goals
1981: 5-8, 10-4½
Born: Wyberton, Lincs., 30 Oct. 1956
Career: Lincolnshire schools football to Derby County on associate schoolboy forms Dec. 1971, (appr.) 1972; Halifax Town May 1975; (Sheffield Wednesday on loan Mar.-Apr. 1976); Barnsley Oct. 1978 (£30,000); CITY Nov. 1979 (£33,000); Chesterfield Aug. 1983 (£8,500); Scunthorpe United Jan. 1984; Boston United Mar. 1986; Spalding United Dec. 1986, Lincoln United Aug. 1987.

Local lad who scored regularly with all his clubs. His Sincil Bank career was badly affected by injuries, but he came good in the 1982-83 season when he was top scorer with 23 goals and hit three hat-tricks before Christmas. Settled in Lincoln and was recently manager of GF Fischer in the Lincoln Sunday League.

BELL, Raymond Lloyd
(1950-1951)

Goalkeeper: 1 app.
1950: 5-11, 12-0
Born: West Seaham, Co. Durham 6 Dec. 1930
Career: Seaham Colliery Welfare; City Jan. 1950 to May 1951; assisted North Scarle United (Lincoln League) and Ruston Bucyrus (Lincoln) as a permit player in the mid-1950's.

A part-time player (he was an electric welder by voca-tion) whose sole League appearance was in a 3-0 victory over Barrow in Dec. 1950. Son of Paddy, pre-war player with Sunderland and Bradford.

BELL, William John
(1924-1925)

Outside-left: 20 app., 3 goals
1925: 5-8, 10-10
Born: Backworth, Newcastle-upon-Tyne 1904
Career: Blyth Spartans; Chopwell Institute (Aston Villa, trial Dec. 1923); CITY Aug. 1924; Mansfield Town May 1925; Leicester City Feb. 1926; Torquay United July 1930 to 1931.

Somewhat surprisingly, this young and promising winger left Sincil Bank after a single season. However, after a few months in a strong Mansfield side (which finished Midland League runners-up in 1925/26) he joined top flight Leicester City. Son of a one-time Glasgow Rangers goalkeeper.

BENNETT, John William
(1900-1901)

Left-half: 4 app.
1904: 5-9, 12-6
Born: Liverpool, 1879
Career: Wavertree FC (Liverpool); Wellingborough; CITY cs 1900 to Jan. 1901; Northampton Town cs 1901; Luton Town cs 1903; Leicester Fosse May 1904; Blackburn Rovers Apr. 1905 to 1906.

"A strong dashing player" reported the Athletic News. Bennett certainly had a sturdy physique to back up the aforesaid strength. His opportunities at Lincoln were restricted and his early release was due to bad conduct.

BENTLEY, Edwin
(1897-1910)
Left-back: 10 app.
Career: St. Mary's (Lincoln); CITY Aug. 1897 to 1910.

Bentley was a local lad who appeared regularly in the reserves throughout his spell on the club's books, filling in for a variety of defensive positions, including goalkeeper on more than one occasion. Five of his first team outings came in 1907-08 and he also appeared seven times for the 1908/09 Midland League championship side. His main role at Sincil Bank was as the club's groundsman, a post he occupied during the early 1900's, and in which he continued after his playing career ceased.

BESTON, James
(1908-1909)
Centre-forward: 3 app.
Born: Houghton-le-Spring, 1880
Career: Houghton; Hebburn Argyle cs 1907; CITY Apr. 1908 to cs 1909.

Beston was a forward recruited from the North Eastern League towards the end of the 1907/08 season, shortly before City were voted out of the League. He failed to win a regular first team place and returned to the north east in the summer of 1909.

BETT, Fred
(1948-1950)
Inside-forward: 14 app., 2 goals
1950: 5-7, 10-8
Born: Scunthorpe, 5 Dec. 1920
Career: Scunthorpe United; Sunderland Dec. 1937; Coventry City May 1946 (£3,000); CITY Sep. 1948 (£2,000); Spalding United Aug. 1950; Holbeach United Aug. 1953; Bourne Town June 1954.

Signed as a Sunderland pro two days after his 17th birthday. City already knew of his talents when he joined them, as he had guested for the club during the War (77 appearances, 36 goals). He scored on his debut at Elland Road but made only 14 appearances - all during the 1948-49 relegation season. Contemporaries described him as *"a small but good player, well built and a strong shot"* and *"unusually deadly from spot kicks"*.

BICKERSTAFFE, John
(1948-1951)
Centre-half: 12 app.
1948: 5-11, 12-0
Born: St. Helens, 8 Nov. 1918
Career: Peasley Cross; Bury during WW2; CITY Dec. 1948; Halifax Town Aug. 1951 to 1953.

Bickerstaffe went straight in the first team on signing but lost his place to Tony Emery after three games and was to remain understudy to him for the rest of his time at Sincil Bank. His longest exposure to first team football came at Halifax late in his career - 37 League appearances.

BIGGINS, Wayne
(1979-1981)
Striker: 8 app., 1 goal
1980: 5-10, 11-0
Born: Sheffield, 20 Nov. 1961
Career: CITY on schoolboy forms Feb. 1977, (appr.) July 1978, (prof.) Nov. 1979; Kings Lynn Aug. 1981; Matlock Town cs 1982; Burnley Feb. 1984 (£7,500); Norwich City Oct. 1985 (£40,000); Manchester City July 1988 (£150,000); Stoke City Aug. 1989 (£250,000); Barnsley Oct. 1992 (£200,000); Celtic Nov. 1993 (part exchange for Andy Payton plus £100,000); Stoke City Mar. 1994 (£125,000).

Striker who came up through the ranks and scored on his debut against Hartlepool in Mar. 1981. At the time City had a surplus of goalscorers with Tony Cunningham, Derek Bell and Gordon Hobson all on the books, and Biggins found himself released two months afterwards. He was later snapped up by Burnley and was the subject of several big money transfers.

BIRCH, Brian
(1952-1956)
Inside-forward: 56 app., 16 goals
1952: 5-7, 10-7
Born: Salford, 18 Nov. 1931
Career: Salford Schools; Manchester United (groundstaff) 1946, (prof.) May 1949; Wolverhampton Wanderers Mar. 1952 (approx. 11,000); CITY Dec. 1952 (£5-6,000); Barrow June 1956 (£2,500); Exeter City Sep. 1958 (£2,000); Oldham Athletic Jan. 1960 (£800); Rochdale Mar. 1961 (£850) to June 1962; when he went to the Phillipines as a coach; Mossley 1963; Boston United Aug. 1963 to Feb. 1964 when he went to Sydney, Australia as a coach; later coached in Malaysia before returning to play for Ellesmere Port to Jan. 1967; Blackburn Rovers coach to juniors Nov. 1967; Galatasary (Turkey) coach 1970.

Honours: England Youth International (1949)

A clever little inside-forward with good ball control - one of the early Busby Babes. After a golden start - youth honours and a Division 1 debut at 17 - his career did not prosper to the extent one would have thought. Scored two on his City debut at home to Leicester but was in and out of the first team. Later found fame as a coach - Galatasary were Turkish Champions in each of his first three seasons in charge.

BIRCHALL, Richard
(1912-1913)
Inside-/outside-left: 7 app., 1 goal
1911: 5-7½, 10-8
Born: Prescot, Lancs., 14 Oct. 1887
Career: Newton-le-Willows 1907; St. Helens Town 1908; Bradford City Mar. 1910; Carlisle United June 1910; Hyde during 1910/11

season; Norwich City May 1911; CITY Aug. 1912; Worksop Town cs 1913; Rotherham Town Dec. 1913; Mexborough cs 1914.

Despite the impressive roll-call of clubs, Birchall's first-class appearances were restricted to 38 (8 FL for the Imps and Bradford City plus 30 Southern League at Norwich). However, his non-League spells were goal productive: 32 for St. Helens Town and 23 at Hyde for example. He was wounded during his WW1 service.

BIRD, Isaac
(1919-1921)

Inside-left: 8 app., 2 goals
1921: 5-9, 11-7
Born: Kimberley, Notts., 14 July 1895
Died: 22 June 1984
Career: Guest player for Notts County during WW1; Ilkeston United; CITY Sep. 1919; Ilkeston United cs 1921.

Initially an amateur at Sincil Bank, Bird appeared regularly in the Midland League championship side of 1920/21 (33 app., 14 goals). When City returned to the League he moved back to Ilkeston and helped them to finish runners-up in the Central Alliance in 1921/22.

BIRKBECK, John
(1952-1955)

Inside-/centre-forward: 2 app.
Born: Lincoln, 1 Oct. 1932
Career: Spilsby (Lincs); CITY Jan. 1952; Boston United July 1955; Skegness Town May 1960; Loughborough cs 1962; Long Eaton; Stamford cs 1965.

A forward who played in the reserves for one and a half seasons, before signing from Spilsby. His only first team opportunities came in the last two games of the 1954/55 season, shortly before his release. He later spent many years on the Midland League scene. Well known in the county as a jazz musician.

BISSETT, James Thompson
(1926-1928)

Right-back: 32 app., 6 goals
1926: 5-11, 13-0
Born: Lochee, Dundee, 19 June 1898
Career: Everton Jan. 1920; Ebbw Vale c.1921; Southend United May 1922; Rochdale May 1923; Middlesbrough May 1924; CITY July 1926 to Apr. 1928 when he joined Dundee as player-manager; Raith Rovers in 1929/30; Dundee secretary-manager 1932 to 1937; Barrow secretary-manager Apr. to Dec. 1937.

Class full-back for whom substantial fees were paid by Middlesbrough and City. Proved a sound and reliable partner for Paddy McConville but after the opening game of 1927/28, was replaced by the newly-signed Albert Worthy, and this match proved to be his last senior appearance.

BISSETT, John
(1898-1899)

Goalkeeper: 18 app.
Career: Dalbeattie; CITY Dec. 1898 to cs 1899.

Bissett was initially signed on a trial basis but impressed sufficiently to be given the first team spot ahead of George Hardie for the final 18 games of the 1898/1899 season.

BLADES, William J.
(1894-1895)

Outside-/inside-right: 3 app., 1 goal
Career: CITY from c.Dec. 1894 to cs 1895.

Most likely a local man, Blades appeared mainly in the Swifts' (reserves) line-up. He scored on his first team debut at home to Leicester Fosse in Apr. 1895 and played in two of the remaining three League games before being released.

BLAKEY, Charles Henry Smithson
(1919-1920)

Goalkeeper: 30 app.
1919: 5-10, 12-0
Born: Lincoln, 1896
Died: 31 Aug. 1962
Career: Lincoln YMCA in 1914/15; Newland Athletic (Lincoln) during WWI; CITY May 1919; Doncaster Rovers July 1920; Boston Town July 1921.

Blakey served three years with the East Yorks. Regiment during the Great War, and made occasional appearances for City from 1916, becoming first choice for the first post-war season. Summed up as *"very quick, resourceful, cool"*. After his football days he worked as a business consultant in the Gainsborough area.

BLAND, G(eorge) Patrick
(1936-1938)

Goalkeeper, 1 app.
1936: 6-1½, 13-0

Born: Tutbury, nr Burton-on-Trent, 24 Feb. 1915
Died: June 1970
Career: Horncastle Town; CITY (amat.) May 1936, (prof.) June 1936; Bradford May 1938; Watford Jan. 1939; Ransomes & Marles cs 1946, Spalding United cs 1947.

Joe McClelland's first signing on taking up the City managership. Owner of a hefty physique, Pat had displayed fine form in Lincolnshire junior football. His FL debut came at home to Rochdale in Nov. 1936 and this was to prove his only peacetime League outing.

BLOOR, Michael B.
(1971-1973)
Right-back: 71 app. + 2 sub
1972: 5-8, 10-10
Born: Wrexham, 25 Mar. 1949
Career: Newport FC (Salop); Stoke City Apr. 1967; CITY May 1971; Darlington Aug. 1973 to 1974.

Bloor was recuited by manager David Herd on a free transfer along with another Stoke reserve player, John Worsdale. He proved a sound partner for both Graham Taylor and George Peden until losing his place early in 1973 and he found himself released at the end of the season.

BLOW, E(dward) Percy ("Corky")
(1901-1907)
Left-half: 162 app., 1 goal
1904: 5-8½, 10-8
Born: North Hykeham, Lincs., 16 Nov. 1877
Died: 9 Mar. 1938
Career: Blue Star (Lincoln); CITY Jan. 1901; Horncastle United Nov. 1907; Bracebridge Sep. 1908.

Regular left-half for five seasons from 1901/02. Blow was highly consistent and said by the great Billy Meredith to have been one of the hardest halves he had ever encountered. Reputedly noted for taking the ball off opponents' heads with a foot! He had two brothers also on City's books - Tom (1900/01) and Fred (1906/07) - but neither made the first team. Percy was a Lincolnshire swimming champion and the Royal Humane Society's youngest holder of their Gold Medal, aged 11, for rescuing two boys who had fallen under ice. A carpenter by trade, hence his nickname, cork being much used. Gassed during WW1, a circumstance that caused his death two decades later.

BOAST, Ernest
(1903-1905)
Goalkeeper: 21 app.
1904: 6-2½, 13-2
Born: Sheffield, 1880
Career: Chelmsford; CITY Nov. 1903 to cs 1905

Made his League debut in a home fixture against Chesterfield, a month after signing, and remained first-choice until the end of the season. However, George Buist, recruited in the summer of 1904, proved an instant hit and Boast spent the whole of the 1904/05 season in the reserves.

BODEN, John G.
(1950-1951)
Centre-forward: 3 app., 2 goals
1950: 5-7, 10-10
Born: Cleethorpes, 4 Oct. 1926
Career: Keelby (Grimsby); Skegness Town cs 1949; CITY Apr. 1950; Skegness Town Aug. 1951; Louth United Oct. 1958; Brigg Town Jan. 1960.

Jackie had a phenomenal scoring record in Lincolnshire junior football and attracted the Imps' attention after netting seven goals in a match for Skegness against City 'A'. At Sincil Bank it was recorded (in 1950/51) that *"he had delighted everyone with his play, and should get a place among the seniors this season.* In the event he had few chances and returned to Skegness where he scored 150 goals over the next three seasons.

BOLAM, David Robert
(1924-1925)
Inside-left: 3 app., 1 goal
1924: 5-7, 10-11
Born: Newcastle-upon-Tyne, 24 Jan. 1898
Died: 1983
Career: Chester-le-Street; CITY May 1924; Exeter City Aug. 1925 to cs 1926; Chester-le-Street 1927.

Engaged to fill the gap left by Archie Kean's transfer to Blackburn, arriving with what was termed *"high credentials in the North Eastern League".* Scored on his debut at home to Wigan Borough but was selected only twice thereafter and was released at the end of the season.

BOLTON, Ian Robert
(1976)
Centre-half: 1 app.
1976: 6-0, 11-9
Born: Leicester, 13 July 1953
Career: Birmingham City, (appr.); Notts County Mar. 1972 (CITY on loan Aug. - Sep. 1976); Watford July 1977 (12,500); Brentford Dec. 1983 (£5,000); Barnet cs 1984; Kettering Town Oct. 1984; Chalfont St. Peters July 1985 - Mar. 1986; Kingsbury Town during 1986/87; Hayes early in 1987/88.

A loan signing from Notts County at the start of the 1976/77 season as cover for Sam Ellis, Bolton appeared in the home FL fixture with Shrewsbury and two League Cup games, before returning to Meadow Lane after a month.

BONHAM, John William
(1921-1922)

Inside-right: 1 app.
1921: 5-7, 11-7
Born: Wallsend, 11 Jan. 1895
Died: 31 Dec. 1973
Career: Wallsend Park Villa; CITY Aug. 1921 to May 1922.

Bonham was signed after impressing as a junior in the North Eastern League where it was said he *"...knows how to beat his man and centre accurately. Has shown best form on the right flank."* He failed to break through into City's first team and made only one appearance, at home to Darlington on Boxing Day, 1921.

BONSON, Joseph
(1966-1967)

Centre-forward: 46 app. + 1 sub., 16 goals
1966: 5-11, 12-5
Born: Barnsley, 19 June 1936
Career: Wolverhampton Wanderers groundstaff, (prof.) July 1953; Cardiff City Nov. 1957 (£5,500); Scunthorpe United June 1960 (part exchange for another player); Doncaster Rovers Jan. 1962 (£4,500); Newport County June 1962 (£3,000); Brentford June 1964 (£6,000), CITY Jan. 1966 (£2,000); Hednesford Town Sep. 1967; Lower Gornal Oct. 1967.

Honours: (Cardiff City) Welsh Cup winner 1959. (Newport Co) Welsh Cup finalist 1963

A much travelled centre-forward who turned out for City late in his career. In total his FL record reads 312 apps., + 1 sub, 132 goals. In his younger days Bonson was regarded as a big, powerful leader, strong at heading and fast - he had been a schoolboy sprint champion. He also appeared at inside-forward.

BOOTH, Dennis
(1974-1977)

Midfield: 162 app., 9 goals
1975: 5-7½, 10-5
Born: Stanley Common, Derbys, 9 Apr. 1949
Career: Charlton Athletic Schoolboy forms June 1964, (appr.) July 1964, (prof.) Apr. 1966; Blackpool July 1971 (£7,000); Southend United Mar. 1972 (£7,000); CITY (loan) Feb. 1974, (perm.) Aug. 1974 (£9,000); Watford Oct. 1977 (£10,000); Hull City May 1980, reserve team coach May 1984, first team coach May 1985, assistant manager 1986 to May 1989; Aston Villa coach July 1989 to June 1991; Stafford Rangers coach Nov. 1991; manager Jan. 1992 to Mar. 1993; Bristol Rovers assistant manager Mar. 1993.

Honours: (City) FL Div. 4 Champions 1976
(Watford) FL Div. 4 Champions 1978

Midfielder who was a member of one of City's most successful teams in recent times. First signed on loan, during which time he hit the only hat-trick in his career in a 4-3 win over Bury. After signing permanently he became a member of the 1975/76 championship side, following Graham Taylor to Watford in 1977. Has since become a respected coach, linking up with Taylor again, whilst at Villa Park, and with John Ward at Bristol Rovers. At Stafford he was manager of the side which knocked City out of the FA Cup in the 1992/93 season.

BOSBURY, Charles Edwin
(1926-1929)

Outside-right: 85 apps, 30 goals
1926: 5-10½, 11-10
Born: Newhaven, Sussex, 5 Dec. 1897
Died: 14 July 1929
Career: Pemberton Billings (Hants); Southampton Dec. 1921; Birmingham Aug. 1922; Preston North End June 1925; CITY May 1926 until his death.

Unusually big for a wingman, Charlie was concisely summed up in 1928 as *"... fast, quick at getting away and a splendid shot on the run".* His final appearance for City was in an FA Cup tie against Leicester, after which he was confined to his bed and died within months from tuberculosis.

BOULLEMIER, Leon Autonin ("Frenchy")
(1895-1897)

Goalkeeper: 49 apps.
Born: Stoke-on-Trent, 1874
Died: 24 Apr. 1954
Career: Northampton; Stoke; Stockport County; CITY Dec. 1895; Reading cs 1897; Brighton United in 1898/99 season.

Despite appearing for City when the club was at a low ebb - the team finished bottom of the League in 1896/97 - Boullemier was regarded as something of a star. After leaving football he was the scorer for Northamptonshire CCC for many years.

BOULTON, Colin Donald
(1980-1982)

Goalkeeper: 4 apps.
1981: 5-10, 13-1
Born: Cheltenham, 12 Sep. 1945
Career: Charlton Kings; Cheltenham Police Cadets; Derby County Aug. 1964 (Southampton loan, Sep. - Oct. 1976); Tulsa Roughnecks (USA) Mar. 1978; Los Angeles Aztecs (USA) May 1979; CITY July 1980, contract cancelled Feb. 1982.

Honours: (Derby County) FL Champions 1972, 1975

A veteran 'keeper who had been ever-present in both Derby's League championship campaigns. Signed for City at the age of 34 but broke a leg in his fourth match, away to Crewe, and never played again. Subsequently became a policeman and represented Dunstall (Staffs) in the final of the National Village Cricket Championship.

BOWERY, Bertram N.
(1976)

Centre-forward: 2 app + 2 sub, 1 goal
1976: 6-1, 13-10
Born: St. Kitts, West Indies, 29 Oct. 1954
Career: Ilkeston Town; Worksop Town; Nottingham Forest Jan. 1975 to Mar. 1977 (CITY on loan Feb.-Mar. 1976); Boston Minutemen (USA) Apr.-Aug. 1976; Team Hawaii (USA) Apr.-June 1977.

Giant striker who arrived on loan from the City Ground with Tony Woodcock. He scored on his debut - a 6-0 victory over Southport - but returned to Forest after his month's loan period had expired.

BOWLER, George Frederick
(1893-1894)

Left-back: 6 app.
Born: Grantham, 1878
Career: CITY Sep. 1893 to 1894.

Bowler was a local lad whose first team appearances all occurred in the first half of the 1893/94 season prior to the signing of James Stothert, the former Blackburn Rover, who took over the position for the remainder of the campaign. He was considered *"not class enough for City"*.

BOWLING, Ian
(1988-1993)

Goalkeeper: 59 app.
1993: 6-3, 14-8
Born: Sheffield, 27 July 1965
Career: Frecheville CA; Stafford Rangers; Gainsborough Trinity cs 1988; CITY Nov. 1988 (£2,000); Hartlepool United, on loan, Aug. 1989; Kettering Town, on loan, Feb. 1990; Bradford City, on loan, Mar. to Apr. 1993; Bradford City Aug. 1993 (£25,000).

Giant goalkeeper whose career at Sincil Bank was badly affeted by injuries. He never made more than 20 appearances (in 1990/91), in any one of his five seasons with Lincoln. His transfer fee to the Valley Parade club was decided by a tribunal.

BOYLEN, John
(1921-1923)

Outside-right: 59 app., 4 goals
1922: 5-5, 10-0
Born: Wishaw, Lanarks, circa 1898
Career: Newmain Juniors (Lanarks.); CITY Oct. 1921; Wigan Borough May 1923; Grimsby Town Jan. to cs 1924; Armadale; Kettering Town Jan. 1926; subsequently returned to Scotland.

Soon made the Imps' first team after his arrival and played brilliantly until substaining a bad injury in Mar. 1922. Held his place the following term (37 FL outings) but appeared only once for Wigan and four times for Grimsby.

BRACEWELL, Kenneth
(1963-1965)

Full-back: 23 app., 1 goal
1959: 6-0, 12-3
Born: Colne, Lancs., 5 Oct. 1936
Career: Trawden; Burnley (amat.) 1955, (prof.) Apr. 1957; Tranmere Rovers May 1959; Canadian football for a period; Norwich City Oct. 1963; CITY Nov. 1963; Margate cs 1965; Bury Dec. 1966; Toronto Falcons 1967; Rochdale Mar. to cs 1968; Toronto Falcons 1968; Atlanta Chiefs 1969 to 1972; Atlanta Apollo 1973; Denver Dynamoes coach, 1974.

Bracewell was working as an engineer in his home town with apparently no thoughts of a career in professional football until meeting Burnley's Dave Cargill during his National Service in the RAF. Cargill persuaded him to go for a trial at Turf Moor and he subsequently signed forms. At Sincil Bank he suffered a broken leg in a reserve match in Nov. 1964 and made no more first team appearances before his release. He later made a career in Canada and the USA, returning to England in July 1984 as a paid director of Tranmere Rovers after the club was taken over by an American businessman. He remained as vice-chairman until Feb. 1987.

BRADBURY, John Jackson Longstaff (1896)

Inside-right: 2 app.
1902: 5-9, 11
Born: South Bank, Middlesbrough, 1878
Career: Stockport County; CITY Jan. 1896; Ashton North End Sep. 1896; Blackburn Rovers Aug. 1897; Ashton North End Nov. 1897; Derby County May 1899; Barnsley June 1900; Bristol City June 1901; New Brompton May 1902; Millwall Athletic May 1904 to 1906; Carlisle United cs 1906; Penrith 1908.

One of the great wanderers of the pre-WW1 period, plying his trade in the Lancashire, Southern and Football League circuits. Shone most in the Southern League where his appearances totalled 126 (Bristol City 30, New Brompton 49 and Millwall 47).

BRADLEY, Brendan (1972-1973)

Centre-forward: 31 app., 12 goals
1972: 6-2
Born: Londonderry, 7 June 1950
Career: Derry Athletic; Derry City 1965; Finn Harps cs 1969 (£100); CITY July 1972 (£8,000); Finn Harps Mar. 1973 (£5,000); Athlone Town late in 1978; Sligo Rovers cs 1979; Finn Harps 1982; Derry City, Jan. 1986.

Honours: League of Ireland (1 cap v Football League 1971)
(Finn Harps) FAI Cup winner 1974
(Sligo Rovers) FAI finalist 1981
(Finn Harps) League of Ireland League Cup finalist 1974, 1975

Bradley was a prolific scorer in Ireland but never really settled at Sincil Bank. Leading scorer in the League of Ireland on four occasions (1969/70, 1970/71, 1974/75 and 1975/76), he set a club record for most goals in a match (6 v. Sligo, Nov. 1975) and a League of Ireland record for highest career aggregate (235). He was League of Ireland Personality of the Year in 1975/76.

BRAILSFORD, James Roberts (1895-1897)

Half-back: 20 app.
Born: Lincoln, c.1877
Career: Casuals (Lincoln League); Newark Town, Feb. 1894; CITY Mar. 1895; Notts County cs 1897 to 1898.

Local-born player who turned out regularly in the 1896/97 season. He only made one FL appearance at Meadow Lane and retired from the game at the early age of 21. Was later employed as a local licensee.

BRAMMER, George (1892-1893)

Left-back: 2 app.
Born: Lincoln, 1873
Career: CITY Sep. 1892 to cs 1893.

Full-back of whom little is known. His two FL appearances came on Good Friday and Easter Saturday 1896 against Walsall Town Swifts and Bootle respectively.

BRANFOOT, Ian G. (1973-1978)

Right-back: 166 app., 11 goals
1974: 5-10, 12-2
Born: Gateshead, 26 Jan. 1947
Career: Redheugh Boys Club; Gateshead; Sheffield Wednesday July 1965; Doncaster Rovers Dec. 1969 (part exchange for another player); CITY July 1973 (£7,500); asst.manager/coach July 1977; Southampton youth team coach Sep. 1978; Reading asst.manger/coach July 1983, manager Jan. 1984 to Oct. 1989; Crystal Palace chief coach, Nov. 1989; Southampton manager June 1991 to Jan. 1994; Fulham manager June 1994.

Honours: (City) FL Div 4 Champions 1976

Experienced full-back who formed a valuable partnership with Dennis Leigh for Graham Taylor's Championship side. A very solid defender with a 'no nonsense' approach whose total of FL appearances (including substitutions) was 358. Had some success as a manager too, winning the FA Youth Cup and Football Combination in his first spell at the Dell and the 3rd Division title with Reading in 1986.

BRANSTON, Terence G. (1970-74)

Centre-half: 99 app. + 1 sub, 1 goal
1971: 6-1, 11-11
Born: Rugby, 25 July 1938

Career: Northampton Town, (amat.) 1957, (prof.) Oct. 1958; Luton Town June 1967; CITY Sep. 1970 (£5,000) to cs 1974 (Long Eaton loan Aug. 1973; Nuneaton Borough, loan Oct. 1973 to cs 1974); Enderby Town manager from cs 1974.

Solid centre-half who was very strong in the tackle. Voted supporters' Player of the Season in 1971/72. His only goal for City against Darlington in the 1972/73 season provided Graham Taylor with his first FL win as a manager. Spent the whole of the following season out on loan. Earlier in his career had been a member of the Northampton Town team which rose from the Fourth Division to the First in the early 1960's. On leaving football he settled in Rugby and qualified as a driving instructor.

BRAZIER, Colin J.
(1983)

Centre-half: 9 app.
1983: 6-1, 11-6
Born: Solihull, 6 June 1957
Career: Alvechurch; Northfield Town; Wolverhampton Wanderers, (appr.) June 1973 (prof.) Aug. 1975; Jacksonville Tea Men (USA) June 1981; Birmingham City Sep. 1982; AP Leamington Mar. 1983; CITY Apr. 1983; Walsall Aug. 1983; Kidderminster Harriers Oct. 1986 to 1990.

Honours: (Wolves) Football League Cup winners 1980 (sub) (Kidderminster) Welsh Cup Finalists 1989

Signed on a short term contract to try and rescue City's promotion challenge towards the end of the 1982/83 season. During his brief spell at Sincil Bank he was sent off in the home match with Wrexham. Whilst with Kidderminster he appeared once for the England Semi-Professional side against Wales in 1987.

BRESSINGTON, Graham
(1987-1993)

Centre-half/midfield: 136 app. + 5 sub, 7 goals
1992: 6-0, 12-6
Born: Slough, 8 July 1966
Career: High Wycombe Schools; Chelsea, juniors; Arsenal, juniors; Wycombe Wanderers; Beaconsfield United; Takaplena (New Zealand); Wycombe Wanderers; CITY Nov. 1987 (£20,000); Southend United July 1993 (£25,000)

Powerful midfielder who also appeared at centre-back and sweeper for City. A promising start to his career - High Wycombe won the ESFA Trophy in 1981 and he had spells at Stamford Bridge and Highbury as a junior - but did not develop his potential until much later. Recruited after performing well for Wycombe against the Imps in a GM Vauxhall Conference match and despite several injuries - he missed nearly all of the 1991/92 season - became a popular player at Sincil Bank. Voted Player of the Season in 1990/91.

BREWIS, Robert
(1907-1908)

Centre-forward: 22 app., 11 goals
1907: 5-8, 10-7
Born: circa 1885
Career: Queens Park Rangers circa 1905; CITY May 1907; Burnley May 1908.

Came to City after seven Southern League outings with QPR. He led the Imps' attack in the first half of the 1907/08 season but lost his place and appeared on only three more occasions.

BRINDLEY, Horace
(1911-1914)

Outside-left: 50 app., 4 goals
1912: 5-8, 11-10
Born: Knutton, Staffs, 1 Jan. 1885
Died: 1971
Career: Stoke 1904/05; Norwich City Jan. 1906; Blackpool June 1907; Crewe Alexandra 1908/09; Queens Park Rangers cs 1910; Sutton Town 1910/11; CITY cs 1911; Chester cs 1914.

First took the City management's eye when playing for Crewe against the Imps in a cup-tie but QPR then secured his signature. A hard running, speedy winger who packed a capital shot. An ever present in City's Central League championship side of 1911/12 (32 app., 6 goals).

BRITTAIN, William
(1894-1895)

Defender: 15 app.
Career: Grantham Rovers; CITY May 1894; Grantham Rovers cs 1895.

Brittain began the season as first choice left-back but later switched to the half-back line. Later returned to Midland League football with Grantham Rovers. Summed up at the time as "…. *undoubtably a good man of his class but his size is very much against him*". Appointed Grantham F.C. trainer in the summer of 1911.

BROADBENT, Albert Henry
(1961-1963)

Inside-left: 38 app., 4 goals
1962: 5-11, 12-0
Born: Dudley, Worcs., 20 Aug. 1934
Career: Dudley Town, Notts County Mar. 1952; Sheffield Wednesday July 1955 (£6,000); Rotherham United Nov. 1957 (part exchange); Doncaster Rovers June 1959 (£2,000); CITY Nov. 1961; Doncaster Rovers Jan. 1963 (exchange for Bob Rooney); Bradford Oct. 1965 (£4,500); Hartlepools United Feb. 1967 (£3,000); Rotherham United Mar. 1968 as player/asst. trainer; after this appeared for a number of minor clubs including Skegness Town in 1972/73, and Sheffield Waterworks in 1977/78.

Honours: (Sheff.W) FL Div 2 champions 1956

A capable, enthusiastic forward who also appeared at outside-left for his other clubs. While on National Service in the mid-1950's often represented the Army. In all made almost 500 FL appearances and was appearing for Sheffield Waterworks in the Yorkshire League at the age of 43.

BROADBENT, John
(1894-1895)

Goalkeeper: 2 app.
Career: Grantham Rovers; CITY May 1894 to cs 1895.

Broadbent was one of four players recruited from Grantham Rovers at this time. First choice at the start of the season he broke a shoulder bone in his second match, away to Darwen, and never appeared in City's Football League side again.

BROOK, Harold
(1958)

Inside-forward: 4 app., 1 goal
1957: 5-10, 11-8
Born: Sheffield, 15 Oct. 1921
Career: Sheffield Schools; Woodbourn Alliance (Sheffield); Fulwood; Sheffield United, (amat.) 1939, (pro) Apr. 1943; Leeds United July 1954 (£600); CITY Mar. to cs 1958; retired.

Honours: (Sheffield United) FL Div 2 champions 1953.

Recruited by Bill Anderson at the very end of his career to aid City's fight against relegation in 1957/58. Scored on his club debut against Middlesbrough but was released at the end of the season and announced his retirement. Later ran a newsagents shop in Meadowcroft, Sheffield and coached Yorkshire League Sheffield FC in the early 1960's. Interestingly he had made his first appearance in senior football for the Blades in a war-time fixture at Sincil Bank back in Sep. 1940 when City won 9-2.

BROOKS, Thomas W.
(1964-1971)

Defender: 103 app. + 10 sub, 1 goal
1966: 5-10, 12-8
Born: Wallsend, 2 Feb. 1948
Career: CITY (amat.) 1963, (appr.) July 1964, (prof.) Feb. 1965 to cs 1971.

Defender whose first appearance for the Imps was in Aug. 1963 as a 15 year old in the reserves. A useful deputy in several positions, his most regular season was 1966/67 when he made 37 FL appearances plus 3 substitutions.

BROWN, Edward H.
(1903-1905)

Centre-forward: 37 app., 9 goals
1904: 5-10, 10-12
Career: Sunderland junior football; CITY Nov. 1903 to cs 1905.

A regular first team choice from signing until the beginning of the 1904/05 season when another north-easterner, John Martin, took over the centre-forward berth. Also appeared on both wings for City.

BROWN, Grant Astley
(1989, 1990-   )

Centre-half: 181 app, 8 goals
1993: 6-0, 11-12
Born: Sunderland, 19 Nov. 1969
Career: Leicester City on YTS forms, (prof.) July 1988; (CITY on loan, Aug.-Nov. 1988); CITY Jan. 1990 (£60,000).

First came to Sincil Bank on an extended loan with Paul Groves as part of the deal which saw Tony James move to Leicester. He was soon back at Lincoln, signing for a fee which equalled City's record outlay for a player. Tall and well built, he has been a regular in the Imps' back four ever since and was club captain during the 1992/93 season.

BROWN, McAndrew
(1923)

Right-half: 17 app.
1923: 5-10, 11-2
Career: Scottish junior football; CITY cs 1923 to Dec. 1923.

Half-back initially signed on a one month trial. He played in 17 of the first 19 games of the 1923/24 season but appears to have been released as he had no further outings at first or reserve-team levels.

BROWN, Michael J.
(1967-1968)

Right-back: 38 app.
1967: 5-10, 9-7
Born: Walsall, 11 July 1939
Career: Gloucester schoolboy football; Hull City (amat.) 1954, (prof.) Oct. 1958; CITY July 1967 (initially on two months trial); Cambridge United player/coach May 1968; Oxford United coach Nov. 1969, asst.manager Jan. 1970, manager Sep. 1975; West Bromwich Albion asst.manager July 1979; Manchester United asst. manager June 1981 -Nov. 1986; Bolton Wanderers coach/asst. manager June 1987; Pahang (Malaysia) coach May 1992; Coventry City asst.manager Nov. 1993.

Balding full-back best remembered at Sincil Bank for being sent off in the FL Cup Round 4 replay at home to Derby when the ground record attendance of 23,196 was established. After his playing career ceased he became a respected coach linking up with Ron Atkinson at West Bromwich and Manchester United. In his younger days played cricket for Gloucestershire II in the Minor Counties.

BROWN, Philip James
(1987-1990)

Forward/midfield: 32 app. + 11 sub, 3 goals
1989: 5-8, 9-7
Born: Sheffield, 16 Jan. 1966

Career: Chesterfield (appr.), Oct. 1983 (prof.); Stockport County Dec. 1986; CITY July 1987 (£6,000), Kettering Town cs 1990.

Phil was signed as part of manager Colin Murphy's rebuilding programme for the 1987/88 Vauxhall Conference campaign and finished leading scorer with 16 goals from 38 appearances plus 2 substitutions. His impact in the Fourth Division was not so great and he returned to the Conference where he was top scorer for Kettering in 1992/93. Twin brother of neil who also played for Chesterfield.

BROWN, Thomas
(1956-1961)
Centre-forward/half-back: 3 app.
1956: 5-11, 10-4
Born: Leven, Fife, 17 Nov. 1933
Career: Newburgh FC; CITY Apr. 1956; Boston United July 1961; Boston FC Aug. 1964 to cs 1967; Lincoln United form cs 1967 where he became part of the coaching staff.

Tom's three FL appearances were all at centre-forward in the 1957/58 season and in the second of these, away to Notts County, he was sent off. Developed into a half-back with the reserves with whom he appeared regularly until his release on a free transfer in May 1961.

BROWN, William
(1896-1897)
Centre-forward: 1 app.
1896; 13-0
Career: Preston North End; Tottenham Hotspur; CITY May 1896 to 1897.

A big burly centre-forward said to have "won golden opinion" when with Tottenham, but spent most of his time at Sincil Bank on the injury list. His sole FL outing with City coming in the home match with Loughborough Town on 3 Oct. 1896.

BRYAN, John Joseph
(1919-1922)
Right-half: 75 app., 1 goal
1921: 5-8½, 11-7
Born: Langwith, Notts., 22 Aug. 1897
Died: 1978
Career: Langwith Red Rose; Mansfield Swifts; Mansfield Town; assisted Notts County and CITY during WW1; Shirebrook; CITY May 1919; Mansfield Town May 1922 to 1928.

A consistent and reliable performer for the Imps, he also made 36 appearances in the Midland League championship side of 1920/21. Once appeared as an emergency goalkeeper - away at Durham in Jan. 1922. At Mansfield (when they were a non-League side) he skippered the team to successive Midland League titles (1923/24 and 1924/25) winning much praise. For example - "... always sure and dependable, particularly in critical situations; knows to a nicety how to upset opposing forward movements, and places the ball with judgement."

BUCKLEY, John William
(1932-1935)
Right-back: 92 app.
1932: 5-9, 12-0
Born: Prudhoe, nr. Newcastle-upon-Tyne, 24 Nov. 1903
Died: 13 Apr. 1985.
Career: Prudhoe Castle; Doncaster Rovers during the 1924/25 season; CITY July 1932; Grantham June 1935 to Mar. 1947.

Reliable full-back who was an ever-present in the 1933/34 campaign when it was reported he was "one of the finest backs in the Second Division". An earlier verdict noted his "sound judgement in tackling, allied to a clean kick". At Doncaster he had made more than 250 FL appearances over eight seasons. On leaving Sincil Bank he became a licensee, firstly in Grantham and later in Doncaster.

BUCKLEY, Steven
(1986-1988)
Left-back: 36 apps. 2 goals
1987: 5-11 11-12
Born: Brinsley, Nottingham. 16 Oct 1953.
Career: Ilkeston Town, June 1970; Burton Albion May 1973; Luton Town Apr. 1974 (£2,500); Derby County Jan. 1978 (£163,000); CITY Aug. 1986; Boston United Nov. 1988 (Eastwood Town on loan Oct. 1990); Shepshed Charterhouse Feb. to May 1991 manager; Boston United July 1991 coach; Kettering Town asst. manager July 1992.

A veteran of more than 500 FL apperances whose first season at Sincil Bank coincided with the club's relegation from the League. One of the few players to be retained, he appeared in 22 Vauxhall Conference games but none at all the following season when he was allowed to join Boston United on a free transfer. The brother of Alan a player with Nottingham Forest, Walsall and Birmingham and manager of Grimsby Town.

BUCKLEY, Walter
(1930-1933)
Left-half: 81 app., 1 goal
1933; 5-8½, 11-0
Born: Eccleshall, Sheffield, 30 Apr. 1906.
Career: Sheffield Schools; Birley Carr; Arsenal Apr. 1923; Bournemouth & Boscombe Athletic Aug. 1926; Mansfield Town Sep. 1926; Bradford May 1927; CITY May 1930; Rochdale Aug. 1933; Runcorn Aug. 1936.

Honours: England Schools inter'l. (2 apps., vs Scotland, Wales 1920)
(City) FL Div 3 (North) champions 1932.

Described (1932) as a "strong defensive half-back and a thorough ninety minutes player, a shade more accuracy in positioning himself and in feeding his forwards would bring him near to the top class". A popular figure at Sincil Bank, he broke a bone in his leg during the promotion season but quickly recovered and was back in the first team by the end of the campaign.

BUICK, Joseph L.
(1955-1962)
Wing-half: 31 app., 3 goals
1960: 5-7, 10-11
Born: Broughty Ferry, Dundee, 1 July 1933
Career: Broughty Athletic; CITY Oct. 1955; Cheltenham Town July 1962, Ruston Bucyrus (Lincoln) in 1963/64.

A baker before turning professional, Buick signed for the Imps in preference to more famous clubs such as Wolves, Blackpool and Celtic. Very much a stalwart of the reserve side during his seven year stay at Sincil Bank - his appearance total reached double figures only once (1957/58, 12 apps). He had played at inside-left for Broughty Athletic.

BUIST, A(lfred) George
(1904-1908)
Goalkeeper: 83 app.
1904: 5-10½, 11-0
Career: Willington Quay; CITY May 1904 to cs 1908; North Shields Athletic cs 1909.

Buist became first-choice 'keeper on arriving at Sincil Bank from the north-east and was ever-present in his first two seasons, losing his place to James Saunders in Oct. 1906. He appeared regularly in the Imps' Midland League side in 1906/07 and 1907/08 but only made two more FL appearances before eventually returning north.

BULGER, Charles Guest
(1935-1936)
Outside-left: 22 app., 10 goals
1935: 5-6½, 11-4
Born: Manchester, 19 Jan. 1915
Died: 18 June 1976
Career: Manchester United (amat.) when 16 year old; Congleton Town; Birmingham May 1934; CITY June 1935; Walsall May 1936 to WW2.

Thickset winger with a ready eye for the scoring opportunity. Given his FL baptism by the Imps after experience in the Cheshire League (Congleton) and Central League (Birmingham). He was also a regular at Walsall where he scored 14 times in 81 League outings.

BURDEN, Brian
(1958-1962)
Goalkeeper: 1 app.
1961: 6-2½, 11-12
Born: West Stockwith, Doncaster, 26 Nov. 1939
Career: West Stockwich (Gainsborough League); CITY (amat.) Aug. 1958, part-time prof. Mar. 1961; Gainsborough Trinity July 1962.

Goalkeeper signed after starring in the West Stockwith side who were runners-up in the 1957-58 Notts Junior Cup final. His only FL appearance for the Imps resulted in a 7-0 defeat at Elland Road, shortly before relegation from Division 2. Afterwards he spent several seasons with Gainsborough in the Midland League.

BURDETT, Thomas
(1936-1939)
Inside-right/centre-forward: 27 app., 12 goals
1936: 5-9, 11-2
Born: West Hartlepool, 22 Oct. 1915
Career: Wheatley Hill Juniors (Co Durham); Hull City June 1933; Fulham June 1935; CITY June 1936; Bury May 1939; retired through injury during WW2.

Tom spent nearly all his FL career as a reserve - he made no senior appearances with Fulham or Bury in peace-time. At Sincil Bank he did well in 1937/38 when deputising for Johnny Campbell - scoring 8 times in 18 outings. He fared slightly better in war- time with 30 goals from 43 games for Bury.

BURKE, James
(1894-1897)
Half-back/inside-forward: 52 app, 7 goals
Career: Third Lanark; Notts County cs 1892; Grantham Rovers cs 1893; CITY May 1894; Grantham Rovers Jan. 1897; Ilkeston cs 1897.

Jimmy was an experienced half-back who had appeared in the Scottish, Football and Midland Leagues before signing for City. A regular for his first two seasons he lost his place at the beginning of 1896/97 and was allowed to return to Grantham.

BURKE, Marshall
(1982-1984)
Midfield: 49 app. + 1 sub, 7 goals
1983: 5-7, 9-1
Born: Glasgow, 26 Mar. 1959
Career: Burnley (appr.), (prof.) Mar. 1977; Leeds United May 1980; Blackburn Rovers Dec. 1980; CITY Oct. 1982 (£2,500); (Cardiff City on loan, Dec. 1983); Scarborough cs 1984; trial at Tranmere Rovers, Sep. 1984; later assisted Northwich Victoria; Colne Dynamoes Aug. 1986; Darwen; Bacup; Clitheroe.

Honours: Scottish Schools international

Stocky little midfield player, signed by Colin Murphy when the Imps were hopeful of gaining promotion to Division 2. Appeared regularly in the 1982/83 campaign but then fell out of favour and after receiving a free transfer he moved into the non-League scene.

BURKE, Michael
(1934-1936)
Outside-/inside-right: 27 app., 2 goals
1935: 5-6, 10-0
Born: Blythewood, Glasgow, 28 June 1904
Died: 16 Oct. 1984
Career: Glasgow Ashfield; Dunfermline Athletic; Aberdeen; Clyde; Dundalk; CITY Aug. 1934; Southport June 1936; Rochdale Aug. 1937 to 1938.

Skilful inside-forward who entered English football late, hence a modest total of 55 FL appearances. Mostly in the reserves at Sincil Bank although he enjoyed a spell as first-choice inside-right from Aug. to Dec. 1935.

BURKE, Stephen J.
(1985)
Winger: 4 apps. + 1 sub
1986: 5-10, 10-6
Born: Nottingham, 29 Sep. 1960
Career: Nottingham Forest (appr.); (prof.) Mar. 1978; Queens Park Rangers Sep. 1979 (£125,000); (Millwall on loan, Oct. 1983; Notts County on loan, Oct. 1984; CITY on loan, Aug. 1985; Brentford on loan, Mar. 1986); Doncaster Rovers Aug. 1986; (Stockport County on loan, Oct. 1987); Shepshed Charterhouse Aug. 1988; Grantham Town Nov. 1988.

Honours: England youth international (1978, 1979).

Solid wing-man recruited by John Pickering at the start of the 1985/86 season. He returned to Loftus Road when his month's loan period was completed. Attracted a large fee from QPR in his younger days, particularly bearing in mind he did not appear in the League for Nottingham Forest.

BURNETT, Alfred P.
(1949-1950)
Centre-forward: 4 app., 1 goal
1949: 5-10, 11-8
Born: Aberdeen, 23 July 1922
Died: Feb. 1977
Career: Dundee; Barrow Dec. 1946; CITY Nov. 1949 to June 1950 when he resigned to join the Lincolnshire Police, subsequently appearing for Skegness Town and Lincs. County Police; CITY as a part-time professional Mar. 1952; Hinckley United Dec. 1953; Gainsborough Trinity June 1956.

Burnett arrived with a respectable record - 32 goals from 87 Northern Section outings with Barrow - but although he scored on his debut for the Imps he received few first team opportunities. He was leading scorer for the reserve team in 1949/50 with 15 goals and won representative honours with the English Police. No FL appearances in his second spell at Sincil Park.

BURNIKELL, William F.
(1929-33)
Right-half: 25 app.
1929: 5-9, 11-0
Born: Southwick, Sunderland, 9 Dec. 1910.
Died: May 1980
Career: Newcastle junior football; CITY Aug. 1929; Bradford City July 1933; Aldershot June 1937; retired during WW2; later coached in Sweden with Helsingborgs IF 1947-49; Landskrona Bois 1949-51; then coach to the Sudan national team and a leading Chilean club before return to England - Halifax Town coach Feb. 1956, manager Apr.-Dec. 1956; Orebro SK (Sweden) coach 1957-59; Degerfors IF (Sweden) coach 1960-61.

Honour: (City) FL Div 3 (North) champions 1932.

Appeared under the name Burnicle during his playing career. Most of his FL games for City came in the 1931/32 season as deputy for the injured Walter Buckley. A contemporary noted that he was a *"... hard working defensive half-back ... still a good deal to learn in the matter of ball distribution"*.

BURNS, Peter
(1893)
Inside-right: 2 app.
Career: CITY Sep. to Oct. 1893

Burns appeared in just two matches for the Imps, at home to Crewe and away to Small Heath. *"A big man and he is pretty fast, but he has not so much dash as Irving"*, was one contemporary view.

BURNS, Robert
(1897)
Centre-half: 1 app.
1897: 5-9, 12-0
Career: Abercorn; CITY June 1897 to Sep. 1897.

"The directors make no secret of the fact that great things are expected of him ... regarded as a valuable capture and in all probability will be made the skipper", was one pre-season verdict on this Scot. Matters turned out rather differently, after appearing at centre-half in the opening game of the season, a 5-0 defeat at Newton Heath, Robert was dropped and shortly afterwards he was released.

BURRIDGE, John
(1993-1994)
Goalkeeper: 4 app.
1991: 5-11, 12-11
Born: Workington, 3 Dec. 1951
Career: Workington (appr.), (prof.) from Dec. 1969; Blackpool Apr. 1971 (£10,000); Aston Villa Sep. 1975 (£100,000); (Southend United on loan, Jan. 1978); Crystal Place Mar. 1978 (£65,000); Queens Park Rangers Dec. 1980 (£200,000); Wolverhampton Wanderers Aug. 1982 (£75,000); (Derby County on loan, Sep. 1984); Sheffield United Oct. 1984 (£10,000); Southampton Aug. 1987; Newcastle United Oct. 1989; Hibernian Aug. 1991 to cs 1993; Scarborough Oct. to Nov. 1993; CITY Dec. 1993 to Jan. 1994; Enfield Feb. to Mar. 1994; Aberdeen Mar. to cs 1994, also employed as a coach by Newcastle from cs 1993.

Honours: (Crystal Palace) FL Div 2 champions 1979
(Aston Villa) Football League Cup winners 1977
(Hibernian) Scottish League Cup winners 1992

Burridge became City's oldest post-War player when he appeared on a non-contract basis at the age of 42. A veteran of many clubs and renowned for his enthusiasm, he was signed as cover over the Christmas period to allow regular 'keeper Mike Pollitt to recover fitness.

BURROWS, David W.
(1977-1981)
Midfield: 1 app.
1980: 5-7, 9-4
Born: Bilsthorpe, Notts, 7 Apr. 1961
Career: CITY associate schoolboy Jan. 1977; (appr.) July 1977; (prof.) Apr. 1979; Kings Lynn cs 1981; Heanor Town; Matlock Town Aug. 1983; Sutton Town Aug. 1985; Alfreton May 1987; Matlock Town July 1988 to 1992; Eastwood Town 1992.

Burrows was a small, lightweight midfielder whose only FL outing for the Imps was as an apprentice under George Kerr's managership. City were beaten 5-0 at home by a Watford side managed by Graham Taylor and Burrows never made the first team again. Has since appeared regularly in the Northern Premier League with various Notts. and Derbyshire clubs.

BUTLER, Joseph H.
(1914-1915)

Goalkeeper: 37 app.
1914: 5-9, 12-0
Born: Lawley Bank, Telford, Salop
Died: Aug. 1941
Career: Stockport County; Clapton Orient cs 1905; Stockport County early in 1906; Glossop early 1908; Sunderland Oct. 1912; CITY May 1914 to cs 1915; assisted Rochdale in 1915/16 season.

Honours: (Sunderland) FL champions 1913
FA Cup finalists 1913

Goalkeeper of the famous Sunderland line-up that came within a whisker of the double in 1913. Summed up as *"... quick, resourceful, alert"* and rightly regarded as a great capture. In fact his skills were well known to the City management for he had *"Always played a great game on Sincil Bank when in the ranks of Glossop and Stockport County"*. In all he made over 450 FL appearances and at Glossop had a run of consecutive outings that stretched over four years.

BUTLER, Lee S.
(1986-1987)

Goalkeeper: 30 app.
1987: 6-2, 14-8
Born: Sheffield, 30 May 1966
Career: Harworth Colliery; CITY June 1986; (Boston United on loan, Jan. 1987); Aston Villa Aug. 1987 £100,000, a record for a non-League club); (Hull City on loan, Mar.-Apr. 1991); Barnsley June 1991 (£165,000).

Butler had signed non-contract froms for City back in Nov. 1985 as cover for an FA Cup tie, but continued to appear for Harworth until joining the Imps full-time in June 1986. Got his break when Trevor Swinburne was injured and appeared on and off until the end of the season when City were relegated to the Vauxhall Conference.

BYRON, Gordon F.
(1974-1975)

Midfield: 3 app. + 3 sub
1975: 5-8½, 10-8
Born: Prescot, Lancs, 4 Sep. 1953
Career: Sheffield Wednesday (appr.), (prof.) July 1971; CITY Aug. 1974 to May 1975; Clifton Town Sep. 1975; Skegness Town Nov, 1975; later emigrated to Australia but returned in the summer of 1980; appeared with Lincoln United in the 1980/81 season.

CALDERHEAD, David (senior)
(1900-1901)

Centre-half: 2 app.
Born: Hurlford, Ayrshire, 19 June 1864
Died: 9 Jan. 1938
Career: Wishaw Swifts; Queen of the South Wanderers 1886; Notts County 1889; CITY as secretary-manager Sep. 1900 to May 1907; Chelsea secretary-manager May 1907 to May 1933.

Honours: Scottish international (1 app vs Northern Ireland, 1889)
Football League (1 app vs Football Alliance, 1891)
(Notts County) FL Div 2 champions 1897
FA Cup winner 1894, finalist 1891

Calderhead was one of the greatest of the pre-1900 players and remained a distinguished figure in the football world for over 40 years. He captained both Queen of the South Wanderers and Notts County and would have won many more caps but for the Scottish selection committee's preference for home-based players. At Lincoln he was principally an adminstrator but twice deputised for Charlie Bannister in the 1900/01 season. As a manager with the Imps he took the club to their highest every position (5th in Division 2, 1901/02) and at Chelsea he led the side to an FA Cup final and two promotions to Division 1 in his 26-year stay. He was also active in the first Players' Union and in 1922 received the Football League's long-service award. His son, David jnr., was City's secretary-manager from 1921 to 1924.

CALLAND, Edward
(1961-1962)

Centre-forward: 7 app., 3 goals
1959: 5-11, 12-0
Born: East Hedleyhope, Co. Durham, 15 June 1932
Career: Langley Park CW, Middlesbrough, (amat.) Mar. 1951; Durham City; Fulham (prof.) Apr. 1952; Cornsey Park Albion; Torquay United Sep. 1952; Exeter City July 1957 (£1,500); Port Vale Aug. 1960 (exchange for another player); CITY July 1961; Cheltenham Town Feb. 1962.

Known for his strong physique, speed and shooting power, Ted scored twice on his City debut in a 3-3 draw at Watford. Shortly afterwards he lost his place to Brian Punter and he moved to Cheltenham early in 1962. One of three brothers who assisted Torquay in the immediate post-war period, his FL aggregate was 77 goals in 172 appearances.

CALLENDER, John
(1936-1938)

Outside-right: 75 app., 26 goals
1936: 5-9, 11-0
Born: Wylam, nr Newcastle-upon-Tyne, 3 Sep. 1912
Died: Dec. 1980
Career: Junior football to Brighton & Hove Albion Apr. 1934; Chesterfield Oct. 1934; Ashington July 1935; CITY Aug. 1936; Port Vale May 1938 to 1939.

A go-ahead right-winger noted for his strong and successful shooting - he scored 16 for City in 1936/37 including two in his first match for the club at Accrington. A cousin of Tom (see below) and Jack, the famous Callender brothers of Gateshead.

CALLENDER, Thomas S.
(1937-1945)

Left-back/left-half: 26 app.
1938: 5-9, 10-6
Born: Wylam, nr Newcastle-upon-Tyne, 20 Sep. 1920
Career: Prudhoe Council School; CITY (amat.) June 1937, (prof.) Sep. 1937; Gateshead as a guest during WW2, signing Nov. 1945 (£500) until 1957.

Honour: England Schools international (3 apps. 1935 vs Scotland, Wales, Ireland)

Callender had attracted City's attention as a schoolboy star and after being given a trial in Oct. 1936 he was employed as a groundstaff boy until reaching his 17th birthday, when he was immediately signed on professional terms. He appeared with Gateshead as a guest from the 1941/42 season and after signing played more than 400 games for them, mostly at centre-half. At one point in his Gateshead days Newcastle United were reported to have offered a then hefty £15,000 for his services.

CAMERON, R.
(1892-1893)

Centre-forward/half-back: 15 app., 3 goals
Career: Glasgow junior football; CITY Sep. 1892 (£18 signing on fee) to cs 1893.

Cameron appeared in City's first ever FL match against Sheffield United and scored their first goal in the new competition when he shot home after 20 minutes play. He had a poor scoring record overall however, and soon lost his place when James Fleming was signed from Aston Villa.

CAMMACK, Stephen R.
(1981-1982)

Forward: 18 app., 6 goals
1982: 5-10, 11-9
Born: Sheffield, 20 Mar. 1954
Career: Sheffield United on schoolboy forms, (appr.) (prof.) May 1971; Chesterfield Jan. 1976 (£11,000); Scunthorpe United Sep. 1979; CITY June 1981 (£20,000 and David Hughes); Scunthorpe United Mar. 1982 (£3,000 and David Hughes); (Port Vale on loan, Dec. 1985; Stockport County on loan, Jan. 1986); Scarborough Oct. 1986; Worksop Town Nov. 1986; Harworth Colliery and later Heanor Town in 1989/90 season; Jan. 1991 Wombwell Town player-coach .

Honour: England youth international (1972)

Stylish striker who had a brief spell with the Imps during a lengthy Football League career in which he made over 400 appearances in all. His two periods with Scunthorpe yielded 110 FL goals, which remains a club record. Continued to appear in non-League football after announcing his retirement in Oct. 1986 due to injury.

CAMPBELL, Andrew
(1927-1929)

Inside-left: 5 app., 4 goals
1928: 5-7, 10-7
Born: Dunfermline
Career: Dunfermline Athletic during season 1922/23; Doncaster Rovers Aug. 1924; Brighton & Hove Albion, trial, cs 1927; CITY Nov. 1927 to cs 1929.

Campbell was initially signed on a one month's trial but impressed sufficiently to be given a contract, although he appeared mostly with City's Midland League side. At Doncaster he had appeared regularly in the 1924/25 season and made a total of 44 Northern Section appearances, scoring 7 goals. After retiring from football he returned to Dunfermline where he worked as a coal merchant.

CAMPBELL, Archibald
(1925-1927)

Right-half: 54 app., 4 goals
1925: 5-7½, 11-0
Born: Crook, Co. Durham, Aug. 1904
Career: Spennymoor United; Aston Villa Dec. 1922; CITY June 1925; Craghead United cs 1927.

A clever footballer considered by City to have been a good buy. Described (1926) as *"a player of style and resource"* who was known for his *"long distance surprise volleys"*. He won junior football honours when representing the Birmingham FA vs the Scottish Junior FA in Apr. 1925, and was a nephew of the Villa 1890's celebrity, John Campbell.

CAMBELL, David A.
(1994)

Midfield: 2 app. + 2 sub, 1 goal
1993: 5-9, 10-7
Born: Eglington, Londonderry, 2 June 1965
Career: Oxford Boys Club (Londonderry); Nottingham Forest June 1983; (Notts County on loan, Feb.-May 1987); Charlton Athletic Oct. 1987; (Plymouth Argyle, on loan Mar. 1989); Bradford City Mar. 1989; (Derry City on loan Dec. 1990); Shamrock Rovers on loan, Jan. 1991, full terms cs 1991; brief trials at Manchester City and Tranmere Rovers before joining Rotherham United Nov. 1992; West Bromwich Albion Feb. 1993; Burnley Mar. 1993; (CITY on loan Feb. 1994).

Honours: Northern Ireland youth international; full international (10 apps. between 1986 and 1988)

Balding midfielder who returned to Turf Moor after his month's loan period was completed. After a promising start which included international honours (his full debut was in the 1986 Mexico World Cup against Brazil) his football career was interrupted by injury in Mar. 1990 and despite the number of clubs has made few FL appearances since.

CAMPBELL, James Charles
(1962-1964)

Inside-right/centre-forward: 63 app., 16 goals
1963: 5-7, 10-8
Born: St. Pancras, London, 11 Apr. 1937
Career: Maidenhead Minors; Maidenhead United 1953 (amat. with Reading and Queens Park Rangers); West Bromwich Albion (amat.) June 1954, (prof.) Oct. 1955; Portsmouth July 1959; CITY May 1962; Wellington Town cs 1964; Hednesford Town coach, Dec. 1966-Oct. 1967; Warley FC.

Broke a leg in Apr. 1958, soon after his senior debut, but recovered fully to give good service to both Pompey and the Imps. Scored 12 goals in 1962/63, making him second-top scorer for the club, but was not so successful in the following campaign and was released in May 1964. Later lived in Sedgley, near Dudley and worked as a painter and decorator.

CAMPBELL, John
(1933-1939)

Forward: 184 app., 104 goals
1936: 5-11, 12-0
Born: Stevenston, Ayrshire, 7 Mar. 1910
Career: Dalry Thistle; Leicester City July 1931; CITY Dec. 1933 (£1,250); Scunthorpe United cs 1939; guest for CITY during WW2; Lincoln Co-op as a permit player Nov. 1946.

Campbell was signed for a club record fee in a vain attempt to aviod relegation from the Second Division, but proved to be well worth the money. He finished leading scorer in each of the following four seasons and his aggregate of 104 goals was a new club record. He hit seven hat-tricks in his Sincil Bank career, including five in 1936/37 and scored all five against Rochdale in Nov. 1936. He later recalled that the Rochdale centre-half had begged him to slow down, for fear of getting

him the sack! He was a qualified pharmacist and optician and when injury brought his retirement from League football he took up full-time employment with Lincoln Co-op, eventually rising to the post of Superintendant Chemist Optician before retiring in 1975.

CAPPER, John
(1956-1959)

Centre-half: 21 app.
1958: 6-1, 11-8
Born: Wrexham, 23 July 1931
Career: Wrexham (amat.) cs 1949, (prof.) Nov. 1949; Headington United cs 1955; CITY Jan. 1956; Chester Sep. 1959 to 1961.

Spent most of his time at Sincil Bank as a reserve, his first team appearances restricted by the presence of Tony Emery for the first three seasons. In all he made over 100 FL app. - 48 at Wrexham and 37 for Chester.

CARBON, Matthew P.
(1993-   )

Defender: 10 app.
1993: 6-2, 12-4
Born: Nottingham, 8 June 1975
Career: Aston Villa (on Schoolboy forms), CITY YTS form cs 1991, (prof.) Apr. 1993.

Left-footed central defender who made his FL debut against Darlington in the final match of the 1992/93 season. He impressed in City's youth side and won representative honours for an England youth XI whilst a YTS player.

CARGILL, David Anderson
(1960-1961)

Outside-left: 9 app.
1960: 5-8, 10-12
Born: Arbroath, 21 July 1936
Career: Junior football; Burnley July 1953; Sheffield Wednesday Sep. 1956 (approx. £4,000); Derby County Apr. 1958 (£4,250); CITY Dec. 1960 (£3,265); Arbroath Feb. 1962.

At his best a speedy, goal-aware wingman, Cargill had found himself a reserve at both Turf Moor and Hillsborough. He rejected City's terms at the end of the 1960/61 season and went back to Scotland, eventually signing for Arbroath for what was reported as a "four-figure fee".

CARLING, Terence P.
(1962-1964)

Goalkeeper: 84 app.
1961: 5-9, 11-2
Born: Otley, Yorks., 26 Feb. 1939
Career: Dawson's P & E (Otley); Leeds United Nov. 1956; CITY July 1962; Walsall June 1964 (exchange for Malcolm White); Chester Dec. 1966; Macclesfield Town cs 1971.

Goalkeeper, comparatively on the small side, who missed just eight matches in his two seasons at Sincil Bank. A reserve at Leeds, playing only 5 League games in almost 6 seasons, he made up for it afterwards, totalling 384 for Lincoln, Walsall and Chester. Later worked as a milkman in Chester.

CARMICHAEL, Matthew
(1989-1993)

Defender/forward: 113 app. + 20 sub, 18 goals
1992: 6-2, 11-7
Born: Singapore, 13 May 1964
Career: Durrington; Salisbury Town; Wycombe Wanderers Oct. 1987; Bromley; Basingstoke Town; CITY Aug. 1989; Scunthorpe United July 1993 (part-exchange for David Hill).

Initially signed on a month's trial having previously been a PT instructor in the Royal Artillery based at Aldershot. His early games were played as a striker (he scored on his debut against Scunthorpe) but he was later converted to a competent central defender. On moving to Glanford Park he was given a more attacking role and became a regular goalscorer. Worn representative honours with the Army and Combined Services in his non-League days. Supporters' Player of the Season in 1991/92.

CARR, David
(1979-1983)

Defender/midfield: 165 app. + 3 sub, 4 goals
1981: 5-11, 11-0
Born: Aylesham, Kent, 31 Jan. 1957
Career: Margate; Luton Town July 1975; CITY July 1979 (£20,500); Torquay United Aug. 1983; Maidstone United cs 1984; Dover Athletic cs 1986; Thanet United in 1987/88; Hythe Town cs 1988; Sittingbourne in 1991.

Versatile player who was a member of the Imps team which won promotion from Division 4 in 1980/81 and came very close to taking the club back to the Second Division the following campaign. Missed only one FL match in his first three seasons at Sincil Bank, he was eventually released in Aug. 1983 and after a season at Torquay returned to his native Kent.

CARSON, A.
(1907)

Left-back: 1 app.
1907: 6-0, 12-7
Born: circa 1886
Career: Potteries junior football to CITY Oct. 1907.

Carson was signed to cover for a spate of injuries and went straight into the first team for the home match against Burnley in Oct. 1907. A report of the game states that he *proved that he has ability as a full-back* but he never appeared for City again, either at first team or reserve level.

CARTWRIGHT, Philip
(1930-1933)

Outside-right: 86 app., 21 goals
1931: 5-9, 11-0
Born: Scarborough, 8 Feb. 1908
Died: Oct. 1974
Career: Scarborough; Middlesborough June 1925; Bradford May 1927; Hull City June 1929; CITY May 1930; Bournemouth & Boscombe Athletic July 1933; Scarborough Feb. 1934; Carlisle United, 1 month trial Sep. 1934.

Honours: (Bradford) FL Div 3 (North) champions 1928
(City) FL Div 3 (North) champions 1932

Dangerous winger, a hard runner liable to score by cutting in at any time. A 1932 source described him thus "... *a speedy and clever winger on his day, though his form is inclined to be variable. He has the ability to beat his man and finish with a drive of tremendous power ...*". Sustained an injury during his first season which was to dog him for the rest of his stay at Sincil Bank. In the late 1930's he was a guesthouse keeper in Scarborough.

CASEY, Paul
(1988-1991)

Full-back/midfield: 44 app. + 5 sub, 4 goals
1988: 5-8, 10-6
Career: Sheffield United (appr.), (prof.) June 1979; Boston United cs 1982; CITY Mar. 1988; Boston United cs 1991.

Signed during the run-in to the Vauxhall conference championship season, Casey's later appearances were badly restricted by a series of knee injuries. Missed the end of the 1990/91 season after he was jailed for grievous bodily harm. He signed for Boston United again during the following close-season, for whom he had earlier appeared at Wembley in the 1985 FA Trophy final, gaining a runners-up medal.

CAVANAGH, John Andrew
(1914-1919)

Inside-forward: 2 app.
1914: 5-8, 11
Born: Newcastle-upon-Tyne, 1891
Career: Ashington; Jarrow Caledonians; Clapton Orient cs 1911; Ashington 1913; CITY June 1914 to 1919.

Did not make the Orient senior side, returning to Ashington where he scored 38 goals in their Northern Alliance championship side of 1913/14. City were attracted by his prolific scoring but he made only two first-team appearances in peace-time, both at inside-left in place of Chesser. He fared rather better in the WW1 years when he played at inside-right, his best season was 1915/16 (34 app, 10 goals). Remained in Lincoln after retiring from football.

CHADBURN, John
(1893-1894)

Outside-right: 25 app., 9 goals
1902: 5-8, 11-7
Born: Mansfield, Feb. 1873
Died: Dec. 1923

Career: Mansfield Greenhalgh's; CITY cs 1893; Notts County Sep. 1894; Wolverhampton Wanderers cs 1897; West Bromwich Albion Jan. 1900; Liverpool May 1903; Plymouth Argyle 1904; Swindon Town 1906; Mansfield Town circa 1907, briefly before retiring.

Winger with speed and stamina who was known for his volatile temperament. In a lengthy career he saw service in both divisions of the Football League and the Southern League, appearing as a right-back from around 1900. Died in Mansfield.

CHAMBERS, Reuben C.
(1926-1927)

Goalkeeper: 7 app.
1926: 5-11, 11-10
Born: Nottingham 1908
Career: Beeston Ericssons; CITY (amat.) Apr. 1926 to cs 1927.

Amateur who signed from a Nottingham works side and deputised for Albert Iremonger in the 1926/27 season. He conceded seven on his debut (a 3-7 defeat at Rochdale on Christmas Day) and let in 21 in his 7 FL matches. It was therefore no surprise when he was released in the summer of 1927.

CHAMBERS, Robert
(1920-1922)

Inside-right/centre-forward: 23 app., 12 goals
1921: 5-11, 11-7
Born: Newcastle-upon-Tyne, 11 Dec. 1899
Died: 1972

Career: Brighton West End (Tyneside League); CITY cs 1920; Burnley Mar. 1922 (£650); Rotherham County May 1923; Torquay United late in 1925; Carlisle United cs 1926; Exeter City Aug. 1927; New Brighton July 1928; Colwyn Bay Oct. 1928; Hurst Aug. 1929.

"A big, bustling fellow, who adds to his knowledge of the game every time he steps on the field" said a 1921 football guide. Bob became a regular towards the end of the 1920/21 Midland League championship campaign in which he scored 8 times in 19 matches and was sold for a sizeable fee to help reduce City's debts. He made 129 FL appearances in all, often turning out at centre-half for his other clubs.

CHAPMAN, Darren P.
(1991-1993)

Midfield: 0 app. + 1 sub
Born: Lincoln, 15 Nov. 1974
Career: Wimbledon on Schoolboy forms; Hykeham United; CITY

on YTS forms, cs 1991; Lincoln United Sep. 1993.

A versatile player who appeared in both midfield and defensive positions for City's youth team. His only Football league experience came in Apr. 1992 whilst still a YTS player when he replaced Dean West for the final four minutes of the 5-1 victory at Chesterfield. He was not given a contract at the end of his period as a trainee and later signed for Lincoln United of the Northern Counties East League.

CHAPMAN, Roy Clifford
(1957-1961, 1965-1967)

Inside-/centre-forward: 172 app. + 1 sub, 77 goals
1960: 6-1, 13-3
Born: Birmingham, 18 Mar. 1934
Died: Mar. 1984

Career: Kingstanding Youths; Kynoch Works (Birmingham); Aston Villa (amat.) Nov. 1951, (prof.) Feb. 1952; CITY Nov. 1957; Mansfield Town Aug. 1961 (£6,000); CITY Jan. 1965 (£5,000); Port Vale Aug. 1967; Chester May 1969; Stafford Rangers player/manager, Oct. 1969; Stockport County manager, Sep. 1975 to May 1976; Stafford Rangers manager Aug. 1977 to Feb. 1980; Walsall Sportsco FC manager.

Chapman was a regular scorer with all his clubs - he netted over 200 FL goals in all - his best haul at Sincil Bank being 20 in 1966/67 towards the end of his playing career. Even when playing badly, he was likely to score. In his second spell he held the title 'player-coach' from Mar. 1965 to Oct. 1966 being in charge of team selection and the playing side of the club. His one appearance as a substitute created club history - when he replaced Bunny Larkin at half-time during the visit to Darlington in Aug. 1965 - becoming the first City substitute in the League. He is the father of Lee Chapman, the well-known centre-forward currently appearing for West Ham

CHEETHAM, Thomas Miles
(1945-1948)

Centre-forward: 47 app., 29 goals
1938: 5-10, 11-8
Born: Byker, Newcastle-upon-Tyne, 11 Oct. 1910
Career: Army football (Royal Artillery in India); Queens Park Rangers (amat.) 1935, (prof.) Aug. 1935; Brentford Feb. 1939 (approx. £4,000); CITY Oct. 1945 (£500); retired cs 1948; appointed club scout for the London area until Sep. 1949 when be became coach to Willesden FC (a QPR nursery).

Turned professional late in life but soon became known as a consistent goalscorer. His QPR aggregate of 80 goals in 116 games earned him an international trial and a transfer to First Division Brentford. During the war he returned to the Army and was wounded at Dunkirk. He later guested for City (49 goals from 51 wartime appearances) before signing for a substantial fee. Despite his age and injuries he was the club's leading scorer in 1946/47 season, but only made two appearances after Sep. 1947.

CHESSER, William Etheridge
(1914-1920)

Inside-left: 76 app., 18 goals
1914: 5-11, 11-0
Born: Stockton-on-Tees, 11 Aug. 1893
Died: 27 Oct. 1949
Career: Stockton; Bradford City Dec. 1911; CITY Feb. 1914 (£600); (Bradford City as a guest in WW1); Merthyr Town June 1920; Wigan Borough Aug. 1921 to 1922; CITY (reserves) Jan. 1924 and Lincoln Claytons in the same season.

At Lincoln he partnered Billy Egerton and earned himself a reputation for his skilful play. In 1914 he was described thus "... *so artistic an inside-left as has ever been seen in the ranks of the Red and Whites*". He returned to Sincil Bank for a brief trial with the Midland League side in the mid-1920's.

CHIPPERFIELD, Francis
(1919-1920)
Centre-/left-half: 23 app.
1920: 5-10, 11-9
Born: Shiremoor, Newcastle-upon-Tyne, 2 Dec. 1895
Died: 8 Mar. 1979
Career: Leeds City; CITY Oct. 1919 (£100); Middlesbrough June 1920 (£1,000); Carlisle United; Ashington June 1923; Frickley Colliery June 1929.

A bargain from the Leeds City auction, Chipperfield gave City a handsome profit for less than a year's service. He only appeared once for Middlesbrough but gave valiant service to Ashington (165 app, 9 goals) in their days in the Northern Section of Division 3.

CLARE, Joseph
(1937-1945)
Outside-left: 71 app., 25 goals
1937: 5-10, 11-10
Born: Westhoughton Lancs 4 Feb. 1910
Died: 23 Sep. 1987
Career: Westhoughton Town; Manchester City (amat.) Aug. 1930 (prof.) Sep. 1930; Wigan Borough Aug. 1931; Westhoughton Town Oct. 1931; Accrington Stanley Nov. 1933; Arsenal 1934 (£700) to farmed him out to their nursery side, Margate for 1935/36; Norwich City May 1936; CITY June 1937; Ruston Bucyrus (Lincoln) Feb.- cs 1946 when appointed coach to Bournemouth & Boscombe Athletic where he remained until 1961.

A great favourite, *"his inward swerve and opportunist shootings make him deadly"* as one critic remarked. He appeared regularly throughout WW2, aggregating a further 150 appearances for the Imps (44 goals). Latterly worked for the Bournemouth & District Water Company, training their football team until 1968.

CLARK, Derek
(1949-1953)
Inside-right: 4 app., 1 goal
1949: 5-8½, 10-8
Born: Newcastle-upon-Tyne, 10 Aug. 1931

Career: Medomsley Juniors; CITY trial Jan. 1949, full terms Mar. 1949 (Durham FC to Dec. 1951 whilst on National Service in the RAF); Ransomes & Marles cs 1953; Boston United cs 1954; Holbeach United cs 1959; Ruston Bucyrus (Lincoln) cs 1961.

Signed as a youngster from Bill Anderson's old club, his early career at Sincil Bank was interrupted by National Service. Scored within 2 minutes of his FL debut against Tranmere in Feb. 1953, but received few first team opportunities. Settled in Lincoln and was heavily involved in the local soccer scene as manager of Lincs. League and Lincoln Sunday League teams.

CLARKE, David Alan
(1987-1994)

Full-back/midfield: 141 app. + 6 sub, 9 goals
1993: 5-10, 11-0
Born: Nottingham, 3 Dec. 1964
Career: Notts County (appr.), (prof.) Dec. 1982; CITY Aug. 1987 (£5,000); Doncaster Rovers Jan. 1994; Gainsborough Trinity on trial Aug. 1994.

Honour: England youth international (1983)

A stylish full-back who spent much of his time at Sincil Bank on the injury list. Signed by Colin Murphy shortly before the Vauxhall Conference season, he played a full part in the championship with 5 goals from 25 appearances plus 4 substitutions.

CLARKE, William
(1898-1900)

Inside-left: 35 app., 7 goals
Career: Aberdeen junior football; CITY June 1898 to Jan.1900

Signed from Aberdeen along with John Henderson, Clarke was a regular in his first season at Sincil Bank, but appeared only 5 times during 1899/1900 and was released at the beginning of Jan. 1900.

CLARKE, William G.
(1909-1911)

Outside-right: 35 app., 1 goal
1909: 5-9, 12-0
Born: Mauchline, Ayrshire, 1880
Died: 1940
Career: Third Lanark 1897; Bristol Rovers cs 1900; Aston Villa Sep. 1901; Bradford City May 1905 (£200); CITY Dec. 1909; Croydon Common Sep. 1911-1912.

Honour: (Bradford C.) FL Div.2 champions 1908

After the 1909/10 season praised as having "... *played pretty and brilliant football and his retention has given much satisfaction"*. Clarke had arrived at Sincil Bank with a considerable reputation as a fast ball-playing winger. Departed for Southern League Croydon Common after City failed to achieve re-election at the end of his second season.

CLAYTON, Rex
(1939)

Inside-right: 3 app., 1 goal
1938: 5-11, 12-6
Born: East Retford, Notts, 1916
Career: Retford Locomotive; Retford Town; Manchester City Nov. 1935; Bristol City June 1938 (£750); CITY July 1939.

Clayton arrived at Sincil Bank with little FL experience (16 matches in all) but appeared in all 3 of City's Northern Section games in 1939/40 until war intervened.

CLEWS, Malcolm Derek ("Maxie")
(1954-1955)

Outside-left: 7 app.
1954: 5-9, 11-0
Born: Ocker Hill, Tipton, Staffs, 12 Mar. 1931
Career: Wolverhampton Wanderers groundstaff during 1946/47 season, (prof.) Mar. 1948; CITY Feb. 1954-cs 1955 when he left to join the Wolverhampton Police Force.

Promising winger whose opportunities at Sincil Bank were restricted by Roy Finch. Left the game in the summer of 1955 to join the police force in Wolverhampton.

CLIFF, Edward
(1974)

Left-back: 3 app.
1974: 5-10, 11-5
Born: Liverpool, 30 Sep. 1951
Career: Burnley (appr.), (prof.) Oct. 1968; Notts County July 1973; (CITY on loan Oct. 1974); Chicago Sting (USA) Mar. 1975; Tranmere Rovers Sep. 1976; Rochdale Sep. 1979 to May 1981.

Cliff was signed as cover for Dennis Leigh and returned to Meadow Lane after his month's loan period was completed. He had made 21 FL appearances for Burnley in 5 years before a Notts County spell which was marred by injuries.

CLINT, Thomas
(1921-1922)

Goalkeeper: 1 app
1921: 5-8½, 10-7
Born: Gateshead, 1892
Died: 1965
Career: Felling Colliery; CITY Aug. 1921 -May 1922

Clint arrived from the Northern Alliance with favourable comments, *"Excellent credentials. Gathers the ball well"*. At Lincoln he was understudy to Bob Bainbridge, his sole FL outing coming in the 2-0 home defeat by Nelson in Sep. 1921.

CLOTWORTHY, Hugh
(1938-1939)
Right-half: 2 app.
1938: 5-8½, 11-0
Born: Kilwinning, Ayrshire 8 Mar 1914
Died: 1984
Career: Irvine Meadow; Glenafton Athletic; Kilwinning Rangers 1936; CITY April 1938-cs 1939.

Described on signing as *"... a player who has individuality and power to express it"*. He had considerable success in Ayrshire junior football and won representative honours with the Scottish Junior FA, but his chances at Sincil Bank were restricted by Billy Bean, and he made only 2 appearances, both in Sep. 1938.

COBB, W(alter) William
(1966-1968)
Wing-half: 67 app., 10 goals
1967: 5-8, 11-0
Born: Newark, 29 Sep. 1940
Career: Ransomes & Marles; Nottingham Forest (amat.) Oct. 1958, (prof.) Sep. 1959; Plymouth Argyle Oct. 1963 (approx. £8,000); Brentford Oct. 1964 (£12,000); CITY Nov. 1966 (£2-3,000); Boston United July 1968-May 1971.

Billy Cobb holds the distinction of being the only man to score a hat-trick on his debut for the Imps - an 8-1 victory over Luton Town at a time when City were struggling at the bottom of the League table. Gave good service to the club in his two seasons, helping them to a best-ever performance in the FL Cup (round 4, replay in 1967/68).

COCKERILL, Glenn
(1976-1979, 1981-1984)
Midfield: 179 app + 7 sub, 35 goals
1981: 6-0, 11-13
Born: Grimsby, 25 Aug. 1959
Career: Ritz Cafe (Louth); Louth United; CITY Nov. 1976; Swindon Town Dec. 1979 (£110,000); CITY Aug. 1981 (£40,000); Sheffield United Mar. 1984 (£140,000); Southampton Oct. 1985 (£225,000); Leyton Orient Dec. 1993.

Cockerill signed from Louth after impressing the City's junior team in the Northern Intermediate League. In his early days he played as a striker but later switched to midfield where he proved to be a powerful and combative performer. Sold by Colin Murphy to Swindon for a then club record fee, but he was given few opportunities at the County Ground and returned to City two years later. One of the stars of the Imps team in the early 1980's he again moved on for a six-figure fee, this time to Bramall Lane. He then had over eight seasons in top-flight football before signing for Orient at the end of 1993. Both his father Ron (Huddersfield Town, Grimsby Town) and his brother John (Grimsby Town) appeared in League football.

COKER, Adewunmi O.
(1974-1975)
Forward: 6 app., 1 goal
1975: 5-9, 10-7
Born: Lagos, Nigeria, 19 May 1954
Career: West Ham United (appr.) July 1970, (prof.) Dec. 1971 (CITY on loan Dec. 1974) contract cancelled Apr. 1976. Moved to USA; Boston Minutemen 1974 to July 1976; Minnesota Kicks August 1976 to April 1978; San Diego Sockers May 1978-1979; Rochester Lancers 1980; San Diego Sockers 1982-1984. Also appeared in the Major Indoor Soccer League with New York Arrows 1979-80; Baltimore Blast 1980-81; San Diego Sockers 1982-1986; St. Louis Steamers 1987-1988.

Striker signed by Graham Taylor on loan from West Ham, returning in Jan. 1975. Ade later emigrated to the United States where he starred in both the NASL and indoor League for several seasons, eventually taking out US citizenship.

COLLINS, Steven M.
(1985-1986)
Full-back: 24 app.
1985: 5-8, 12-4
Born: Stamford, 21 Mar. 1962
Career: Peterborough United (appr.), (prof.) Aug. 1979; Southend United Aug. 1983; CITY on loan Mar.-May 1985, signing permanently cs 1985; Peterborough United on loan Dec. 1985, permanently Jan. 1986; Kettering Town Aug. 1989; Boston United cs 1991; Corby Town cs 1992.

Lincolnshire-born full-back who impressed sufficiently in his extended loan period to be signed on full terms but later fell out of favour following the change in manager from John Pickering to George Kerr. Most of his FL experience was with Peterborough where he made over 200 appearances in his two spells.

COMMONS, Michael
(1958-1961)
Centre-forward: 2 app, 1 goal
1960: 5-9, 11-7
Born: Doncaster, 18 May 1940
Career: Wath Wanderers; CITY May 1958; Workington July 1961; Chesterfield July 1964- 1965.

Commons was signed from the famous Wolves' nursery side, Wath Wanderers, but despite finishing at the head of the reserves' goalscoring charts in each of his three seasons, first team opportunities were restricted at Sincil Bank. He scored on his debut for the Imps against Cardiff in February 1960 but received only one more chance before joining Workington on a free transfer. He totalled 36 goals in 74 League outings for the Cumbrian outfit, but eventually returned to Lincoln when his football career was over and worked for European Gas Turbines (Rustons).

COMRIE, James
(1910-1911)
Centre-half: 12 app., 1 goal
1912: 5-11½, 12-4
Born: Denny, Stirling., 31 Mar 1881
Career: Third Lanark; Reading 1906; Glossop cs 1907; Bradford City Sep. 1908 to cs 1910; CITY Nov. 1910 to cs 1911; Grantham Oct. 1911; Stenhousemuir Nov. 1911; Reading May 1912-15 (assisted Boston Swifts Jan.- cs 1914).

Scot signed by the Imps in an unsuccessful attempt to escape re-election in the 1910/11 season. Placed on the offers list at £100 but eventually the player reduced this to £20 on appeal. Retained connections with Lincolnshire on leaving Sincil Bank - he appeared for Boston Swifts while on the Reading injury list awaiting an operation. Worked as an attendant at Bracebridge Asylum for many years. Killed in action fighting with the Northumberland Fusiliers during the Great War.

CONNOR, J. Edward
(1907-1908)
Inside-left: 4 app.
Born: 1890
Career: Eccles Borough (CITY as an amateur, November 1907); Manchester United cs 1909; Sheffield United cs 1911; Bury cs 1912; Exeter City 1919-20; Rochdale cs 1920.

Connor was one of three men signed on amateur forms in Nov. 1907, all appeared in the away fixture at Glossop which was abandoned, the other two (Percy Hayden and Herbert Rothwell) never played for the Imps again. His form at Eccles in the following season's Lancashire Combination campaign earned him a transfer to Manchester United which was the start of a lengthy Football League career. A versatile forward known for his sportsmanship.

CONNOR, James
(1939)
Goalkeeper: 7 app.
1939: 6-0, 12-0
Born: Cleland, Lanarks, c.1917
Career: Glenavon; Coltness United; CITY Mar. 1939.

Due to Dan McPhail's indisposition and Jack Thacker missing his rail connection, third choice Connor took the goalie's jersey for the Good Friday fixture against Oldham Athletic. He did well and played in all the remaining Northern Section matches that season.

COOK, Mark R.
(1988-1990)
Defender/midfield: 7 app.
1990: 6-0, 11-11
Born: Boston, Lincs, 7 Aug. 1970
Career: CITY on YTS July 1986, (prof.) Aug. 1988 (Bromsgrove Rovers on loan, Feb. 1989); Boston United Jan. 1990 to cs 1991.

Lincolnshire-born midfielder who came up through the ranks. Made his first team debut at Exeter in May 1989 but failed to win a regular first team place and moved on to York Street in the 1989/90 season. Retired from senior football wich a back injury at the age of 21.

COOPER, Joseph
(1932-1933)
Inside-forward: 24 app., 3 goals
1930: 5-11¾, 11-2
Born: Newbold, Chesterfield, 1899
Died: 22 Jan. 1959
Career: Army football; Sheepbridge Works (trials with West Bromwich Albion and Sheffield Wednesday); Chesterfield cs 1921; Notts County Mar. 1923 (£1,500); Grimsby Town Sep. 1924 (approx. £1,000); CITY July 1932-cs 1933.

Classy, ball-playing inside man signed by the Imps to strengthen the side on their return to Divison Two. His one season at Sincil Bank was the final one of a FL career in which he aggregated 272 appearances and scored 70 goals. A schoolmaster by profession and a useful club cricketer.

COOPER, Richard D.
(1985-1897)
Midfield/defender: 57 app + 4 sub, 2 goals
1986: 5-10, 10-8
Born: Brent, London, 7 May 1965
Career: Sheffied United (appr.) June 1981, (prof.) May 1983; CITY non-contract Aug. 1985, full terms Jan. 1986 (also assisted Gainsborough Trinity in 1985/86); Exeter City July 1987; Weymouth Mar. 1989; Yeovil Town Nov. 1990.

Hard tackling midfield player who first joined the Imps on a non-contract basis after being released by Sheffield United. Both his seasons at Sincil Bank ended in relegation, and he found himself released when City went down to the Vauxhall Conference. Cooper also made more than 50 appearances for Exeter and has remained in the West Country since leaving them.

COOPER, Terence
(1971, 1971-1979)

Defender/midfield: 268 app. + 2 sub, 12 goals
1975: 5-9, 11-0
Born: Croesyceiliog, Carmarthen, 11 Mar. 1950
Career: Newport County July 1968; Notts County July 1970; CITY on loan Dec. 1971, and again July 1972, signing permanently Aug. 1972 (£5,000); (Scunthorpe United on loan, Nov. 1977); Bradford City June 1979 (£10,000); Rochdale Aug. 1981-1982.

Honours Wales youth international
(City) FL Div. 4 champions 1976

Terry, who had captained the Welsh youth side, first came to Sincil Bank at the end of 1971 as a midfield player on loan from Meadow Lane. He was signed permanently the following summer and later switched to central defender where he formed a successful partnership with Sam Ellis in Graham Taylor's side of the mid-1970's. He was twice voted supporters Player of the Year (1974/1975 and 1978/79) and on leaving football became a milkman.

COPLEY, Dennis I.
(1946-1948)
Inside-right: 1 app.
Born: Misterton, Notts., 21 Dec. 1921
Career: Norwich City (amat.); CITY Sep. 1946; Boston United Aug. 1948; Corby Town 1949; Lincoln Claytons in 1953/54.

Local lad who was in the forces based at RAF Swinderby when he signed for City. His sole FL appearance came in a Northern Section fixture at Barrow in May 1947. Looked upon as an inside-forward but later reverted to wing-half. The club's 1948 brochure noted him to be *"keen and a trier"*.

CORBETT, Frederick William
(1936-1939)
Left-back: 103 app.
1936: 5-9, 13-0
Born: Birmingham, 8 Oct. 1909
Died: 20 Nov. 1974
Career: Worcester City; Torquay United May 1929; Manchester City Mar 1930; CITY June 1936-cs 1939 when he left to join the Birmingham Fire Brigade.

"... Very sound and steady, and reliable and resourceful in emergencies" noted a contemporary. Corbett came to City after a six year spell at Maine Road when he had been unable to gain a regular first team place. He fared better at Sincil Bank, occupying the left-back slot until Jan.1939 when he was replaced by Tom Callender. His brother Victor assisted Manchester City and Southend United.

CORK, Alan G.
(1977)
Centre-forward: 5 app.
1980: 6-0, 12-0

Born: Derby, 4 Mar. 1959
Career: Derby County (junior), (prof.) July 1977, (CITY on loan, Sep. 1977); Wimbledon Feb. 1978; Sheffield United Mar. 1992; Fulham Aug. 1994.

Honour: (Wimbledon) FA Cup winner 1988

Cork was a young light-weight centre-forward who failed to score in his loan period at Sincil Bank. Signed by Wimbledon on a free transfer he developed into a powerful and assertive striker, staying 14 years during which time he established club records for Football League appearances (352 + 78 as substitute) and goals (145), appearing in all four divisions.

CORNER, J(ames) Norman
(1967-1969)

Centre-forward: 44 app. + 1 sub, 12 goals
1964: 6-2, 12-0
Born: Horden, Co Durham, 16 Feb. 1943
Career: Horden Colliery Welfare; (Wolverhampton Wanderers amat.); Hull City Aug. 1962; CITY Oct. 1976 (£1,000); Bradford City Jan. 1969 (£4,000); Bradford March 1972; South Shields July 1973.

Tall, gangly striker who showed considerable skill in the air - he once scored a hat-trick of headers in an away match at Bradford (Apr. 1968). Also appeared as a centre-half for his other clubs and made over 100 FL appearances at Valley Parade. Later went into business in South Shields and coached schools' teams in the area.

CORNFORTH, John Michael
(1990)
Midfield: 9 app. 1 goal
1990: 6-1, 11-5
Born: Whitley Bay, 7 Oct. 1967
Career: Whitley Bay Youths; Sunderland (appr.) (prof.) Oct 1985 (Doncaster Rovers on loan Nov 1986); (Shrewsbury Town on loan Nov 1986); (CITY on loan Jan-Mar 1990); Swansea City Aug.1991 (£50,000).

Tall left-sided midfield player whose performances in an extended loan period pursuaded City to try and sign him permanently. However, he returned to Roker Park and later joined Swansea.

COSTELLO, Peter
(1991, 1992-1994)

Forward: 31 app. + 10 sub, 7 goals
1993: 6-0, 11-3
Born: Halifax: 31 Oct. 1969
Career: Bradford City on YTS, (prof.) July 1988; Rochdale July 1990 (£10,000); Peterborough United Mar. 1991 (£30,000); (CITY on loan, Sep. 1991); CITY Sep. 1992-April 1994 (£15,000); (Halifax Town on loan, Oct. 1993; Dover Aug. 1994.

Alert and skilful striker who could also perform in midfield, signed permanently 12 months after a brief loan period at Sincil Bank. Lost his first team place early in the 1993/94 season and had loan spells in the Vauxhall Conference with Halifax and Kettering.

COSTIGAN, Thomas
(1910)

Inside-left: 2 app., 1 goal
1910: 5-8, 10-12
Career: Wallsend Park Villa; Seaham Harbour; CITY May-Dec. 1910

Costigan signed together with his inside partner Welsh (who did not make the Imps' FL team), in the summer of 1910. A football annual of the time remarked *"not of big physique but was one of the brilliant forwards in the North-Eastern League. Twice scored a hat-trick in 1909/10. City had tried to sign him before"*. Appeared in the first two games of the 1910/11 season, scoring in a 3-1 defeat at Burnley but was released three months later and returned to the North-East.

COTTAM, John Edward
(1973)

Centre-half: 1 app.
1971: 5-10, 11-10
Born: Worksop, 5 June 1950
Career: Nottingham Forest (appr.) Aug. 1966, (prof.) May 1967 (Mansfield Town on loan, Nov. 1972; CITY on loan Mar. 1973); Chesterfield Aug. 1976; Chester July 179; Scarborough May 1982-Oct. 1984 as player-manager; Burton Albion 1984/85; Metropolitan Police in 1987/88.

Rated an outstanding prospect in his youth at Forest, however, he had to wait three years for his senior debut. Cottam was a solid defender who impressed in his performance in the home match with Chester in Mar. 1973, but was quickly recalled to the City Ground. He aggregated 332 appearances plus 6 as substitute in his FL career before moving into non-League football.

COULTON, Charles
(1892-1893)

Right-back: 12 app.
Career: Birmingham St. Georges Sep. 1890; CITY Sep. 1892-1893.

Full-back signed from the disbanded Birmingham St. Georges club prior to City's entry into the Football League. He had appeared in all St. Georges' Football Alliance games the previous season and played in the Imps' first 12 fixtures of 1892/93. Brother of Frank (Aston Villa).

COWLEY, B(ernard) John
(1899-1902)

Left-half: 68 app., 3 goals
1899: 5-8, 11-7
Born: Burton-on-Trent, 1877
Died: 21 Dec. 1926
Career: Winshill St. Marks; Trinity Strollers; Hinckley Town; CITY May 1899; Swindon Town Sep. 1902; retired Apr. 1906

Spotted quite by chance by a City director, Jack developed into a sound wing-half for both the Imps and Swindon Town. A regular in his first two seasons before losing his place to Percy Blow in 1901/02. For Swindon he is recorded as having made 77 Southern League appearances, scoring 4 goals.

COX, Mark L.
(1976-1978)

Forward: 3 app. + 2 sub
1977: 5-6, 10-1
Born: Birmingham, 4 Oct. 1959
Career: CITY (appr.) July 1976, (prof.) Sep. 1977; Doncaster Rovers Sep. 1978; Boston FC cs 1979; Boston United May 1980; Shepshed Charterhouse cs 1983; Alfreton Town Dec. 1983; Shepshed Charterhouse Jan. 1984.

Small striker who had an excellent scoring record in City's junior and reserve teams but received few opportunities at first-team level. Made his FL debut when still an apprentice (as a sub. at Crystal Palace, May 1977) but after signing full terms that Sep. he was released in May 1978. Had a season at Doncaster before switching to the non-League scene.

COXON, William George
(1958)

Outside-left: 11 app., 1 goal
1958: 5-8, 11-6
Born: Derby, 28 Apr. 1933
Career: Derby Schools; Derby County groundstaff, (prof.) May 1950; Ilkeston Town; Norwich City May 1952; CITY Mar. 1958 (£4,000); Bournemouth & Boscombe Athletic Nov. 1958; Poole Town July 1966.

Fast wingman signed by Bill Anderson from Norwich at a time when City looked doomed to relegation from

Divison 2. They escaped the drop but Coxon's stay at Sincil Bank lasted only seven months before he moved to Bournemouth where he stayed eight seasons and made 199 appearances plus 1 as substitute, scoring 37 times. Later settled in the Bournemouth area.

CRAWFORD, John
(1900-1903)

Centre-half: 85 app., 1 goal
1903: 5-9½, 11-2
Born: Renton, Dunbart., 23 Feb. 1880
Career: Renton FC; CITY Aug. 1900; Nottingham Forest Feb. 1903 to 1905.

Came to Lincoln on the recommendation of David Hannah of Sunderland's *'Team of all the Talents'*, who had also assisted Renton in his early career. He received the following write-up (1904): *"He is a rare worker who never seems to tire, which is remarkable for one of his build. He covers a tremendous amount of ground and would be even more useful if he did not so frequently indulge in tricks of an acrobatic nature"*. Played in one of City's best ever teams but was sold to Forest for financial reasons.

CRAWLEY, Felix Patrick ("Frank")
(1923-1924)

Left-back: 1 app.
1923: 5-10, 11-7
Born: Paisley, 22 May 1894
Died: Apr. 1945
Career: Croy Celtic; Kirkintilloch Rob Roy; Blackburn Rovers Oct. 1921; CITY Sep. 1923; Accrington Stanley Aug. 1924, registration cancelled Jan. 1925. Emigrated to North America - assisted Toronto Bell Telephone and Toronto Dunlops and coached Detroit All Stars.

Honours: Canadian International (3 apps during 1927 tour of New Zealand)

Injured a knee on his debut for the Imps in a 'derby' match with Grimsby and only recovered fitness in time to appear in the reserves' final match of the season (as a centre-forward). His Canadian link apparently started with a visit in the summer of 1922. He died in Detroit.

CREANE, Gerard M.
(1978-1983)

Defender: 6 app. + 1 sub
1980: 6-0, 13-6
Born: Lincoln, 2 Feb. 1962
Career: Witham Wanderers (Lincoln); CITY schoolboy form Oct. 1976, (appr.) July 1978, (prof.) Feb. 1980; (Yaro, Finland, on loan Apr.-Oct. 1982); Tsuen Wan, Hong Kong, on loan Oct. 1982-Jan. 1983; Stafford Rangers on loan Jan. 1983; Yaro, Finland, on loan Apr.-Oct. 1983); Boston United Oct. 1983; Kettering Town Nov. 1988; Kings Lynn cs 1989; Grantham 1991; Lincoln United July 1992.

Local boy who appeared in City's reserve side at the age

of 15. Made his FL debut as a striker when still an apprentice (Apr. 1979) but later converted to a defender. Had very few first team opportunities at Sincil Bank and spent long periods abroad. He eventually joined Boston United with whom he stayed five seasons, appearing in the 1985 FA Trophy Final in which they lost to Wealdstone.

CROMBIE, Dean M.
(1977-1978, 1991)

Defender: 33 app + 1 sub
1980: 5-11, 11-7
Born: Lincoln, 9 Aug. 1957
Career: CITY as a junior then on non-contract forms June 1976; Ruston Bucyrus (Lincoln) Aug. 1976; CITY Feb. 1977; Grimsby Town Aug. 1978 (Reading on loan, Nov. 1986); Bolton Wanderers Aug. 1987; CITY Jan.-cs 1991.

Dean appeared in City's junior sides and was then released, only to be re-signed six months later. He became a first team regular under George Kerr, but was dropped when Willie Bell arrived and was again released. It was very much Grimsby's gain as a 1983 commentator put it: *"an accomplished back-four player ... snapped up by the Mariners Dean has been one of their most consistent players ... now playing full-back, on occasion centre-back. An explosive shot"*. 320 FL outings for Grimsby, 95 for Bolton. Returned to Sincil Bank to assist Steve Thompson when he made one further appearance as substitute. His brother Allen was also on City's books.

CROSBY, Gary
(1986-1987)

Midfield: 6 app + 1 sub
1990: 5-7, 9-11
Born: Sleaford, Lincs, 8 May 1964
Career: CITY on schoolboy forms Oct. 1979, non-contract Sep. 1980; Ruston Sports; Lincoln United 1982, (CITY, non-contract Aug. 1986); Grantham Town Oct. 1987; Nottingham Forest Dec. 1987 (£20,000), (Grimsby Town on loan, Aug. 1993).

Honours: (Nottingham Forest) FA Cup finalist 1991
FL Cup winner 1990

Another local player who was released after appearing for the juniors and re-signed at a later date. Crosby played a handful of games under George Kerr but was again allowed to drift back into non-League football. He was soon snapped up by Nottingham Forest and quickly established himself in their first team, going on to make well over 100 appearances in top flight football.

CROSS, Graham Frederick
(1979)

Central Defender: 19 app.
1978: 6-0, 13-0
Born: Leicester, 15 Nov. 1943
Career: Leicester City (amat.), (prof.) Nov. 1960; (Chesterfield on loan, Mar. 1976); Brighton & Hove Albion May 1976; Preston North End July 1977; Enderby Town Jan. 1979; CITY Mar. 1979;

Enderby Town Aug. 1979

Honours: England Under-23 international (11 apps)
(Leicester) FL Div.2 champions 1971
FA Cup finalist 1963, 1969
FL Cup winner 1964, finalist 1965

Veteran central defender signed on a short-term contract by Colin Murphy to shore up City's back four in the 1978/79 campaign. His FL career stretched for 19 seasons in which he aggregated 617 appearances plus 3 as substitute - the vast majority were for Leicester but he also appeared in promotion sides at Brighton and Preston. A Leicestershire cricketer from 1961 to 1976.

CROUCH, Nigel J.
(1979)
Left-back: 7 app.
1979: 5-8, 10-7
Born: Ardleigh, Essex, 24 Nov. 1958
Career: Ipswich Town (appr.), (prof.) Aug. 1978; (CITY on loan, Aug. 1979); Colchester United July 1980; Harwich & Parkeston cs 1981 where he remained for several years.

Full-back signed on loan to cover for Phil Neale's absence playing cricket at the start of the 1979/80 season. He saw little first-team action at Layer Road before moving on to Isthmian League Harwich & Parkeston.

CULLEN, Joseph
(1899-1900)
Goalkeeper: 12 app.
1897: 5-7½, 12-0
Died: 27 Oct. 1905
Career: Junior Hawthorn; Glasgow Benburb; Celtic Jan. 1892; Tottenham Hotspur May 1897; CITY Sep. 1899-1900.

Honours: Scottish League (1 app. vs Irish League 1894)
(Celtic) Scottish League champions 1893, 1894
Scottish Cup winner 1892; finalist 1893, 1894.

A Scottish junior international highly regarded at Celtic Park where he held sway until ousted by Dan McArthur. Once the recipient of a gold watch from a Celtic fan following a particularly dazzling display. At Tottenham he made 55 Southern League and FA Cup appearances. He apparently left football after his season at Sincil Bank as in 1900 he was reported to be unemployed. Cullen's early death was caused by pneumonia.

CULLEY, James
(1938-1939)
Goalkeeper: 5 app.
1938: 5-11, 12-0
Born: Condorrat, nr Glasgow, 20 July 1915
Died: 30 July 1981
Career: Bankrock Juveniles; Camelon Juniors; Hibernian 1935; CITY June 1938; Alloa Athletic cs 1939.

Culley was one of four goalkeepers used by City in 1938/39 (Connor and McPhail were also Scots). He had appeared in 33 matches with Hibs. spread over four seasons and returned to Scotland after his season at Sincil Bank.

CUMBERLAND, Thomas William
(1902-1903)
Goalkeeper: 5 app.
Born: Derby, 1882
Career: Notts East End; Southwell St. Marys 1902; CITY May 1902; Southwell St. Marys cs 1903; Grantham Avenue cs 1905; Southwell St.Marys; Brentford cs 1908; Sutton Junction cs 1909.

Cumberland impressed in Notts. junior football but mostly appeared for the Imps' reserve side, his first team opportunities being very much restricted by the presence of Alfred Webb. Moved to Grantham Avenue for their entry to Midland League football before spending a season in Brentford's reserves. Cumberland was also an enthusiastic member of Nottingham City Operatic Society.

CUMMING, Robert
(1987-1989)
Midfield: 40 app. + 1 sub, 5 goals
1990: 5-8, 10-5
Born: Airdrie, 7 Dec. 1955
Career: Albion Rovers; Baillieston Juniors; Grimsby Town (appr.) July 1973, (prof.) March 1974; CITY July 1987; Albany Capitals (USA) May 1989; CITY August 1989; Grimsby Borough Jan. 1990; Albany Capitals (USA).

A brave and skilful player who proved an inspirational force in the 1987/88 Vauxhall Conference championship campaign. He had previously appeared in over 350 games with the Mariners. Cumming returned to Sincil Bank after a brief spell in the USA but injured an ankle in the FA Cup tie with Billingham Synthonia in Nov. 1989 and never played in City's first team again. Supporters' Player of the Year in 1987/88.

CUNNINGHAM, Anthony E.
(1979-1982)
Centre-forward: 111 app. + 12 sub, 32 goals
1980: 6-1, 12-0
Born: Kingston, Jamaica, 12 Nov. 1957
Career: Kidderminster Harriers; Stourbridge cs 1977; CITY May 1979 (£20,000); Barnsley Sep. 1982 (£80,000); Sheffield Wednesday Nov. 1983; Manchester City July 1984 (£100,000); Newcastle United Feb. 1985 (£75,000); Blackpool Aug. 1987 (£25,000); Bury July 1989 (£40,000); Bolton Wanderers Mar. 1991 (£70,000); Rotherham United Aug. 1991 (£50,000); Doncaster Rovers July 1993; Wycombe Wanderers Mar. 1994; Gainsborough Trinity cs 1994.

Tony Cunningham made a sensational debut for City in a League Cup-tie with Barnsley, outplaying his marker, the former England international Norman Hunter, and scoring a fine goal. He obviously impressed Hunter who later paid a hefty fee to bring him to Oakwell which was the start of a career which seemed to take him round a large proportion of the clubs in northern England. To date he has made over 400 FL appearances and scored a century of goals.

CURTIS, Albert Victor
(1922-1923)

Right-back: 1 app.
Born: Bradford 1899
Died: Oct. 1967
Career: Robeys (Lincoln); CITY (amat.) Dec. 1922, (prof.) Feb. 1923; Gainsborough Trinity cs 1923.

Curtis was one of several local men recruited in the 1922/23 season to assist the reserves when the club was in financial crisis. His one League outing for the Imps came in a 9-1 defeat at Wigan Borough in Mar. 1923.

DAGG, Henry C.
(1946-1947)

Centre-forward: 1 app., 1 goal
Born: Sunderland, 4 Mar. 1924
Career: Boston United; CITY (amat.) Dec. 1946; Boston United cs 1947; Sunderland; Horden Colliery; Boston United Jan. 1950 to cs 1951.

Centre-forward who signed amateur forms for City when based at RAF Cranwell. He made his only appearance for the Imps on 21 December 1946 at Stockport, scoring once in a 3-2 defeat. On demobilisation he moved back to the north-east, appearing with Sunderland's reserves and 'A' teams. His twin brother John also signed for Lincoln but did not appear in the first team.

DAILLY, John
(1897)

Inside-left: 1 app.
Career: Hibernian; CITY Aug.-Sep. 1897.

Inside-forward recruited from Scotland who appeared in the opening game of the 1897/98 season - a 5-0 defeat at Newton Heath. He did not impress and lack of fitness led to his being released almost immediately.

DANIEL, Peter William
(1985-1987)

Full-back/midfield: 35 app., 2 goals
1987: 5-9, 11-5
Born: Hull, 12 Dec. 1955
Career: Hull City on schoolboy forms Oct. 1969, (amat.) 1971, (prof.) Sep. 1973; Wolverhampton Wanderers May 1978 (£182,000); Minnesota Strikers (USA) May 1984; Sunderland Sep. 1984 (£15,000); CITY Nov. 1985 (£20,000), appointed caretaker-manager Mar.-May 1987; Burnley July 1987-cs 1989; North Ferriby United as player-coach, appointed manager June 1991.

Midfield player with a vast amount of experience who was recruited by John Pickering shortly before he vacated the manager's post. On the departure of Pickering's successor, George Kerr, Daniel was appointed caretaker-manager. He was unable to produce an upturn in the club's fortunes and following defeat at Swansea in the final match of the campaign, City became the first team to be automatically relegated from the League. Given a free transfer, he moved on to Turf Moor where he spent two more seasons before moving on to the non-League scene.

DANIELS, John F.
(1946-1948)

Goalkeeper: 17 app.
1948: 6-1, 12-3
Born: St. Helens, 8 Jan. 1925
Career: British Sidac (St. Helens Combination); CITY May 1946; New Brighton (amat.) Jan. 1948, (prof.) Mar. 1948-May 1949.

Daniels was City's regular 'keeper for the start of the 1946/47 season but lost his place through injury and never appeared in the first team again. Moved on to New Brighton where he made just three FL appearances. Nephew of Welsh international inside-forward, Richard Jones.

D'ARCEY, Harry Carlill H.
(1894-1898)

Inside-forward: 3 app.
Born: Lincoln, 1874
Died: 10 Sep. 1930
Career: Nondescripts (Lincoln); CITY Sep. 1894-around 1898; Adelaide (Lincoln) 1899-1906.

Local-born player who appeared mostly with the City Swifts (reserves) team. His Football League outings were widely spread out - one in Mar. 1895, and a couple two years later. He was well-known in Lincoln for his activities with the Liberal Party at the time of his death.

DAVIDSON, James
(1897)

Outside/inside-right: 9 app., 1 goal
1897: 5-7½, 11-2
Born: Edinburgh 1876
Career: Leith Athletic; Celtic 1892; Burnley cs 1895 (CITY on loan Mar.-Apr. 1897); Tottenham Hotspur May 1897; Brighton United May 1898; Burnley Apr. 1900-cs 1902.

Honour: (Celtic) Scottish League champions 1893

Davidson was loaned to City along with Jimmy Hartley as a favour by Burnley at a time when the Imps were in deep trouble both on and off the field. He later moved on to Tottenham whose 1897 handbook recorded *"he can play in any position forward and is a very clever lad with his feet and a deadly shot at goal"*. At Celtic he had been given the nickname 'Tooty'.

DAVIDSON, Roger
(1971-1972)

Midfield: 6 app.
1971: 5-8, 11-6
Born: Islington, London, 27 Oct. 1948
Career: Islington Schools; Arsenal (appr.) July 1964, (prof.) Oct. 1965; Portsmouth May 1969; Fulham Sep. 1970; CITY Oct. 1971; Aldershot Feb.-June 1972.

Honour: England schools international (4 app., 1964)

Roger came to Lincoln on a one month trial but stayed four months in all, appearing in midfield and as a sweeper. Despite the number of clubs his FL appearances totalled only 22 plus 1 as substitute. Captained England Schools on two occasions.

DAVIES, Alexander M.
(1945-1949)

Outside-right: 37 app., 9 goals
Born: Dundonald, Ayrshire, 21 May 1920
Career: Sheffield Wednesday during WW2; CITY 1945; Frickley Colliery Aug. 1949; Denaby United cs 1952; Ransomes & Marles cs 1953.

Alec was a regular in City's 1946/47 side but only had two more League outings in the next two seasons. Later saw service in the Midland League with Frickley and Denaby and the Central Alliance (Ransomes).

DAVIS, Darren J.
(1988-1991)

Defender: 97 app. + 5 sub, 4 goals
1989: 6-0, 11-0
Born: Sutton-in-Ashfield, Notts., 5 Feb. 1967
Career: Notts County (appr.), (prof.) Feb. 1985; CITY Aug. 1988; Maidstone United Mar. 1991 (£27,500) to cs 1992; Boston United Nov. 1992; Eynesbury Rovers Jan. 1993; Frickley Athletic Feb. 1993; Scarborough Aug. 1993.

Honour: England youth international (2 apps. 1984)

Tall and versatile defender who made his FL debut for Notts County in Division 1 when still an apprentice. A regular first-team player and club captain at Sincil Bank, but moved on to Maidstone on the transfer deadline in March 1991. When the Kent club folded he drifted into non-League football only to return to FL action with Scarborough at the start of the 1993/94 season.

DAWS, Anthony
(1994-)

Forward: 14 app., 3 goals
1993: 5-8, 11-10
Born: Sheffield, 10 Sep. 1966
Career: Notts County (appr.), (prof.) Sep. 1984; Sheffield United Aug. 1986; Scunthorpe United July 1987; Grimsby Town Mar. 1993 (£50,000); CITY Feb. 1994 (£50,000)

Honours: England Schools international (1 app. 1982 vs. Scotland) England youth international (1 app. 1984)

Small, nippy striker who established himself as a proven goalscorer in his Scunthorpe days (166 app. + 17 sub, 63 goals). Became one of the few players to have appeared for all three Lincolnshire sides in the Football League when recruited by Keith Alexander to boost City's attack.

DAWSON, Carl M.
(1949-1951)

Goalkeeper: 1 app.
Born: Dovercourt, Essex, 24 June 1934
Career: Nottingham junior football to CITY cs 1949 (amat.) to cs 1951; Grantham on trial, Oct. 1952.

Signed by City on amateur forms when just 14 years old, Dawson made only one first team appearance - a 3-1 defeat at Barrow in Apr. 1951. He was released by the Imps shortly afterwards and later had a short trial at Grantham with their reserve side.

DEACON, Richard
(1936-1939)

Inside-left: 113 app., 22 goal
1938: 5-8, 10-7
Born: Glasgow, 26 June 1911
Died: May 1986
Career: Darlington junior football with Alliance Juniors, Albert Hill United and Darlington Juniors (Wolverhampton Wanderers and Fulham on trial during 1928/29 season); Cockfield; Wolverhampton Wanderers Jan. 1930; West Ham United cs 1931; Chelsea June 1934; Glentoran 1935; Northampton Town Oct. 1935; CITY Aug. 1936-Sep. 1939; post-war on Darlington's training staff for around 30 years.

A 1938 annual desbrided Dicky as *"The 'little wonder' ... a real artist with the ball, and gives defenders a headache in trying to define him as an inside or outside forward. He is really neither but both"*. Deacon was born in Glasgow of Irish parents but raised in Darlington where he had begun his working life as an apprentice fitter in the locomotive works. Younger brother of the well known Jimmy Deacon (Wolves inside-left, 1929-4).

DICKINS, Matthew
(1991-1992)

Goalkeeper: 27 app.
1991: 6-4, 14-0
Born: Sheffield: 3 Sep. 1970
Career: Sheffield United on YTS forms, (prof.) July 1989 (Leyton Orient on loan Nov. 1989 -Jan. 1990); CITY non-contract Feb. 1991, full terms May 1991; Blackburn Rovers Mar. 1992 (£250,000); (Blackpool on loan, Jan-Apr 1993; CITY on loan Nov. 1993).

Tall, well-built 'keeper who had his introduction to League Football at Sincil Bank. Produced some impressive performances and was on his way to Ewood Park 12 months later for a club record transfer fee. Appeared regularly for Blackpool during an extended loan period but had no FL outings with City when he returned briefly, also on loan, at the end of 1993.

DICKINSON, Sydney
(1934-1935)

Inside-/outside-left: 14 app., 3 goals
1934: 5-8, 11-0
Born: Nottingham, 17 Aug. 1906
Died: 2 Feb. 1984
Career: Dale Rovers (Nottingham); Nottingham Forest (amat.) Jan. 1924; Mansfield Town cs 1925; Bradford Feb. 1927; Port Vale Nov. 1933; CITY Aug. 1934; Grantham Aug. 1935.

Honour: (Bradford) FL Div.3 (North) champions 1928

"A clever and energetic forward who is at all times quick to sieze goal-scoring opportunites" a critic wrote in the mid-1920's. This remained the case subsequently when Syd also appeared at left-half. He had 156 FL outings with Bradford but was principally a reserve at Sincil Bank, his first team appearances coming in four different positions.

DILSWORTH, Eddie
(1967)

Wing-half: 2 app.
1967: 5-11½, 13-0
Born: Freetown, Sierra Leone, 16 Apr. 1946
Career: Fulham (amat.); Wealdstone 1964; CITY (amat.) Mar.-Apr. 1967; Barking cs 1967; Chelmsford City Oct. 1967; Brentwood cs 1968; Chelmsford City in the early 1970's; Kettering Town cs 1973; subsequently appeared for a number of teams including Ilford, Hemel Hempstead and Woodford Town.

Honours: (Wealdstone) FA Amateur Cup winner 1966.

Dilsworth was on Wealdstone's books when he appeared for City and they suspended him when they discovered he had played for the Imps without their permission. The ban was quickly lifted but he moved on to Barking at the end of the season and then a succession of non-League clubs. The first African born player to appear in the League for Lincoln.

DINSDALE, William Arthur
(1926-1929, 1930-1931)

Centre-forward: 126 app., 89 goal
1926: 5-11, 13-0
Born: Darlington, 12 July 1903
Died: 21 Feb. 1984
Career: Rise Carr Juniors; St. Martins; Rise Carr (amat.) Aug. 1921; Darlington Railway Athletic; Crook Town; Aston Villa Mar. 1925; CITY May 1926; Bradford Mar. 1929 (£1,200); CITY May 1930; Darlington cs 1931-1932.

Dinsdale came to Sincil Bank from Villa where he had made a handful of appearances, being understudy to Len Capewell and Bill Walker, but developed into one of City's all-time greats. A contemporary described him as *" ... a big bustling type of player with no great ball control ... an enthusiastic team man, could give or take hard knocks with equal equanimity, and was as happy as a sandboy when his side scored a goal"*. Inspired the Lincoln crowd to chant *"give it to Dinny"*. Despite his robust nature on the field he was considered very much a gentleman off it.

DIXON, Benjamin
(1991-)

Winger: 6 app. + 7 sub
1993: 6-1, 11-0
Born: Lincoln, 16 Sep. 1974
Career: Washingborough Youths; CITY on YTS forms cs 1991, (prof.) Nov. 1992. Witton Albion on loan Oct. 1993.

Skilful wingman who made his FL debut as a substitute at Gillingham when he was a first year YTS player. His performances for City's junior side attracted the attention of scouts from other clubs and he was given a professional contract before his YTS period had been completed. Won representative honours with an FA Youth XI but has yet to establish himself as a regular first team player.

DIXON, Edward
(1905-1907)

Right-back: 35 app., 3 goals
1906: 5-9½, 11-12
Born: Easington, Co. Durham, 1884
Career: Tynevale; Sunderland; CITY June 1905; Hull City Mar. 1907.

Dixon signed from Sunderland with no League experience but appeared regularly for City in 1905/06. He did not fare so well the following season and moved on to Hull where he had just three FL outings. Also deputised for the Imps as a centre or inside-forward when required.

DIXON, Frederick
(1935-1937)

Left-back: 1 app.
1935: 5-8, 10-10
Born: Lincoln, c.1917
Career: Blue Star Rangers; Lincoln Corinthians; CITY July 1935; Newark Town cs 1937; Lincoln Claytons Aug. 1939.

Fred was recruited from top local amateur side Corinthians but was restricted to Midland League football by the presence of Fred Corbett. His one League appearance came on 2 Jan.1937, a 2-1 defeat at Southport.

DIXON, John
(1900-1902)
Centre-forward: 17 app., 4 goals
Born: c.1882
Died: 7 Nov. 1942
Career: St. Marys (Lincoln); CITY Feb. 1900; Gainsborough Trinity Aug. 1902; Newark Town cs 1907; later assisted Billinghay (Lincs.).

A local lad who appeared in 17 of the first 18 FL fixtures of the 1901/02 season. At Gainsborough he made 128 League appearances, scoring 23 times in their Second Division days. Was later well known as a local referee and became a hospital worker.

DIXON, Joseph
(1926)
Goalkeeper: 1 app.
1926: 5-11½, 11-7
Born: c.1902
Career: Penrhiwceiber (Glamorgan); CITY Apr. 1926; Boston Town July 1926.

Although City had ample goalkeeping resources at the time, Dixon was considered promising enough to be signed on and was given his chance at Halifax in the final match of the 1925/26 season. Shortly afterwards he departed for Midland League Boston.

DOBSON, Paul
(1991-1992)
Forward: 13 app. + 8 sub, 5 goals
1991: 5-9, 10-6
Born: Hartlepool, 17 Dec. 1962
Career: Hartlepool United (amat.); Newcastle United non-contract; Hartlepool United Nov. 1981; Horden Colliery cs 1983; Hartlepool United Dec. 1983; Torquay United July 1986; Doncaster Rovers July 1988 (£20,000 plus player-exchange); Scarborough Feb. 1989 (£40,000); (Halifax Town on loan, Oct. 1990; Hereford United on loan Nov. 1990); CITY Jan. 1991 (£40,000); Darlington Aug. 1992; Gateshead on loan Feb. 1993, permanent Mar. 1993.

Small striker who scored regularly throughout his career (his FL aggregate was 246 appearances plus 69 as substitute, 111 goals). Popular with the fans but suffered an ankle injury at Hereford two months after signing and on recovering fitness was mostly used as a substitute. At Torquay he scored an injury-time goal against Crewe in the final match of the 1986/87 season which sent City down to the Vauxhall Conference.

DOCHERTY, Edward
(1895)
Inside/outside-left: 5 app., 2 goals

Career: Duntocher Harp; CITY June-Oct. 1895

Glasgwegian recruited along with Gavin Thomson in the summer of 1895. Scored twice in a 5-2 defeat by county rivals Grimsby but departed soon afterwards, again with Thomson.

DOCHERTY, Thomas
(1947-1950)

Outside-left: 45 app., 3 goals
1950: 5-9, 10-9
Born: Penshaw, Co. Durham, 15 Apr. 1924
Career: Murton Colliery; CITY July 1947; Norwich City June 1950 (£1,000); Reading July 1953; Newport County June 1955; Kings Lynn cs 1958; subsequently assisted March Town and Parson Drove before retiring in 1966.

Very fast, thrustful player packing a hard shot. Shared the outside-left berth with Willie Windle in 1948/49 and 1949/50. A part-time player who also worked as a plasterer.

DODDS, Ephraim ("Jock")
(1948-1950)

Centre-forward: 60 app., 38 goals
1949: 6-0, 14-8
Born: Grangemouth, Stirlings., 7 Sep. 1915
Career: Medomsley Juniors; Huddersfield Town (amat.) June 1932, (prof.) Sep. 1932; Sheffield United May 1934; Blackpol Mar. 1939 (£10,000); Shamrock Rovers cs 1946; Everton Nov. 1946; CITY Oct. 1948 (£6,000); retired Sep. 1950.

Honours: Scottish wartime international (8 app.)
(Sheffield United) FA Cup finalist 1936

A big, powerful centre-forward, considered one of City's best in the post-war period. Well known for both his heading ability and lightness of foot. Scored a century of goals at Bramall Lane, finishing with a FL aggregate of 201 goals from 308 matches. A former colleague of manager Bill Anderson at both Medomsley Juniors and Sheffield United, he justified the hefty fee paid for him by finishing leading scorer in both his seasons at Sincil Bank. Retired from the game after he was expelled from the Football League in June 1950 over his role as a recruiting agent for the Millionarios Club of Bogota (the Columbian League in which they played was not affiliated to FIFA). Later a successful Blackpool businessman.

DODGIN, William
(1933-1934)

Right-half: 46 app., 1 goal
1933: 5-10, 12-7
Born: Gateshead, 17 Apr. 1909
Career: High Fell (Gateshead); Huddersfield Town (amat.) Oct. 1929, (prof.) Nov. 1929; CITY Mar. 1933; Charlton Athletic Aug. 1934; Bristol Rovers May 1936; Clapton Orient July 1937; Southampton June 1939 appointed coach, and Jan. 1946 manager; Fulham manager Aug. 1949 - Sep. 1953; Brentford manager Oct. 1953-Apr. 1957; Sampdoria (Italy) manager/coach May 1957-Feb. 1958 followed by a spell as advisor to the club's chairman; Yiewsley manager Mar. 1959 - Dec. 1960; Bristol Rovers chief scout Aug. 1961, caretaker-manager July 1969, manager Nov. 1969 - July 1972 when he reverted to chief scout until retiring in 1983.

Honour: (Charlton) FL Div. 3 (South) champions 1935

Workmanlike, efficient wing-half who also appeared at centre-half and inside-right for City. Left Sincil Bank for Charlton when the Imps were relegated from Division Two at the end of the 1933-34 season. Spent over half a century in the game later becoming a respected manager and coach. Father of Bill Dodgin jnr. an England under-23 international who also became a manager.

DOOLEY, Derek
(1945-1947)

Centre-forward: 2 app., 2 goals
1949: 6-3, 12-8
Born: Sheffield, 13 Dec. 1929
Career: Sheffield YMCA; CITY (amat.) Nov. 1945; Sheffield

Wednesday June 1947-July 1953; later employed by Wednesday to run their Development Fund, Oct. 1962 - Jan. 1971 when appointed team manager, until Dec. 1973; Sheffield United commercial manager Nov. 1974 and later a Director and Managing Director at Bramall Lane.

Honour: (Wednesday): FL Div.2 champions 1952

Sheffield based amateur who was leading scorer for City's Midland League side in 1946/47 with 13 goals. Given two first team outings at the end of that season, scoring in both, but Wednesday came in ahead of City to sign him. A prolific scorer at Hillsborough (62 goals in 61 FL games) before suffering a broken leg at Preston in Feb. 1953. Gangrene set in and the limb had to be amputated. Later worked for both Sheffield clubs in administrative roles.

DOUGHERTY, Joseph
(1924)

Right-half: 2 app.
1924: 6-0, 13-0
Born: Darlington, c.1892
Career: Darlington Forge; Leeds City Feb. 1914; Oldham Athletic Apr. 1919 (£100); Hartlepools United Mar. 1921 - Jan. 1923; CITY Jan. 1924 - Feb. 1924

Joe was signed for a trial period following the departure of McAndrew Brown. He was not successful and was released shortly afterwards. Had played at centre-forward earlier in his career.

DOVEY, Donald
(1924-1927)

Outside/inside-right: 14 app., 3 goals
1926: 5-7, 10-7
Born: Lincoln, 13 Apr. 1900
Died: 1979
Career: Horncastle Town; CITY Sep. 1924; Newark Town cs 1927.

Hard working and popular reserve who performed *"with considerable success"* in the wing positon in 1925/26. His longest run in the first team came in Sep. and Oct. 1926 when he deputised for Charles Bosbury for nine consecutive matches.

DOWALL, William
(1936-1938)

1936: 5-10, 11-0
Born: Thornliebank, Renfrewshire.
Career: Kilbirnie Ladeside; Motherwell late 1929; St. Mirren during 1934/35; Bury July 1935; CITY Aug. 1936; Notts County cs 1938

Honour: (Motherwell) Scottish League champions 1932

Bill began the 1936/37 season as City's first choice left-winger, but soon lost his place and appeared only once more - at left back. A 1937 source noted *"... has proved himself capable of filling either half-back or full-back positions with credit. Generally seen out with the Reserves"*. At Motherwell he appeared at right-back in their championship side and aggregated 43 goals from 118 Scottish League matches with the Fir Park club.

DOWLING, Michael
(1914-1920)

Forward: 28 app., 4 goals
1914: 5-9, 12-0
Born: Jarrow, 1889
Career: St. Mirren; Sheffield Wednesday May 1910; Portsmouth June 1911; Jarrow 1913; CITY July 1914; Ebbw Vale June 1920.

Described as promising and *"a sturdy, fast and dashing forward"* on signing from North-Eastern League Jarrow. Returned after serving in the Royal Navy in the Great War for a final season before departing for Ebbw Vale, then a prominent Southern League side.

DOWNIE, Mitchell
(1954-1959)

Goalkeeper: 157 app.
1952: 5-11, 12-4
Born: Troon, Ayrshire, 9 Feb. 1923
Career: Troon Juveniles; Kilmarnock Juniors; Hibernian c.1941; Troon Athletic briefly before joining Kilmarnick 1944; Airdrieonians Oct. 1947; Bradford Aug. 1950 (£5,000); CITY May 1954 (£6,000); Goole Town Aug. 1959; Bradford City Sep. 1959; Doncaster Rovers Sep. 1963; Altrincham Nov. 1963; Stalybridge Celtic.

Consistently dependable Scottish 'keeper who had a reputation for saving penalties. A part-timer at Lincoln (he also worked in the confectionary trade in Bradford), he was a regular in four of the five campaigns he spent with the club. In all made more than 100 appearances for three different clubs - City, Bradford and Bradford City. On leaving the game worked as a licensee in West Riding.

DOWNIE, Robert
(1897)

Outside-left: 6 app., 1 goal
1897: 5-10, 11/12-0
Career: Albion Rovers; CITY July-Oct. 1897; reported to be assisting McKeesport (Pittsburgh, USA) in 1911.

Scottish winger who played in the first six games of the 1897-98 season before being released. An 1897 comment *"... has the reputation of being speedy and fearless, and can swing the ball well across into goal from the wing"*.

DRANSFIELD, George Ronald
(1936-1937)

Outside-right: 3 app., 1 goal
1936: 5-6½, 10-1
Born: Ecclesfield, Sheffield, 12 Oct. 1914
Career; Barnsley junior football; CITY on trial Feb. 1936, (prof.) Mar. 1936; Macclesfield Aug. 1937.

Dransfield was introduced to Northern Section football soon after signing. He scored on his debut (against Halifax Town at home) and also appeared in the season's remaining two fixtures. At the end of the campaign it was said he *"should prove very effective in the position from which goals were not particularly frequent last season"*, but he made no more first team appearances before being released. Later signed for Cheshire League Macclesfield.

DRYSDALE, Brian
(1959-1965)

Defender: 20 app.
1963: 5-7, 11-0
Born: West Hartlepool, 24 Feb. 1943
Career: Thornley CW Juniors; CITY (amat.) Aug. 1959, (prof.) Sep. 1960; Hartlepools United July 1965; Bristol City June 1969 (£10,000); (Reading on loan, Feb.-May 1977); Oxford United July 1977; Frome Town cs 1978, appointed manager cs 1979; later manager at Minehead, Shepton Mallett and Clandown.

Drysdale chose to join City in preference to Sunderland who had also offered him trials but he remained a reserve throughout his time at Sincil Bank. His career took off after the Imps gave him a free transfer and he made over 450 FL appearances for Hartlepools and Bristol City, mostly at left-back. Small in height yet a resilient player. After leaving football he worked as a postman in the Bristol area. Father of Jason Drysdale (Watford).

DUCKWORTH, Robert William W.
(1894-1895)

Inside-right: 24 app., 5 goals
Born: Bury 1872
Died: 23 Apr 1924
Career: Burnley 1888 to Apr 1890; Rossendale cs 1890; CITY June 1894; Rossendale cs 1895.

Duckworth formed a successful right-wing partnership with Frank Smallman during the 1894-95 season. He appeared only five times in Burnley's FL side, but had several years experience of good quality non-league football in the Lancashire League with Rossendale. Like most of the players at the time he was a part-time player, his occupation (according to an 1895 court case) being that of a 'bottle washer'.

DUNKLEY, Malcolm
(1989)

Centre-forward: 9 app. + 2 sub, 4 goals
1990: 6-5, 14-0
Born: Wolverhampton, 12 July 1961
Career: Ettingshall; Bromsgrove Rovers; Stafford Rangers cs 1987; Rovaniemen Palloseura (Finland) Dec. 1987-Sep. 1990 (Bromsgrove Rovers Feb. 1989; CITY Feb.-Mar. 1989)

Giant striker who signed for the Imps on a short-term contract during the Finnish close season. Showed tremendous promise on his debut, scoring twice against Cambridge United but his later form was disappointing. He had three seasons in Finland appearing in UEFA Cup action and finishing with a record of 20 goals from 76 appearances (including substitutions).

DUNNE, John
(1914-1915)

Left-back: 23 app.
1914: 5-7, 11-10
Born: Donnybrook, Dublin, c.1890
Career: Shelbourne c.1911; CITY June 1914; (during WW1 appeared for Rustons Aircraftmen 1916/17; CITY 1917/18; RAF Cranwell 1918/19); Mid-Rhondda June 1919; Boston Town 1921; Horncastle Town.

Honours: Irish League (1 app. vs Scottish League, 1914)
(Shelbourne) Irish Cup winner 1911

Irishman whose promising Sincil Bank career was curtailed by the Great War. Made occasional appearances for City throughout the war and was a regular in the 1917/18 season. *"A little on the short side, perhaps, he is fast, dashing and fearless"* wrote one critic during Dunne's prime.

DUNPHY, Sean
(1990-)

Centre-half: 48 apps. + 5 sub., 2 goals.
1993: 6-3, 13-5
Born: Maltby, Rotherham, 5 Nov. 1970
Career: Barnsley on YTS forms, (prof.) June 1989; CITY June 1990 (£30,000); (Goole Town on loan, Oct. 1991; Doncaster Rovers trial, Mar. 1992; Matlock Town loan, Mar. 1992; Doncaster Rovers loan, Oct. 1993).

Dunphy was brought to Sincil Bank by Allan Clarke under whom he had played at Barnsley, but he had the misfortune to suffer a severe knee injury in a pre-season match with Leeds in Aug. 1990. He did not appear in the League for City until the home encounter with Maidstone - almost two years after signing - and has since been in and out of the first team.

DUNWELL, Peter M.
(1957-1962)

Outside-left: 14 app., 1 goal
1960: 5-6, 9-10
Born: Ecclesfield, Sheffield, 22 Nov. 1938
Career: Ecclesfield F.C.; City (amat.) Nov 1957 (prof.) Sep 1958; Ramsgate Aug.1962.

Peter was a PT student at Sheffield University when he first appeared for City's Lincolnshire League side, and later became a schoolteacher. Given a chance towards the end of the 1959/60 season but was unable to win a permanent first team place and eventually left on a free transfer. *"Needs a little more weight"*, wrote a commentator of the time.

DWANE, Edwin John
(1920-1924)

Inside-forward/wing-half: 46 app., 3 goals
1923: 5-9, 10-11
Born: Valletta, Malta, 17 July 1896
Died: 10 Feb. 1973
Career: Royal Engineers (Chatham Depot); CITY July 1920; Boston Town Aug. 1924; Newark Town cs 1925; CITY cs 1926-cs 1927; Worksop Town Oct. 1928.

Despite his birthplace, Dwane was considered a local lad and signed for City on demobilisation. He was introduced to first team action in the 1920/21 Midland League campaign (4 app., 3 goals) but was principally a reserve. *"Consistent, steady and never left the side down"*, was a 1923 verdict. No FL outings in his second spell at Sincil Bank.

DYE, Dean C.
(1991)

Forward: 9 app. + 2 sub

1991: 5-9, 11-0

Born: Lincoln, 14 Mar. 1969

Career: Lincoln Schools; Nettleham cs 1985; Lincoln United cs 1987; Boston FC Jan. 1985; Sutton Town cs 1989; Lincoln United cs 1990; Charlton Athletic July 1991 (£3,000); CITY non-contract Oct. 1991; Lincoln United Dec. 1991; Boston FC Mar. 1992; Lincoln United cs 1992.

Dean had performed impressively in local football to attract FL scouts but his career at Charlton was affected by a change in manager. A brief trial at Sincil Bank followed before he returned to Lincoln United.

DYKES, Donald W.
(1947-1959)

Defender/inside-forward: 95 app., 4 goals

1954: 5-11, 10-11

Born: Ashby by Partney, Lincs, 8 July 1930

Career: British Crop Driers (Metheringham); CITY (amat.) Aug. 1947, (prof.) Aug. 1949; Boston United July 1959; Ruston Bucyrus (Lincoln) cs 1961.

Dykes was signed on amateur forms after impressing in a trial game and stayed with City for 12 seasons, although he only appeared in more than half the first team fixtures on one occasion (1957-1958: 23 app.). Very useful player who deputised in a variety of positions. In his early days at inside-forward he displayed accurate shooting but nevertheless was thought better fitted to be a right-half.

EASTHAM, George Richard
(1948-1950)

Inside-forward: 27 app., 1 goal

1949: 5-10, 11-7

Born: Blackpool, 13 Sep. 1913

Career: Cambridge Juniors (Blackpool); South Shore Wednesday (Blackpool); Bolton Wanderers (amat.) May 1932, (prof.) Aug. 1932; Brentford June 1937 (£4,000); Blackpool Nov. 1938 (approx. £5,000); Swansea Town Aug. 1947; Rochdale June 1948; CITY Dec. 1948; Hyde United Sep. 1950; Ards player-manager July 1953-1955, manager to Oct. 1958; Accrington Stanley manager Oct. 1958; Distillery manager June 1959 - Mar. 1964; Ards manager late 1964 - Mar. 1970; Stoke City scout; Hellenic FC (South Africa) manager late 1971; Glentoran manager late 1972.

Honour: England international (1 app. vs Holland 1935)

Star inside-foward recruited at the very end of his League career to assist in the fight against relegation in 1948-49. City were unsuccessful and Eastham made just a handful of appearances the following season before moving on. In pre-war days known as "Diddler" for his brilliant, mazy dribbling which mesmerised top-class defences. Father of George Eastham (Newcastle, Arsenal and Stoke) who was also an England international.

EDEN, Alan
(1977-1979)

Forward: 5 app. + 2 sub

1978: 5-9, 10-8

Born: Sunderland, 8 Oct. 1958

Career: Lambton Street Boys Club (Sunderland); CITY July 1977; (Boston United on loan Mar. 1979); Runcorn in 1979/80 season.

Alen Eden was one of four lads recruited by City from a Sunderland junior team in the summer of 1977. All four played League soccer for the Imps - and two (Mick Harford and Mick Smith) subsequently had lengthy careers in the game. Eden never established himself as a first-team player and moved on to join the former Lincoln coach Jim McCalliog at Runcorn.

EDWARDS, Roy
(1947-1949)

Inside-left: 6 app.,

1947: 5-10½, 12-7

Born: Sheffield, 26 Nov. 1920

Career: Sheffield junior football; Army football; CITY June 1947; Denaby United Aug. 1949; Grimsby Borough Police cs 1951 until early 1960's.

Signed when still a sergeant in the Royal Artillery. A keen performer, Roy's enthusiasm was demonstrated by his travelling each evening from his Newark-based unit for training at Sincil Bank with other part-time players. Afterwards joined Grimsby Police at a time when their chief constable was recruiting ex-professionals to boost the force soccer team and appeared for them in the Lincolnshire League for many seasons. Played representative matches for both the Army and the English Police.

EDWARDS, Wilfred James
(1931-1932)

Outside-left: 1 app.

1928: 5-8½, 10-10

Born: Fenton, Stoke-on-Trent, 1904

Career: Stoke City; Crewe Alexandra June 1924; Stafford Rangers Sep. 1926; Crewe Alexandra Aug. 1928; Burton Town Aug. 1929; Loughborough Corinthians 1930; CITY Oct. 1931-May 1932.

Despite a lengthy career Wilf had very little FL experience (no app. for Stoke, and 12 in his two spells with Crewe). His one first team outing at Sincil Bank came soon after signing in a 1-0 victory at Rotherham in Oct. 1931, otherwise restricted to Midland League Football.

EGAN, T(homas) William
(1896-1897)

Centre-/inside-forward: 16 app.

Born: Chirk, Denbighs, 1872

Died: late 1946

Career: Chirk FC 1889; Fairfield (Manchester) 1892; Ardwick Nov. 1893; Burnley Mar. 1894; Ashton North End May 1895; Sheffield United Nov. 1895; CITY Oct. 1896-Apr. 1897; Birdwell Nov.

1897; Altofts Oct. 1898; Darwen June 1899; Royston United Aug. 1901; Stockport County Sep.-Oct. 1901.

Honours: Welsh international (1 app. vs. Scotland 1892) (Chirk) Welsh Cup Winner 1892.

William Egan arrived with an excellent footballing background but had the misfortune to appear in one of City's worst-ever teams. The club's record in his 16 outings was drawn 2, lost 14. In earlier days he had been reckoned a good shot besides being tenacious and fast.

EGERTON, William
(1914-1920)

Centre-forward: 76 app., 25 goals
1914: 5-10, 12-6
Born: Bollington, Cheshire 1891
Died: 1934
Career: Bollington FC; Bolton Wanderers 1911; Chesterfield Town Aug. 1913; CITY Jan. 1914; Mid-Rhondda June 1920 as manager; later associated with Pembroke Dock.

Signed from Midland League Chesterfield, Egerton quickly established a goal productive partnership with another new recruit, Billy Chesser. Appeared regularly for the Imps during the Great War and was particularly prolific in 1915/16 when he scored 30 goals from 32 outings and hit five in a 7-3 victory over Sheffield United. *"Travels fast, can break through most defences, fine shot"*, observed a 1919 commentator. Later settled in Pembroke, where he died.

ELLIS, Keith D.
(1965-1966)

Centre-forward: 7 app.
1964: 6-1, 12-8
Born: Sheffield, 6 Nov. 1935
Career: Sheffield Wednesday (amat.) 1953, (prof.) Apr. 1955; Scunthorpe United Mar 1964 (£9/10,000); Cardiff City Sep. 1964 (in exchange for Dick Scott and a small fee); CITY May 1965-Mar. 1966.

Honour: (Cardiff City) Welsh Cup winner 1965 (Second leg only)

A free transfer signing from Cardiff and whose appearances at Sincil Bank were restricted by injury. His most productive spell was during his time at Wednesday where he made his League debut as an amateur and totalled 54 goals from 103 outings over 11 years.

ELLIS, Samuel
(1973-1977)

Centre-half: 173 app., 33 goals
1975: 6-0, 13-5
Born: Ashton-under-Lyne, Lancs., 12 Sep. 1946
Career: Smiths FC (Manchester Works League); Sheffield Wednesday Sep. 1964; Mansfield Town on loan Jan. 1972, permanent Mar. 1972 (£10,000); CITY May 1973 (£7,000); Watford July 1977 (£15,000), coach cs 1979; Blackpool manager June 1982-Mar.

1989; Bury manager May 1989-Dec. 1990; Manchester City asst.-manager Dec. 1990-Aug. 1993; helped with coaching duties at CITY on a casual basis from Mar. 1994, appointed manager May 1994.

Honours: England under-23 international (3 apps)
(Wednesday) FA Cup finalist 1966
(City) FL Div.4 champions 1976
(Watford) FL Div.4 champions 1978

Tall and powerful central defender who established a fine partnership with Terry Cooper in the middle of City's defence which proved vital to the success of Graham Taylor's 1970's side. Ellis was club captain at Sincil Bank and won a reputation as a cool penalty taker - which helped him to finish as the club's leading scorer in 1974/75 with 13 goals. A very popular figure with the supporters who voted him Player of the Season in 1975/76 and 1976/77 and gave him the nickname "Super Sam". Later followed Graham Taylor to Watford before moving into coaching and management. He had chosen a career in football in preference to banking (he did well at school, gaining 13 GCE's) and appeared in an FA Cup Final for Wednesday only a few weeks after making his FL debut.

ELLIS, William Thomas
(1929-1930)

Outside-left: 31 app., 11 goals
1929: 5-8, 11-0
Born: Wolverhampton, 5 Nov. 1895
Died: Oct. 1971
Career: Highfield Villa; Bilston Juniors; Sunderland Mar. 1919; Birmingham Nov. 1927; CITY Aug. 1929; York City Nov. 1930-Jan 1931.

William had been Sunderland's regular outside-left for five seasons, earning a reputation as a crafty dribbler and a fine provider of chances for the likes of Charlie Buchan. A moderately successful year at Sincil Bank - the team finished fifth in the Northern Section and Ellis was second top scorer.

ELMORE, E.
(1903-1904)
Inside-left: 1 app.

Career: St. Botolphs (Lincoln); St. Swithins Athletic (Lincoln) 1901; Liberal Club (Lincoln) 1902; CITY Sep. 1903; Liberal Club cs 1904; Adelaide (Lincoln); Grantham Avenue Oct. 1905.

Elmore (his name also appeared as Elmer) was a local lad recruited to assist City's Midland League side. His only FL outing for the Imps came in a midweek match in Mar. 1094 and resulted in a 6-2 home defeat by Bristol City.

EMERY, Anthony J.
(1945-1959)

Centre-half: 402 app., 1 goal
1954: 6-1, 12-6
Born: Lincoln, 4 Nov. 1927

Career: CITY (amat.) Aug. 1945, (prof.) Aug. 1947; Mansfield Town June 1959 (£2,500)-1961.

Honour: (City) FL Div.3 (North) champions 1952

One of City's finest and most loyal post-war products. He made his club debut in a 1945/46 FA Cup tie and established himself as the regular first choice centre-half early in 1949 following the retirement of Tom Johnson. Made the position his own for the next decade, choosing to stay with the Imps despite the attention of bigger clubs. Honoured in the summer of 1955 when he was chosen to tour the West Indies with an FA representative team. He scored the only goal of his career at Chester in April 1951 when he was put into the forward line after suffering a badly cut head. In addition to the club record number of Football League appearances he also played in 22 FA Cup ties for City. Later employed in a builders' merchants. Tony was the son of Bob (a City reserve in 1922/23) and nephew of Fred (holder of the Doncaster Rovers FL appearance record, and later manager of Doncaster, Bradford and Carlisle).

ETCHES, Harry
(1902-1903)
Inside-forward: 2 app.

Career: Adelaide (Lincoln); Boston Town cs 1901; Adelaide cs 1902; CITY Oct. 1902-cs 1903; Adelaide Feb. 1904.

Harry was one of the many talented players in local junior football who assisted City in the early 1900's. Mostly a reserve with two first team outings in Jan. 1903 - at home to Preston and away at Burslem Port Vale.

EVANS, A(ndrew) Clive
(1987-1989)
Defender: 42 app., 2 goals
1988: 5-10, 11-5
Born: Birkenhead, 1 May 1957

Career: Tranmere Rovers (appr.) 1975, (prof.) Mar. 1977; Wigan Athletic July 1981 (£25,000); Crewe Alexandra Aug. 1982; Stockport County Aug. 1983; CITY Sep. 1987; Bangor City 1989; Stalybridge Celtic Feb. 1990; Leek Town Aug. 1990; Caernarvon Town cs 1991; Accrington Stanley.

Defender with the knack of scoring goals, he joined the Imps from Colin Murphy's old club, Stockport County. Proved an important member of the Vauxhall Conference championship winning team (36 app., 8 goals) and stayed a further season before leaving the club in May 1989. A FL career total of 429 appearances plus 10 as substitute with 60 goals. A defender at Sincil Bank but also appeared as an occasional striker in his earlier days.

EVANS, William
(1900-1901)
Centre-forward: 3 app.
Born: Llansantffraid, nr Aberystwyth

Career: London Welsh; Queens Park Rangers; CITY May 1900 to cs 1901.

Welsh centre-forward who appeared nine times with QPR in their first Southern League season. His first team appearances at Lincoln were limited by the competition (McCairns, Proudfoot and Scott were all on the club's books) and latterly by injuries which led him to announce his retirement at the end of his Sincil Bank season.

EYRE, Thomas
(1895-1898)
Left-back: 65 app., 1 goal.

Career: Dalziel Rovers; Glasgow Ashfield; CITY Oct. 1895 to Mar. 1898; Hamilton Academicals cs 1898.

Scottish junior international signed by City on the recommendation of the Blackburn Rovers secretary and became the club's regular left-back for the next three seasons. Summed up (1895) as *".... has a very taking style .... a clean and powerful kick, and a good turn of speed"*.

FAIRGRAY, Norman Murray
(1905-1907)

Outside-left: 60 app., 6 goals
Born: Dumfries, 28 Oct. 1880
Career: Dumfries Primrose; Maxwelltown Volunteers; Kilmarnock Nov. 1903; Maxwelltown Volunteers July 1904; CITY Dec. 1905; Chelsea Sep. 1907; Motherwell May 1914; Queen of the South Aug. 1919.

Was really introduced to the first class game at Lincoln (he made only one appearance for Kilmarnock). Norrie was quick, dribbled cleverly and on occasions was brilliant. He followed David Calderhead to Chelsea and was later considered good enough to be selected for a Scotland trial match. Settled in Dumfries and was employed in a local motor works in the early 1920's.

FAIRLEY, Peter Lindsay
(1907)
Inside-left: 4 app.
Career: Edinburgh junior football; CITY Oct.-Nov. 1907.

One of several players recruited from the Edinburgh area at this time having been recommended by Hugh McPhee (a City player in the later 1880's). In addition to his FL outings, Fairley also appeared in one Lincolnshire Cup tie (in which he scored) and one reserve match (at left-half) before departing.

FARMER, Michael C.
(1965-1966)
Left-half: 21 app. + 1 sub
1965: 6-0, 11-12
Born: Leicester, 22 Nov. 1944
Career: Birmingham City (appr.) Aug. 1961, (prof.) Apr. 1962; CITY May 1965; Skegness Town cs 1966; Arnold Town; Skegness Town; Grantham Town cs 1970; Oadby Town cs 1973; Grantham Town Feb. 1974.

Wing-half signed on a free transfer in the summer of 1965. Farmer never established himself as a regular first-teamer and moved on to Midland League soccer. At St. Andrews he had scored in his solitary FL outing.

FARRALL, Alec
(1965-1966)
Left-half: 20 app., 2 goals
1964: 5-8, 11-0
Born: West Kirby, Cheshire, 3 Mar. 1936
Career: Wirral Schools; Everton (prof.) Mar. 1953; Preston North End May 1957; Gillingham July 1960 (£5,000); CITY May 1965; Watford July 1966 to cs 1968.

Honours: England schools international (5 app., 1950 & 1951) (Gillingham) FL Div.4 champions 1964

Farrall had his best years at Gillingham where he made 202 FL appearances and was an important member of their championship side. Left Sincil Bank on a free transfer after one season and moved on to Third Division Watford.

FASHANU, John
(1983-1984)
Centre-forward: 31 app. + 5 sub, 11 goals
1984: 6-1, 11-12
Born: Kensington, London, 18 Sep. 1962
Career: Cambridge United, trial; Norwich City (appr.) Dec. 1978, (prof.) Oct. 1979 (Crystal Palace on loan, Aug. 1983); CITY on loan Sep.-Nov. 1983, when he signed permanently (£15,000); Millwall Nov. 1984 (£55,000); Wimbledon Mar. 1986 (£125,000).

Honours: England international (2 app. vs Chile & Scotland 1989) (Wimbledon) FA Cup winner 1988

Powerful all-action centre-forward who proved very effective at breaking down third division defences. Signed permanently by Colin Murphy despite a sending off in the second match of a loan period. Later won international honours at Wimbledon where to date he has scored over 100 goals from 250 plus appearances in top flight football. More recently has been building a career as a television presenter and developing links with African nations. Brother of Justin (Norwich, Nottingham Forest and Notts County).

FAWELL, Derek S.
(1965)

Centre-forward: 3 app.
Born: Hartlepool, 22 Mar. 1944
Career: Spennymoor United; Notts County Oct. 1964; CITY Sep. 1965; Wisbech Town Nov. 1965; Ilkeston Town early in 1966 to cs 1967; Redditch United Aug. 1968; Lockhead Leamington cs 1969.

Centre-forward who had a two month trial period at Sincil Bank later moving on to Southern League Wisbech, before switching to the midlands' non-league scene.

FEENEY, Thomas Wilfred
(1933-1934)

Inside-left: 10 app.
1933: 5-8½, 11-12
Born: Grangetown, North Yorks, 26 Aug. 1910
Died: 5 Mar. 1973
Career: Witby United; Newcastle United Dec. 1930 (£25); Notts County June 1932 (£500); CITY June 1933 (in exchange for Harold Riley); Stockport County Feb. 1934; Halifax Town Aug. 1934; Chester May 1937; Darlington Feb. 1938 to cs 1939.

Tom was first choice inside-left at the beginning of City's 1933/34 Second Division campaign but soon lost his place and departed for Stockport the following Feb. Also appeared at wing-half and centre-forward with his other clubs.

FELGATE, David Wynne
(1980-1985)

Goalkeeper: 198 app.
1981: 6-1, 13-3
Born: Blaenau Ffestiniog, Merioneth, 4 Mar. 1960
Career: Blaenau; Bolton Wanderers Aug. 1978 (Rochdale on loan, Oct. 1978; Bradford City on loan July 1979; Crewe Alexandra on loan Sep. 1979; Rochdale on loan Mar. 1980); CITY on loan Sep. 1980, permanent Dec. 1980 (£25,000) (Cardiff City on loan Dec. 1984; Grimsby Town on loan Feb.-Apr. 1985); Grimsby Town July 1985 (£27,500), (Bolton Wanderers on loan Feb. 1986; Rotherham United on loan Dec. 1986); Bolton Wanderers Feb. 1987 (£16,000); Wolverhampton Wanderers Aug. 1983; Chester City Oct. 1993.

Honours: Wales schools international
Wales international (1 app. vs Romania 1984)

Brilliant goalkeeper whose form earned him the honour of becoming one of the very few City players to win an international cap while with the club when he appeared as a second half substitute for Wales against Romania. Initially came to Sincil Bank on loan as a replacement for Colin Boulton who had suffered a broken leg. Departed for Grimsby after five seasons, the fee being set by a tribunal. Has aggregated over 500 FL appearances to date.

FELL, James Irving
(1964-1966)

Outside-left: 64 app., 10 goals
1964: 5-10, 11-6
Born: Cleethorpes, 4 Jan. 1936
Career: Waltham FC (Grimsby); Grimsby Town (amat.), (prof.) Apr. 1954; Everton Mar. 1961 (approx. £17,000); Newcastle United Mar. 1962 (£3,000 plus another player); Walsall July 1963 (£5,000); CITY Jan. 1964; Boston United Jan 1966 to cs 1969; Skegness Town in 1969/70; Ross Group in 1970/71.

Came to Sincil Bank at the end of a lengthy career which included a brief sample of top flight football at Everton. A City regular in his first two seasons but only appeared twice in 1965/66. Played in a total of 326 FL matches, scoring 69 times. Later employed at the Grimsby Sports Centre.

FENCOTT, Kenneth S.W.
(1964-1967)

Outside/inside-right: 67 app. + 6 sub, 13 goals
1965: 5-8, 9-12
Born: Walsall, 27 Dec. 1943
Career: Walsall schools; Aston Villa (amat.) Mar. 1959, (prof.) Jan. 1961; CITY June 1964; Tamworth Aug. 1967; Blakenall in 1968/69 season.

Fencott scored on his debut for the Imps against Hartlepools, but never really established himself as a regular first teamer in any one position. He appeared for City in all five forward placings, and also had the distinction of being the first player named as a substitute for the club although he was not brought on. After leaving football he ran a driving school in Birmingham.

FENWICK, Robert William
(1920-1923, 1925-1926)

Centre-half: 76 app., 2 goals
1921: 5-10, 12-10
Born: Walker, Newcastle-upon-Tyne, 29 Sep. 1894
Career: Ashington; CITY July 1920; Notts County Feb. 1923; CITY Jan. 1925; Shirebrook June 1926; Newark Town cs 1927; Horncastle Town Sep. 1928.

Fenwick arrived from Ashington having represented the North Eastern League against the Central League, and was an ever-present in City's Midland League championship side of 1920/21 (38 app., 3 goals). Departed for Meadow Lane during the financial crisis of February 1923 when several players were sold to raise funds, but later returned to serve the Imps for another two seasons. A 1921 writer described him as *"sturdy, energetic, full of tricks, uses his brains at centre-half, where City have a tradition of being well served"*.

FERN, Thomas Edward
(1909-1913)

Goalkeeper: 127 app.
1912: 5-10½, 13-4
Born: Measham, Leics., 1 Apr. 1886
Died: Mar. 1966
Career: Mafeking Rovers; Worksop Albion; Worksop Town 1905; CITY May 1909; Everton Dec. 1913 (£1,500); Port Vale June 1924; Colwyn Bay Aug. 1927.

Honour: (Everton): FL champions 1915

One of City's finest discoveries of the pre-WW1 era. Tommy missed only two matches (both through injury) in four and a half seasons at Sincil Bank, appearing in 142 consecutive league and cup games from Feb. 1910 until his departure. Not so lucky at Everton where he suffered several injuries (*"... always in the thick of the action"*) but played in 433 FL games in a career lasting 18 years.

FERNE, George Edward
(1898-1899)

Outside-left: 24 app., 3 goals
Born: Burton-on-Trent 1874
Died: 19 May 1955
Career: Hinckley Town; CITY June 1898; Millwall Athletic May 1899; Watford cs-October 1900; Fulham Dec. 1900.

Positive left-winger who appeared regularly in his Sincil Bank season. Later saw Southern League action with Millwall, Watford and Fulham, totalling a further 21 senior outings.

FINCH, A. Roy
(1949-1959)

Outside-left: 275 app., 56 goals
1955: 5-7, 10-7
Born: Barry Island, Glamorgan, 7 Apr. 1922
Career: Barrians FC (Cardiff) and Swansea during WW2; West Bromwich Albion (amat.) June 1944, (prof.) Sep. 1944; CITY Feb. 1949 (£3,000); retired 1959.

Honour: (City) FL Div.3 (North) champions 1952

Roy Finch made soccer history in Feb. 1949 when he flew to Southampton to sign in time to play in City's match at The Dell (a 4-0 defeat). He was unable to prevent the Imps being relegated that season, but made a major contribution to their return to Division Two three years later. A regular in City's first team for eight seasons and on the books for 11 before retiring to run a newsagents shop in Winn Street. Turned out for East End Athletic in the Lincoln Sunday League in the early 1960's.

FINNEY, Kevin
(1991-1993)
Midfield: 31 app. + 6 sub, 2 goals
1992: 6-0, 12-0
Born: Newcastle-under-Lyme, Staffs., 19 Oct. 1969
Career: Port Vale YTS, (prof.) June 1987; CITY July 1991; Leek Town cs 1993; Stafford Rangers Dec. 1993.

Left-footed midfield player recruited on a free transfer from Vale Park. Kevin appeared regularly in his first season without making any one position his own, but fell out of favour in his second campaign and returned to Staffordshire at the start of the 1993/94 season.

FISHER, John
(1928-1930)
Outside-right: 19 app., 3 goals
1929: 5-8½, 11-10
Born: Hodthorpe, Derbys, 4 Aug. 1897
Died: 22 June 1954
Career: Brodsworth Collier; Chesterfield cs 1920; Burnley Mar. 1922 (£1,000); Chesterfield Apr. 1923 (in exchange for George Beel); Mansfield Town June 1927; Staveley Town June 1928; CITY Oct. 1928; Denaby United Aug. 1930; Hurst Sep. 1931.

An experienced winger but mainly a reserve at Sincil Bank. Jackie had been a great favourite at Chesterfield where he totalled 174 Northern Section games (32 goals) in his two spells and was known for his speed, trickery and an ability to cross the ball when going full tilt. A deeply religious man who refused to play in Good Friday matches. Fisher was also a useful cricketer and played three matches for Derbyshire, 1921-22.

FITZSIMONS, Arthur Gerard
(1959)
Inside-forward: 7 apps.
1959: 5-8, 10-7
Born: Dublin, 16 Dec. 1929
Career: Shelbourne; Middlesbrough May 1949 (£18,000); CITY Mar. 1959 (£5,000); Mansfield Town Aug. 1959 (£6,000); Wisbech Town July 1961 to 1962; Drogheda United player coach 1967-69; Shamrock Rovers coach cs 1969. Also coached the League of Ireland representative side and Libya.

Honours: Eire international (26 app.)
League of Ireland (2 app. vs Irish League, 1949)
(Shelbourne) FAI Cup finalist 1949

Classy inside-forward who came to Sincil Bank after more than 200 FL outings with Middlesbrough. He stayed only briefly but won the last of his international caps while on City's books, appearing against Czechoslovakia in a European Championship tie in May 1959.

FLEMING, James
(1892-1893)
Centre-forward: 11 app., 5 goals
Born: Leith, Edinburgh, Sep. 1864
Died: Aug. 1934
Career: Vale of Leven; Army football with the 93rd Argyle & Sutherland Highlanders (Southampton St. Mary's Oct.-Dec. 1891); Aston Villa May 1892; CITY Oct. 1892; Larkhall Saints May 1893.

City were bottom of the table by the Oct. of their first FL season and so recruited Fleming, an aggressive centre-forward, and veteran defender Bob Roberts in an attempt to reverse their fortunes. Fleming scored two on his debut against Burton Swifts but moved back to Scotland later in the season. The short Southampton association came after he starred in an exhibition match for his army team against them.

FLEMING, John J.
(1975-1980)
Midfield: 109 app. + 12 sub, 17 goals
1977: 5-8, 10-2
Born: Nottingham, 1 July 1953
Career: Oxford United July 1970; CITY July 1975; Port Vale Mar. to cs 1980. Coach of Wollongong (Australia) in 1989.
Honours: (City) FL Div.4 Champions 1976.

Fleming proved a bargain free transfer signing from Oxford where he had been captain of the reserve side. A regular in City's 1975/76 championship line-up (39 app. + 1 sub, 8 goals). He left Sincil Bank after five seasons and later emigrated to Australia. In 1989 he was coaching in New South Wales.

FLEMING, Neil
(1972-1974)
Centre-half: 1 app.
Born: Felixstowe, 9 Jan. 1950
Career: Lincoln United; Gainsborough United; Lincoln Claytons; CITY (amat.) Apr. 1972; Grantham Town Nov. 1974.

Local amateur given a FL outing in the final home match of the 1973/74 season against Northampton. Also appeared for Swiss Cottage in the Lincoln Sunday League.

FLETCHER, H(orace) Robert
(1897-1898)
Inside-left: 28 app., 6 goals
Born: Rotherham, 1876
Died: Sep. 1931
Career: Mexborough; CITY Sep. 1897; Rotherham Town 1898

Yorkshire-born player who had a useful season in City's colours - although the club had to seek re-election it was a great improvement on the previous campaign when they nearly folded. Also deputised occasionally at outside-right for City.

FLETCHER, J(ames) Rodney
(1967-1971)

Centre-forward: 86 apps. + 6 sub, 29 goals
1970: 5-8, 11-2
Born: Preston, 23 Sep 1945
Career: Colne; Leeds United Dec.1962; Madeley College (Staffs); Crewe Alexandra Mar 1967; CITY Aug.1967; Scunthorpe United June 1971 (£2,500); Grimsby Town Nov.1973; Immingham Town.

A schoolteacher who was a part-time professional at Sincil Bank. Fletcher finished leading scorer in 1969/70 and 1970/71 but lost his place at the end of the following campaign and was allowed to move on. Appeared as an outside-left in his early career.

FLEWITT, Albert William
(1893-1895)

Inside-left: 56 app., 30 goals
Born: Beeston, Notts, Feb. 1872
Died: 1943
Career: Mansfield Greenhalgh's; CITY cs 1893; Everton cs 1895; West Bromwich Albion Jan. 1896; Bedminster June 1899 to 1900.

Honour: Football League (1 app. vs Southern League 1895)

Recruited from Mansfield junior football along with John Chadburn in the summer of 1893. Flewitt was reported to have a terrific shot, to work hard and have a touch of elegance. Leading scorer for the Imps in 1894/95 with 17 goals.

FLITCROFT, David
(1993)

Midfield: 2 app.
1993: 5-11, 12-0

Born: Bolton, 14 Jan. 1974
Career: Preston North End YTS, (prof.) May 1992, (CITY on loan Sep. 1993); Chester City Dec. 1993.

Flitcroft made his City debut as a substitute in the home leg of the League Cup tie with Everton, but appeared in only two more games before returning to Preston.

FOOTITT, Donald
(1946-1949)

Goalkeeper: 24 app.
1949: 5-9, 11-7
Born: Grantham, 24 May 1929
Career: Grantham St. Johns; CITY (amat.) cs 1946, (prof.) Jan. 1947; Crewe Alexandra July 1949; Ransomes & Marles cs 1952.

Lincolnshire-born goalkeeper who got his first team chance in an FA Cup tie with Wrexham due to Daniels' injury and kept his place until the end of the season. Turned professional in January 1947 for which City rewarded Grantham St. Johns at a later date by sending a cheque for £10. Called up for National Service in the summer of 1947 and was restricted to one reserve team appearance a month. At Crewe he made only one appearance in three seasons before returning to play for Ransomes in the Central Alliance.

FORBES, James
(1921-1923)

Centre-half: 16 app.
1921: 6-1, 12-0
Born: Walker, Newcastle-upon-Tyne, 14 Mar. 1896
Died: 29 Mar. 1939
Career: Walker Celtic; Carlisle United; CITY June 1921; Leadgate Park Feb. 1923; Scunthorpe United cs 1923; Blackpool Oct. 1923; Southport June 1924; Bolton Wanderers Jan. 1925; Bristol Rovers June 1926; Workington July 1928 as player coach.

City had to compete with several First Division clubs to sign Forbes from North-Eastern League Carlisle United. He replaced the injured Bob Fenwick at the end of the 1921/22 season but only had one more FL outing with the Imps. Left on a free transfer when faced with the prospect of a cut in wages. *"Clever and methodical in all his work"* commented a 1921 observer. Served in the Navy during the Great War and was employed as a licensee in the 1930's.

FORD, Clive
(1967-1968)

Forward: 48 app. + 1 sub, 16 goals
1966: 5-8, 11-8
Born: Hateley Heath, West Bromwich, 10 Apr. 1945
Career: Wolverhampton Wanderers (appr.), (prof.) Oct. 1962; Walsall Dec. 1964; CITY Feb. 1967; Los Angeles Wolves (USA) May-Sep. 1968.

Burly centre-forward who had nearly all his Football League experience at Lincoln. Appearing for the Imps against Bradford in Dec. 1967 he scored twice in the first minute and completed his hat-trick in the 11th minute in a game which City won 5-1. Departed on a free transfer and that summer appeared in the NASL with Los Angeles (11 app., 3 goals).

FORMAN, Reginald George
(1936-1939)

Right-half: 2 app.
1938: 5-9½, 11-0
Born: Louth, Lincs., 3 Sep. 1917
Died: 1978
Career: CITY (amat.) cs 1936, (prof.) Sep. 1936; Gainsborough Trinity cs 1939; Louth Town Mar. 1947; Louth United cs 1948.

Former Louth Grammar School pupil who made his senior debut for City in a Northern Section Cup match at Doncaster in Oct. 1937 (a 2-7 defeat). Given two FL outings the following Sep. with similar results (0-3 vs Hull, 0-6 vs Crewe) and left at the end of the season for Midland League Gainsborough on a free transfer.

FOSTER, Albert William
(1906-1912)

Outside-right: 67 app., 1 goal
1912: 5-6, 10-8
Born: Sleaford, Lincs., c.1885
Died: 29 May 1959
Career: Grantham Avenue; CITY (amat.) Nov. 1906, (prof.) Dec. 1906-cs 1912; Grantham FC in 1913; CITY Oct. 1914.

Bertie quickly became a regular first teamer at Sincil Bank and remained so until he suffered a broken collarbone in Oct. 1909. *"A thorough worker"* and *"... lacking in inches but a bustler with excellent speed and trickiness"* were two contemporary comments. Returned to play a solitary reserve fixture shortly after WWI commenced. Later a licensee in his native Sleaford for many years.

FOSTER, Samuel Bernard
(1920)

Centre-forward: 1 app.
1920: 5-9½, 11-7
Born: Southwell, Notts., 12 Nov. 1897
Died: 31 Mar. 1965
Career: Southwell Federation; CITY Jan. 1920; Mansfield Town cs 1920; Coventry City Oct. 1920; Mansfield Town cs 1921; Newark Town cs 1922.

Amateur centre-forward whose only appearance for City was in the home match with Leicester in March 1920 (a 3-0 defeat). Also had 10 FL outings with Coventry, scoring four goals.

FOULKES, Charles Edward
(1927-1930)

Centre-half: 64 app., 1 goal
1928: 5-9½, 11-10
Born: Bilston, Staffs., 7 Feb. 1905
Career: Fryston Red Triangle; Frickley Colliery; Fryston Colliery; Bradford City Nov. 1923; Bournemouth & Boscombe Athletic May 1925; CITY July 1927; Boston Town Aug. 1930; Hurst Oct. 1931.

"Quietly efficient" centre-half who was a regular for nearly two seasons before Alf Hale took over the position in February 1929. Arrived with no previous Football League experience. Foulkes was a miner at Fryston Colliery and bother of Richard and Jabez who both appeared in League Football.

FOX, Kevin
(1978-1981)

Goalkeeper: 4 app.
1980: 5-11, 11-2
Born: Sheffield, 22 Sep. 1960
Career: Sheffield Rangers; CITY on schoolboy forms Oct. 1976, (prof.) March 1978; (Boston United on loan; Hull City on loan Mar. 1981); Kettering Town cs 1981; Rushden Town; Wellingborough Town cs 1983; Rushden Town; Rushden & Diamonds.

A produce of City's Sheffield nursery side who appeared with the Imps junior team from Nov. 1976. Played in the last four games of the 1979/80 season after Eric McManus was recalled to Stoke and also in a League Cup-tie at Swindon the following Sep. as replacement for broken-leg victim Colin Boulton. He had no further opportunities and was released in May 1981.

FRANKLIN, Neil J.
(1986-1988)

Defender: 15 app. + 1 sub
1987: 6-0, 12-0
Born: Lincoln, 10 Mar. 1969
Career: Leicester City on schoolboy forms; CITY YTS Oct. 1986, (prof.) cs 1987; Nÿkopings BIS (Sweden); CITY Oct. 1988 (non-contract); Gainsborough Trinity Jan. 1989.

Youngster who was given a first team chance by George Kerr soon after signing YTS forms. He made several first team appearances in 1986/87 but had only three Vauxhall Conference outings the following season. Later returned after a season in the Swedish Second Division, appearing once more as a substitute in the FL, and in the FA Cup tie at Altrincham.

FRANKS, Albert John
(1961-1964)

Wing-half: 58 app., 5 goals
1962: 5-11, 12-6
Born: Boldon, Co. Durham, 13 Apr. 1936
Career: Boldon Colliery Welfare; Newcastle United Dec. 1953 (£50); Rangers Mar. 1960 (£6,500), (Morton on loan, Aug. 1961); CITY Nov. 1961; Queen of the South Jan. 1964; Scarborough July

1964 - Dec. 1965 as player-manager.

Powerful wing-half with a mighty throw. A regular first team player until the summer of 1963 when he went into dispute with the club over terms. He never played for City again and was granted a free transfer by a Football League tribunal in Dec. 1963. Represented the RAF during his National Service.

FRANKS, Charles Robert
(1922-1923)
Centre-forward: 1 app
1922: 5-8½, 10-0
Born: Gateshead, 15 Oct. 1892
Died: 1978
Career: Close Works (Gateshead); CITY June 1922-Feb. 1923.

"Comes with a good reputation from Gateshead Close Works, acclaimed to be a terrific shot, which is what the club wants", said a 1922 football handbook. Made his solitary FL appearance at home to Rochdale in Sep. 1912. One of a number of men from the north-east who left the club on a free transfer in Feb. 1923, at a time of financial crisis.

FRASER, David
(1896)
Inside-left: 1 app.
1896: 5-9½, 11-9
Career: St. Bernards; Leith Athletic; CITY May-Sep. 1896

Scottish player whose only Football League outing for the Imps was in the opening match of the 1896/97 season at home to Blackpool. Described (1897) as *"a well balanced player with all the making of a fine footballer"* he did not perform as well as expected and was soon released.

FRASER, George
(1901-1911)

Right-half: 265 app., 4 goals

1904: 5-8, 10-7
Born: Elgin, c.1874
Died: 21 Oct. 1951
Career: Elgin City; Sunderland cs 1899; CITY July 1901 to cs 1911; assisted Nettleham FC in 1913/14 season; CITY secretary-manager Sep. 1919-Mar. 1921; Grimsby Town secretary-manager Mar. 1921-Mar. 1924.

City's regular right-half for about a decade, George Fraser had the distinction of making more League appearances than any other player in the pre-WW1 era. Described as a *"quiet, gentlemanly and useful player"*. Badly injured in a car crash whilst serving with the Lincolnshire Yeomanry Regiment during the Great War which resulted in a lengthy spell in hospital. On leaving the club he was a local licensee until succeeding his brother-in-law, Jack Strawson, as City's secretary-manager. Later worked for 25 years as the steward of the Iron and Steel Club in Scunthorpe.

FREEMAN, James Alfred
(1927-1928)
Wing-half: 2 app.
1927: 5-8½, 11-7
Born: Ilkeston, Derbys., 13 July 1904
Died: Jan. 1986
Career: Sutton Town (Notts.); Blackpool during the 1925/26 season; CITY June 1927; Mansfield Town Oct. 1928; Frickley Colliery June 1929.

Freeman appeared twice for City's League team, once in each of the wing-half positions, but was unable to dislodge either of the regular occupants, Bassnett and Hale. Later a member of Mansfield's 1928/29 Midland League championship side.

FREEMAN, Ronald Peter ("Percy")
(1970-1973, 1975-1977)

Centre-forward: 138 app. + 14 sub, 64 goals
1975: 6-0, 13-10
Born: Newark, 4 July 1945

Career: Stourbridge 1964; West Bromwich Albion Apr. 1968 (£2,500); CITY June 1970; Reading Jan. 1973 (£11,500); CITY Jan. 1975 (£1,500); Boston United Aug 1977; retired Nov. 1977; Nettleham manager cs 1989- cs 1991; Boston FC manager cs 1991; Stamford Town manager Dec. 1993 (with Dave Smith as his assistant). Also managed Ivy Tavern in the Lincoln Sunday League.

Honour; (City) FL Division 4 Champions 1976

Very popular robust centre-forward who arrived on a free transfer from the Hawthorns. His style of play upset opposing defences and he also had the knack of scoring spectacular goals. Transferred to Reading shortly after Graham Taylor became manager, but came back two years later and made a major contribution to the Fourth Division championship side with 23 League goals. Has returned to the game in recent years as manager of several Lincs. non-League sides. A lorry driver before signing for West Bromwich.

FRETTINGHAM, John Henry Abel ("Jimmy") (1894-1896)
Outside-left: 56 app., 20 goals
1903: 5-10, 12-0
Born: Nottingham, 1871
Died: 17 May 1904
Career: Long Eaton Rangers; CITY May 1894; New Brompton cs 1896-1903.

"A good dribbler, but has not the slightest idea of holding his forwards together" was an 1894 opinion of this capable, goalscoring winger. Later joined New Brompton for their first season of Southern League football and went on to make over 150 appearances for them. His death at Derby was the result of a football injury.

GALLACHER, Samuel (1928-1929)
Centre-half: 13 app.
1928: 6-0, 11-10
Born: Annbank, Ayrshire, 23 Dec. 1904
Career: Larkfield Juveniles; Cadzow St. Annes; Bradford City May 1924; Crystal Palace June 1927; CITY Aug. 1928; York City Sep. 1929 (trial).

Sam performed as deputy for Bassnett and Foulkes during the 1928/29 season. Earlier in his career had made 40 appearances in the Second Division with Bradford City. No senior outings with Palace. Worked as a miner.

GALLAGHER, Jackie C. (1975-1978)
Midfield: 1 app.
1977: 5-10½, 12-4
Born: Wisbech, Cambs., 6 Apr. 1958

Career: March Town; CITY on trial Sep. 1975, full terms Feb. 1976; Kings Lynn; Wisbech Town; Peterborough United Apr. 1980 - Sep. 1981; spell in Hong Kong; Torquay United Aug. 1982; Wisbech Town cs 1983; Peterborough United cs 1985; Wolverhampton Wanderers June 1987; Wisbech Town Feb. 1989; Kettering Town Mar. 1989; Wisbech Town cs 1989; Boston United Sep. 1989; Kings Lynn Feb. 1990.

Jackie's only League appearance with City came in May 1977 in the home match with Peterborough which was to be Graham Taylor's last before his departure. Later developed into a bustling striker, aggregating a total of 138 FL appearances plus 37 as substitute, scoring 31 times in a career which also saw plenty of non-League action.

GAMBLE, S(imon) William (1984-1989)
Centre-forward: 44 app. + 20 sub, 14 goals
1988: 5-9, 11-7
Born: Cottam, Notts., 5 Mar. 1968
Career: CITY (appr.) July 1984, (prof.) Mar. 1986, (Grantham Town on loan, Feb.-cs 1988); Boston United June 1989; Shepshed Charterhouse Feb. 1990; Harworth Colliery early 1991; Brigg Town cs 1993; Glapwell later in 1993/94.

Speedy striker who made his first team debut as a 17 year old apprentice. Always on the fringe of the first team without gaining a regular place, Willie was released on a free transfer in May 1989. Later worked as a bricklayer.

GARDNER, Andrew (1909-1920)
Centre-half: 151 app., 9 goals
1909: 5-11½, 12-0
Born: Airdrie, c.1888
Died: 2 June 1934
Career: Petershill; CITY Aug. 1909-1920

"Consistent, cool, deliberate; never plays to the gallery but makes his points and, at his best, has no superior in the Second Division - no stars barred" was a 1913 verdict on Andy. City's regular centre-half through to the 1918/19 season, he also made one post-WW1 appearance. Before coming to Lincoln he won three Scottish junior caps. His death occurred suddenly, the day after commencing work in a local engineering factory, following a three year period of unemployment.

GARNER, Herbert A. (1921-1922)
Left-back: 6 app.
1921: 5-10, 10-7
Born: Mexborough, Yorks., c.1899
Career: Mexborough Great Central Loco; Denaby United cs 1920; CITY May 1921; Wombwell cs 1922; Rotherham Town June 1924; Mansfield Town May 1925; Leicester City during the 1925/26 season; Stockport County cs 1930.

Signed after performing well for Denaby against City. Garner appeared mostly in the Midland League team, deputising for Ward and Atkin on a handful of occasions in the early part of the 1921/22 season. Arrived at First Division Leicester after touring the Midland League circuit but made no senior appearances in five years at Filbert Street.

GARRATY, William
(1910-1911)

Inside/centre-forward: 16 app., 2 goals
1905: 5-9, 12-0
Born: Saltley, Birmingham, 6 Oct. 1878
Died: 6 May 1931
Career: Highfield Villa; Aston Shakespeare 1895; Aston Villa Aug. 1897; Leicester Fosse Sep. 1908 (£250); West Bromwich Albion Oct. 1908 (£270); CITY Dec. 1910 (£100); retired cs 1911.

Honours: England international (1 app. vs Wales 1903)
(Villa) FL champions 1900
FA Cup winner 1905

Veteran forward signed in an unsuccessful attempt to boost City's attack during the 1910/11 season. In earlier days Billy was known as a robust inside-forward and had headed the League scoring list for season 1899/1900. Also won junior international honours with the Birmingham FA. From 1923 until his death worked as a lorry driver for Ansells Brewery in Birmingham.

GARVIE, John
(1950-1956)

Inside-right: 184 app., 78 goals
1955: 5-8, 10-9
Born: Bellshill, Lanarks., 16 Oct. 1927
Career: Carfin Boys Club; Hibernian; Preston North End Aug. 1949; CITY Aug. 1950 (£750); Carlisle United May 1956; Boston United Aug. 1957; Corby Town; Stamford Town; Ilkeston Town cs 1962.

Honour: (City) FL Div.3 (North) champions 1952

Scottish-born inside-forward who formed a very productive partnership with Andy Graver during City's best post-WW2 seasons. Had a fine goalscoring record and topped the club scoring charts in 1950/51 and 1954/55. Gave City five seasons of excellent service before moving back to the Northern Section with Carlisle. On leaving the professional game was steward of Corby Trades and Labour club.

GASH, Robert
(1894-1895)

Half-back: 14 app., 1 goal
Career: Grantham Rovers; CITY May 1894; Grantham Rovers 1895; Gainsborough Trinity 1896; later assisted several Grantham teams: Amateurs; Avenue cs 1902; Hornsby's Engineers cs 1903.

One of several recruits from Grantham Rovers in the early 1890's, Gash appeared in all three half-back positions during his season at Lincoln. Later at Gainsborough in their first Football League campaign. A private in the Lincolnshire Regiment.

GASTON, Ray
(1970)

Centre-forward: 4 app., 1 goal
1970: 6-2
Born: Belfast, 22 Dec. 1946
Career: Coleraine; Wolverhampton Wanderers May 1965; Coleraine; Oxford United Sep. 1968 (CITY on loan Feb. 1970); Finn Harps cs 1970-1971.

Honours: Northern Ireland international (1 app. vs Israel 1969)
Northern Ireland under-23 international (1 app. vs Italy 1969)

Gaston scored freely at Coleraine but did not fare so well in England (he totalled 16 FL appearances, 3 goals). Scored on his debut for City at Scunthorpe but returned to Oxford when his month's loan period was completed.

GEDNEY, Christopher
(1961-1966)

Inside-left: 9 app, 1 goal
Born: Boston, Lincs, 1 Sep. 1945
Career: Holbeach United; CITY (amat.) Dec. 1961, (Birmingham City on loan Jan. 1966); Spalding United cs 1966; Alverchurch cs 1967; Nuneaton Borough cs 1969; Alvechurch; Walton & Hersham 1970.

Amateur who made his first team debut as a 16 year old schoolboy in a friendly fixture with Grimsby. Mostly a reserve he combined football with his studies at Boston Grammar School and then at Birmingham University. Won representative honours with Lincolnshire Grammar Schools (in the same team as Graham Taylor) and toured New Zealand in the summer of 1969 with an FA XI. Later a schoolteacher in Wolverhampton and Croydon.

GERRY, James
(1911)
Centre-forward: 2 app.
Career: Larkhall Thistle; CITY Apr. to cs 1911; Scunthorpe United (on trial) 1911; Leicester Imperial in 1913/14 season.

Scottish forward recruited at the very end of the 1910/11 season as City struggled to avoid re-election. They failed and were voted out of the League for the second time in four years.

GIBB, James M.
(1938-1939)
Inside-right: 3 app.
1938: 5-10½, 11-0
Born: East Calder, Lothian, c.1918
Career: Newtongrange Star, Manchester United Jan. 1937; CITY May 1938; Hibernian cs 1939.

Gibb was one of a number of Scottish players signed by Joe McClelland in the late 1930's. His appearances all came in Sep. 1938 at the beginning of a season when the Imps had to wait until their tenth match before securing a victory. *"Has speed and swerve and is a powerful shot"* said a 1938 football guide.

GIBSON, Colin Hayward
(1956-1957)
Inside-right: 36 app, 12 goals
1956: 5-11, 11-4
Born: Normanby, North Yorks., 16 Sep. 1923
Career: Penarth Pontoon; Cardiff City Aug. 1942; Newcastle United July 1948 (£15,000); Aston Villa Feb. 1949 (£17,500); CITY Jan. 1956 (£6,000); Stourbridge July 1957

Honours: England 'B' international (1 app. vs Holland 1949)
Football League (1 app. vs League of Ireland 1949)
(Cardiff) FL Div. 3 (South) champions 1947

Arrived from Villa Park with a good footballing pedigree to assist City in their Second Division days. Fair-haired winger, in his earlier days known for his ball control and good shot. A marine engineer in the South Wales dockyards before joining Cardiff, Colin became a licensee in Hagley, Worcs. on leaving the game.

GIBSON, Robert H.
(1951-1955)
Centre-forward: 43 app., 20 goals
1951: 5-10, 12-7
Born: Ashington, Northumberland, 5 Aug. 1927
Career: Ashington; Aberdeen Jan. 1949; Hull City Nov. 1949; Ashington cs 1950; CITY May 1951; Peterborough United cs 1955; Gateshead Mar. 1957 to 1959.

Honour: (City) FL Div.3 (North) champions 1952

Understudied Andy Graver until the latter was sold to Leicester in Dec. 1954. Bob maintained a good scoring record when called up for first team duties. His career record in the League shows an excellent 52 goals from 104 appearances.

GIBSON, Robert James
(1912-1914)
Inside-right: 1 app.
1912: 5-8, 12-7
Born: Scotswood, Newcastle-upon-Tyne, 1887
Career: Middlesbrough Sep. 1910; Newcastle United Aug. 1911 (£50); CITY May 1912; Third Lanark May 1914

After a good start to his senior career (31 First Division and FA Cup appearances with Middlesbrough) Gibson made little progress. His solitary FL outing for City came in the home game with Bury in April 1913. Also appeared as an outside-right.

GIBSON, William
(1898-1903)
Left-back: 130 app., 1 goal
1895: - , 14-4
Born: c.1869
Died: 15 Sep. 1911
Career: Flemington Thistle; Cambuslang 1887; Sunderland Aug. 1888; Rangers May 1894; Sunderland Sep. 1895; Notts County 1896; CITY May 1898 to 1903.

Honours: Scottish League (1 app. vs Irish League 1895)
(Sunderland) FL champions 1892, 1893
(Notts County) FL Div.2 champions 1897

One of City's most distinguished pre-1914 players. Will was also one of the heaviest outfield players of his time - in his Rangers days it was said he *"carries his weight like a war horse"* and by the time he came to Lincoln he was reputed to weigh around 17st. Club captain in what was the Imps' best ever period at the turn of the century. Even in late career he had lost none of his ability *"... his kicking is as true and accurate as ever"*, noted a 1902 commentator. He had earlier been left-half in Sunderland's 'Team of All the Talents' switching to full-back when he went to Notts County. On leaving football worked as a licensee in Lincoln until his death.

GILBERT, David J.
(1979-1982)
Midfield: 15 app + 15 sub, 1 goal
1981: 5-4, 10-6
Born: Lincoln, 22 June 1963
Career: CITY (appr.) July 1979, (prof.) June 1981; Scunthorpe United Sep. 1982; Boston United Oct. 1982; Northampton Town June 1986; Grimsby Town Mar. 1989 (£55,000).

Diminutive left-sided midfield player who made his debut for the Imps while still an apprentice. Regularly brought on as substitute in the 1981-82 season when City came so close to a return to the Second Division, but was released that summer. Appeared at Wembley for Boston United in the 1985 FA Trophy final and eventually re-entered League football with Northampton. Has since accumulated a further 300 FL outings.

GILLESPIE, Matthew
(1895-1896)

Inside-left: 36 app., 10 goals
Born: 24 Dec. 1869
Career: Glasgow Thistle; Blackburn Rovers June 1892; Accrington 1893; Leith Athletic Aug. to Dec. 1894; CITY Sep. 1895; Newton Heath Nov. 1896 to 1900.

Scottish recruit who revitalised the Imps' attack in the early part of the 1895/96 season after signing with his younger brother William. Departed for Manchester during one of City's periodic financial crises, staying for four seasons (73 apps, 18 goals).

GILLESPIE, William Jardine
(1895-1897)

Centre-forward: 37 app., 16 goals
1903: 5-8½, 11-10
Born: Strathclyde, 2 Oct. 1873
Career: Strathclyde; CITY Oct. 1895; Manchester City Jan. 1897 to 1905

Honours: (Manchester City) FA Cup winners 1904
FL Div.2 champions 1899, 1903

William signed shortly after his brother Matthew and was an immediate goalscoring success, scoring two on his debut in a 13-0 trouncing of Peterborough in an FA Cup tie. Followed Matthew to Manchester where he had a very productive eight years spell with the City club, scoring 125 goals in 218 FL appearances before emigrating to South Africa.

GILLIGAN, James Martin
(1982, 1987)

Centre-forward: 11 app. + 3 sub, 1 goal
1987: 6-2, 11-7
Born: Hammersmith, London, 24 Jan. 1964
Career: Stevenage Minor League; Watford (appr.) July 1980, (prof.) Aug. 1981 (CITY on loan, Oct. 1982); Grimsby Town July 1985 (£110,000); Swindon Town June 1986 (£100,000), (Newport County on loan, Feb. 1987) CITY Mar. 1987 (£35,000); Cardiff

City July 1987 (£20,000); Portsmouth Sep. 1989 (£215,000); Swansea City Aug. 1990 (£175,000); retired through injury Feb. 1993; Boreham Wood; Stamco (Sussex County League) cs 1993.

Honours: England Youth international (3 app., 1982)
(Cardiff) Welsh Cup winner 1988

Tall striker who never really produced his best form in two spells at Sincil Bank. Initially came on loan but returned to Watford without making the starting line-up. His return coincided with City's relegation out of the League. The subject of big money transfers both before and after his permanent move to the Imps.

GILLIVER, Alan H.
(1971-1972)

Centre-forward: 33 apps. + 4 sub, 8 goals
1971: 6-1½, 13-0
Born: Swallownest, Sheffield, 3 Aug. 1944
Career: Huddersfield Town (amat.) June 1960, (prof.) Aug. 1961; Blackburn Rovers June 1966 (£12,000); Rotherham United May 1968 (in exchange for another player); Brighton & Hove Albion July 1969; CITY Feb. 1971 (£10,000); Bradford City June 1972 (£4,000); Stockport County June 1974; Baltimore Comets (USA) May 1975; Boston United Sep. 1975 (Buxton on loan, Mar. 1976); Gainsborough Trinity Aug. to Oct. 1976; Bradford City (non-contract) Aug. 1978

Big, experienced striker recruited by David Herd from Brighton in Feb.1971 along with Nobby Lawton. Injured in his second match at home to Bournemouth, but recovered to play a full role the following season. Also a talented cricketer who appeared for Sussex II and played as a professional in the Bradford League.

GILLOTT, Edward
(1924-1928)

Centre-half: 14 app.
1924: 5-9, 11-0
Born: Sheffield, 14 Dec. 1902
Died: 14 Jan. 1984
Career: Sheffield Forge; CITY (amat.) Sep. 1924, (prof.) Oct. 1924; Shirebrook June 1928; Scarborough 1929.

Reserve centre-half who came to Sincil Bank from Sheffield junior football. *"Resourceful, good anticipation, and developed his powers considerably last season"* wrote a critic prior to the opening of the 1927/28 season.

GLADDING, Charles
(1892-1895)

Outside-left: 2 app.
Born: Louth, Lincs., 1874
Career: Lincoln junior football; CITY Dec. 1892; Gainsborough Trinity cs 1895; Blue Star (Lincoln) 1897.

Local lad who appeared regularly for the City Swifts (reserve) side. His two FL outings came in Mar. and Apr. of 1895 at Leicester and Walsall respectively.

GODBOLD, Harold
(1966-1967)

Outside-left: 22 app. + 1 sub, 3 goals
1962: 5-9. 10-6
Born: Springwell, Co. Durham, 31 Jan. 1939
Career: Ushworth Colliery; Sunderland Aug. 1956; Hartlepool United Jan. 1961; Boston United Aug. 1963; Boston FC cs 1964; CITY Mar. 1966; Spalding United cs 1967; Boston FC Dec. 1967; Gateshead 1968.

Harry joined the Imps after nearly three seasons in non-League football and appeared regularly towards the end of the 1965/66 campaign. Returned to the Lincs. non-League scene after being given a free transfer in May 1967.

GOLDSBOROUGH, John
(1911-1920)

Goalkeeper: 36 app.
1912: 5-8, 11-0
Born: Sheffield, c.1893
Career: Industry (Sheffield Licensed Victuallers League); CITY cs 1911; Boston Town 1920; Llanelly manager May 1921 and trainer July 1924.

Signed after starring for a Sheffield public house team, Goldsborough waited two years for his FL debut, finally getting his chance when Tommy Fern was sold to Everton. A popular player described (1913) as *"... daring and dashing; can hold his own in a tough time and has grit - makes up in pluck what little he may lack in inches"*. Appeared regularly for the Imps during the Great War and was later associated with the Llanelly club until the 1940's.

GORDON, James S.
(1974-1978)

Goalkeeper: 4 app.
1974: 5-10, 12-0
Born: Stretford, Manchester, 3 Sep. 1955
Career: Blackpool (appr.); Luton Town Sep. 1973; CITY July 1974; Reading Aug. 1978; Scunthorpe United Aug. 1979; Gainsborough Trinity Aug. 1981; Boston United Jan. to Mar. 1982; Skegness Town Feb. 1983 later assisted Saxilby (Lincs.) in season 1989/90.

Honours: England schoolboy international (5 app. 1971)

Jimmy played superbly on his debut at Mansfield in an FA Cup tie but received few first team opportunities because of the form of Peter Grotier. Moved on to Reading on a free transfer but later returned to live in Lincolnshire. Now runs a newsagents business in Saxilby.

GORMLIE, William Joseph
(1939)

Goalkeeper: 3 app.
1938: 5-10½, 11-7
Born: Blackpool, 1911
Died: July 1976

Career: Fleetwood Windsor Villa; Blackburn Rovers (amat.) July 1930, (prof.) May 1931; Northampton Town July 1935; CITY July 1939. Appointed coach to Belgian national side Jan. 1947, subsequently coaching Aderlecht for 15 years and later Ostend and Racing Club Jette.

Stylish 'keeper whose Lincoln career was restricted to the first three games of the 1939-40 season before war intervened. Bill had been working as a page boy at Blackpool Tower when signed by Blackburn and had aggregated 183 FL appearances, before arriving at Sincil Bank, despite suffering a serious kidney injury, in Oct. 1933. Described by a contemporary as *"... brilliant and spectacular, he has created tremendous impressions on several grounds"*. After spending the period 1939-46 as a PT instructor in the Army he was appointed coach to the Belgian national team on the recommendation of Stanley Rouse. When his coaching career was over he worked as a night manager at the Hilton in Brussels. Died in Belgium.

GORRINGE, Frederick Charles
(1928-1929)

Inside-forward: 6 app., 3 goals
1928: 5-10, 11-7
Born: Salford, 1903
Died: 1965
Career: St Cyprians; Manchester Ship Canal; Manchester City Sep. 1926; CITY July 1928; Crewe Alexandra July 1929; Bolton Wanderers Dec. 1929; Reading May 1931 to 1932.

A reserve with all his FL clubs except for Crewe, but scored regularly when given the opportunity; for example two on his Manchester City debut and one in his first game for the Imps. Gorringe worked as a docker before entering professional football.

GORTON, Andrew William
(1989-1990)

Goalkeeper: 20 app.
1990: 5-11, 11-4
Born: Salford, 23 Sep. 1966
Career: Oldham Athletic (amat.) June 1983, (prof.) July 1985; (Stockport County on loan, Dec. 1986; Tranmere Rovers on loan, May 1988); Stockport County Aug. 1988; CITY Aug. 1989 (£15,-000); Glossop Aug. 1990 (£3,000); Oldham Athletic Feb. 1991; Crewe Alexandra (non-contract) Apr. 1991; Witton Albion Sep. 1991; Mossley Oct. 1991; Bury July 1992; (Altrincham on loan, Mar. 1993).

Brave and talented goalkeeper who had been talked of as a future England prospect in his Oldham days. Unfortunately a promising career was damaged by off-the-field activities. Departed from Lincoln because *"he was unable to comply in a manner with the rules and regulations of the club"*.

GOULD, Geoffrey
(1968)

Outside-left: 1 app.
1967: 5-8½, 9-4

Born: Blackburn, 7 Jan. 1945
Career: Bradford (amat.) at 15, (prof.) Jan. 1962, (CITY on trial, Feb. 1968); Notts County July 1969.

Trialist winger who appeared in just one first team match for City before suffering a broken leg when playing for the reserves at Halifax. Had a lengthy career at Park Avenue totalling 145 League and FA Cup matches.

GRAHAM, Douglas
(1951-1957)

Full-back: 182 app.
1950: 5-10, 12-2
Born: Ashington, Northumberland, 15 July 1921
Died: Nov. 1993
Career: Barrington United; Newcastle United Aug. 1940 (£20); Preston North End Nov. 1950 (£8,000); CITY Dec. 1951; St. Gallen (Switzerland) July 1957 as player-coach. Later manager of Blyth Spartans; trainer of Gateshead in the mid-1960's.

Honour: (City) FL Div.3 (North) champions 1952

Cultured left-back signed to replace the injured Varney. Unable to break into the first team at Preston, but gave the Imps five and a half seasons of splendid service before moving into coaching. On leaving football he worked in the motor trade in the Newcastle area.

GRAHAM, Peter
(1973-1978)
Forward: 142 app. + 16 sub, 47 goals
1975: 5-10, 10-4
Born: Worsborough Common, nr Barnsley, 19 Apr. 1947
Career: Worsborough Bridge; Barnsley Jan. 1967 (Halifax Town on loan, Mar. 1970); Darlington June 1970; CITY Sep. 1973 (£12,500); Cambridge United June 1978 to cs 1980 when he was appointed assistant manager; manager Newmarket Town from Feb. 1989.

Classy striker who was one of City's most skilful and stylish players of the 1970's. Injury kept him out of much of the 1975/76 championship campaign, but he stayed a couple more seasons, occasionally appearing at centre-half. Later remained in the Cambridge area where he was running a grocery store in 1989.

GRAHAM, William
(1893-1894)
Outside-left: 20 app., 2 goals
Career: Burnley c.1891; CITY Apr. 1893 to cs 1894.

Graham was recruited at the very end of the 1892/93 season after spending the previous two campaigns at Burnley. He appeared regularly for City throughout the following season before departing.

GRAINGER, Arthur
(1926)
Outside-left: 1 app.
1926: 5-10, - .
Career: Wath Athletic; CITY Aug. to Sep. 1926

Short stay triallist from Midland League Wath whose solitary FL appearance for the Imps came in the home game with Tranmere in Sep. of 1926.

GRAINGER, John
(1957-1959)
Outside-right: 42 app., 14 goals
1958: 5-11, 11-9
Born: Havercroft, West Yorks, 3 Apr. 1924
Died: 10 Jan. 1983
Career: Frickley Colliery; Rotherham United 1945; CITY June 1957 (£4,000); Burton Albion July 1959; Denaby United July 1961.

Honours: England 'B' international (1 app. vs Scotland 1953)
(Rotherham) FL Div.3 (North) champions 1951

Veteran winger who came to Sincil Bank after 12 seasons at Rotherham where he had made over 350 FL appearances. In his younger days known as a tall and speedy winger who attracted the First Division scouts to Millmoor. Brother of Colin (an England international) and cousin of Jack and Dennis who both played League football. A former miner.

GRATTON, Dennis
(1959-1961)
Centre-half: 45 app.
1960: 5-10, 11-7
Born: Bramley, nr Rotherham, 21 Apr. 1934
Career: Sheffield junior football, Worksop Town cs 1951; Sheffield United Aug. 1952; CITY Sep. 1959 (£5,000); Boston United Aug. to Nov. 1961; Worksop Town cs 1962.

A sound investment from Sheffield United, City showing a remarkable improvement in fortunes after he was signed at the start of the 1959/60 season. A reserve in his seven years at Bramall Lane, where he had only six League outings. Later worked as a miner.

GRAVER, Andrew Martin
(1950-1954, 1955 & 1958-1961)

Centre-forward: 274 app., 143 goals
1955: 5-10, 11-11
Born: Craghead, Co. Durham, 12 Sep. 1927
Career: Willington Athletic; Annfield Plain cs 1947; Newcastle United Aug. 1947; CITY Sep. 1950 (£3,000); Leicester City Dec. 1954 (£27,250 plus Eric Littler); CITY June 1955 (£13,000); Stoke City Nov. 1955 (£12,000); Boston United Sep. 1957 (£1,000); CITY Oct. 1958 (£2,500); Skegness Town July 1961; Ilkeston Town July 1962; retired Nov. 1963. Appointed CITY youth team coach cs 1964 to Oct. 1965 and scout from Oct. 1965..

Honour: (City) FL Div.3 (North) champions 1952

One of Lincoln's all-time 'greats' and the most prolific goalscorer in the history of the club. Andy arrived having played just one first team match for the Magpies, but scored on his debut for City against Halifax and went on to hit 20 League and cup goals in his first season. He was even more successful during the following campaign with 36 from 35 FL outings and it was said that his *"fine opportunism"* was the leading factor in the Imps' promotion. During that season he scored hat-tricks against Darlington and Oldham and six goals in the 11-1 victory over Crewe, which still stands as a club record. Had three spells at Sincil Bank and made his final League appearance for City at Brighton in Apr. 1961. His football career was ended when he suffered a broken ankle playing for Ilkeston reserves. Later worked as a financial consultant in the Lincoln area and was involved in coaching and scouting at Sincil Bank. Son of Fred (who played for Grimsby Town and Leeds in the 1920's) and brother of Alf who also joined the Imps but did not appear in the FL side.

GRAVES, Robert E.
(1959-1965)

Goalkeeper: 79 app.
1962: 6-1, 11-6
Born: Marylebone, London, 7 Nov. 1942
Career: Kirton FC (Lincs.); CITY (amat.) Feb. 1959, (prof.) Apr.

1960; retired May 1965.

Bob made his debut for City as a 17 year old amateur in the home match with Rotherham in Dec. 1959. He was on the club's books for over six years but only saw regular action in the 1961/62 season (35 appearances). Also turned out for Old Aldenhamians in the Arthur Dunn Cup (a competition for public schools old boys' teams). Switched to rugby union for the 1965/66 season, appearing for the Boston club.

GRAY, Alfred
(1934-1936)

Centre-half: 32 apps.
1934: 5-11½, 11-10
Born: Bolton, 30 Aug. 1910
Died: 1974
Career: Daisy Hill; Oldham Athletic May 1930; Torquay United cs 1932; Liverpool May 1933; CITY May 1934; Newark Town cs 1936 to 1939. Appeared for Ransomes & Marles in Dec. 1947.

Alf was a regular in his first season at Sincil Bank but later on his appearances were restricted by injury. No FL outings at Oldham or Liverpool but made 21 Southern Section appearances with Torquay. Younger brother of Matt Gray (Oldham Athletic 1928-1945).

GRAY, Ernest
(1898-1899)

Left-half: 6 app.
Born: c.1875
Career: Mexborough; CITY June 1898; New Brompton cs 1899.

Recruited from Mexborough where he was said to have played under the name 'Jack Roberts'. Gray was deputy to George Morris in his Lincoln season before moving on to Southern League New Brompton.

GRAY, Robert
(1949-1951)

Outside-/inside-right: 2 app.
1950: 5-9, 11-6
Born: Cambuslang, Lanarks., 18 June 1927
Career: Blantyre Victoria; Wishaw cs 1948; CITY Oct. 1949-March 1951; Hamilton Academicals Sep. 1951.

Bobby came to Sincil Bank from Scottish junior football, making both his FL appearances in the 1949/50 season. After his release he returned to live in Cambuslang and eventually signed for Hamilton. Said to be keen and *"... as comfortable on the wings as at inside-forward"*.

GREAVES, George Henry
(1921-1924)

Full-back: 72 app.
1923: 5-8, 10-9

Born: Nottingham, 20 June 1897
Career: Army football; Lincoln Rovers; Chesterfield May 1920; CITY Aug. 1921; Scunthorpe United July 1924; Boston Town cs 1925; Lincoln Claytons cs 1928.

"Consistent and persistent. Has no fireworks to show, but a steady, reliable player" was a 1922 verdict, and a year later, *"not too robust but gives the club every ounce of effort, and had proved his worth repeatedly"*. George was a local lad and in 1933 was working as a lorry driver in Lincoln.

GREAVES, Ian Denzil
(1960-1961)
Right-back: 11 app.
1960: 5-11, 12-10
Born: Oldham, 26 May 1932
Career: Buxton; Manchester United May 1953; CITY Dec. 1960 (£2,500); Oldham Athletic May 1961 (£2,000); Altrincham June 1963 to cs 1964; worked in Zambia as a coach then Huddersfield Town coach, Aug. 1964, manager June 1968; Bolton Wanderers asst. manager Aug. 1974, manager Oct. 1974 to Jan. 1980; Hereford United asst. manager; Oxford United manager Dec. 1980; Wolverhampton Wanderers manager Feb. to Aug. 1982; Mansfield Town manager Jan. 1983 to Feb. 1989. Subsequently at Bury (coach); Manchester United (scout); Emley (manager) and Manchester City (scout).

Honours: (Man Utd) FL champions 1956
FA Cup finalist 1958

Full back signed as cover for broken leg victim Ron Allen during City's last season of Division Two football. Stayed only briefly before moving on to Boundary Park. Ian became a respected manager taking Huddersfield (1970) and Bolton (1978) to Second Division championships and Mansfield to a Wembley victory in the 1987 Freight Rover Trophy.

GREEN, Albert
(1935-1936)
Inside-left: 23 app., 6 goals
1935: 5-10, 11-0

Born: Hanley, Stoke-on-Trent, c.1907
Career: Denaby Rovers; Denaby United; Sheffield Wednesday Apr. 1927; Denaby United in 1928/29; Gainsborough Trinity cs 1930; West Ham United Feb. 1934; CITY June 1935; Newark Town cs 1936; Gainsborough Trinity cs 1938.

Shared the inside-left slot with the young Bernard Towler in his single campaign at Sincil Bank. No FL experience with Wednesday or West Ham, he spent most of his career in Midland League circles. One of several Gainsborough Trinity players signed by the Hammers in the 1930's.

GREEN, Horace
(1949-1955)

Right-back: 212 app., 14 goals
1952: 5-9, 12-0
Born: Barnsley, 23 Apr. 1918
Career: Worsborough Bridge Old Boys; Halifax Town (amat.) Nov. 1936, turning prof. soon afterwards; CITY Feb. 1949 to cs 1955.

Honour: (City) FL Div. 3 (North) champions 1952

Horace was approaching his 31st birthday when signed by the Imps but this stalwart defender still gave the club five years of excellent service. Had a spell as penalty taker which accounts for most of his goals. On leaving football worked on the railways and later in a steelworks.

GREEN, N(orman) Russell
(1951-1955, 1957-1964)
Defender: 125 app., 8 goals
1960: 5-10, 11-13
Born: Donington, Lincs., 13 Aug. 1933
Career: Quadring (Spalding Intermediate League); CITY Aug. 1951; Corby Town July 1955; CITY May 1957; Gainsborough Trinity July 1964 to May 1971 as player-coach.

Russell made his first team debut for City in a Festival of Britain match when he was only 17, but was allowed to leave for Corby without having any FL experience.

City kept his registration however, and offered him terms two seasons later. He went on to make over 100 appearances in six different positions, including several as an occasional centre-forward and not without success - he scored a hat-trick against Newport in Apr. 1962. Later employed as a manufacturing technician by Rustons.

GREGSON, John
(1967-1968)

Outside-right: 31 app. + 5 sub, 3 goals
1966: 5-9, 10-6
Career: Skelmersdale Town; Blackpool May 1957; Chester May 1962; Shrewsbury Town Apr. 1963; Mansfield Town Nov. 1964 (£12,000); CITY June 1967; Cambridge United cs 1968 to 1972.

John began his FL career as understudy to Stanley Matthews at Blackpool but had only three first team outings at Bloomfield Road before moving on. He was an ever-present in the 1967/68 Football League Cup run which saw the Imps go out in a fourth round replay but received a free transfer at the end of the season. Played for Cambridge in their first season of League football. A career aggregate of 228 appearances plus 7 as substitute, and 20 goals.

GREIG, Andrew
(1909-1910)

Centre-forward: 2 app.
1909: 5-10, 12-7
Born: Inverness, c.1887
Career: Inverness Clachnacuddin; CITY Aug. 1909 to Feb. 1910.

Andrew was known for his versatility at Clachnacuddin - appearing in practically every outfield position before switching permanently to centre-forward in 1907. Attracted scouts from Scottish League clubs but chose to come south to Lincoln. His two FL outings came in the first two fixtures of the 1909/10 season after which he appeared only in the Midland League side.

GRESHAM, James
(1891-1893, 1894)

Outside-left: 27 app., 6 goals
Born: Liverpool 1875
Career: Lincoln junior football; Doncaster Rovers cs 1890; CITY Dec. 1891 (£20); Rossendale Oct. 1893; CITY cs Oct. 1894; Gainsborough Trinity cs 1895; Thames Ironworks 1896-1899.

After participating in the Imps' first season of League football, Gresham had a season in the Lancashire League with Rossendale. Broke a collar-bone shortly after re-signing for City and was then released. Subsequently sued the club for loss of earnings - he was said to have earned 30 shillings (£1.50) a week as a footballer but only 18 shillings (90p) working as a higgler. Later played for Thames Ironworks (forerunners of West Ham) in their first Southern League season. Brother of William.

GRESHAM, William
(1892-1893, 1894)

Goalkeeper: 35 app.
Born: Liverpool, 1870
Career: Gainsborough Trinity; CITY cs 1892 to cs 1893; CITY Jan. -cs 1894

William kept goal in all of City's fixtures in their first season of League football, later re-signing for a short spell the following campaign. Older brother of James.

GREYGOOSE, Dean
(1985)

Goalkeeper: 6 app.
1985: 5-11, 11-5
Born: Thetford, Norfolk, 18 Dec. 1964
Career: Cambridge United (appr.), (prof.) Nov. 1982, (Orient on loan, Mar. 1985; CITY on loan Sep. 1985); Orient Dec. 1985; Crystal Palace on loan Aug. 1986, permanent Dec. 1986; Crewe Alexandra on loan Aug. 1987, permanent Dec. 1987; Northwich Victoria Nov. 1993.

Honours: England youth international (5 app., 1982, 1983)

Young 'keeper who came on loan to cover for Stuart Naylor. Settled after a rather nervous debut against Brentford but returned to Cambridge after two months without signing permanently.

GRIFFIN, Ronald Henry George
(1938)

Outside-right: 1 app.
1938: 5-8, 11-3
Born: Camberwell Green, London, 18 Oct. 1919
Died: Feb. 1987
Career: St. Mirren c.1936; CITY July to Sep. 1938; Brentford Oct. 1938; Watford May 1939.

Short term signing whose solitary FL appearance for the Imps came in a 4-2 home defeat by Barnsley at the end of August 1938. Later returned to the London area.

GRIFFITHS, Charles
(1907)

Centre-forward: 1 app.
Career: Luton Town; Barrow; Preston North End cs 1907; CITY Nov. to Dec. 1907

"Not a success" said a newspaper report of Griffiths' only one FL outing for City - at home to Leicester Fosse in Nov. 1907. Apparently missed several easy chances in both this and a subsequent Midland League game before being released.

GRIFFITHS, Thomas
(1922-1923)

Centre-forward: 22 app., 7 goals
1922: 5-7, 11-0
Born: Willington Quay, Northumberland, c.1902
Career: Willington St. Aidans; CITY Aug. 1922; Jarrow Feb. 1923; Ashington June 1923; Jarrow Feb. 1924.

Despite an early departure, Tommy finished joint leading scorer with Harry Pringle in his single Sincil Bank season. With the club in financial trouble he chose to take a free transfer rather than a cut in wages and returned to the north-east.

GROCOTT, Frederick
(1922-1925)
Right-back: 60 app.
1922: 5-7, 10-7
Born: c.1900
Career: Wallsend 1919; Walker Celtic 1921; CITY May 1922 to cs 1925

City recruited more or less a whole team from the north-east of England in the summer of 1922, most of whom returned with free transfers the following Feb. when the club were in serious financial difficulties. Grocott initially announced he would go too, but changed his mind and stayed to give two more years service. A 1924 opinion was *"a steady, consistent right-back who has never yet played a poor or even moderate game for the club. Not spectacular but sound and reliable"*.

GROTIER, Peter D.
(1974-1979)
Goalkeeper: 233 app.
1977: 5-11, 12-2
Born: Stratford, London, 18 Oct. 1950
Career: West Ham United (appr.), (prof.) Mar. 1968, (Cardiff City on loan, Nov. 1973); CITY on loan Aug. 1974, signing permanent-ly Oct. 1974 (£16,666); Cardiff City on loan Dec. 1979, signing permanently Feb. 1980 (£25,000), (Gillingham on loan, Sep. 1981); Grimsby Town Mar. 1982 (£5,000) to Sep. 1986, latterly on coaching staff.

Honour: (City) FL Div.4 champions 1976

The Imps found themselves without an experienced goal-keeper at the start of the 1974/75 season and signed Grotier on loan from West Ham to cover the vacancy. He proved a great success and was signed permanently for a then club record fee - a portion of the money being raised by a public appeal. After making his debut he went on to complete 134 consecutive League appearances and proved a key figure in Graham Taylor's 1975/76 championship side. In the late 1980's was reported to be living in Chelmsford and helping to run a family shoe business.

GROVES, Frederick
(1909-1910)
Inside-/centre-forward: 7 app., 1 goal
1911: 5-9, 11-6
Born: Lincoln, 6 May 1892
Died: 8 Dec. 1980
Career: South Bar (Lincoln League); CITY Aug. 1909; Worksop Town cs 1910; Sheffield United June 1911 (£100); Huddersfield Town Aug. 1912 (£50); Worksop Town 1913; Pontypridd Sep. 1914; Tranmere Rovers 1919; Stoke Nov. 1921 (£1,000); Crystal Palace Aug. 1924; Rhyl Athletic cs 1926; Sutton Town (Notts.) July 1927.

Local discovery who made his League debut for City as a 17 year old in the opening march of the 1909/10 campaign. A lengthy career in the professional game followed, taking in all four FL divisions and good class non-League football.

GROVES, J(ames) Albert
(1903-1904)
Right-back: 29 app., 2 goals
1903: 5-8, 10-7
Born: South Bank, Middlesbrough, July 1883

Career: South Bank FC; CITY June 1903; Sheffield United Apr. 1904; Middlesbrough Aug. 1907; Wingate Albion 1912.

Light-weight full-back known for his thoughtful play. Albert came close to an England cap, playing in an international trial for the North vs South in 1905. Left Sheffield United because they felt someone faster and more robust would be better suited.

GROVES, Paul
(1989)
Midfield: 8 app., 1 goal
1989: 5-11, 11-6
Born: Derby, 28 Feb. 1966
Career: Belper Town; Burton Albion Nov. 1986; Leicester City Apr. 1988 (£12,000); (CITY on loan, Aug. 1989); Blackpool Jan. 1990 (£60,000); Grimsby Town Aug. 1992 (£125,000).

Signed with Grant Brown for an extended loan period as part of the deal which saw Tony James move to Leicester. City did not pursue a permanent signing and he returned to Filbert Street. Has since developed into a strong midfield player and was leading scorer for the Mariners with 12 goals in the 1992/93 season. Won an FA Trophy runners-up medal with Burton Albion in 1987. Previously a bricklayer.

GRUMMETT, James senior
(1943-1952)

Wing-half/inside-forward: 165 app., 12 goals
1949: 5-7, 12-0
Born: Barnsley, 31 July 1921
Career: Barnsley junior football; CITY (amat.) Aug. 1943, (prof.) Sep. 1943; Accrington Stanley Sep. 1952; Boston United July 1953 to cs 1954; Ruston Bucyrus (Lincoln) in 1957/58 season.

Honour: (City) FL Div.3 (North) champions 1948

A miner who also guested for Halifax Town in WW2, Jim scored on his City debut, at Notts County on Christmas Day 1943, and went on to make a total of 51 wartime appearances for the Imps. A dour, gritty performer and stalwart of Lincoln's late 1940's teams, he could take both wing-half positions and also appeared at inside-left. On leaving football was employed in a local engineering works. Father of Jim, junior.

GRUMMETT, James junior
(1962-1971)
Half-back: 246 apps. + 5 sub, 19 goals
1970: 5-10, 12-5
Born: Barnsley, 11 July 1945
Career: Lincoln Schools; Ruston Bucyrus (Lincoln); CITY (amat.) Sep. 1962, (prof.) June 1963; Aldershot July 1971 (£4,000); Chester June 1973 (part exchange for another player); Rochdale Dec. 1973 to Dec. 1974; (Denver Dynamoes, USA, May to Aug. 1974); Boston United Dec. 1974.

Honour: England youth international (3 app. 1963)

Son of Jim senior, above, who served the club as well as his father. Jim junior was a determined defender, club captain for a while and versatile when required. Principally a left-half, he appeared in every outfield position for the club on at least one occasion and took over the goalkeeper's jersey when John Kennedy was injured in an FA Cup replay with Chester in Dec. 1968. An ever-present in the 1966/67 and 1967/68 seasons in a run of 105 consecutive FL appearances. Later settled in the Doncaster area and worked as a sales executive.

GRUNDY, Harry
(1908-1910)
Outside-left: 6 app.
Career: Chirk; Neston; Everton c.1905; Reading 1906; CITY Apr. 1908 to cs 1910.

Winger who appeared in the last three matches of the 1907/08 season and regularly in the 1908/09 Midland League championship side (36 app., 6 goals). Lost his place to Tommy Yule at the start of the following campaign and was restricted to reserve football, often taking the centre-half position.

GUEST, Brendan J.
(1976-1980)
Full-back: 99 app. + 5 sub, 2 goals
1978: 5-10½, 10-9
Born: Nottingham, 19 Dec. 1958
Career: CITY (appr.) July 1975, (prof.) Dec. 1976; Swindon Town July 1980; Bath City 1980; Forest Green Rovers Feb. 1981.

Honour: England youth international (1977)

Talented youngster who won England youth honours and made his first team debut as a 17 year old. Released by Colin Murphy after four seasons at Sincil Bank, he had a brief trial at Swindon before a move into non-League football, where he went on to win an FA Vase winners medal with Forest Green in 1982. Later joined the Lincolnshire Police Force and has turned out in Sunday League football in recent years.

GUNSON, F.
(1895-1899)
Half-back: 1 app.
Career: Casuals (Lincoln); CITY Oct. 1895; Adelaide (Lincoln) cs 1899.

Recruit from local junior football who was a stalwart of the City Swifts (reserve) side in his four seasons at the club. The solitary FL appearance came at the end of Jan. 1897 - an 8-0 defeat at the hands of Notts County.

HAILS, William
(1953-1955)
Inside-forward: 9 app.
1960: 5-8, 10-9
Born: Nettlesworth, Co. Durham, 19 Feb. 1935
Career: Kimblesworth Juniors; CITY Mar. 1953; Peterborough United July 1955; Northampton Town Nov. 1962 (£4,000); Luton Town June 1964; Nuneaton Borough July 1965 as a player and asst. manager, later becoming player-manager; Rugby Town cs 1967 player-manager; Peterborough United coach Aug. 1968, appointed manager Nov. 1978 to Feb. 1979; Watford coach 1979 to 1987.

Honours: (Peterborough) FL Div.4 champions 1961
(Northampton) FL Div.3 champions 1963

Initially signed on amateur forms as a 15 year old, becoming a part-time professional at 18. Spent most of his time playing in the reserves but refused to accept the terms offered in July 1955 and moved on. At Peterborough he was a member of the team which won five consecutive Midland League titles followed by the Fourth Division on entry into the League. Billy was later involved in coaching for many years. Had been an electrician in his earlier days. Father of Julian (Fulham).

HAINES, Keith H.
(1960-1963)
Defender 13 app.
1960: 6-3, 13-0
Born: Wigston, Leicester, 19 Dec. 1937
Career: Matlock Town, Leeds United May 1959; CITY July 1960; Hinckley Athletic July 1963; Rugby Town; Lockheed Leamington Aug. 1965; Burton Albion Dec. 1966; Rugby Town in 1967/68; Atherstone United cs 1968.

Honour: England youth international (1956)

Keith signed on a free transfer from Leeds where he had appeared in the Central League team. He was unable to win a regular first team place at Sincil Bank and moved on to the non-League scene after three seasons.

HALE, Alfred ("Pally")
(1925-1930)
Centre-/left-half: 156 app., 4 goals
1926: 5-9, 11-2
Born: Kiveton Park, Sheffield, 24 Jan. 1906

Died: Dec. 1972
Career: Kiveton Park CW; Wales United; Kiveton Park CW; CITY Apr. 1925; Luton Town July 1930; Llanelly 1933; Halifax Town cs 1934; Dinnington Athletic cs 1936.

"A good defensive player, whole hearted in his methods ... his proficiency with his head made him very useful in the pivotal position" was a contemporary view of this reliable half-back. Added a further 48 FL appearances with Luton and Halifax to take his career aggregate over 200.

HALL, B(erthold) Allan C(ouldwell)
(1931-1933)

Centre-forward: 72 app., 65 goals
1931: 5-10½, 12-0
Born: Deepcar, Sheffield, 29 Mar. 1908
Died: 9 Feb. 1983
Career: Victoria Hall Juniors (Sheffield); Park Labour Club (Sheffield) 1924; Doncaster Rovers cs 1926; Middlesbrough Mar 1928; Bradford City June 1930; CITY May 1931; Tottenham Hotspur June 1933 (£3,000); Blackpool Mar. 1934; Gainsborough Trinity July 1935 to WW2.

Honour: (City) FL Div. 3 (North) champions 1932

Allan Hall was a prolific goalscorer at all levels who created club history with a record seasonal total of 42 League goals in the 1931/32 championship campaign. Later sold to Tottenham for a club record fee but was considered a little too slow for the top class game. Particularly successful in the Midland League - 50 goals for Bradford City reserves in the 1930/31 season and a further 160 (207 in all games) in four seasons at Gainsborough. He joined the Northolme club after Blackpool put him on their retained list at a prohibitive fee. A 1932 comment was *"... distributes the ball with discretion ... quite unselfish ... possesses that coolness at the critical moment, which enables him to place the ball past a goalkeeper, rather than endeavour to break the net with a pile-driver"*. Returned to guest for City during WW2. Died at Saxilby, Lincs.

HALL, Edward
(1897-1898)
Outside-right: 18 app., 3 goals
Career: Beeston Humber (Nottingham); CITY Sep. 1897; Loughborough Town Mar. 1898; Wellingborough cs 1898.

Hall was City's regular wingman for most of the 1897/98 season but lost his place to Fletcher towards the end of the campaign and quickly moved on to Loughborough, who were then also members of the Second Division.

HALL, Harry
(1921-1922)
Outside-right: 16 app.
1921: 5-8½, 10-10
Born: c.1900
Career: Pinxton (Derbys Senior League); CITY Apr. 1921 to cs 1922; appeared for Darlington in season 1923/24.

Appeared as an amateur in the final three matches of the 1920/21 Midland League season, signing professional shortly afterwards. Described (1921) as *"... a well known sprinter, clever dribbler and centres accurately"*.

HALL, John
(1923-1924)
Inside-right: 1 app.
1924: 5-9, 11-6
Born: Bolton, c.1905
Career: Bolton junior football; CITY Aug. 1923; Accrington Stanley July 1924; Manchester United May 1925 to cs 1927.

His solitary FL appearance for the Imps came on the opening day of the 1923/24 season in the home match with Halifax Town. A reserve at his other clubs too, making five Northern Section appearances for Accrington and three in the First Division at Old Trafford where he deputised for the England international Joe Spence.

HALLAM, Henry
(1913-1914)
Right-back: 2 app.
1913: 5-7, 12-6
Born: Sleaford, Lincs.
Career: Peterborough GN Loco; CITY May 1913 to early 1914; Gainsborough Trinity cs 1914.

A recruit from the Central Alliance, Hallam's experience of League football was limited to two outings at the end of Sep. 1913, deputising for the suspended Clem Jackson. At Peterborough Loco he was said to have developed *"a reputation for watchfulness and powerful kicking"*.

HALLIDAY, John Hastings
(1931)
Centre-forward/inside-left: 9 app., 7 goals
1931: 5-8½, 11-0
Born: Dumfries, 20 Feb. 1908

Career: Queen of the South; Boston Town Aug. 1929; CITY Jan. 1931; Doncaster Rovers Dec. 1931; Boston Town Aug. 1932; Stockport County Aug. 1933; Hurst Oct. 1933; Burton Town cs 1934.

Youngster who had an excellent scoring record for both first and reserve teams at Sincil Bank. Halliday hit four hat-tricks for the Midland League side in the second half of the 1930/31 season and scored twice on his first team debut but was still not considered to be good enough for a regular place. A contemporary critic noted that he was *"a clever footballer"* but *"... too lightly built for heavy grounds, and his only scoring foot was his left"*. A younger brother of David Halliday (a well-known centre-forward with Dundee and Sunderland).

HAMILTON, William
(1926-1928)
Outside-left: 15 app., 3 goals
1926: 5-10, 12-0
Born: Belfast, c.1906
Career: Dundela FC; CITY May 1926; Notts County Aug. 1928; Gainsborough Trinity Nov. 1928.

Signed after a successful season in Irish Intermediate League football which had seen him score 33 goals from the left wing and win junior international caps against Scotland and Wales. At Lincoln his first team appearances were said to alternate between brilliant and moderate and he lost his place to the more consistent Frank Pegg. No FL outings in his brief spell at Meadow Lane.

HAMMOND, George
(1902-1903)
Centre-forward: 1 app.
Career: Barrow; CITY May 1902 to cs 1903.

Hammond had his single FL appearance for the Imps in Nov. 1902 when he deputised for Peter Proudfoot in the home match with Blackpool. Otherwise he was restricted to Midland League outings during his time at Sincil Bank.

HAMMOND, John
(1934-1935)
Goalkeeper: 1 app.
Born: Birtley, Co. Durham
Career: RAF football; CITY (amat.) Feb. 1934, (prof.) Aug. 1934 to cs 1935.

John played in a pre-season trial in the summer of 1933 but did not sign forms until Feb. of the following year when he became a regular in the reserve team. He made his first team debut as deputy for Dan McPhail against Walsall in a Northern Section Cup match in Feb. 1935, making his solitary FL appearance at Rotherham the following Saturday (a 5-0 defeat). Prior to signing full terms he had spent six years in the RAF, most recently stationed at Cranwell.

HANCOCK, Edmund
(1938-1939)

Outside-/inside-right: 30 aps., 4 goals
1938: 5-7, 11-7
Born: Rotherham, 29 Mar. 1907
Career: Denaby United; Gainsborough Trinity; Liverpool Jan. 1931; Burnley Feb. 1933; Luton Town Nov. 1936; CITY July 1938; Frickley Colliery cs 1939.

Honour: (Luton) FL Div.3 (South) champions 1937

Stocky former miner who appeared mostly on the wing for City. A forceful player with excellent shooting and ball control skills. Ted actually signed for Northwich Victoria in June 1938 but the Cheshire League club released him when City came along.

HANNAH, Gardiner
(1896-1898)

Right-half: 56 app.
1895: 5-6½, 11-9
Born: Baillieston, Lanarks, 4 Feb. 1871
Career: Baillieston Thistle; Airdrieonians Mar. 1894; Blackburn Rovers Mar. 1895; CITY May 1896 to cs 1898.

Former Scottish junior international recruited from Ewood Park where although mainly a reserve it was said he was a *"fearless tackler, stubborn worker, possessed a safe kick and if given the chance would trouble goal-keepers"*. City regarded him as a fine capture and he was considered to be *"among the best halves seen in Lincoln"*.

HANNAH, George
(1957-1958)

Inside-right: 38 app., 4 goals
1957: 5-8, 9-12
Born: Liverpool, 11 Dec. 1928
Died: 5 May 1990
Career: Everton (amat.); Linfield; Newcastle United Sep. 1949 (£23,000 including another player); CITY Sep. 1957 (£4,500); Manchester City Sep. 1958 (£10,000 and John McClelland); Notts County July 1964 (£2,000); Bradford City Oct. 1965 (about £1,000); retired May 1966.

Honours: Irish League (1 app. vs Scottish League, Sep. 1949) (Newcastle) FA Cup winner 1955

George is considered by many to have been one of the most skilful players to appear for the Imps in the post-WW2 period. He arrived with a sound background in top class football, staying almost exactly 12 months before returning to the First Division with Manchester City. His career aggregate was 374 FL games plus 1 as substitute over 17 seasons during which he was honoured by being selected for several FA tours including West Africa (1957), the Far East (1961) and New Zealand (1964). On leaving football he ran a news-agents shop in Manchester and later worked for British Telecom.

HARBERTSON, Ronald
(1958-1960, 1961-1962)

Centre/inside-forward: 86 app., 25 goals
1960: 5-10, 11-11
Born: Redcar, 23 Dec. 1929
Career: North Shields; Newcastle United Jan. 1949 (£750); Bradford City July 1950; Brighton & Hove Albion Oct. 1951; Bradford City Mar. 1952; Grimsby Town July 1954 (in exchange for another player); Ashington cs 1955; Darlington Jan. 1957; CITY Mar. 1958 (£2,500); Wrexham Mar. 1960 (£7,000); Darlington Jan. 1961 (£1,000); CITY July 1961; Grantham July 1962 to cs 1968.

Honours: (Wrexham) Welsh Cup winner 1960

A much travelled centre-forward who had two spells at Sincil Bank. He had an eventful baptism with City, the story being that manager Bill Anderson was forced to scale an outer wall and break into the Darlington ground at midnight on the night before Ron's debut for the Imps at Anfield in order to retrieve his boots! Lincoln appeared doomed to relegation at the time but won their final six games to escape the drop with Harbertson scoring nine goals in the last 11 games. The Imps were not so fortunate when they signed him a second time and the season ended with the club relegated to the Fourth Division for the first time. Later worked for many years as a prison officer before becoming a caretaker for sheltered housing.

HARDIE, George
(1898-1899)

Goalkeeper: 12 app.
1898: 5-10, 12-0
Born: Stanley, nr Shardlow, Derbys., 1873
Career: West Hallam aged 15; Denaby Wanderers c.1893; Conisborough (South Yorkshire League); Mexborough; Grimsby Town February 1897 (£50); Mexborough cs 1897; CITY June 1898 -Feb. 1899.

Originally a centre-forward, switching to goalkeeper during his Denaby Wanderers' days. At Mexborough earned the reputation as *"one of the cleverest goal-tenders in the Midland League"*. George was City's first choice 'keeper until replaced by new signing James Bissett at the end of Dec. 1898 and departed soon afterwards. A more than useful club cricketer who was employed as a professional by Conisborough Town CC.

HARDING, Alan
(1973-1979)

Midfield: 203 app. + 6 sub, 38 goals
1976: 5-9, 11-0
Born: Sunderland, 14 May 1948
Career: Spennymoor United; Darlington Jan. 1970; CITY Mar. 1973 (£7,000 plus Frank McMahon); Hartlepool United Mar. 1979 (£4,000) to 1983. Scout for Reading in the late 1980's.

Honour: (City) FL Div.4 champions 1976

Skilful left-sided midfield player who was one of Graham Taylor's early signings and proved to be an excellent buy. Harding gave City seven years of fine, consistent service and performed a vital role in the 1975/76 championship side. Moved on after the Imps were relegated from Division Three in 1979.

HARDY, John Henry
(1939-1949)

Wing-half: 19 app.
1939: 5-8, 11-10
Born: Chesterfield, 15 June 1910
Died: 1978
Career: Chesterfield League football; Unstone FC (Sheffield); Chesterfield late 1934; Hull City July 1937; CITY May 1939, appointed player-coach of the 'A' team cs 1947 to cs 1949; appeared for Skellingthorpe (Lincoln League) in 1950/51 season.

Honour: (Chesterfield) FL Div. 3 (North) champions 1936

A career very much affected by the war for Jack appeared once for City in Sep. 1939 and a further 18 times during the 1946/47 campaign. He had been a regular performer for the Imps in wartime football, totalling a further 200 appearances. Later involved in coaching the club's youngsters when his first team days were over. Nephew of Sam Hardy the England international goalkeeper.

HARFORD, Michael Gordon
(1977-1980)

Centre-forward: 109 app. + 6 sub, 40 goals
1979: 6-1, 12-4
Born: Sunderland, 12 Feb. 1959
Career: Lambton Street Boys Club (Sunderland); CITY July 1977; Newcastle United Dec. 1980 (£180,000); Bristol City Aug. 1981 (£160,000); Birmingham City Mar.1982 (£100,000); Luton Town Dec. 1984 (£250,000); Derby County Jan. 1990 (£450,000); Luton Town Sep. 1991 (£325,000), Chelsea Aug. 1992 (£300,000); Sunderland Mar. 1993 (£250,000); Coventry City July 1993 (£200,000); Wimbledon Aug. 1994 (£50,000).

Honours: England international (2 app, vs Israel 1988, Denmark 1989)
England 'B' international (1 app, vs Malta 1987)
(Luton) FL Cup winner 1988; finalist 1989

Mick was signed as an 18 year old midfield player from Sunderland junior football but was quickly converted to the striker's role. Made his Fourth Division debut within five months of becoming a professional and never looked back. Strong in the air and skilful on the ground it was almost inevitable that he would go on to a bigger club and after hitting three hat-tricks during 1980 he moved on to St. James' Park for a then club record fee. He was later the subject of several large transfer fees and became one of the very few Sincil Bank products to go on to win England international honours.

HARFORD, Raymond Thomas
(1967-1971)

Centre-half: 191 app., 9 goals
1970: 6-1, 12-12
Born: Halifax, 1 June 1945
Career: South London schools; Charlton Athletic (amat.) May 1961, (prof.) May 1964; Exeter City Jan. 1966 (£750); CITY July 1967; Mansfield Town June 1971 (£6,000); Port Vale Jan. 1972; Colchester United on loan Jan. 1973, permanent Feb. 1973; Romford July 1975; Colchester United coach Sep. 1975; Fulham coach July 1981, caretaker Apr. 1984, manager May 1984; Luton Town coach July 1986, manager June 1987 - Jan. 1990; Wimbledon asst. manager Mar. 1990, caretaker June 1990, manager Dec. 1990; Blackburn Rovers asst. manager Oct. 1991.

A tall and dependable centre-half, one of several signings made by Ron Gray in the summer of 1967 as he successfully sought to reverse the dismal performances of the early 1960's. Ray was an ever-present in his first season and a regular thereafter apart from injuries and suspensions. His senior career was ended by two cartilage operations in his time at Colchester. Has since become a respected coach and manager, currently working as asst. to Kenny Dalglish at Ewood Park.

HARRISON, Francis N.
(1985-1986)

Midfield: 0 app. + 1 sub
1988: 6-1, 12-6
Born: Eston, Middlesbrough, 19 Sep. 1963
Career: Guisborough Town; Middlesbrough Sep. 1982; CITY (non-contract) Aug. 1985; Guiseley; Halifax Town Aug. 1986, appointed youth team coach in late 1989.

Frank was a student at Carnegie College, Leeds whilst on City's books, his sole FL outing coming in Nov. 1985 when he came on as substitute for Andy Toman at Wigan. At Halifax, where he appeared as a left-back, he made a total of 48 appearances plus 6 as substitute, recovering from a lengthy spell out injured following a broken leg in Nov. 1987.

HARRISON, John G.
(1968-1969)

Outside-right: 4 app.
Born: Worksop, Notts., 18 May 1946
Career: Worksop Town; Sheffield United Jan. 1967; CITY July 1968; retired Sep. 1969.

Winger who came on a free transfer from Bramall Lane in the summer of 1968. A promising career was only just starting when he suffered a dislocated knee joint in a reserve match against Halifax in Apr. 1969. He never played again and received a benefit match in Apr. 1970.

HART, Harry
(1894-1895)

Right-half: 1 app.
Career: St. Andrews (Lincoln); CITY cs 1894 to cs 1895.

A product of local junior football who appeared regularly for the City Swifts (reserve) team in his season with the club. His sole FL outing came in a home match with Burton Wanderers on 30 Mar. 1895.

HART, John Thomas
(1894-1895)
Goalkeeper: 1 app.
Career: St. Andrews (Lincoln); CITY cs 1894 to cs 1895.

Hart got his first team chance in Sep. 1894 after Broadbent broke a shoulder bone. He was not a success - City lost 5-2 at home to Rotherham and a newspaper report noted of him *"he was out of his class altogether, seemed nervous and lacked judgement"*. Afterwards appeared only occasionally with the Swifts side.

HARTLEY, James
(1897, 1899-1903)
Inside-/centre-forward: 138 app., 52 goals
1987: 5-6, 11-4
Born: Dumbarton, 29 Oct. 1876
Career: Dumbarton 1894; Sunderland Oct. 1895; Burnley Nov. 1896 (CITY on loan, Mar. 1897); Tottenham Hotspur May 1897; CITY May 1899; Rangers cs 1903; Port Glasgow Athletic c.1904; Brentford cs 1905; New Brompton cs 1906 to 1908.

Jimmy was one of City's best and most consistent forwards of the pre-WW1 era and the first to aggregate a total of 50 League goals for the club. He could take any of the forward positions apart from outside-left, having been converted from a defensive role by Dumbarton. Brother of Araham ("Daisy") Hartley, centre-forward in Everton's 1897 FA Cup final line-up.

HARTSHORNE, John
(1936-1946)
Right-back: 93 app.
1939: 6-0, 13-6
Born: Willenhall, Staffs., 25 Mar. 1907
Died: 1971
Career: Short Heath (Wolverhampton); Stoke City May 1932; Macclesfield 1934; CITY Aug. 1936; Grantham cs 1946; Boston United cs 1948.

A late League debutant (for City when aged 29) yet a first-rate signing. Tall and weighty, Jack was a popular player at Sincil Bank, summed up as *"strong kicking and tackling, likes nothing better than ploughing through, with a strong shot at goal"*. He returned after the war (having served in the RAF), to make one further appearance for the Imps in Nov. 1945 during which he was injured and he later departed for Midland League football.

HAVELOCK, P(eter) Henry W.
(1925-1926)
Centre-forward: 27 app., 17 goals
1925: 5-10, 12-7
Born: Hull, 20 Jan. 1901

Died: 31 May 1973
Career: Army football (16th Hussars); Hull City Oct. 1923; CITY June 1925; Portsmouth Mar. 1926; Crystal Palace Nov. 1927; Hull City May 1931; Folkestone June 1932.

A bustling centre-forward whose weight and build made him very difficult to knock off the ball and who was also a deadly finisher with his head. Harry scored regularly throughout his career (114 FL appearances, 68 goals). His brother John played for Bristol Rovers, whilst his father was an England rugby union international. Latterly lived for many years in the Yorkshire coastal town of Hornsea.

HAWKINGS, Barry
(1956-1957)
Centre-forward: 15 app., 6 goals
1957: 5-9, 11-0
Born: Birmingham, 7 Nov. 1931
Career: Coventry City groundstaff Jan. 1949, farmed out to Rugby Town (Birmingham Combination) early 1953, recalled cs 1953; CITY Mar. 1956; Northampton Town June 1957; Gravesend & Northfleet June 1959.

Signed from Coventry after the transfer deadline and City needed permission from the FL to play him on the two occasions he appeared at the end of the 1955/56 season. Scored twice on his debut against Stoke (a 2-1 win) but never won a regular place and departed in the summer of 1957.

HAWKSBY, John F.
(1964-1966)
Inside-/outside-left: 64 app. + 1 sub, 4 goals
1966: 5-9, 10-11
Born: York, 12 June 1942
Career: York schools; Leeds United (amat.) July 1957, (prof.) June 1959; CITY Aug. 1964; York City Mar. 1966 (£4,000); Kings Lynn July 1968 to cs 1970; Cambridge City cs 1970; Kettering Town Aug. 1972; Dunstable July 1974 (£4,000); Stevenage Athletic; Rushden Town; Desborough Town.

Honour: England youth international 1959

Hawksby was recruited for a "substantial" fee from Elland Road where he had made his FL debut at 18 deputising for Don Revie. A regular in his first campaign at Sincil Bank, but in and out of the side after that. Very much a 'supplier' rather than a goalscorer as the following comment shows: *"... has a reputation for fetching and carrying for his co-forwards"*.

HAWKSWORTH, Derek M.
(1960-1961)
Centre-forward/outside-left: 36 app., 14 goals
1960: 5-11, 12-0
Born: Bradford, 16 July 1927
Career: Bradford (amat.); RAF football; Huddersfield Town (amat.) c.1948; Bradford City Oct. 1948; Sheffield United Dec. 1950 (£12,500); Huddersfield Town May 1958 (part exchange for another player); CITY Feb. 1960 (£3,000); Bradford City Jan. 1961 (£3,000); Nelson July 1962.

Honours: England 'B' international (1 app. vs France 1952 (Sheffield United) FL Div.2 champions 1953

Derek's Sincil Bank career began successfully - he netted on his debut against Hull and scored 10 goals from 13 outings at the end of the 1959/60 season. The following campaign he switched to the wing position and there was a consequent reduction in his goal tally. A cousin of Malcolm Devitt (Bradford City, 1958-1963). Later ran a newsagents shop.

HAYCOCK, Frederick
(1910-1911)

Inside-forward: 25 app., 5 goals
1909: 5-7; 11-4
Born: Smethwick, 1886
Died: 1955
Career: Smethwick Victoria; Coombes Wood; West Bromwich Albion June 1904; Crewe Alexandra July 1907; Luton Town cs 1908; Portsmouth cs 1909; CITY Oct. 1910; Burslem Port Vale cs 1911; Dudley Town 1913; Shrewsbury Town 1915.

Alert, energetic and experienced forward who was signed from Southern League Portsmouth. At the end of his season at Sincil Bank the Imps were voted out of the League and Haycock moved on to Port Vale who were to become City's main rivals for the Central League championship in the 1911/12 campaign.

HEATH, R(ichard), Terence
(1973-1975)

Midfield: 17 app., 1 goal
1973: 5-8, 11-0
Born: Leicester, 17 Nov. 1943
Career: Leicester City (prof.) Nov. 1961; Hull City May 1964 (£8,000); Scunthorpe United Mar. 1968 (£5,000); CITY on loan Feb. 1973, signing permanently May 1973 (£2,000); retired through injury July 1974.

Honour: (Leicester City) FL Cup winner 1964

Cultured midfield player whose time at Lincoln was badly affected by the knee injury which was to force his retirement. His best years were at Scunthopre (177 FL outings, 50 goals). On leaving the game Terry worked as a stores foreman and in a steelworks before running a Newquay guest house.

HEATH, Seamus, M.J.P.
(1982)

Defender: 6 app. + 1 sub
1982: 5-9, 10-5
Born: Belfast, 6 Dec. 1961
Career: Luton Town Apr. 1979; (CITY on loan, Aug.- Oct. 1982); Wrexham Aug. 1983; Tranmere Rovers Aug. 1984; Northwich Victoria Sep. 1987; Oswestry Town; Ekenas IF (Finland) Apr. 1986; Rhyl Sep. 1987; Caernarfon Town Oct. 1988; BK-46 (Finland) 1989; Glentoran Sep. 1990; Distillery July 1992, becoming player/coach.

Honours: Northern Ireland schoolboy and youth international

Defender initially signed on a month's loan as cover for Phil Neale at the end of the cricket season. Seamus made no FL appearances with Luton but totalled a further 38 plus 11 as sub. at Wrexham and Tranmere. After a lengthy career divided between the Northern Premier League and Finland, he returned to Northern Ireland. Currently runs a shop in Belfast and coaches on a part-time basis with the Irish F.A.

HEATH, William
(1893-1896)

Full-back: 10 app.
Career: Lindum (Lincoln); CITY Sep. 1893 to cs 1896.

Youngster who was barely out of his teens when he first appeared in City's FL side - winning praise for his *"fearless and dashing game"*. Heath was a former Lincoln Grammar School boy and secretary of the Lindum club for a while. He broke a collar-bone in Feb. 1896 and did not make the first team again.

HEATH, William H.M.
(1958-1962)

Goalkeeper: 84 app.
1960: 6-0, 13-2
Born: Bournemouth, 15 Apr. 1954
Career: Bournemouth & Boscombe Athletic groundstaff, (prof.) Dec. 1951; CITY Nov. 1958; Cambridge City July 1962; appeared for Newmarket Town in the late 1960's.

Burly goalkeeper signed after a seven year spell at Bournemouth where he was understudy to the Eire international Tommy Godwin, being restricted to a total of 34 FL outings. Bill was first choice for much of his time at Sincil Bank but lost his place to Bob Graves in the 1961/62 campaign and departed at the end of that season. Later employed running a schools sportswear agency in East Anglia.

HEATHCOTE, James
(1924-1925)

Inside-left: 33 app., 13 goals
1924: 5-10, 12-0
Born: Bolton, 17 Jan. 1894
Career: Bolton junior football to Blackpool c.1917; Notts County June 1922 (£1,500); Pontypridd cs 1923; CITY June 1924; Mansfield Town May 1925; Coventry City July 1926; Accrington Stanley Jan. -Mar. 1929.

A clever inside man with a good goalscoring record - his FL aggregate was 84 goals from 204 appearances. Jimmy moved on to Mansfield after his season at Sincil Bank, helping the Stags to finish Midland League runners-up in 1925/26 with 30 goals from 35 games.

HELLINGS, Dennis ("Dan")
(1945-1949)
Centre-/inside-forward: 3 app.
Born: Lincoln, 9 Dec. 1923
Career: Lincoln Rovers; Ransomes & Marles cs 1945; CITY Oct. 1945 (amat.), Dec. 1945 (prof.); Grantham Aug. 1949; Skegness Town cs 1952; Alford United cs 1955.

Local-born player recruited from Midland League football in the 1945/46 season. Dan was mainly used as a reserve by City, his three FL outings all coming in the 1946/47 campaign.

HELLIWELL, David
(1969-1970)
Inside-forward: 11 app. + 2 sub, 1 goal
1970: 5-8, 9-12
Born: Blackburn, 28 Mar. 1948
Career: Blackburn Rovers (amat.), (prof.) May 1966; CITY May 1969 (£4,000); Workington July 1970; Rochdale July 1976 to 1977.

Slightly built inside-forward who was unable to establish himself as a first team regular under Ron Gray at Sincil Bank. Moved on a free transfer to Workington where he had greater sucess, totalling 184 outings plus 13 as substitute and scoring 20 goals.

HEMPSALL, Ernest
(1924-1927)
Right-half: 1 app.
1924: 5-9, 11-0
Born: Lincoln 1901
Career: Lincoln Claytons; CITY on trial Feb. 1924, permanently cs 1924; Lincoln Claytons cs 1927.

A local lad who was a stalwart of the reserve side, as a 1926 commentator noted, "... done yeoman service with the Midland League side. Consistent and a sound defender; good man in emergency in goal; cool-headed and strong in clearance". Made his solitary FL appearance in the home game with Halifax Town on 19 Dec. 1925.

HENDERSON, John Kenneth
(1898-1900)
Inside-right/outside-left: 76 app., 9 goals
Born: Dumfries, 1871
Died: Aug. 1930
Career: 5th Kirkcudbrightshire Rifle Volunteers (Maxwelltown); Celtic Jan. 1896; CITY May 1898; Leicester Fosse Dec. 1900 (£100); Small Heath Mar. 1901; Leicester Ivanhoe 1902.

Honour: (Celtic) Scottish League champions 1898

Skilful forward said to be "exceptionally speedy and tricky". Henderson was a regular throughout his time at Sincil Bank but made only 17 further FL appearances. Later returned to Scotland and was reported to be running a newsagents shop in Dumfries in 1923.

HETHERINGTON, James ("Jos")
(1925-1926)
Inside-right: 3 app., 1 goal
1925: 5-9, 11-9
Born: Monkwearmouth, Sunderland, 11 Apr. 1892
Died: 6 Apr. 1971
Career: Sunderland Royal Rovers; Southwick FC (Sunderland); South Shields May 1920; Preston North End June 1924; CITY Nov. 1925 -Jan. 1926; Durham City; Norwich City Aug. 1927; Guildford City Sep. 1929.

Triallist forward whose career was badly affected by a broken leg suffered in his fifth outing with Preston. After his release from Sincil Bank he made just one further FL appearance (at Norwich).

HEWARD, Brian
(1961-1964, 1964-1967)
Centre-half: 97 app., 2 goals
1963: 5-9, 11-0
Born: Lincoln, 17 July 1935
Career: Scunthorpe United (amat.) 1953, (prof.) Mar. 1954; CITY July 1961; Bankstown (Australia) June 1964; CITY Nov. 1964; retired cs 1967.

Solid and reliable centre-half who had totalled 135 FL outings with Scunthorpe. Brian played no first team football for the Imps after Apr. 1966 although he remained on the club books for a further season before retiring. Remained in the Lincoln area and now runs an insurance brokers business. Was chairman of the Red Imps Association for a while.

HEWITT, Ronald
(1946-1949)
Goalkeeper: 3 app.
1948: 6-0, - .
Born: Chesterfield, 25 Jan. 1924
Career: Youlgreave FC (Derbyshire); Sheffield United Oct. 1944; CITY Aug. 1946; Worksop Town Aug. 1949; Grantham cs 1952; Spalding United 1957.

Reserve goalkeeper whose three FL outings came as deputy for George Moulson in the 1948/49 season. Ron had spent much of the previous campaign on the injury list with a broken wrist. A part-time professional who worked as a miner in the Chesterfield area.

HEWS, Harold Burston
(1909-1911)
Goalkeeper, 2 app.
1909: 6-1½, - .
Born: Honiton, Devon, 1888
Died: 7 Jan. 1922
Career: Sleaford Town (Lincs); CITY Oct. 1909 to cs 1911.

Hews had two first team outings in March 1910 when he deputised for Tommy Fern, otherwise he was restricted to Midland League appearances where he also took the left-back position. A competent cricketer with Sleaford CC, appearing once for Lincolnshire in the Minor Counties competition in 1914. His early death was due to bronchial pneumonia.

HIBBERD, Stuart
(1979-1983)

Midfield: 36 app. + 6 sub, 3 goals
1982: 6-0, 11-13½
Born: Sheffield, 11 Oct. 1961
Career: Sheffield Rangers; CITY (appr.) July 1978, (prof.) Oct. 1979; Boston United June 1983 to 1984; Alfreton Town; Gainsborough Trinity Nov. 1987.

A tall midfield player, Hibberd was one of a number of youngsters who emerged from City's Sheffield nursery side of the late 1970's and went on to represent the club in the Football League. Stuart played his best football in the 1981/82 season when he won a regular place in the second half of the campaign at the end of which the Imps almost got back into Division Two.

HIBBERT, Henry Crookes
(1909-1910)

Left-half: 4 app., 1 goal
1909: 5-11, 12-0
Born: c.1887
Career: Hathersage; Sheffield Wednesday cs 1907; Stockport County 1908; CITY July 1909 to cs 1910; Rotherham County cs 1911; Sheffield United Apr. 1913; Chesterfield Town in 1916/17 season.

Made all his FL appearances in the early part of his Sincil Bank season, afterwards being appointed captain of the Midland League side. Despite the number of clubs he made a total of only seven League appearances in all.

HIGGINS, Thomas
(1903)

Centre-forward: 6 app.
1903: 5-6, 11-2
Career: Darlington St. Augustines; CITY May to Nov. 1903.

A recruit from the Northern League, Higgins began the season as first choice but soon lost his place and was given an early release due to bad conduct.

HILL, Amos
(1935-1936)

Outside-left: 14 app., 5 goals
1936: 5-8½, 10-7
Born: Wath-on-Dearne, Yorks, 21 June 1910
Died: 1973
Career: Mexborough; Wath National OB; Hawson Street (Wombwell); CITY Aug. 1935; Mansfield Town Oct. 1936 to 1937.

Nearly all of Hill's League outings came during a run of consecutive matches in the 1935/36 season when he formed a goal-productive partnership with Bernard Towler on City's left-wing. Lost his place through injury and later moved on to Mansfield where he linked up again with former Imps' manager Harry Parkes.

HILL, David
(1993-)

Midfield: 27 app. + 5 sub, 3 goals
1993: 5-9, 10-3
Born: Nottingham, 6 June 1966
Career: Notts County schoolboy; Arnold Town; Scunthorpe United Feb. 1985; Ipswich Town July 1988 (£80,000); Scunthorpe United on loan, Mar. 1991, permanent Sep. 1991 (£30,000); CITY July 1993 (£17,500 plus Matt Carmichael).

Experienced right-sided or central midfield player who possesses a powerful long-range shot. Has aggregated a total of 250 plus Football League appearances to date.

HILL, Kenneth G.
(1974)

Centre-half: 1 app.
1975: 6-0, 11-3
Born: Canterbury, Kent, 7 Mar. 1953
Career: Gillingham (appr.), (prof.) Mar. 1971 to Dec. 1976; (Baltimore Comets, USA, May to Aug. 1974; CITY on loan, Dec. 1974); Washington Diplomats, USA, Apr. to Aug. 1977; Maidstone United cs 1978; Folkestone Town July 1983.

Tall central defender who deputised for Sam Ellis in the home match with Reading in Dec. 1974 and also made one FA Cup appearance before returning to Kent. Later appeared for the England semi-professional team whilst on Maidstone's books.

HILL, Leonard George
(1927-1929)

Goalkeeper: 69 app.
1927: 5-11, 13-0
Born: Islington, London, 15 Feb. 1899
Died: 1979
Career: Cranley Rovers (Leigh-on-Sea); Southend United cs 1919; Queens Park Rangers Aug. 1920; Southampton June 1925; Rochdale June 1926; CITY July 1927; Grays Thurrock United July 1929.

Safe and consistent 'keeper who had earlier won representative honours for a Football League XI vs The Army, Nov. 1921, and an FA XI vs Oxford University, Nov. 1923. First choice at Sincil Bank until replaced by Jack Kendall in Feb. 1929. Later worked as a cricket coach at Watford Grammar School and in 1933 was reported to be coaching at the Hercules Sports Club in Utrecht, Holland.

HINDSON, Edward
(1903-1904)

Outside-/inside-right: 11 app.
1903: 5-7, 10-10
Born: Easington, Co. Durham
Career: Southwick (Sunderland); CITY Sep. 1903 to 1904.

Hindson was signed by David Calderhead after impressing in a match against Seaham. Mostly a reserve in his season at Sincil Bank, his first team outings came as deputy for Denis O'Donnell and Watson.

HIRST, Lee
(1993-1994)

Centre-half: 7 app.
1993: 6-2, 12-7
Born: Sheffield, 26 Jan. 1969
Career: Scarborough Feb. 1990; Coventry City July 1993 (CITY on loan, Dec. 1993 to Feb. 1994); Gainsborough Trinity on trial Aug. 1994.

Massive central defender who appeared for the Imps during an extended loan period without impressing sufficiently for the club to pursue a permanent signing. A rather surprise recruit by Coventry after being released by Scarborough on a free transfer.

HOBBS, William T.
(1926-1927)

Inside-left: 1 app.
1926: 5-9, 11-7
Born: Lurgan, Co. Armagh, c.1904
Career: Lurgan FC; CITY May 1926; Belfast Celtic cs 1927

Operated in both inside-forward positions and signed "... as a man who has gained a material reputation in Irish District League Football". His single FL outing came when he replaced Stan Sayer in the home match with Hartlepools in Sep. 1926.

HOBSON, Gordon
(1977-1985, 1988-1990)

Forward: 321 app. + 12 sub, 96 goals
1985: 5-9, 10-7
Born: Sheffield: 27 Nov. 1957
Career: Sheffield Rangers; Manchester Villa (Chesterfield); CITY Dec. 1977; Grimsby Town June 1985 (£35,000); Southampton Nov. 1986; CITY Sep. 1988 (£60,000); Exeter City Aug. 1990; Walsall, non-contract, Sep. 1991; Farnborough Town Nov. 1991; Salisbury Dec. 1991.

Winger signed from Sheffield local football after a two week trial who went on to become one of the most prolific scorers for City since the war. Netted on his League debut against Cambridge in Apr. 1978 and after that scored regularly throughout both his spells at Sincil Bank. Top scorer in five of his ten seasons at Lincoln, hitting five hat-tricks in all. His best tally came in the 1980/81 season when he scored 21 goals, including four in the 8-0 win over Northampton. Just as effective as a goal-maker for others, although as his career progressed he became an out and out striker. His transfer from First Division Southampton equalled the club record fee paid for a player.

HODGES, Harry James
(1924-1925)

Centre-forward: 7 app.
1924: 5-9½, 11-9
Born: Edmonton, London, 1897
Died: 12 Dec. 1966
Career: Sterling Athletic (Dagenham); West Ham United June 1921; CITY Aug. 1924 to Jan. 1925

Distinguished himself by failing to score at all during his time at Sincil Bank, despite regular appearances for both first and reserve teams in over half a season's football with the club. Only 2 FL outings at Upton Park where he had been reckoned *"a skilful player and sharpshooter"* and had been a member of the Hammers' reserve team that won the London Combination in 1923/24.

HODGKINSON, Vincent Arthur
(1933)

Inside-forward: 1 app.
1933: 5-9, 11-7
Born: Wollaton, Notts., 1 Nov. 1906
Died: 28 June 1990
Career: Magadalene Amateurs; Nottingham Forest Aug. 1925; Blackpool May to Sep. 1927; CITY Sep. to Oct. 1933; Lysaghts Sports (North Lindsey League) cs 1935 to WW2

Triallist who won a quick promotion to City's first team after playing just once for the reserves. Played his only FL match for the Imps on 21 Oct. 1933 at home to Plymouth Argyle. Better known for his cricketing skills - he was on the groundstaff of Notts CCC in 1926 and appeared 44 times for Lincolnshire in the Minor Counties (1936-1952), taking 162 wickets.

HODSON, Simeon Paul
(1986-1987)

Full-back/midfield: 54 app. + 2 sub
1986: 5-9, 10-2
Born: Lincoln, 5 Mar. 1966
Career: Notts County (appr.), (prof.) Mar. 1984; Charlton Athletic Mar. 1985; Lincoln United Dec. 1985; CITY Jan. 1986; Newport County July 1987; West Bromwich Albion Mar. 1987 (£5,000); Doncaster Rovers Sep. 1992; Kidderminster Harriers Jan. 1993; Mansfield Town Feb. 1993; Kidderminster Harriers July 1993.

Local-born player who appeared as a teenager with Notts County and Charlton, returning to live in Lincoln after his release from the South London club. Signed by George Kerr after a very brief spell at Ashby Avenue, he was a regular in the Imps' side which was relegated out of the League at the end of the 1986/87 season. Skippered Kidderminster during their famous FA Cup run and Vauxhall Conference championship of 1993/94, when he also won England non-League representative honours.

HOGG, George H.
(1925-1926)

Right-back: 5 app.
1925: 5-9, 11-0
Born: Kiveton Park, Sheffield, 1900
Career: Anston FC (Sheffield); CITY Apr. 1925; Southend United June 1926; Peterborough & Fletton United cs 1927; Mansfield Town June 1928 to 1931.

Hogg was one of six men tried in the right-back position in the 1925/26 campaign, his opportunities coming in Jan. and Feb. of 1926. At Mansfield during their last three seasons before entry to the Football League where he was summed up as *"... a bustling, hefty player and a relentless tackler"* (his weight had by then risen to 12½ stone).

HOLDER, Alan M.
(1955-1956)

Right-half: 1 app.,
1954: 5-10, 11-0
Born: Oxford, 10 Dec. 1931
Career: Army football (6th Bttn. RAOC); Nottingham Forest (amat.) 1951/52, (prof.) Apr. 1952; CITY July 1955; Tranmere Rovers Dec. 1956; Headington United July 1958 to cs 1959.

Rose to the professional ranks with Forest via a highly successful Army team. His solitary appearance for the Imps came in Mar. 1956 when he deputised for Fred Middleton at Fulham. Despite seven seasons in the professional game he saw little first team action at any of his clubs - totalling just 17 FL outings in all.

HOLMES, Maxey Martin
(1938-1939)

Wing-half/forward: 21 app., 1 goal
1939: 5-9, 11-0
Born: Pinchbeck, Lincs., 24 Dec. 1908

Career: London University; Spalding United; Grimsby Town in 1931/32; Hull City May 1935; Mansfield Town July 1927; CITY Aug. 1938 to Sep. 1939; guested for Grimsby Town in WW2.

Honour: (Grimsby Town) FL Div. 2 champions 1934

Max was a fine all-round sportsman and only switched to soccer after damaging a shoulder playing rugby union for the Northampton club. He represented the Midland Counties at rugby and Lincolnshire in Minor Counties cricket. At Sincil Bank he was considered a fast and clever player who could take a variety of positions, although he was mostly used at centre-forward or wing-half. A graduate of London University and a school-master by profession. In early 1994 he was reported to be living in retirement in Cleethorpes and still a season ticket holder at Blundell Park.

HOLMES, Roger W.
(1958-1972)

Inside-forward/wing-half: 276 app. + 2 sub, 36 goals
1965: 5-9, 10-4
Born: Scunthorpe, 9 Sep. 1942
Career: Limestone Rangers (Gainsborough League); CITY (amat.) May 1958, (prof.) Sep. 1959 to May 1971; reverted to amat. status cs 1971 appearing with CITY, Lincoln United in late 1971 and Skellingthorpe (Lincs. League) in Apr. 1972 while assisting with the youth team at Sincil Bank; appointed manager of City's 'A' team cs 1972.

Among the most skilful players to appear for the Imps in the last 30 or so years. Roger was signed on amateur forms as a 15 year old and made his debut for the reserves four days after his 16th birthday. By Sep. 1959 he had become a part-time professional and quickly won a regular first team place. Turned full-time in Jan. 1964 and was regularly reported to be attracting the attention of top clubs. He was leading scorer in 1967/68 but suffered a badly broken leg the following October in a home match with York. He never really recovered his old form and was released in May 1971, returning as an amateur the following season when he made one further

FL appearance and turned out for the reserves in their midweek matches. On leaving the game he worked as a chemist in a steelworks and then for a finance company.

HOOD, Derek
(1987)
Midfield: 9 app.
1987: 5-11, 12-8
Born: Washington, Co. Durham, 17 Dec. 1958
Career: West Bromwich Albion (appr.), (prof.) Dec. 1976; Hull City Aug. 1977; York City Feb. 1980 (£2,000), (CITY on loan, Mar. to May 1987) retired through injury cs 1988; Harrogate Town Jan 1989; Goole Town.

Honour: (York City) FL Div. 4 champions 1984

Experienced midfield player recruited by caretaker-manager Peter Daniels during his brief spell in charge which ended when the Imps were relegated to the Vauxhall Conference. A career aggregate of over 300 FL appearances, most of which were with York.

HOOD, Richard Parker
(1904-1909)
Centre-half/right-back: 130 app., 1 goal
1904: 5-7½, 10-12
Born: Seaham, Co. Durham, 1881
Career: Seaham Rovers; CITY May 1904 to cs 1909

The skipper of Seaham Rovers who made the considerable jump from minor football to the Second Division with some ease. A regular at Sincil Bank in his first four seasons but in and out of the side in his final campaign when the Imps were in the Midland League (1908/09: 23 app.). Returned to the north-east in the summer of 1909.

HOOPER, Charles ("Carl")
(1925-1926)
Centre-forward: 34 app., 6 goals
1926: 5-7, 10-0
Born: Darlington, 23 Oct. 1903
Died: 10 Aug. 1972
Career: Crook Town; CITY Mar. 1925 to cs 1926; Shildon; Notts County Jan. 1927; York City Nov. 1927; Chesterfield Mar. 1928; Norwich City Nov. 1928 to Jan. 1929; Darlington Wire Works; Sheffield Wednesday June 1929; Worksop Town cs 1930; West Stanley Aug. 1931.

"... rather on the light side, but has the chance to render the club further service", wrote a critic after the 1924/25 season. Most of Carl's FL experience was at Sincil Bank, for he made only six appearances elsewhere - three each for Chesterfield and Norwich. From a famous footballing family. Brother of Mark (of Wednesday's inter-war League championship and FA Cup winning sides), Fred (Oldham and Darlington) and Dan (a triallist at Sincil Bank in Sep. 1924) and nephew of Charlie Roberts (Manchester United and England).

HORNE, Alfred
(1932-1936)

Right-half/forward: 166 app., 36 goals
1934: 5-8, 11-0
Born: Birmingham, 1903
Died: Apr. 1976
Career: Alvechurch; West Bromwich Albion (amat.); Stafford Rangers; Hull City May 1925; Southend United May 1927; Manchester City Mar. 1928; Preston North End Sep. 1929 (£2,000); CITY June 1932; Mansfield Town Dec. 1936 to cs 1938.

Versatile player summed up as *"... could hardly fail anywhere, but his footcraft is best shown at right-half back. Can build up an attack from the start. Deadly penalty taker"*. Alf scored a hat-trick of penalties in the home match with Stockport in Sep. 1935. Later followed Harry Parkes to Field Mill where his FL career was concluded. Aggregated 315 appearances, 63 goals.

HOUGHTON, H(arry) Brian ("Bud")
(1963-1965)
Centre-forward: 54 app., 22 goals
1964: 6-0, 12-8
Born: Madras, India, 1 Sep. 1936
Career: St. Wilfreds Youth Club (Bradford); Bradford Oct. 1955; Birmingham City Oct. 1957 (approx. £5,000); Southend United Oct. 1958 (£1,000); Oxford United Mar. 1961 (£2,000); CITY Oct. 1963 (£6,000); Chelmsford City July 1965; Cambridge United cs 1966; Wellington Town Feb. 1968; Cheltenham Town; Morris Motors (Oxford).

Bustling centre-forward who did well in his first season at Sincil Bank (14 goals from 24 outings) but was put on the open to transfer list at the end of the following campaign, moving on to Southern League football. A regular goalscorer in the lower divisions, his final FL figures were 206 appearances, 78 goals.

HOUGHTON, Keith
(1983-1985)
Defender: 26 app.
1983: 6-2, 12-10
Born: Backworth, Northumberland, 10 Mar. 1954
Career: Newcastle United (appr.), Blyth Spartans; Carlisle United Jan 1980; CITY Aug. 1983 (£25,000); retired through injury July 1985.

Solid defender who could also play in midfield. Keith did not make the first team at Newcastle but later won England semi-professional honours with Blyth which led to a return to the Football League. His time at Sincil Bank was badly disrupted by the injuries which eventually led to his retirement from the game, after over 12 months on the sick list. A former policeman.

HOULT, Alan J.
(1978)
Forward: 2 app. + 2 sub, 1 goal
1978: 5-8, 10-8
Born: Burbage, Leics., 7 Oct. 1957
Career: Mid-Leicester schools; Leicester City (schoolboy), (prof.) Sep. 1975; (Hull City on loan, Jan. to Mar. 1978; CITY on loan Mar. to Apr. 1978); Bristol Rovers July 1978 to cs 1979; Nuneaton Borough; Bedworth United.

Honour: England schools international (4 app., 1973)

Small striker who spent a month at Sincil Bank towards the end of the 1977/78 season, scoring in the 3-3 draw at home to Rotherham. His only other FL experience was in the loan spell at Hull (3 app., 1 goal).

HOULT, Russell
(1991)
Goalkeeper, 2 app.
1991: 6-4, 13-2
Born: Leicester, 22 Nov. 1972
Career: Leicester City on YTS, (prof.) Mar. 1991; (CITY on loan Aug. 1991; Cheltenham Town on loan Dec. 1991; Blackpool on loan Mar. 1992; Kettering Town on loan Aug. 1993; Bolton Wanderers on loan Nov. 1993); CITY on loan Aug. 1994.

Teenaged 'keeper signed on loan from Filbert Street as cover for injuries to Matt Dickins and Ian Bowling. Hoult had an impressive start but returned to Leicester after appearing in the 6-0 home defeat by Barnet.

HOWARD, Fred
(1897)
Outside-right: 1 app.
Born: Hoyland, nr. Barnsley
Career: Sheffield United cs 1895; CITY Nov. to Dec. 1897; Barnsley 1898 to 1900.

One of four players given their debuts for Lincoln in the home match with Newton Heath on 6 Nov. 1897. Fred was considered no better than Hall, the regular wingman and although he later received several run-outs with the Swifts (reserves) he did not appear in the League again. He had more success at Barnsley where he made 49 appearances in their first two FL seasons.

HOYLAND, Ernest
(1939-1946)
Outside-right: 2 app.
1939: 5-8, 11-4
Born: Thurnscoe, Rotherham, 17 Jan. 1914
Career: Sheffield junior football (CITY on trial, c.1936); Halifax Town during 1936/37 season; Blackpool Feb. 1938; West Bromwich Albion May 1938; CITY June 1939; Grantham Mar.1946 (in part exchange for Jack Earnshaw) to cs 1946.

Hoyland's two FL appearances for City came shortly before the outbreak of war at the beginning of the 1939/40 season. Returned to Sincil Bank in 1945 after serving in the Army, but played only twice in the final year of war-time football before moving on to Midland League Grantham.

HUBBARD, Archibald ("Ranji")
(1912-1913)
Inside-left: 12 app., 3 goals
1912: 5-8½, 11-8
Born: Leicester, 1883
Died: 1967
Career: Leicester Imperial; St. Andrews FC (Leicester); Leicester Fosse May 1903; Fulham May 1907; Watford Jan. 1908; Norwich City May 1909; Grimsby Town Nov. 1910; CITY Aug. 1912; Leicester Imperial Sep. 1913.

Hubbard was by reputation enthusiastic, dashing and clever with a good shot. With the Imps towards the end of his career he appeared at wing-half on occasion. A career total of 99 FL outings and a further 79 in the Southern League at Watford and Norwich.

HUBBARD, Philip John
(1965-1971, 1976-1979)
Utility: 249 app. + 11 sub, 52 goals
1979: 5-11, 12-2
Born: Lincoln, 25 Jan. 1949
Career: Lincoln United (in 'A' team) 1963/64; Blanchards Sports (Lincoln Sunday League) in 1964/65; CITY (appr.) Oct. 1965, (prof.) July 1966; Norwich City Dec. 1971 (£20,000); Grimsby Town Oct. 1972 (approx. £20,000); CITY Aug. 1976 (Columbus Magic USA, on loan Apr. to Sep. 1979); Boston United Nov. 1979; Skegness Town May 1982 as player-manager; Ruston Sports (Lincoln) Apr. 1983.

Local-born player who was one of City's first apprentices following the introduction of a youth scheme in the mid-1960's. Had already made his League debut before signing full terms and by the age of 19 he had a regular first team place. At different times in his career he played full-back, in midfield and as a striker with equal effectiveness, although it was his goalscoring exploits which eventually led to his transfer to Norwich for a five figure fee at Christmas 1971. By then he had scored 15 times in only 20 League games, this following 18 goals in the 1970/71 season when he had been voted Plyer of the Year by the supporters. Never really broke through at Norwich and soon moved on. Was later brought back to Sincil Bank by Graham Taylor to strengthen the midfield after City were promoted to Division Three and gave the club three more years of fine service.

HUCKERBY, Darren Carl
(1992-)
Forward: 0 app. + 6 sub, 1 goal
Born: Nottingham, 23 Apr. 1976
Career: CITY on YTS cs 1992, prof. 1994.

Small striker given first team experience after scoring regularly with the junior side. Scored within five minutes of coming on the field in his senior debut at Shrewsbury in Mar. 1994.

HUDSON, Geoffrey Alan
(1965-1966)
Full-back: 33 app.
1965: 5-6, 11-0
Born: Leeds, 14 Oct. 1931
Career: Bradford Dec. 1949; Bradford City Feb. 1957; Halifax Town Aug. 1959; Exeter City July 1961; Crewe Alexandra July 1962; Gillingham July 1963; CITY May 1965; Rotherham United June 1966 as player-coach; Cambridge United cs 1967 trainer-coach; Southend United trainer-coach cs 1968, manager Oct. 1969 to 1970.

Honour: (Gillingham) FL Div. 4 champions 1964

Full-back who came to Sincil Bank at the end of a lengthy career in which he made over 300 FL appearances. An ever-present in his Sincil Bank season until Mar. when he lost his place to Jeff Smith.

HUGHES, David T.
(1978-1981, 1982)
Midfield: 61 apps. + 1 sub, 1 goal
1981: 5-9, 12-5
Born: Birmingham, 19 Mar. 1958
Career: Aston Villa (appr.) June 1974, (prof.) Feb. 1976; CITY Apr. 1978 (£4,000); Scunthorpe United June 1981 (in part exchange for Steve Cammack); CITY Mar. 1982; Worcester City cs 1982; Moor Green 1987.

Midfield player who was hit by a series of injuries after signing for the Imps. Recovered to become a mainstay of the 1980/81 promotion campaign during which he made 37 appearances plus 1 as substitute. No senior outings in his second spell at Sincil Bank.

HUGHES, Gordon
(1968-1971)
Outside-right: 117 app., 9 goals
1970: 5-6, 10-11
Born: Washington, Co. Durham, 19 June 1936

Career: Fatfield Juniors; Easington Lane; Tow Law Town; Newcastle United Aug. 1956; Derby County Aug. 1963 (£12,000); CITY Mar. 1968 (£6,000); Boston United Mar. 1971; retired Mar. 1972.

Popular bald-headed winger who came to Lincoln in his thirties after considerable experience at Newcastle and Derby. Gordon broke a leg soon after his senior debut in 1956/57 season, but returned to make an aggregate 434 FL appearances, scoring 46 goals.

HULME, Arthur
(1897-1898)
Inside-right: 29 app., 12 goals
Career: Staffs junior football; CITY June 1897; Gravesend United cs 1898.

Arthur missed only one game in his season with Lincoln, moving on to Southend League football with Gravesend for the following campaign. A contemporary noted of him *"He is said to be a smart shot, and to possess a good command over the ball"*.

HULME, Eric Martin
(1972-1974)
Goalkeeper: 23 app.
1973: 5-10, 11-3
Born: Houghton-le-Spring, Co. Durham, 14 Jan. 1949
Career: Spennymoor United; Nottingham Forest Mar. 1970; CITY on loan Sep. 1972, permanent Oct. 1972 (£4,000); (Gainsborough Trinity on loan Jan. 1973); Worksop Town cs 1974.

Goalkeeper signed following a successful loan period after previously performing consistently well with Forest's Central League side. Lost his place when John Kennedy returned from injury, spending the second half of the 1972/73 season on loan at Gainsborough before eventually being given a free transfer.

HULMES, Samuel ("Bob")
(1899-1900)
Defender: 2 app.
1899: 5-9, 11-0
Career: Heywood (Lancs. League); CITY May 1899; New Brompton cs 1900.

One of several professional recruits made by City in a bid to improve their reserve strength in time for the second string's entry into the Midland League. Bob had two first team outings towards the end of his Sincil Bank campaign, but more success with Southern League New Brompton where he made 19 appearances in the 1900/01 season.

HUMPHRIES, Glenn
(1987)
Centre-half: 9 app.
1987: 6-0, 12-0
Born: Hull Aug. 1964
Career: Doncaster Rovers (appr.), (prof.) Aug. 1982, (CITY on loan Mar. to May 1987); Bristol City Oct. 1987 (£20,000);

Scunthorpe United Mar. 1991 (£55,000); Frickley Athletic cs 1993 to Feb. 1994 when he moved to play in Hong Kong.

Honour: England youth international (1983)

Well-built central defender who had the misfortune to be sent off after only six minutes of his debut appearance for the Imps at Hartlepool. Returned to Doncaster at the end of the season following City's relegation out of the League.

HUNT, S(amuel) Walter
(1933-1934)

Centre-forward: 3 app.
1938: 5-11½, 11-12
Born: Doe Lea, Derbys., 9 Jan. 1909
Died: 2 Aug. 1963
Career: Welbeck Colliery Welfare; CITY May 1933; Mansfield Town July 1934; Torquay United June 1935; Rochdale Aug. 1936; Stockport County Dec. 1937 (£400); Accrington Stanley July 1938; Carlisle United Oct. 1938 to WW2.

Signed from Notts. junior football in City's Second Division days, Hunt proved more successful on moving down to the Northern Section. At Carlisle he led the divisional scoring list in 1938/39 with 34 goals, including four in one match against the Imps. Also a talented cricketer with Derbyshire (6 matches in 1936) and later Northumberland and the Central Lancashire League.

HUNTER, Cyril
(1929-1930)

Centre-half: 14 app., 1 goal
1929: 5-11, 12-0
Born: Pelaw, Newcastle-upon-Tyne, 1898
Career: Brentford 1921; South Sheilds cs 1924 to 1928; Boston Wonder Workers (USA); Fall River Marksmen (USA); CITY June 1929 to cs 1930.

Recruited from US football where he had spent a season following a lengthy period of suspension at South Shields. A hard worker but considered crude and too wary of upsetting referees after his earlier experiences. Never really settled at Sincil Bank and was in and out of the side.

HUNTER, George Irwin
(1965-1966)

Goalkeeper: 1 app.
1959: 6-0, 11-10
Born: Troon, Ayrshire, 29 Aug. 1930
Died: 10 May 1990
Career: Neilston Juniors; Celtic Jan. 1949; Derby County June 1954; Exeter City Aug. 1955; Yiewsley July 1960; Darlington June 1961; Weymouth July 1962; Burton Albion July 1963; CITY Sep. 1965; Matlock Town July to Sep. 1966.

Honour: (Celtic) Scottish Cup winner 1951

Veteran 'keeper who was signed by City on a match-by-match arrangement to cover for Peter Wakeham, Burton having first call on him when he was not in City's first team. Appeared once - in the home match with Halifax Town, Sep. 1965. Earlier in his career had won a Scottish Cup winners medal before reaching the age of 21.

HUNTER, William
(1909-1911)

Centre-forward: 32 app., 8 goals
1909: 5-9½, 11-9
Born: Sunderland, 1888
Career: Sunderland West End; Liverpool 1908; Sunderland May 1909; CITY Nov. 1909; Wingate Albion cs 1911; South Shields; Barnsley cs 1912; Manchester United; Clapton Orient cs 1913; Exeter City cs 1914.

Hunter was a regular choice in his first campaign but fared less well the following season when he suffered a bad injury which required hospital treatment. On his release in March 1911 he was sent back to Sunderland to recuperate. Saw little first team action elsewhere, his senior outings in the FL and Southern League totalling just 19.

HUTCHINSON, James Arthur
(1946-1949)

Inside-right: 85 app., 55 goals
1949: 5-8, 11-0
Born: Sheffield, 28 Dec. 1915
Career: Aqueduct FC (Sheffield); Sheffield United Sep. 1937; Bournemouth & Boscombe Athletic June 1946; CITY Nov. 1946; Oldham Athletic Feb. 1949 to Aug. 1950; Denaby United.

Honour: (City) FL Div.3 (North) champions 1948

Jimmy was known to the Imps' management after appearing as a war-time guest during Royal Navy service (28 app., 15 goals). A strong forward, difficult to dispossess, fast off the mark and a sharpshooter. Leading scorer with 32 goals in the 1947/48 championship campaign, but lost his place to Jock Dodds the following season and moved on to Oldham. Father of Barry (see below).

HUTCHINSON, J(ames) Barry
(1965-1966)

Centre-forward: 24 app., 18 goals
1966: 6-0, 12-2
Born: Sheffield, 27 Jan. 1936
Career: Bolton Wanderers (amat.); Chesterfield Apr. 1953; Derby County July 1960 (£2,025 and two players); Weymouth July 1964; CITY July 1965; Darlington Feb. 1966 (£5,000 plus Ken Allison); Halifax Town Nov. 1966 (approx. £2,500); Rochdale July 1967 (£2,850); Bangor City Aug. 1968; Hyde United Sep. 1968.

Signed after finishing top scorer in the Southern League with Weymouth in the 1964/65 season (45 goals). His scoring run continued at Lincoln and despite appearing in an unsuccessful team he averaged nearly a goal a game: 20 goals in 27 League and Cup outings. His overall record in the Football League was 362 matches (plus 2 subs.), 115 goals. Son of Jimmy.

INSKIP, John
(1912-1914)

Left-half: 1 app.
1913: 5-9, 11-7
Born: Glengarnock, Ayrshire
Career: Tyneside junior football; CITY Aug. 1912 to cs 1914.

Reserve half-back who replaced Andy Gardner for the fixture at Fulham in Apr. 1913 (a 3-1 defeat). Later returned to live in South Shields.

IREMONGER, Albert
(1926-1927)

Goalkeeper: 35 app.
1926: 6-5, 13-2
Born: Wilford, Notts., 15 June 1884
Died: 9 Mar. 1958
Career: Jardines' FC (Nottingham); (Nottingham Forest, trial, Mar. 1903); Notts County 1904; CITY May 1926; retired cs 1927.

Honours: Football League (2 app. vs Irish League & Southern League, 1912)
(Notts County) FL Div.2 champions 1914, 1923

Veteran goalkeeper recruited after 22 seasons at Meadow Lane during which he had established a club record of 564 FL appearances. Regarded as one of the greatest custodians of the time in his younger days and considered a fine capture by City even though he was 42 years old. Justified the optimism with some star performances for the club, using his exceptionally long reach to good effect and showing great enthusiasm. A capable cricketer too, appearing for Notts. between 1906 and 1910 and later as a professional for Aberdeen CC and as coach for The Leys School, Cambridge. On retirement became a licensee in his native Wilford. Younger brother of James, Nottingham Forest and England full-back and a Notts. cricketer.

IREMONGER, Sidney
(1919-1920)

Outside-right: 3 app., 1 goal
Career: Lincoln junior football; CITY Aug. 1919 to cs 1920. Grantham Sep. 1921; Newark Town Aug. 1922.

Signed after impressing in City's pre-season trial. Given a few first team opportunites at the start of the 1919/20 season but the outside-right position was taken over by Fred Linfoot after signing in Oct., and Iremonger was confined to the reserves. His surname also appeared as Ironmonger in the local press.

IRVING, John
(1889-1895, 1895-1897)

Forward: 51 app., 10 goals
Born: c.1867
Died: 20 Nov. 1942
Career: Queen of the South Wanderers c.1887; CITY Nov. 1889; Newark Town Feb. 1895; CITY in late 1895; retired cs 1897.

One of the very best of City's early professional imports and a regular goalscorer in their Midland League and Football Alliance days. He had switched to inside-forward by the time the club entered the Football League but remained a first choice until around 1894 after which he appeared mostly for the Swifts (reserve) side. Remained involved in the game for many years after he ceased playing, serving City as trainer for two brief spells and as a director from Mar. 1897 to 1901 - one of the very few players in the history of the game to have served a club as player and director at the same time. He was also secretary of top local junior side Adelaide for several years. Became a licensee in Lincoln and two of his sons also served on the Imps' board of directors from the early 1920's.

IVERSON, Robert Thomas James
(1933-1935)

Inside-right: 41 app., 13 goals
1934: 5-10½, 11-7
Born: Folkestone, 17 Oct. 1910
Died: 20 June 1953
Career: Folkestone Aug. 1926; Tottenham Hotspur May 1932, assisting their nursery side Northfleet in 1932/33 season; Ramsgate Press Wanderers June 1933; CITY Sep. 1933; Wolverhampton Wanderers Feb. 1935; Aston Villa Dec. 1936; retired late 1949 and appointed coach to the Villa junior side, Aston Villa Amateurs.

Honour: (Villa) FL Div.2 champions 1938

Bob made his debut in League football with the Imps and proved a most effective performer, soon attracting the attention of scouts from the bigger clubs. An ever-present in the 1934/35 season until his inevitable departure to Molineux. Developed into a tough yet constructive half-back in his Villa days helping them to victory in the 1944 League (North) Cup.

JACK, J(ames) Ross
(1983-1985)

Forward: 52 app. + 8 sub, 16 goals
1984: 5-10, 11-2
Born: Avoch, Ross-shire, 21 Mar. 1959
Career: Ross County; Everton (appr.), (prof.) Feb. 1977; (Cardiff City on loan Oct. 1979); Norwich City Dec. 1979 (£20,000); CITY Aug. 1983 (£15,000); Dundee July 1985; Dunfermline Athletic Oct. 1987; Kilmarnock July 1991 (£50,000); (Sligo Rovers on loan Jan. to Mar 1993); Montrose Mar. 1993; Ayr United Oct. 1993.

Honour: (Dunfermline) Scottish League Div. 2 champions 1989

Scottish-born striker who spent two seasons at Sincil Bank during Colin Murphy's first spell as manager, also appearing in midfield. Had greater success north of the border, finishing top scorer for Dunfermline in three consecutive seasons.

JACKLIN, Alfred
(1903-1905)

Wing-half: 3 app.
Career: Liberal Club (Lincoln); CITY Dec. 1903 to cs 1905.

Local lad who made his FL debut when deputising for George Fraser at Blackpool in Jan. 1904. He also appeared at right-half in the final two matches of the 1903/04 campaign but was restricted to Midland League football in his second season with the Imps.

JACKSON, A.
(1892-1893)

Right-back: 2 app.
Career: CITY Sep. 1892 to cs 1893. Lincoln Lindum Oct. 1895.

Jackson occupied the right-back slot for the fixtures at Darwen and Crewe in Jan. 1893 following the departure of Charles Coulton. Joined Lindum as a replacement for Heath when the latter signed for the Imps.

JACKSON, Alan E.
(1958-1961)

Outside-right: 4 app.
1960: 5-9, 10-4
Born: Scunthorpe, 14 Feb. 1938
Career: Ashby Institute; Brigg Town cs 1958; CITY Nov. 1958 to May 1961; Brigg Town cs 1961 until the early 1970's.

Reserve winger who played in a handful of first team games towards the end of City's Second Division days. Released on a free transfer when the club were relegated to Division Three and returned to Lincolnshire League Brigg Town.

JACKSON, A(lfred) Clement
(1909-1920)

Right-back: 184 app.
1909: 5-9½, 11-0
Born: Kimberley, Nottingham, 1886
Died: 28 Aug. 1960
Career: Kimberley St. Johns; Eastwood Rangers; CITY Jan. 1909 to 1920.

Recruit from Notts. junior football who became one of the club's great servants of the early twentieth century. Won considerable praise for his performances in City's defence, reported as "cool and calculating and never a shirker" and, "kicks strong and clean, tackles promptly and determinably". In addition to his FL outings Clem was an ever-present in the 1911/12 Central League championship side (32 app.) and made over 100 appearances during the Great War. Was given the title 'honorary player-manager' for a brief period in the summer of 1919 before George Fraser was appointed to the secretary-manager's position. Subsequently a licensee in Lincoln for many years.

JACKSON, Brian H.
(1964)

Wing-half/inside-forward: 10 app., 1 goal
1963: 5-7; 10-9
Born: Walton-on-Thames, Surrey, 1 Apr. 1933
Career: Weybridge Schools; Chase of Chertsey (Arsenal amat.); Leyton Orient Oct. 1950; Liverpool Nov. 1951 (£6,500 and another player); Port Vale June 1958 (£3,000); Peterborough United July 1962 (£2,000); CITY May 1964; Burton Albion Dec. 1964; Boston United cs 1965.

Honours: England schools international (1 app. vs Wales, 1947) (Port Vale) FL Div. 4 champions, 1959

Experienced half-back who joined City for a 'nominal fee' at the very end of his professional career. Soon after arriving at Sincil Bank he was made club captain and given the responsibility of assisting manager Bill Anderson. Brian made over 100 FL appearances for both Liverpool and Port Vale.

JACKSON, Robert
(1955-1964)

Right-back/half-back: 235 app.
1960: 5-10, 12-2
Born: Middleton, Lancs., 5 June 1934
Career: Oldham Athletic (amat.) June 1949, (prof.) Aug. 1951; CITY Mar. 1955; Wisbech Town cs 1964 to Oct. 1966.

Bob was signed as a right-back but did not make the breakthrough to regular first team football until Jan. 1957, nearly two years after his arrival at Sincil Bank. A sound defender who stayed with the club 10 seasons, switching to the half-back line in later years. On leaving football he worked in a local engineering factory before taking up employment at Bevercotes Colliery in Nottinghamshire.

JACQUES, Joseph
(1964-1965)

Left-half: 22 app.
1964: 5-11, 12-3
Born: Consett, Co. Durham, 12 Sep. 1944
Died: 4 Feb. 1981
Career: Preston North End (amat.), (prof.) Sep. 1961; CITY May 1964; Darlington July 1965; Southend United Oct. 1969 (£8,000); Gillingham Oct. 1972 to cs 1974; Hartlepool Jan. 1976 to cs 1977.

Joe had his introduction to League soccer with the Imps but his career only really took off when he left the club. Developed into a solid centre-half (also occasionally

turning out at centre-forward), aggregating 335 FL appearances plus 5 as substitute, and scoring 6 goals.

JAMES, Anthony C.
(1988-1989)

Centre-half: 24 app. + 5 sub
1989: 6-3, 13-8
Born: Sheffield, 27 June 1967
Career: Sheffield Club; Gainsborough Trinity Aug. 1988; CITY Aug. 1988 (£6,000); Leicester City Aug. 1989 (£150,000); Hereford United June 1994.

Central-defender who impressed Colin Murphy so much in a pre-season match that he signed him soon afterwards. Tony had a reputation for his long throw-ins and clean tackling and was voted Supporters' Player of the Year in 1988/89 season. After early success at Leicester he suffered a bad injury at the start of the 1991/92 season.

JEAVONS, Patrick
(1966)

Goalkeeper: 1 app.
1966: 5-10, 13-0
Born: Deptford, London, 5 July 1946
Career: Gravesend; CITY on trial Feb. 1966, permanent Apr. 1966 (£250) to Sep. 1966; Wisbech Town Nov. 1966.

Given his chance at Southport on Easter Monday 1966 after regular 'keeper Peter Wakeham had been sent home for refusing to join the other players in watching a show at Morecambe on the night before the match. City lost 5-1 and Jeavons was reported to have had a 'nightmare game'. His performances with the reserves alternated between the very good and the poor.

JEFFREY, Alick James
(1969-1970)

Inside-forward: 19 app. + 3 sub, 3 goals
1968: 5-10½, 13-4
Born: Rawmarsh, West Yorkshire, 29 Jan. 1939

Career: Doncaster Rovers (amat.), (prof.) Feb. 1956; retired through injury Feb. 1959; Skegness Town as a permit player Mar. 1959; Prague FC (Sydney, Australia) Feb. 1961; Auburn (Sydney); Doncaster Rovers as player-coach Dec. 1963; CITY Jan. 1969; Drumcondra on trial, Aug. 1970; Worksop Town Aug. 1970; Retford Town in season 1971/72; Gainsborough Trinity Sep. 1972 to Jan. 1973.

Honours: England schools international (4 app., 1954)
England youth international (1955)
England and Great Britain amateur international (4 app., 1955-56)
England Under-23 international (2 app., 1957)
(Doncaster Rovers) FL Div.4 champions 1966,1969

Extremely talented as a teenager, winning international honours at several levels but then suffered a badly broken leg playing for England U-23 against France in Oct. 1956. The injury was so serious that it was believed his career was over and he received an insurance pay-off. Suffered a second break in Aug. 1959 when making a comeback with Skegness but bravely fought his way back to fitness and a full-time career. Came to City at the age of 30 and was in and out of the side, by this time he had lost some of his speed but still impressed with his skilful touches. Later a licensee in Doncaster.

JENKINS, Evan Thomas
(1929-1930, 1933-1934)
Outside-right: 44 app., 13 goals
1929: 5-6½, 10-8
Born: Ynyshir, Porth, Glamorgan, 26 June 1906
Died: 27 Dec. 1990
Career: Denaby United; CITY Mar. 1929; Burnley May 1930; CITY Sep. 1933; York City Aug. 1934 to 1935; later assisted Crittall's Athletic (Braintree).

Diminutive winger said to be full of grit and undaunted by the heftiest of defenders. Impressed in his second season at Sincil Bank and was soon transferred to First Division Burnley. Returned to play for City during the 1933/34 campaign when they were relegated back to the Northern Section. A former miner.

JENKINS, Reginald
(1926-1927)
Outside-right: 5 app.
Career: Chester cs 1926; CITY Nov. 1926 (£300); Chester Sep. 1927.

Wingman who briefly replaced the injured Bosbury in City's line-up shortly after signing from Chester, who were then members of the Cheshire League. Released on a free transfer after he failed to settle in Lincoln.

JEPSON, Arthur
(1948-1950)
Goalkeeper: 58 app.
1939: 5-10, 11-0
Born: Selston, Notts., 12 July 1915
Career: Mansfield Town late 1934; Grantham; Port Vale June 1938; Stoke City Sep. 1948; CITY Dec. 1948; Northwich Victoria

Aug. 1950; Gloucester City Oct. 1951; Hinckley United as player-manager 1953; later scouted for Coventry City and Middlesbrough and had a spell as Hinckley Athletic manager from July 1963.

First choice 'keeper throughout his time on the club's books and considered by a 1949 critic to be *"... one of the best goalkeepers seen at Sincil Bank for many years and [he] rapidly inspired confidence"*. Well known as a Notts. cricketer from 1939 to 1959 and from 1960 a first-class umpire who stood in Test matches.

JEWETT, Alfred William
(1923-1924)
Centre-half: 37 app., 3 goals
1924: 5-11, 12-0
Born: Bitterne, nr. Southampton, 15 Nov. 1899
Died: 13 July 1980
Career: Bitterne United; Southampton (amat.); Thorneycroft Works; Arsenal; CITY Sep. 1923 to cs 1924; Wigan Borough Aug. to Sep. 1926.

Considered a great capture for the Imps despite doubts over his fitness - he had suffered a bad knee injury earlier in his career. He played almost a full season at Lincoln, before his knee gave way in the final matches of the campaign. He announced his retirement and Arsenal visited Sincil Bank for a benefit match in Oct. 1925. However, he was later pronounced fit again only for the knee to break down a third time on his comeback appearance for Wigan against Stoke City.

JOHNSON, Alan Keith
(1994-)
Defender: 16 app.
1994: 6-0, 12-0
Born: Billinge, Wigan, 19 Feb. 1971
Career: Wigan Athletic YTS, (prof.) Apr. 1989; CITY Feb. 1994 (£40,000 plus a further £20,000 after 50 app.).

No-nonsense defender who was a product of Wigan's youth policy. Highly regarded at Springfield Park and the Latics were said to have turned down an offer of £100,000 for him. The fee paid by City was set by a Football League tribunal.

JOHNSON, David Alan
(1993-)
Forward: 38 app. + 3 sub, 8 goals
1993: 6-2, 13-8
Born: Dinnington, South Yorks., 29 Oct. 1970
Career: Sheffield Wednesday YTS, (prof.) July 1989, (Hartlepools United on loan Oct. 1991 and again Nov. 1992); CITY Sep. 1993 (£32,000).

Skilful right-sided forward, capable of beating defenders and delivering a measured cross. Instantly popular with the Imps' fans who gave him the nickname 'Magic' after the US basketball player.

JOHNSON, George J.
(1951-1956)

Outside-left: 3 app., 1 goal
1951: 5-9, 11-0
Born: Esh, Co. Durham, 6 Oct. 1932
Career: Langley Park Juniors; CITY Sep. 1951; Grantham July 1956.

An apprentice joiner when he signed for the Imps, Johnson made all his frst team appearances in the early part of the 1951/52 season (his goal came in the record 11-1 victory over Crewe Alexandra). Missed the following season due to National Service and spent the rest of his time at Sincil Bank in the reserves, eventually moving on to Midland League Grantham.

JOHNSON, Joseph R.
(1952-1953)

Inside-forward: 11 app., 2 goals
1951: 5-9, 12-0
Born: Greenock, 13 Sep. 1920
Career: Arthurlie; Rangers July 1946 (Falkirk on loan Nov. 1950 to early 1951); CITY Oct. 1952 (£750); Workington July 1953 (in exchange for Dan McDowall) to 1954.

Honour: (Rangers) Scottish League champions 1950

Joe began his City career with a run of nine consecutive first team appearances but dropped to the reserves when Johnny Garvie became fit again and was exchanged for the much younger McDowall the following summer. A former farmer (hence his nickname 'Farmer Joe' at Ibrox) and schools PT instructor.

JOHNSON, Robert Simon
(1983)

Full-back; 4 app.
1983: 5-6, 9-12
Born: Bedford, 22 Feb. 1962
Career: Luton Town (appr.), (prof.) Aug. 1979, (CITY on loan Aug. -Sep. 1983); Leicester City Aug. 1989; Barnet cs 1991.

Honour: (Luton Town) FL Cup winner 1988

Full-back signed as a stand-in for Phil Neale while he completed the 1983 cricket season with Worcestershire. Later played over 90 games in the top flight with Luton.

JOHNSON, Tom
(1946-1948)

Centre-half: 75 app.
1938: 5-11, 12-7
Born: Ecclesfield, Sheffield, 4 May 1911
Died: 19 Aug. 1983
Career: Ecclesfield United; Sheffield United Sep. 1928; CITY Mar. 1946; retired Dec. 1948; became club's Yorkshire area scout Feb. 1949.

WILLS'S CIGARETTES

Honours: (Sheffield United) FA Cup finalist 1936
(City) FL Div.3 (North) champions 1948

Veteran defender signed after appearing as a guest for City during the war and going on to skipper the 1948 championship side. Keen, forceful and a tower of strength in the defence, he played his best football in the pre-war period, captaining the Blades at Wembley in the 1936 FA Cup final. Both his father William and brother Harry played for Sheffield United and when Tom joined the Imps it broke a run of 50 years in which members of the same family had turned out for the Bramall Lane club. Later worked as an electrical engineer in Sheffield.

JOHNSON, William Thomas
(1901-1902)

Winger: 6 app.
Career: Wrockwardine Wood; Walsall cs 1896; Gravesend United cs 1897; Chatham cs 1898; CITY Aug. 1901 to cs 1902.

A regular with Walsall (17 app., 4 goals) and Southern League Chatham (56 apps., 12 goals) but mostly a reserve at Sincil Bank where he usually turned out as a centre- or inside-forward with the Midland League team. However, nearly all his first team opportunities came on the wing.

JONES, Alan
(1977-1979)

Outside-right: 24 app. + 2 sub, 4 goals
1979: 5-6, 10-11
Born: Grimethorpe, West Yorks, 21 Jan. 1951
Career: Huddersfield Town (appr.), (prof.) Dec. 1968; Halifax Town Aug. 1973 (£4,500); Chesterfield Sep. 1976 (£9,000); CITY Nov. 1977 (£11,500) (Columbus Magic, USA, on loan Apr. 1979); Bradford City Sep. 1979; Rochdale Aug. 1980 to cs 1981.

Right-sided forward who appeared regularly under Willie Bell's management but never made the starting line-up after the arrival of Colin Murphy in Nov. 1978. A career aggregate of 258 appearances plus 11 substitutions, 22 goals.

JONES, Alfred
(1962-1967)

Full-back: 179 app. + 1 sub, 3 goals
1966: 5-9, 12-3
Born: Liverpool, 2 Mar. 1937
Career: Marine; Leeds United Apr. 1960; CITY June 1962 (£4,000); Wigan Athletic cs 1967; Horwich RMI 1968 to early 1970's.

"A steady, reliable defender" was one observer's verdict on this tough tackling player. Alf spent five seasons as City's regular right-back before being released on a free transfer and joining Wigan Athletic, then members of the Cheshire League. Worked in a car factory on leaving the full-time game.

JONES, David T.
(1923-1924)

Goalkeeper: 3 app.
1923: 5-10, 12-0
Born: Troed-y-rhiw, Cardigan
Career: Merthyr Town season 1919/20; Chesterfield Aug. 1922; CITY June 1923; Penrhiwceiber 1924; Barry Town Aug. 1925.

Welsh 'keeper who was a reserve with all his senior clubs, hence an aggregate of only 17 FL appearances from his three clubs. At Sincil Bank he was understudy to Jack Kendall getting his first team experience when the latter was sold to Everton towards the end of the 1923/24 campaign.

JONES, Frederick William
(1893)

Goalkeeper/full-back: 7 apps.
Born: Llandudno, 1869
Died: 27 Dec. 1910
Career: Gloddaeth 1886 to 1890; Llandudno Swifts 1890 (Burslem Port Vale Sep. 1890; Newton Heath Oct. 1890); Small Heath Dec. 1892; CITY Aug. to Nov. 1893; Reading in 1895/96; Llandudno Swifts 1896-1900; Caernarvon Ironopolis Nov. 1901 to 1902; Llanrwst Mar. 1903.

Honours: Wales international (1 app. vs Scotland 1893)

Turned out for City in seven of the first eight 1893/94 League fixtures, although only two were in his recognised full-back position. He was known in Wales as 'Fred Fawr' (big Fred), embarking on an up-and-down career, as a teenager. Employed as a bookmaker, Jones founded Llandudno Corinthians FC and acted as secretary of the local Wednesday League. Died from pneumonia, his body being found in a Llandudno street.

JONES, Gary
(1993)

Forward: 0 app. + 4 sub, 2 goals
1993: 6-1, 12-9
Born: Huddersfield, 6 Apr. 1969
Career: Rossington Main; Doncaster Rovers Jan. 1989; Grantham Nov. 1989 (£8,500); Kettering Town Jan. 1990 (£17,500); Boston United Aug. 1991 (£3,000); Southend United June 1993 (£25,000) (CITY on loan Sep. to Oct. 1993).

Striker who earned a transfer to Second Division Southend after scoring regularly with Boston United in the Conference (73 app., 43 goals). Netted the equaliser against Bury (2-2) on his debut for the Imps but returned south when his loan period was completed.

JONES, James Alfred
(1951-1954)

Goalkeeper: 76 app.,
1950: 5-10, 12-6
Born: Birkenhead, 3 Aug. 1927
Career: Everton (amat.) May 1945, (prof.) Dec. 1945; Ellesmere Port Town in season 1946/47; Everton Aug. 1948; New Brighton Aug. 1950; CITY Aug. 1951 (£750); Accrington Stanley Feb. 1954 (£550); Rochdale Sep. 1955 (£750); retired June 1961; City reserve team trainer Dec. 1965.

Honour: (City) FL Div.3 (North) champions 1952

Goalkeeper who missed only two games in his first season as City won the Northern section title, but later had to share the position with Jerry Lowery. Totalled 331 FL outings, appearing in contact lenses towards the end of his career. Became a licensee at Scopwick near Lincoln on retiring from the game and now lives near Horncastle.

JONES, J(ohn) Merfyn
(1963)

Outside-left: 1 app.

1962: 5-6, 10-0

Born: Bangor, Caernarfons, 30 Apr. 1931

Career: Bangor City; Liverpool Nov. 1951; Scunthorpe United July 1953; Crewe Alexandra June 1959 (£3,000); Cheshire Aug. 1961 to cs 1963; CITY Oct. 1963 (trial); Gainsborough Trinity July 1964 to cs 1965.

Welsh winger who had a month's trial at Sincil Bank before being released. His only first team game for the Imps was in the home match with Carlisle on 30 Oct. 1963. He had earlier made a total of 391 FL appearances, mostly with Scunthorpe.

JUDGE, Alan G.
(1985)

Goalkeeper: 2 app.

1985: 5-11, 11-6

Born: Kingsbury, London, 14 May 1960

Career: Luton Town (appr.) 1967, (prof.) Jan 1978; Reading on loan Sep. 1982 and Nov. 1982 to cs 1983, signing permanently July 1983; Oxford United Dec. 1984 (£10,000); (CITY on loan Nov. 1985; Cardiff City on loan Oct. to Dec. 1987); Hereford United July 1991; Bromsgrove Rovers Aug. 1994.

Honour: (Oxford United) FL Cup winner 1986

Goalkeeper who appeared briefly for the Imps during an injury crisis. Made his debut in a home match with Bristol City, but the team lost 7-0 in his next outing at Derby and Judge was one of four members of that side who never played for City again.

KABIA, Jason Thomas
(1992-)

Forward: 17 app. + 11 sub, 4 goals

1993: 5-11, 12-0

Born: Sutton-in-Ashfield, Notts., 28 May 1969

Career: Clipstone Welfare; Oakham United Oct. 1991; CITY non-contract Jan 1992, full terms Mar. 1992 (Doncaster Rovers on loan Jan. 1993; Stafford Rangers on loan Nov. 1993; Valletta, Malta, on loan for a period from Dec. 1993).

Recruit from the Central Midlands League who was given his League debut soon after signing full terms. Did not appear in the Imps first team after Nov. 1992, having returned from his loan spell at Doncaster with torn knee ligaments which resulted in a long lay off. Brother of Jim (Chesterfield and Boston United).

KEAN, Archibald
(1922-1924)

Inside-forward: 76 app., 11 goals

1923: 5-7, 11-0

Born: Parkhead, Glasgow, 30 Sep. 1894

Career: Croy Celtic; Clapton Orient July 1921; CITY Aug. 1922; Blackburn Rovers Apr. 1924; Grantham Sep. 1925.

Archie was known as a clever footballer, particularly skilled at dribbling *("a real wizard with the ball")* who was more of a provider of goals than a scorer. Did not make the first team at Ewood Park and returned to Midland League football the following campaign.

KEARNS, Peter V.
(1968-1969)

PETER KEARNS
LINCOLN CITY

Inside-forward: 45 app. + 1 sub, 11 goals

1967: 5-8, 10-2

Born: Wellingborough, 26 Mar. 1937

Career: Wellingborough Town; Plymouth Argyle Apr. 1956; Corby Town June 1961; Aldershot Dec. 1962; CITY Mar. 1968; Weymouth July 1969.

Peter scored five goals in 12 outings at the end of the 1967/68 season after being signed by Ron Gray at transfer deadline time. However, he was not so successful in the following campaign and was released on a free transfer. Finished with an aggregate FL total of 294 matches plus 2 substitutions, 83 goals.

KEATING, Reginald E.
(1927-1928)

Centre-forward: 2 app.

1927: 5-9½, 11-0

Born: Halton, nr. Swillington Common, Leeds, 14 May 1904

Died: 13 Oct. 1961

Career: Annfield Plain; Scotswood United; Newcastle United Oct. 1926; CITY July 1927; Gainsborough Trinity June 1928; Scarborough May 1929; Stockport County May 1930; Birmingham June 1931; Norwich City May 1932; North Shields Aug. 1933; Bath City Oct. 1933; Cardiff City Dec. 1933; Doncaster Rovers June 1936; Bournemouth & Boscombe Athletic Nov. 1936; Carlisle United Aug. 1937 -1938.

Keating finished top scorer for City's reserve team with 35 goals but his first team opportunities were limited by the presence of Billy Dinsdale. On leaving Sincil Bank he embarked on a lengthy and varied career but only appeared regularly in the Football League with Cardiff (70 appearances, 36 goals). Brother of Albert (Bristol City and Blackburn Rovers).

KEELEY, Nolan Bruce
(1980-1982)

Full-back: 52 app. 3 goals
1981: 5-11, 11-2
Born: East Barsham, Norfolk, 24 May 1951
Career: Great Yarmouth Town; Scunthorpe United July 1973; CITY Jan. 1980 (£7,000) to May 1982; Corby Town (trial) Aug. 1982; Kings Lynn Sep. 1982; Great Yarmouth Town later in season 1982/83. Was subsequently player-manager of Swaffham in the early 1990's and manager of Fakenham from 1991.

Stylish player signed by Colin Murphy after a successful spell at Scunthorpe (255 app. + 4 sub, 37 goals). His career at Sincil Bank was badly affected by injuries and he was eventually released in May 1982, more than 12 months after he had last appeared in City's first team. Has since been involved in the East Anglian non-League scene, including Sunday football, and played for Hobbies United (Norwich) when they won the FA Sunday Cup in 1985.

KEETLEY, Frank
(1931-1933)

Inside-right: 42 app., 27 goals
1932: 5-9, 11-6
Born: Derby, 23 Mar. 1901
Died: 13 Jan. 1968
Career: Victoria Ironworks (Derby); Derby County Feb. 1921; Doncaster Rovers June 1926; Bradford City Nov. 1929; CITY May 1931; Hull City Feb. 1933; Margate Aug. 1933; Worcester City cs 1934, appointed player-manager cs 1935.

Honour: (City) FL Div.3 (North) champions 1932

A provider of goals for Allan Hall at Doncaster, Bradford City and Lincoln. Described by a contemporary as *"a hardworking inside-forward, an excellent support to his wing partner and the centre-forward, and a strong finisher with both head and feet"*. Frank created a Football League record by scoring six times in the second half against Halifax on 16 Jan. 1932, including five in a 21 minute spell. Member of a famous footballing family including Tom (see below). Later a licensee in Worcestershire.

KEETLEY, Thomas
(1933-1934)

Centre-foward: 10 app., 5 goals
1933: 5-7½, 11-10
Born: Derby, 16 Nov. 1898
Died: 19 Aug. 1958
Career: Victoria Ironworks (Derby) (Derby County amat.); Bradford Apr. 1920; Doncaster Rovers July 1923; Notts County June 1929; CITY June 1933; Gresley Rovers cs 1934.

Honour: (Notts County) FL Div.3 (South) champions 1931

The most prominent of the five Keetley brothers who appeared in League football in the inter-war period. Tom netted 281 goals in 366 appearances including six for Doncaster against Ashington in Feb. 1929. All his

first team outings for City were in the early part of the 1933/34 campaign. Subsequently entered the licensing trade.

KELLY, Errington Edison
(1983)

Forward: 0 app. + 2 sub
1983: 5-8, 11-7
Born: St. Vincent, Windward Islands, 8 Apr. 1958
Career: Leamington; VS Rugby; Ledbury Town; (Hereford United on trial, CITY on trial, Sep. 1981); Bristol Rovers Sep. 1981; CITY Jan. 1983 on a non-contract basis; Bristol City Mar. 1983; Coventry City Aug. 1983; Peterborough United on loan Mar. to May 1984, permanent Aug. 1984 (£3,000) to 1989.

Non-contract player who appeared as a substitute in the home matches with Southend and Plymouth in Feb. 1983. Both were lost and City, who had led the table since early season, gradually drifted away from the promotion positions. Kelly had more success with Peterborough for whom he made 118 League appearances (including substitutions), scoring 28 goals.

KELLY, James
(1892)

Inside-left: 8 app., 1 goal
Career: Glasgow junior football; CITY Sep. 1892 (£22 signing on fee) to around Dec. 1892.

Recruited from Glasgow along with Cameron for City's entry to the Football League. Although considered a skilful midfield player his shooting was poor and he lost his place when Isaac Moore was switched from the half-back line.

KELLY, Martin
(1905-1907)

Inside-left: 24 app., 3 goals
1906: 5-7, 10-6
Career: Liberal Club (Lincoln); CITY Feb. 1905; Oldham Athletic Sep. 1907; later appeared for Liberal Club again in season 1909/10.

Kelly was signed from a top local side but had to wait 12 months for his League debut against Burton United when he scored two goals in a 5-1 victory. No FL appearances at Oldham and he soon returned to Lincoln League football. Joined up with Kitchener's Army at the start of the Great War.

KELLY, Terence J.
(1962-1963)

Centre-forward: 8 app., 2 goals
1960: 5-10, 10-0
Born: Gateshead, 14 May 1942
Career: Newcastle United May 1960; CITY July 1962 to May 1963; Cambridge United cs 1963; Stamford Town later in 1963; Skegness Town Oct. 1967; Retford Town cs 1968; Sutton Town later in season 1968/69; Heanor Town Oct. 1969; Long Eaton United Dec. 1970; Boston FC cs 1971 to cs 1972.

Developed in Newcastle's nursery team and listed in 1960 as a half-back, Terry switched to centre-forward before leaving the Magpies. Never established himself in the first team at Sincil Bank and after a brief trial with Cambridge United reserves he joined Stamford, the first of many Midland League clubs he was associated with over the next decade.

KENDALL, John William
(1922-1924, 1928-1930)

Goalkeeper: 117 app.
1923: 6-0, 12-0
Born: Broughton, nr. Brigg, Lancs., 9 Oct. 1905
Died: Oct. 1961
Career: Broughton Rangers (North Lindsey League); CITY Mar. 1922; Everton Apr. 1924 (£1,250); Preston North End May 1927; CITY July 1928; Sheffield United Mar. 1930 (£1,125); Peterborough United July 1934 to cs 1938.

Initially signed after a trial with the reserves and soon became regarded as one of the Northern Section's best 'keepers. Summed up at the time as *"... a cool, fearless player, has a keen eye, and possesses an enormous reach"*. His career at both Everton and Preston was badly affected by injuries. He had not played football at school and became a goalkeeper by accident when his junior team's regular man failed to turn up. Jack went in goal, saved two penalties and was snapped up by the Imps soon afterwards. Had previously worked on Lord Yarborough's estate at Broughton.

KENNEDY, David ("Jack")
(1971-1972)
Centre-forward: 6 app. 2 sub, 1 goal
1971: 6-1, 13-8
Born: Sunderland, 30 Nov. 1950
Career: Leeds United May 1968; CITY July 1971 to Sep. 1972.

Central defender signed by David Herd on a free transfer. Kennedy made a promising start by scoring on his full debut at Stockport but was mainly used in the reserves or when City wanted to play a fifth defender in away games. Quit League football in Sep. 1972.

KENNEDY, George
(1906-1908)
Left half: 42 app.
1906: 5-8½, 10-8
Born: Dumfries, c.1885
Died: Dec. 1917
Career: Maxwelltown Volunteers; CITY May 1906; Chelsea May 1908; Brentford cs 1910 to 1913.

One of a number of players recruited from the Dumfries area in the early 1900's. Kennedy later followed manager David Calderhead to Chelsea where he received a limited amount of top flight experience: 10 FL plus two FA Cup ties. Later made 73 Southern League appearances at Brentford. Killed in action at Paschendaele in the Great War.

KENNEDY, John
(1967-1974)
Goalkeeper: 251 app.
1970: 6-2, 11-10
Born: Newtownards, Co. Down, 4 Sep. 1939
Career: Distrillery c.1954; Celtic Mar. 1965; CITY July 1967 to May 1974; Lincoln United July 1974 to May 1976 and again in season 1978/79.

Honours: Northern Ireland amateur international (1 app. vs Scotland 1959)
Great Britain amateur international
(Distillery) Irish Cup finalist 1963

Tall, consistent 'keeper who was an ever-present in his first campaign with the Imps and rarely missed a match in the following seven seasons, apart from when injured. Proved to be one of Ron Gray's best signings when he arrived on a free transfer from Celtic. John was popular with the fans who voted him the first ever Player of the Season in 1969/70. A part-time professional who combined football with a career as a schoolteacher.

KERR, David ("Jock")
(1937-1938)
Centre-forward: 5 app.
1937: 5-9½, 11-2
Born: c.1913
Career: Clyde; Stonehouse Violet; Glentoran; returned to Scotland for a while but then assisted Bangor Town (Irish League) in 1936/37 season; CITY July 1937; Newark Town cs 1938.

Centre-forward who found his first team opportunities limited by the presence of Campbell and Burdett. Appeared regularly for the reserves in the Midland League, finishing leading scorer with 29 goals.

KERR, James
(1952-1954)
Outside-left: 15 apps., 1 goal
1955; 5-8, 10-4
Born: Lemington, Northumberland, 3 Mar. 1932
Career: Newcastle United; Blyth Spartans cs 1952 on completing National Service; CITY Nov. 1952; Oldham Athletic June 1954; signed for North Shields Aug. 1956 but was unable to play as he had taken compensation for injury sustained when with Oldham.

Winger most noted for a turn of speed that could open up the opposition defence. Appeared fairly regularly for the Imps in 1952/53 but only once in the following campaign. Jimmy's career was ended by a knee injury sustained at Boundary Park against Scunthorpe on 24 Dec. 1955. Afterwards employed as an audit clerk in the Newcastle area.

KERRIGAN, Donald M.
(1969)
Inside-left: 12 app.
1968; 10-0, 12-0
Born: Seamill, Ayrshire, 7 May 1941
Died: Dec. 1990
Career: Drumchapel Amateurs; Johnstone Burgh; St. Mirren c.1959; Aberdeen Oct. 1963; Heart of Midlothian May 1965 (in exchange for another player); Dunfermline Athletic Mar. 1967 (in exchange for another player); Fulham Mar. 1968 after a two month trial, (CITY on loan Mar. to cs 1969); Portadown late in 1969.

Honour: Scotland schools international
Scotland youth international
(St. Mirren) Scottish Cup finalist 1962

Experienced and versatile player who moved south after a decade in Scottish League football. Made only 6 appearances (including subs) at Fulham but was a regular at Sincil Bank during his extended loan period. Lost his life in an accident at work.

KILLIN, H(arold) Roy
(1952-1954)
Left-back: 7 app.
1950; 5-9, 11-7
Born: Toronto, Canada, 18 July 1929
Career: Manchester United Apr. 1949; CITY Aug. 1952; Peterborough United July 1954 to cs 1958.

Canadian-born defender who served as understudy to Doug Graham. Made no first team appearances at Old Trafford and all his senior experience at Lincoln (7 FL and 3 FA Cup outings) came in the second half of the 1953/54 season.

KILMORE, Kevin
(1986-1987)
Forward: 40 app. + 6 sub, 6 goals
1986; 5-9, 11-10
Born: Scunthorpe, 11 Nov. 1959
Career: Scunthorpe United Jan 1977; Grimsby Town Sep. 1979 (£60,000); Rotherham United Aug. 1983; KFC Geel (Belgium) cs

1985; CITY Jan 1986 to May 1987; Gainsborough Trinity Aug. to Nov. 1987; Crowle United cs 1988; Grimsby Charltons Mar. 1989; Shepshed Charterhouse Aug. 1989. Later signed for Brigg Town reserves towards the end of the 1990/91 season and has since appeared in Scunthorpe Sunday League football.

Honours: England youth international (1978)
(Grimsby Town) FL Div.3 champions 1980

Skilful striker signed by manager George Kerr for whom he had also played at Grimsby and Rotherham. Left the Imps when they were relegated out of the League and has since been employed as a licensee, firstly in Grimsby and more recently in Scunthorpe. A career aggregate of 285 FL appearances plus 49 as substitute, 81 goals.

KIRK, James J.
(1909-1911)
Right-back: 5 app.
1909; 5-10½, 11-7
Born: c.1882
Career: Southwell St. Marys (Notts County, amat. from Nov. 1902); Newark Town cs 1903; CITY Aug. 1909; Worksop Town cs 1911.

Recruit from the Notts non-League scene who was reserve for Clem Jackson in his two seasons at Sincil Bank. He had earlier made one League appearance for Notts County back in Feb. 1903.

KIRKLAND, William
(1938)
Centre-half: 3 app.
1938; 5-11, 11-0
Born: c.1915
Career: Stonehouse Violet c.1931; Third Lanark 1936; CITY June to Sep. 1938.

One of a number of Scots signed by manager Joe McClelland in the late 1930's. He appeared in the first three matches of the season but was dropped after a poor performance against Chester and shortly afterwards returned to Scotland.

KIRTON, John William
(1896-1897)
Outside-left: 27 app., 5 goals
1986; 5-8, 10-4
Born: Pinxton, Derbys., 2 Nov. 1873
Died: 27 Sep. 1970
Career: Staffordshire junior football; Glossop North End; Oldham County; CITY May 1896; Small Heath cs 1897; Swindon Town May 1898; Sunderland May 1899; Swindon Town cs 1900; Millwall Athletic May 1901 to 1902.

A 'thickset' youngster who was known *"both for speed and the command he has over the ball, two qualities that do not usually go together"*, as a contemporary noted. Appeared for Lincoln in perhaps their worst ever season but missed only three games and finished joint leading scorer.

KITCHING, Harry
(1928-1931)

Inside-/centre-forward: 58 app., 28 goals
1929: 5-9, 11-7
Born: Grimsby 1905
Career: Municipal College (Grimsby); Grimsby Town (amat.) Aug. 1923 (Leeds University when a student there); Boston Town Aug. 1926; Worksop Town 1927; CITY May 1928; Tranmere Rovers Aug. 1931; New Brighton Aug. 1932 to 1936.

Kitching was leading scorer for the reserves in 1928/29 and when given his chance in the first team following the sale of Dinsdale to Bradford he responded by scoring in nine consecutive matches, finishing the season with a remarkable 15 goals from 17 League outings. A critic noted of him: *"... a very brainy type of forward, most artistic in his methods, and a good shot"*. A schoolmaster by profession he was appointed headmaster of Heswall Council School, Birkenhead in Apr. 1946.

KNIGHTON, Thomas
(1919)

Forward: 2 app.
Career: Glossop Sep. 1914 (amat.); Manchester United cs 1915 (guested for Watford, Tottenham Hotspur and Grimsby Town during the Great War); CITY Sep. to Oct. 1919.

Tom made his FL debut for Glossop at Sincil Bank but made only one further appearance for the Derbyshire club. He enlisted in the Officer Training Corps during the Great War and was initially based at Berkhamsted, Herts before being posted as a lieutenant to the South Humber Garrison. He joined City on amateur forms but did not perform particularly well and was soon released.

KOERNER, Frederick Albert
(1898-1900)

Full-back: 3 app., 1 goal
Born: Eccleshall, nr. Sheffield
Career: Army football; CITY Oct. 1898 to 1900.

A private in the Army who appeared occasionally for the Imps when based at the Lincoln Barracks. In the summer of 1900 he was reported to be fighting with the 1st Yorkshire & Lancashire Regiment in the Boer War.

KRZYWICKI, Ryzard Lech ("Dick")
(1974-1976)

Outside-right: 55 app. + 13 sub, 11 goals
1975: 5-10, 11-0
Born: Penley, Flintshire, 2 Feb. 1947
Career: Leek Youth Club; West Bromwich Albion (appr.), (prof.) Feb. 1965; Huddersfield Town Mar. 1970 (£45,000); (Scunthorpe United on loan Feb. 1973; Northampton Town on loan Nov. 1973 to Jan. 1974); CITY July 1974; retired Nov. 1976.

Honours: Wales international (8 app.)
Wales Under-23 international (3 app.)

(West Brom) FL Cup finalist 1970 (sub)
(City) FL Div.4 champions 1976

Exceptionally fast, tricky winger who was one of the best in the lower divisions when fit. His career was badly affected by injuries and he was eventually forced to retire with hamstring trouble. Later returned to live in Yorkshire and was employed in a Batley engineering works and then as a group manager with the Football in the Community scheme. Born in Wales of Polish parents.

KURILA, John
(1971-1972)

Midfield: 23 app. + 1 sub
1972: 6-0, 12-12
Born: Glasgow, 10 Apr. 1941
Career: Blantyre Celtic; Celtic 1959; Hamilton Steelers (Canada) in the summer of 1962; Northampton Town Aug. 1962; Hamilton Steelers summer 1963; Bristol City Aug. 1963; Northampton Town Nov. 1963 (£5,000); Southend United July 1968; Colchester United May 1970; CITY Dec. 1971; Dover Aug. 1972; Atherstone Town.

Honour: (Northampton) FL Div.3 champions 1963

Strong, hard tackling midfield player who impressed in his brief spell with the club which ended when the Imps just missed out on promotion to the Third Division. Came to Sincil Bank at the very end of his career in which he totalled 315 FL matches (plus 4 as sub), scoring 9 goals.

LAMMING, Walter George
(1919-1920, 1921-1922)

Winger: 6 app.
Born: Lincoln, 2 Sep. 1896
Died: 2 Jan. 1962
Career: Boston Town Sep. 1914 to early 1915; Army football; Rustons Staff cs 1917; CITY from early 1918, (prof.) cs 1919; Merthyr Town Oct. 1920; CITY Sep. 1921; Robeys (Lincoln) Aug. 1922.

Local lad who appeared regularly on City's left wing in the 1918/19 season. Made his FL debut at outside-right in the opening match of the first season of peacetime football, but was soon dropped and next played for the Imps' League team in Nov. 1921. Later prominent in local club cricket and a bowls player of near county standard. Uncle of the football writer and historian Doug Lamming.

LANCASTER, Raymond
(1967-1968)

Wing-half: 24 app.
1967: 5-11½, 11-5
Born: Rotherham, 17 Aug. 1941
Career: Rotherham United Nv. 1958; Grimsby Town Dec. 1964 (£5,000); CITY Jan. 1967; Boston United July 1968; Skegness Town May 1969; Boston FC in season 1974/75; Louth United cs 1975; Immingham Town in season 1976/77.

Wing-half who was one of Ron Gray's early signings as he attempted to rebuild the City team who were then lying near the foot of the Division Four table. Ray made only five appearances in his second campaign and was released on a free transfer in the summer of 1968.

LANGHAM, William
(1907-1910)

Forward: 58 app., 21 goals
1900: 5-10, 10-7
Born: Nottingham, 1876
Career: Stapleford; Hucknall Portland c.1894; South Shore (Blackpool) later in 1894/95 season; Notts County cs 1896; Bristol City cs 1898; Leicester Fosse Nov. 1900; Doncaster Rovers cs 1901; Gainsborough Trinity cs 1903; Doncaster Rovers cs 1906; CITY Mar. 1907 (£75) to 1910. Appointed Lincoln coach in Jan. 1920 and trainer/groundsman cs 1920.

Honour: (Notts County) FL Div.2 champions 1897

Regarded mainly as a wingman in his earlier career, Billy also appeared regularly at centre-forward for the Imps. He was particularly successful in the 1908/09 campaign when he scored 30 goals in 26 Midland and United League matches before an injury put him out of action. *"Has a fine turn of speed and is a rare goal-getter"*, was one contemporary's opinion of him. Later worked as a licensee in Gainsborough.

LARKIN, Bernard Patrick ("Bunny")
(1964-1966)

Wing-half/inside-forward: 25 app. + 2 sub, 3 goals
1965: 5-8½, 11-5
Born: Birmingham, 11 Jan. 1936
Career: Lea Hall Youth Club (Birmingham); Rockwood Albion; Birmingham City (amat.) 1952, (prof.) July 1954; Norwich City Mar. 1960 (£10,000); Doncaster Rovers Oct. 1961 (£6,000); Watford May 1962 (£4,000); CITY Nov. 1964; Wisbech Town Aug. 1966; Nuneaton Borough cs 1968; Kings Lynn May 1969; Stevenage Athletic cs 1970. Coach of Attleborough FC (Norfolk) 1975-77.

Versatile player who appeared in five different positions for the Imps without ever having a lengthy run in the first team. Recovered from a broken leg at 17 to enjoy a solid career, totalling 219 appearances and 2 substitutions, 53 goals. After leaving the game worked as a salesman in the Norwich area.

LATCHFORD, Robert Dennis
(1985-1986)

Centre-forward: 14 app. + 1 sub, 2 goals
1985: 6-1, 12-8
Born: Kings Heath, Birmingham, 18 Jan. 1951
Career: Birmingham City (appr.) May 1967, (prof.) Aug. 1968; Everton Feb. 1974 (a fee and two players, total estimated value £350,000); Brisbane Lions (Australia) summer 1981; Swansea City July 1981; NAC Breda (Holland) Feb. 1984; Coventry City June 1984; CITY July 1985; Newport County on loan Jan. 1986, permanent Apr. 1986; Hamrun Spartans (Malta) in late 1986; Merthyr Tydfil Nov. 1986.

Honours: England international (12 app.)
England Under-23 international (6 app.)
England Youth international (1969)
Football League (1 app. vs Scotland League, 1974)
(Everton) FL Cup winner 1977
(Swansea City) Welsh Cup winner 1982, 1983
(Merthyr Tydfil) Welsh Cup winner 1987

Bustling striker who joined City on a free transfer at the end of a career in which he had made over 400 appearances in top class football and won international honours. Bob was injured on his debut for the Imps and never really impressed after that, eventually moving on to Newport (he still lived in south Wales while on Lincoln's books). His brothers David and Peter also appeared in League football, both as goalkeepers.

LAVERICK, Charles
(1904-1907)

Right-back: 66 app.
1904: 5-10½, 12-0
Born: 1881

Career: Newcastle junior football; Doncaster Rovers cs 1902; CITY May 1904 to 1907.

An ever-present in his first season, but he eventually lost his place to Dick Hood. *"Played a strong, fearless and vigorous game"*, noted a commentator of the time. Also occasionally appeared at left-back for the Imps.

LAW, John
(1907-1908)

Outside-left: 19 app.
1907: 5-10, 11-0
Born: c.1887
Career: Maxwelltown Volunteers; Rangers; CITY May 1907; Gainsborough Trinity May 1908; Carlisle United May 1909.

"A speedy youth", noted Athletic News of this player who appeared regularly for the Imps in the first half of the 1907/08 season. At the end of the campaign Lincoln were voted out of the League and Law moved on to Gainsborough, then a member of the Second Division, where he played a further nine matches.

LAWRENCE, George Harold
(1925-1926)

Goalkeeper: 5 app.
1923: 6-1, 13-0
Born: Ilkeston, Derbys., 10 Mar. 1889
Died: 3 Mar. 1959
Career: Ilkeston Primitives; Ilkeston United cs 1909; Derby County May 1910; Bristol City Sep. 1924 (£100); CITY Aug. 1925; Ilkeston Town Nov. 1926.

Honour: (Derby County) FL Div.2 champions 1915

Veteran goalkeeper who arrived at Sincil Bank in his late 30's having spent much of his earlier career in the Derby reserve side (137 FL outings in 10 seasons of peacetime football). A reserve at Lincoln too, deputising for first choice 'keeper Sissons when required.

LAWTON, Norbert ("Nobby")
(1971)

Wing-half: 20 app.
1971: 5-9, 11-7
Born: Manchester, 25 Mar 1940
Career: Manchester United (amat.) in 1956/57 season, (prof.) Apr. 1958; Preston North End Mar. 1963 (£14,000); Brighton & Hove Albion Sep. 1967 (£8,000); CITY Feb. 1971; retired on medical advice Dec. 1971.

Honour: (Preston) FA Cup finalist 1964

Experienced half-back whose career began as a 'Busby Babe' at Old Trafford in the late 1950's. Captained Preston in the 1964 FA Cup final when they lost to West Ham. Nobby came to Lincoln on a free transfer at the same time as Alan Gilliver, but was forced to retire due to injuries after only a brief spell with the

club. Received a testimonial match in Mar. 1972. Served on the Executive Committee of the P.F.A. from the mid-1960's .

LAX, Walter
(1929-1931)

Outside-left: 45 app., 18 goals
1930: 5-8½, 10-4
Born: Gainsborough, 22 Mar. 1912
Career: Albion Works (Gainsborough League); CITY Aug. 1929; Blackpool July 1931; Coventry City Aug. 1933; York City Nov. 1933; Scunthorpe United Aug. 1934; Lysaghts Sports (North Lindsey League) cs 1935.

One of the best local discoveries of the 1920's. *"... is skilful and excellently judges his passes"*, was one contemporary's view while another noted he was *"very cool for one so young, and a deadly shot within range of goal"*. Lax suffered a broken leg playing for Blackpool reserves in Oct. 1932 and never reached his full potential, quickly dropping down to local football by his mid-20's.

LAYBOURNE, Keith E.
(1977-1979)

Full-back: 18 app., 1 goal
1978: 5-10, 10-11
Born: Sunderland, 27 Jan. 1959
Career: Lambton Street Boys Club (Sunderland); CITY July 1977; Runcorn Sep. 1979; Scarborough 1980.

Young full-back who was one of four players signed from a Sunderland junior team in July 1977 who all made City's League side in their first season of professional football. Played fairly regularly in 1978/79 when the Imps were relegated from the Third Division but then fell out of favour. Moved to Runcorn on a free transfer where he linked up with former Lincoln player Jim McCalliog.

LEACH, Thomas ("Tony")
(1938-1939)

Centre-half: 25 app., 2 goals
1938: 5-11, 11-0
Born: Wincobank, Sheffield, 23 Sep. 1903
Died: 1970
Career: Wath Athletic (trial with Liverpool); Sheffield Wednesday Oct. 1925; Newcastle United June 1934 (£1,100); Stockport County July 1936 (£300); Carlisle United Feb. 1937; CITY Sep. 1938; retired cs 1939.

Honours: England international (2 app. vs Wales, N. Ireland, 1930)
Football League (1 app. vs Scottish League, 1930)
(Sheffield Wednesday) FL champions 1929, 1930
(Stockport County) FL Div.3 (North) champions 1937

Considered a find defensive player and expert header of the ball in his days with Wednesday where he made over 200 FL appearances and won international honours. Involved in a minor scandal towards the end of his career, receiving a four week suspension and £20 fine for accepting 'incentives' from a Stockport director during the run-in to the 1936/37 season (Stockport had wanted Carlisle to beat Lincoln to boost their own chances of promotion). Ironically Leach was on City's books at the time the case was heard and the club was forced to seek a delay to the suspension to enable him to appear in the FA Cup tie at Portsmouth.

LEANING, Andrew J.
(1994-)
Goalkeeper: 8 app.
1993: 6-0, 13-0
Born: Howden, Yorkshire, 18 May 1963
Career: Rowntree Mackintosh; York City June 1985; Sheffield United May 1987; Bristol City on loan Sep. 1988, permanent Nov. 1988 (£12,000); CITY Mar. 1994.

Experienced 'keeper recruited close to the transfer deadline by manager Keigh Alexander. Had spent long periods in the reserves at Ashton Gate but went straight in City's first team and appeared in all but one of the season's remaining fixtures.

LEE, Jason Benedict
(1991-1993)
Centre-forward: 86 app. + 7 sub, 21 goals
1991: 6-3, 13-8
Born: Forest Gate, London, 9 May 1971
Career: Charlton Athletic YTS Oct. 1987, (prof.) June 1989 (Fisher Athletic on loan Aug. 1989; Stockport County on loan Feb. 1991); CITY Mar. 1991 (£35,000); Southend United on loan Aug. 1993, permanent Sep. 1993 (£150,000); Nottingham Forest Mar. 1994 (£200,000).

Tall, lean striker who appeared raw and inexperienced when first signed. Developed into a hustling forward, capable of laying the ball off to perfection, a style that soon attracted the scouts from bigger clubs and earned him a big money transfer to Second Division Southend.

LEES, Joseph W.D.
(1921-1922)
Inside-forward: 33 app., 9 goals
1921: 5-7½, 11-7
Born: Coalville, Leics., 1892
Died: 26 July 1933
Career: Coalville PSA; Whitwick Imperial cs 1911; Barnsley Aug. 1913; Rotherham County June 1919; CITY June 1921 to cs 1922; Guildford United Aug. 1923; Halifax Town Apr. 1924; Scunthorpe United (trial) Nov. 1924; Newport County (trial) Oct. 1925; Wombwell Nov. 1925.

"... a young player of small physique but clever feet from Whitwick who attracted a great deal of attention", said the Athletic News in 1913 when reviewing Barnsley's prospects. Lees put in a couple of good seasons with Rotherham County (51 matches, 17 goals) before his 1921/22 stint as City's regular inside-left. Awarded the Military Medal in the Great War.

LEES, William ("Donald")
(1893-1895)
Centre-forward: 52 app., 24 goals
Career: Celtic in early 1890's; CITY Sep. 1893; Celtic June 1894; CITY Oct. 1894 to cs 1895; Barnsley St. Peters May 1895; Darwen in 1896/97; Barnsley Aug. 1898; Watford May 1904 to Feb. 1905; Barnsley later in 1904/05 season; Denaby United.

Considered to be one of the club's best players of the 1890's and, as a critic noted, *"an exceptionally good shot at goal"*. Lees received £5 when re-signing for the Imps in the summer of 1894 but then also signed forms for Celtic. Lincoln complained to the Football League who placed the Glasgow club on their "boycott list", prompting a dispute with the Scottish FA which was only resolved when Lees returned to play for City. Appeared mostly as a centre-half in later career.

LEIGH, Dennis
(1973-1979)

Full-back: 201 app. + 5 sub, 3 goals
1976: 5-8½, 10-11
Born: Barnsley, 26 Feb. 1949
Career: Doncaster Rovers (appr.), (prof.) Mar. 1967; Rotherham United Feb. 1968 (a deal in which Leigh, Graham Watson, also later of City, and about £8,000 were exchanged for three Rotherham players); CITY Feb. 1973 (£4,000); Boston United Aug. 1979 to June 1983.

Honours: (City) FL Div.4 champions 1976

Made almost 200 League appearances for Doncaster and Rotherham before becoming Graham Taylor's first signing as manager for the Imps. Leigh was a two-footed player who remained a first choice in City's defence apart from injuries or suspensions for the next six seasons. Later employed as an advertising manager by the Lincolnshire Echo.

LEMONS, Charlie
(1921-1922)

Inside-forward: 22 app., 4 goals
1921: 5-11, 11-7
Born: Sheffield, 3 Dec. 1887
Died: 1952
Career: Beighton Recreation (Sheffield); Scunthorpe United cs 1920; CITY May 1921; York City cs 1922; Gainsborough Trinity July 1923.

Charlie was given an extended run in City's first team after Chambers was sold to Burnley in Mar. 1922, but was considered too slow for the Northern Section and he soon returned to Midland League football. Highly popular at Scunthorpe where he had been one of the team's stars.

LESTER, Abraham Bennett
(1947-1949)

Centre-forward: 37 app., 10 goals
1948: 6-0, 11-0
Born: Sheffield: 10 Feb. 1920
Career: Newhall Colliery; Army football; Selby Town cs 1946; Hull City Sep. 1946; CITY Dec. 1947; Ransomes & Marles Aug. 1949; Stockport County Aug. 1949 to 1951.

Honour: (City) FL Div.3 (North) champions 1948

Snapped up by Hull City after netting eight goals in four matches for Selby Town, he maintained an excellent scoring rate at Boothferry Park: 18 goals in 27 FL appearances. Not as prolific at Lincoln but demonstrated an ability to keep the line moving and was regarded as a fine header of the ball.

LEWIS, F(rederick) Jack
(1967-1970)

Forward: 47 app. + 15 sub, 9 goals
1970: 5-9, 10-9
Born: Long Eaton, Derbys., 22 Mar. 1948
Career: Long Eaton Albion; Long Eaton United Nov. 1966; CITY Mar. 1967; Grimsby Town Jan. 1970 (£3,000); Blackburn Rovers Aug. 1977; Doncaster Rovers Aug. 1978; Scarborough 1980.

Honours: Wales Under-23 international (1 app. vs Scotland 1976)
(Grimsby Town) FL Div.4 champions 1972

Versatile forward who made his debut as a teenager but always remained on the fringe of the first team despite some good performances. Moved on to Blundell Park where he made over 200 FL appearances, scoring 74 goals and winning Welsh Under-23 honours as an 'over-age' player.

LINCOLN, Andrew
(1931-1932)

Inside-forward: 3 app., 2 goals
1930: 6-1, 12-7
Born: Seaham Harbour, Co. Durham, 17 May 1902
Died: 1977

Career: Speedwell; Glen Rose; Halifax Town Aug. 1921; Boldon Villa cs 1922; Peterborough & Fletton United cs 1923; Millwall Athletic June 1924; Northampton Town June 1928; Stockport County July 1929; CITY June 1931; Gateshead Aug. 1932; Workington 1933.

Andrew scored twice on his City debut in a 6-0 win over Hartlepools but was mainly a reserve at Sincil Bank, as he had been at all his clubs except Stockport (81 matches, 40 goals). He had earlier won Southern League championship medals with Peterborough (1923/24) and Millwall reserves (1925/26).

LINFOOT, Frederick
(1919-1920)

Outside-right: 29 app., 3 goals
1920: 5-11, 11-1
Born: Whitley Bay, Northumberland, 1901
Career: Smith's Dock (Newcastle); Leeds City Mar. 1919; CITY Oct. 1919 (£250); Chelsea July 1920; Fulham Mar. 1924 to 1926.

Signed along with Ashurst and Chipperfield from the Leeds City players auction, and soon established himself as a regular first-teamer. Snapped up by David Calderhead senior's Chelsea when the Imps were voted out of the League but played only 34 FL games in almost four seasons at Stamford Bridge before moving on to Fulham.

LINNECOR, Albert R.
(1957-1964)

Left-half/inside-left: 264 app., 52 goals
1960: 5-8, 10-6
Born Nechells, Birmingham, 30 Nov. 1933
Career: Brookhill Juniors; Birmingham City (amat.) Feb. 1950, (prof.) May 1952; CITY Apr. 1957 (part exchange for Dick Neal); Boston FC Aug. 1964; Grantham July 1967; Worksop Town June 1969; Bourne Town Jan. 1970 to cs 1973 as player-coach; coach of CITY's junior team cs 1973; Ruston Sports (Lincoln) manager cs 1974.

Quickly established himself in City's first team and gave the club seven years fine service. A regular goalscorer who had the distinction of hitting a hat-trick against Liverpool at Anfield in Apr. 1960. Later appeared for several Midland League clubs and was still turning out for Gatehouse in the Lincoln Sunday League in the mid-1970's when over 40 years old.

LISHMAN, William Joseph
(1921-1922)
Right-half: 4 app.
1921: 5-8½, 10-11
Born: Newcastle-upon-Tyne, 28 Apr. 1899
Career: Hebburn Argyle; Close Works (Gateshead); CITY May 1921; Gateshead Town cs 1922; Leadgate Park later in 1922/23.

"A resourceful tackler, with speed on his side", was a contemporary verdict on Lishman who arrived at Sincil Bank with experience of Northern Alliance and North-Eastern League soccer. Mainly a reserve with Lincoln, deputising for Jack Bryan when needed.

LITTLEDYKE, Robert
(1935-1936)
Centre-foward: 9 app.
1936: 5-8½, 11-6
Born: Chester-le-Street, Co. Durham, 5 July 1913
Career: Durham City; CITY Nov. 1935; Mansfield Town June 1936; Grantham May 1937.

Reserve centre-forward who received few opportunities at first team level and followed manager Harry Parkes to Mansfield at the end of the season. Made a further nine Northern Section appearances at Field Mill, scoring once.

LITTLER, J(oseph) Eric
(1954-1955)
Centre-forward: 6 app., 2 goals
1954: 5-11, 11-0
Born: St. Helens, 14 Apr. 1929
Career: Stubshaw Cross (Wigan); Leicester City May 1951; CITY Dec. 1954 (part exchange for Andy Graver); Wrexham June 1955 (part exchange for Tommy Bannan); Crewe Alexandra Dec. 1955; Chorley Aug. 1956.

Littler had a brief run in the first team after signing but soon lost his place to Bob Gibson. Saw more League action when stepping down to the Northern Section but finished with a total of only 33 appearances, 7 goals.

LIVINGSTONE, James
(1922-1923)
Outside-left: 2 app.
1922: 5-7, 11-0
Born: Wallsend, 1898
Career: Walker Celtic; CITY May 1922 to Feb. 1923.

Livingstone was one of a group of players recruited from north-eastern junior football in the summer of 1922, several of whom departed in Feb. 1923 when given the choice of a free transfer or a cut in wages. On signing it was said *"... he has credentials as a resourceful tackler and strong kicker"*.

LLOYD, Raymond
(1950-1951)
See entry under BELL, Raymond Lloyd.

LONG, H(erbert) Raymond
(1958-1960)
Centre-half: 1 app.
1959: 6-0, 12-3
Born: Stickney, Lincs., 4 Oct. 1936
Career: Spilsby (Lincs.); CITY (amat.) Feb. 1952; Louth United; CITY (prof.) Dec. 1958; Louth United cs 1960; Boston United June 1962; Skegness Town June 1963; Boston FC Aug. 1966.

Centre-half who combined a career in football firstly with his studies at Loughborough College and later with a teaching post at Stickney, near Boston. His solitary League appearance came in the Second Division match at Leyton Orient in Sep. 1959.

LORD, Walter
(1956-1958)
Inside-right: 1 app.
1957: 5-9½, 10-3
Born: Grimsby, 1 Nov. 1933
Career: Grimsby Town Aug. 1951; CITY May 1956; Alford United (Lincs. League) cs 1958; later appeared for Spalding United and Brigg Town from cs 1962.

Forward recruited on a free transfer from Blundell Park who made his only appearance for the Imps against Liverpool at Anfield in Nov. 1956. Grimsby were earlier said to be asking a £3,000 fee for his signature.

LORMOR, Anthony
(1990-1994)

Forward: 90 app. + 10 sub, 30 goals
1990; 6-1, 12-3
Born: Ashington, Northumberland, 29 Oct. 1970
Career: Newcastle United YTS, permanent Feb. 1988, (Norwich City on loan Nov. 1988); CITY Jan. 1990 (£25,000) to cs 1994, (Halifax Town on loan Feb. to cs 1994); Peterborough United cs 1994.

Impressed for City after stepping down from the top flight, finishing leading scorer in his first three seasons with the club. He then suffered a severe knee injury which forced him to miss the whole of the 1992/93 campaign. Never really recovered his old form and was released on a free transfer at the end of the 1993/94 season.

LOUGHLAN, Anthony John
(1993-1994)

Midfield: 4 app. + 8 sub, 2 goals
1992; 6-0, 12-3
Born: Croydon, Surrey, 19 Jan. 1970
Career: Leicester City (appr.); Leicester United; Nottingham Forest Aug. 1989; Kettering Town cs 1993; CITY on non-contract basis Oct. 1993 to cs 1994.

Midfield man who scored in the first minute of his FL debut for Forest at Wimbledon in Mar. 1991. Made only one more first team appearance at the City Ground and was released after recovering from a long spell on the injury list. Proved useful for the Imps as a substitute but was unable to establish himself in the first team and was given a free transfer in the summer of 1994.

LOWERY, Jeremiah
(1952-1954)

Goalkeeper: 51 app.
1957; 5-9½, 11-10
Born: Newcastle-upon-Tyne, 19 Oct. 1924
Career: Leicester City (amat.) when 14 years old; Parsons Athletic (Newcastle); Newcastle United June 1947; CITY Feb. 1952 (£750); Peterborough United July 1954; Barrow June 1956; Crewe Alexandra June 1958; Wisbech Town 1959.

Jerry made seven appearances for City as a wartime guest but was then signed by his home town club where he had just six FL outings in almost five seasons. Shared the goalkeeper's position at Sincil Bank with Jimmy Jones. He aggregated 147 League appearances with his four clubs (Peterborough were then members of the Midland League). Later became an attendant at a Cheshire Home in East Anglia.

LOXLEY, Anthony D.
(1976-1980)

Centre-half: 1 app.
1979; 6-2½; 12-6
Born: Nottingham, 14 Dec. 1959

Career: CITY (appr.) July 1976, (prof.) Dec. 1977; Sydney Olympic (Australia) June 1980; Melita Eagles (Australia) Nov. 1981; Boston FC Oct. 1982; Skegness Town Jan. 1983; later appeared for Alfreton Town and Lincoln United.

Tall central defender whose sole League appearance for the Imps came in the 6-0 defeat at Swindon on 3 Mar 1979. Has latterly worked as a sports organiser for Lincoln City Council. Son of Bert (see below).

LOXLEY, Herbert
(1966-1967)

Centre-half: 7 app.
1963; 6-1, 12-10
Born: Bonsall, Derbys., 3 Feb. 1934
Career: Bonsall FC; Notts County Mar. 1952; Mansfield Town July 1964; Lockhead Leamington Sep. 1965; CITY as trainer/coach July 1966, appointed team manager May 1970 to Mar. 1971 before reverting to trainer/coach a post he held until cs 1987.

Bert came to Sincil Bank as a member of the training staff but was forced to resume his playing career because of an injury crisis. His FL career was ended for a second time when he dislocated an elbow in Nov. 1966, although he recovered fitness later in the season and made a few more appearnaces for the reserves. He had earlier played 245 matches for Notts County in a 12 year period at Meadow Lane. Left City's backroom staff when the club were relegated out of the League after which he set up his own business as a sports physiotherapist. Father of Tony.

LUDKIN, Daniel
(1922-1924)

Centre-half: 14 app., 1 goal
1923; 5-10½, 11-9
Born: Ryton, Co. Durham, 1 May 1894
Died: Jan. 1945
Career: Close Works (Gateshead); CITY June 1922 to cs 1924 when he was appointed reserve team trainer, became assistant trainer under Ted Wynter in 1927 and then shared the post with Wynter for a couple of years to cs 1933.

One of several players from north-eastern junior clubs who were signed in the summer of 1922. Ludkin was given a lengthy run in City's first team after Bob Fenwick was sold to Notts County in Feb. 1923. Summed up at the time as, *"robust and watchful; the sentinel of the defence"*. A former miner, he remained in Lincoln after his playing career was over and spent several years on the club's backroom staff.

LUND, Gary J.
(1986-1987)

Forward: 41 app. + 3 sub, 13 goals
1986; 5-11, 11-0
Born: Grimsby, 13 Sep. 1964
Career: Grimsby Town (appr.), (prof.) July 1983; CITY Aug. 1986 (exchange for Phil Turner); Notts County June 1987 (£27,000), (Hull City on loan Aug. 1993 and again Jan. 1994).

Skilful striker who was one of the few successes of the 1986/87 campaign which ended with the club relegated to the Vauxhall Conference. Gary was the Imps leading scorer and moved on to Second Division Notts County where he has since completed seven seasons with the Magpies and made over 150 FL appearances.

LYNES, James
(1896-1897)

Outside-right: 19 app., 4 goals
Born: Cheltenham, 1869
Career: Leicester Fosse; CITY May 1896; Halifax cs 1897.

A regular on the right-wing during one of the club's worst ever seasons. Jimmy attracted favourable comments from contemporaries: *"He knows no fear and will tackle the strongest defence without regard to his own safety"*. Signed by Halifax as a goalkeeper. Also a capable cricketer serving the Lindum CC as professional in the 1896 season.

McALEER, Joseph
(1934-1935)

Outside-left: 6 app., 5 goals
Born: c.1911
Career: Bridgetown Waverley; Rochdale July 1931; Glenavon July 1933; Northampton Town later in 1933; CITY July 1934; Clapton Orient July 1935; Gillingham Aug. 1936; Wrexham cs 1937 to 1938.

Reserve winger who was given a few first team outings after Jackie Wilkinson was sold to Sunderland. Hit a hat-trick in the 6-0 home win over Barrow on Good Friday 1935, but was released at the end of the season.

McCAIRNS, Thomas
(1899-1901)

Centre-forward: 35 app., 14 goals
1897: 5-9, 11-10
Born: Dinsdale, nr. Darlington, 22 Dec. 1873
Died: 1932
Career: Middlesbrough Ironopolis; Whitby 1891; Grimsby Town Sep. 1893; Bristol Rovers cs 1898; Notts County May 1899; CITY Nov. 1899 to Sep. 1900 and again Jan. to cs 1901; Barnsley Aug. 1901; Wellingborough May 1902; Queens Park Rangers cs 1903; Brighton & Hove Albion Dec. 1903; Kettering cs 1904.

Honour: Football League (1 app. vs Irish League 1896)

Experienced forward who had been at his peak when with Grimsby, scoring 104 goals in 154 FL and FA Cup matches including six against Leicester Fosse in Apr. 1896. Had his contract terminated by City shortly after the arrival of David Calderhead senior. as secretary-manager, but returned four months later and completed the 1900/01 season at Sincil Bank before moving on. Praised by contemporaries as, *"a crack centre ... an expert in dribbling and shooting"*, and, *"... wonderfully fast considering his weight"* (his recorded weight in 1902 was 13 stone).

McCALLIOG, James
(1978-1979)

Midfield: 9 app.
1979: 5-9, 10-5
Born: Glasgow, 23 Sep. 1946
Career: Leeds United (amat.); Chelsea Sep. 1963; Sheffield Wednesday Oct. 1965 (£37,500); Wolverhampton Wanderers July 1969 (£70,000); Manchester United Mar. 1974 (£60,000); Southampton Feb. 1975 (£40,000); Southampton Feb. 1975 (£40,000); Chicago Sting (USA) Apr. 1977; Lynn Oslo (Norway) early 1978 as player-coach; CITY Sep. 1978 as player-coach to Mar. 1979; Runcorn July 1979 as player-manager to 1980. Later coached Halifax Town's junior players before serving as manager Apr. 1990 to Oct. 1991; Leyton Orient scout 1992.

Honours: Scotland international (5 app.)
Scotland Under-23 international (2 app.)
Scotland youth international
Scotland schools international
(Sheffield Wednesday) FA Cup finalist 1966
(Wolves) UEFA Cup finalist 1972
(Manchester United) FL Div.2 champions 1975
(Southampton) FA Cup winner 1976

McCalliog came to Sincil Bank at the end of a very distinguished career and took over as caretaker-manager following Willie Bell's sudden departure in Oct. 1978. Did not appear in City's first team after Colin Murphy was appointed manager and was released the following spring. Became a licensee when his playing career finished.

McCANN, Henry
(1908-1909)

Inside-left: 17 app, 6 goals
Careers: Edinburgh junior football; CITY Jan. 1908 to cs 1909.

Signed during an injury crisis. McCann went straight into City's first team and remained a regular over the next season and a half. Made 25 appearances scoring 6 goals in the Imps' Midland League championship side of 1908/09.

McCARRICK, Mark Bernard
(1984-1986)
Full-back: 42 app. + 2 sub
1985: 5-8, 10-8
Born: Liverpool, 4 Feb. 1962
Career: West Bromwich Albion (appr.); Witton Albion 1982; Birmingham City May 1983; CITY July 1984; Crewe Alexandra Feb. 1986; Kuopion Pallotoverit (Finland) Apr. 1986; Runcorn Sep. 1986; Tranmere Rovers Aug. 1987; Altrincham Mar. 1991; Northwich Victoria Aug. to Sep. 1991. Later at Marine; Winsford United Oct. 1993.

Free transfer signing who appeared regularly in the first team to start with but lost his place after the 7-0 defeat at Derby in Nov. 1985 and was released shortly afterwards. His best senior spell was at Tranmere where he made 125 FL appearances, scoring 14 goals.

McCLAREN, Stephen
(1987)
Midfield: 8 app.
1987: 5-7, 9-8
Born: Fulford, York, 3 May 1961
Career: Hull City (appr.) cs 1977, (prof.) Apr. 1979; Derby County July 1985 (£70,000), (CITY on loan Feb. 1987); Bristol City Feb. 1988 (£50,000); Oxford United Aug. 1989 (in exchange for another player).

Light-weight midfield man who impressed with his skill during a brief period at Sincil Bank. Returned to the Baseball Ground when his loan period was over.

McCLELLAND, John B.
(1958-1961)
Outside-right: 121 app., 32 goals
1960: 5-8, 10-10
Born: Bradford, 5 Mar. 1935
Career: Manchester YMCA; Manchester City Sep. 1953; CITY Sep. 1958 (part exchange for George Hannah); Queens Park Rangers Sep. 1961 (£14,000); Portsmouth May 1963 (£10,000); Newport County July 1968; retired May 1969.

Fast, skilful winger always a first choice at Sincil Bank. Provided a good supply of goals too - finishing leading scorer in the 1959/60 season with 18. A career record of 370 FL matches plus 1 sub, 104 goals.

McCLELLAND, John T. ("Jack")
(1968-1969)
Goalkeeper: 12 app.
1968: 5-11½, 12-7
Born: Lurgan, Co. Armagh, 19 May 1940
Died: 15 Mar. 1976
Career: Glenavon; Arsenal Oct. 1960 (£7,000); Fulham Dec. 1964 (CITY on loan Dec. 1968 to Mar 1969); Barnet May 1969 to May 1975.

Honours: Northern Ireland international (6 app.)
Northern Ireland amateur international (1 app.)
Irish League (2 app. vs Scottish League, Football League 1960)

Spent three months on loan at Lincoln covering for the injured John Kennedy. A solid reliable 'keeper who won representative honours at an early age and had seen a good deal of top flight service at both Highbury and Craven Cottage. His untimely death was caused by cancer.

McCONVILLE, Patrick ("Paddy")
(1925-1932)
Full-back: 138 app.
1929: 5-9½, 12-0
Born: Gilford, Co. Down, c.1902
Career: Portadown Celtic; Glenavon; CITY Nov. 1925; Glenavon cs 1932.

Honour: (City) FL Div.3 (North) champions 1932

Extremely popular man: *"a doughty left-back, unquestionably amongst the finest in the Third Division, whether for dash or judgment as a tackler"*, noted a 1931 commentator. Lost his place through injury to Andy Yorke but fought back and eventually regained it towards the end of the 1929/30 season.

McCORMICK, James ("Boy")
(1947-1949)
Outside-right: 64 app., 6 goals
Born: Rotherham, 26 Apr. 1912
Died: 3 Jan. 1968
Career: Rotherham YMCA; Rotherham United (amat.) Sep. 1930, (prof.) Apr. 1931; Chesterfield Aug. 1932; Tottenham Hotspur Mar. 1933 (£1,500); Fulham Nov. 1945; CITY Aug. 1947; Crystal Palace Feb. 1949; Sliema Wanderers (Malta) player-coach June 1949; Turkish Football Federation coach May 1950; Wycombe Wanderers coach 1951 to 1952; Sheffield United asst. trainer/coach; York City manager May 1953 to Sep. 1954.

Honour: (City) FL Div.3 (North) champions 1948

Experienced forward who proved a valuable member of the 1948 championship side. An interesting feature was that the team were all part-time professionals - McCormick ran a sports outfitters shop near to Harringay Stadium at the time. He had earlier won a reputation as a goalscoring inside-forward in his Tottenham days (he made over 100 FL appearances at White Hart Lane). On leaving football worked as a licensee. Died in a road accident in Marbella whilst on holiday.

McCREADIE, Thomas S.
(1950-1951)
Inside-forward: 11 app., 1 goal
1950: 5-8, 12-0
Born: Port Glasgow, 28 Sep. 1923
Career: Clyde; Cowdenbeath; Hartlepools United Aug. 1949; CITY Aug. 1950; Grantham Sep. 1951; Spalding United Nov. 1951 to cs 1952; Lincoln Claytons cs 1954.

Scottish-born inside-forward who appeared regularly at the beginning of the 1950/51 season but then lost his place and was put on the open to offers list the following May.

McCUBBIN, Alexander C. ("Sandy")
(1911-1915)
Inside-right: 59 app., 15 goals
1912: 5-9, 11-6
Born: Greenock, 1888
Career: Volunteer Amateurs (Greenock); Greenock Morton c.1904; Huddersfield Town May 1910; CITY cs 1911 to cs 1915; Newland Athletic (Lincoln) 1916; Lincoln Corinthians 1919 to 1921.

Clever inside-forward: *"... knows all the tricks ... a tactician and an artist"*, as one admirer put it. Appeared in all but one of the 1911/12 Central League matches (31 app., 16 goals) and remained on the books at Sincil Bank for four seasons although injuries and loss of form prevented him from appearing in City's League team after March 1914. Emigrated to San Francisco in Sep. 1921.

McCULLOCH, Alexander
(1919-1920)
Inside-right: 13 app., 3 goals
1919: 5-8, 11-0
Born: Edinburgh
Career: Heart of Midlothian; CITY July 1919; Merthyr Town cs 1920.

Scottish forward who failed to establish himself as a first team player during his season at Sincil Bank. One of several Lincoln men who moved to South Wales in the summer of 1920 but had little success there either, making only a further three FL appearances. Appeared for Hearts against St. Mirren in the Scottish Victory Cup final of 1919.

McCULLOCH, Gordon
(1913-1914)
Inside-/centre-forward: 11 app.
1913: 6-0, 12-0
Born: Hinckley, Leics., c.1888
Career: Ilkeston United; Ripley 1910; Sutton Town; Notts County cs 1911; Sutton Town cs 1912; CITY May 1913; Bentley Colliery (Sheffield Association League) cs 1914.

Reserve forward who deputised in a number of positions during the 1913/14 campaign. He signed for Bentley Colliery the following summer but never actually appeared for them - he was an Army reservist and was called up on the outbreak of war. Reported to be servimg at 'the front' in Sep. 1914.

McDERMID, Robert
(1893)
Right-back: 2 app.
Born: c.1870

Career: Renton Thistle; Renton; Newcastle West End; Sunderland Albion; Accrington 1890; Burton Swifts 1891; Stockton 1892; CITY Mar. to cs 1893; Renton cs 1893; Dundee Wanderers; Newcastle United 1894; Hebburn Argyle; Warmley; South Shields 1899.

Experienced defender of whom it was said at Lincoln: " *He did not play so well as he was represented to be able to, but he gave a fair exhibition.*" Played in the final two matches of City's opening League campaign. His name also appeared as 'McDermott' in the contemporary press.

McDONALD, George
(1899-1900)
Inside-left: 2 app.
Career: Newcastle United; CITY Nov. 1899 to Jan 1900

Short-stay recruit who appeared twice in Nov. 1899 - against New Brighton at home and Grimsby away. Returned to Scotland after being released by City.

McDOUGALL, Angus
(1913-1914)
Left-half: 9 app.
1913: 5-9½, 12-0
Born: Glasgow, c.1891
Career: Bathgate Linlithgow; CITY Sep 1913; Hartlepools United July 1914

Reserve half-back from Scottish junior football who briefly replaced Tommy Wield in City's Second Division line-up. Moved on to North Eastern League Hartlepools for the following campaign.

McDOWALL, Daniel
(1953-1954)
Inside-forward: 17 app., 4 goals
1954: 5-7½, 11-0
Born: Kirkintilloch, Dumbartonshire, 22 May 1929
Career: Middlesbrough Feb. 1947; Kilmarnock late 1949 (£1,000); Celtic 1950; Workington Aug. 1951; CITY July 1953; (in exchange for Joe Johnson); Millwall June 1954 to 1956.

Solid Scot who made his Imps' debut in an 8-0 win over Blackburn Rovers in August 1953. Made a few appearances when Garvie was out injured but never established himself as a regular and moved on at the end of the season.

McEVOY, Donald William
(1959-1960)
Centre-half: 23 app.
1959: 5-11, 12-8
Born: Golcar, Huddersfield, 3 Dec. 1928
Career: Kirkheaton Rovers; Bradley United (Huddersfield); Huddersfield Town Sep. 1947; Sheffield Wednesday Dec. 1954

(£15,000); CITY Jan 1959 (£2,000); Barrow June 1960; Halifax Town coach July 1963; Barrow Manager July 1964; Grimsby Town manager July 1967 to Jan. 1968; Southport Manager Feb. 1968 to Jan. 1970; Halifax Town scout.

Honour: (Sheffield Wednesday) FL Div. 2 champions 1956

Sturdy, powerful centre-half who arrived with plenty of experience of the top flight with Huddersfield and Wednesday. A regular until losing his place to the newly signed Dennis Gratton in the early part of the 1960/61 season. Had a lengthy career in management before leaving the game to become a licensee in Brighouse.

McFADDEN, John
(1913-1914)
Right-half: 19 app.
1913: 5-9, 12-0
Born: Glengarnock, Ayrshire, c.1891
Career: Ayrshire junior football; Barrow Aug. 1912; CITY July 1913 to Oct. 1914; Barrow Nov. 1914

"... a right-half of power and persistency. Clean kicking and incisive work are his specialities", noted a reporter of this Scot who had starred in Barrow's 1912/13 FA Cup ties. McFadden returned to the north-west shortly after the outbreak of war.

McFARLANE, Archibald E.
(1894-1896, 1897-1898)
Full-back: 61 app.
Born: Scotland
Career: Glasgow junior football; CITY Nov. 1894; Glossop North End cs 1896; CITY May 1897; Gravesend Feb. 1898; Sheppey United cs 1898.

A popular defender from the 1890's, described by one critic as *"... a magnificent flying kicker and altogether a really brilliant back"*. It was reported during McFarlane's Glossop season that First Division Stoke were keen to acquire his services but he returned to Lincoln in the following close season.

McFARLANE, David
(1913-1914)
Inside-/centre-forward: 7 app., 2 goals
1913: 5-9½, 11-8
Born: c.1890
Career: Campsie Minerva; Kirkintilloch Harp (Scottish Junior League) Aug. 1913; CITY Oct. 1913 to cs 1914

One of several players tried in the centre-forward position after Donald Slade was sold to Arsenal in Dec. 1913. Scored on his debut, a 2-1 home win over Bristol City, but was unable to establish himself as a first team regular.

McGEOUGH, James
(1972-1974)
Midfield: 61 app. + 4 sub
1973: 5-7½, 10-7
Born: Belfast, 14 July 1946
Career: Sheffield Wednesday (appr.); Derry City; Waterford Dec. 1965 (£1,000); CITY June 1972 (£6,000) (Hartlepool on loan Mar. 1973); Waterford Oct. 1974.

Honours: Irish League (1 app. vs League of Ireland 1965)
League of Ireland (1 app. vs Irish League 1967)
(Derry City) Irish Cup winner 1964
(Waterford) FA of Ireland Cup finalist 1968

Recruited by manager David Herd from his former club, Waterford, McGeough had been a star on both sides of the Irish border but never really showed his best form at Lincoln. Had earlier spent several years on the books at Hillsborough without making the first team.

McGINLEY, John
(1984-1986, 1987-1989)
Forward: 105 app. + 7 sub, 18 goals
1985: 6-2, 13-8
Born: Rowlands Gill, Co. Durham, 11 June 1959
Career: Ashington; Gateshead; Sunderland Jan. 1982 (£3,000); Gateshead May 1982 (£1,000); Charleroi (Belgium) 1983; CITY Oct. 1984; Rotherham United Sep. 1986 (£3,000 plus Tony Simmons), (Hartlepool United on loan Jan. 1987); CITY Jan. 1987 (£8,000); Doncaster Rovers May 1989; Boston United May 1990 to 1992.

McGinley was originally signed as an orthodox winger but later switched to a more central role. Proved effective in his early days with the club but then suffered a bad injury. Returned after a brief spell at Millmoor and finished second in the scoring list in the 1987/88 season with 15 goals, but damaged an achilles tendon in the final match against Wycombe and never fully recovered fitness, eventually leaving on a free transfer.

McGLEN, William
(1952-1953)
Left-half: 13 app.
1952: 6-0, 12-0
Born: Bedlington, Northumberland, 27 Apr. 1921

Career: Blyth Spartans; RAF football; Manchester United May 1946; CITY July 1952; Oldham Athletic Feb. 1953 (in exchange for Jimmy Munro); retired Aug. 1956; CITY asst. trainer cs 1956, trainer July 1957 to June 1967 (reverting to asst. for the period Jan. to Nov. 1965); Skegness Town manager/coach June 1967 to Aug. 1968.

Solid, hard-working defender signed after making over 100 FL appearances at Old Trafford. Spent less than a year at Sincil Bank before moving back to Lancashire, however, returned to Lincoln when his playing career was over and spent a further 10 years on the backroom staff. Later lived in the Lincolnshire village of Burgh-le-Marsh.

McGRAHAN, James
(1922-1923, 1925-1927)
Right-half: 51 app.
1926: 5-8½, 11-4
Born: Leadgate, Co. Durham, 1 Mar. 1898
Career: Leadgate Park; CITY May 1922; Wigan Borough Feb. 1923; Boston Town Oct. 1924; CITY Oct. 1925; Scarborough as player-coach July 1927; had a spell at Fleetwood in the early 1930's and scouted for Notts County before leaving the game. Was subsequently manager Boston United Apr. 1948 to Apr. 1949.

Wing-half signed from the north-each to replace Jack Bryan. McGrahan's first spell at Sincil Bank was only brief and early in 1923 he was sold to Wigan along with Yaffer Ward when the Imps were in serious financial trouble. Returned to Lincoln and appeared regularly for the first team in the early part of the 1926/27 season. At the time of his appointment as manager of Boston United he was working as a foreman for Vickers Armstrong in Blackpool.

MACHIN, Peter
(1905-1907)
Inside-right: 54 app., 21 goals
1906: 5-7½, 11-0
Born: c.1883
Career: Wallsend Park Villa; CITY May 1905 to cs 1907.

Recruit from Northern Alliance football who occupied the inside-right position for the final two seasons of David Calderhead senior's time as secretary-manager. A regular goalscorer, particularly in his first campaign when he netted 16 in 33 FL outings. His name also appeared as 'Mackin' in the contemporary press.

McINALLY, John S.
(1970-1972)
Goalkeeper: 22 app.
1970: 5-10, 11-6
Born: Gatehouse of Fleet, Kirkcudbright, 26 Sep. 1951
Career: Manchester United Mar. 1969; CITY Aug. 1970; Colchester United Nov. 1972 to 1975.

Honour: Scotland schools international

Talented youngster who arrived on a free transfer from

Old Trafford with no senior experience. Served as understudy to John Kennedy for a couple of years before moving south to Colchester where he made a further 27 FL appearances.

McINNES, Ian
(1986-1987)
Midfield: 38 app. + 5 sub, 4 goals
1988: 5-8, 9-9
Born: Hamilton, Lanarkshire, 22 Mar. 1967
Career: Rotherham United (appr.), (prof.) Sep. 1984; CITY Jan. 1986; Kilmarnock Aug. 1987; Stranraer Oct. 1988; Stirling Albion cs 1990.

Honour: (Stirling Albion) Scottish League Div.2 champions 1991

Teenaged recruit from George Kerr's former club who scored twice in a dream debut for the Imps against Bury. Failed to sustain the early promise shown and returned to Scotland on a free transfer.

McINNES, Thomas
(1900-1903)
Outside-left: 79 app., 20 goals
1902: 5-6, 10-11
Born: Glasgow: 29 Aug. 1870
Died: Dec. 1937
Career: Dalmuir Thistle; Cowlairs; Newcastle East End; Clyde; Nottingham Forest June 1892 to cs 1899; CITY Sep. 1900 to cs 1903.

Honour: Scotland international (1 app. vs Ireland 1889)
(Nottingham Forest) FA Cup winner 1898

Among the most distinguished of Lincoln's early players and a Scottish cap while still a teenager. "... tricky, a fine shot and plays the combination game to a nicety", according to a reporter of the time. At Forest he made well over 100 FL appearances and played at outside-right in their 1898 FA Cup-winning side.

McKENZIE, Aiden
(1979-1980)
Forward: 4 app. + 2 sub
Born: Athlone, 15 July 1959
Career: Athlone Town; Galway Rovers; CITY Dec. 1979; Finn Harps cs 1980.

Young recruit from League of Ireland football who deputised for Gordon Hobson on a handful of occasions in a brief spell at Sincil Bank which ended when he was released on a free transfer.

MACKENZIE, Ronald
(1909-1910)
Inside-left: 28 app., 6 goals
1909: 5-9, 12-0
Born: in Scotland, c.1885
Career: Inverness Clachnacuddin; Chelsea Sep. 1907; CITY May 1909; Inverness Clachnacuddin cs 1910.

Developed in Highland League football where he was reckoned to have been one of the finest Inverness products up to that time. Did not appear in Chelsea's first team but scored 37 goals for the club's reserves in his first season at Stamford Bridge. Partnered another Scot, Tommy Yule on City's left-wing during his time at Sincil Bank.

MACKEY, James Alfred
(1923-1924)
Outside-right: 21 app., 2 goals
1923: 5-8, 11-7
Born: Ryton, Co. Durham, 1898
Career: Newburn Colliery; Coventry City during the 1920/21 season; Carlisle United cs 1922; Notts County cs 1923; CITY Sep. 1923; Luton Town July 1924; Crewe Alexandra cs 1925; Torquay United June 1927 to 1929.

Highly thought of winger who shared the outside-right position with Harry Pringle during his season at Sincil Bank. His final career aggregate was 148 FL matches of which 67 were in his final years at Torquay.

MACKIN, John
(1969)
Right-back: 3 app.,
1970: 5-9, 11-5
Born: Glasgow, 18 Nov. 1943
Career: Northampton Town (amat.), (prof.) Nov. 1963; CITY July 1969; York City Sep. 1969 (Darlington on loan Mar. 1973); Corby Town July 1973.

Sound defender who had a two month trial with City at the start of the 1969/70 season. Saw plenty of League action at both Northampton (95 app. plus 9 sub.) and York (157 app. plus 3 sub.) before joining Southern League Corby.

MACKIN, Peter
(1905-1907)
See entry under MACHIN, Peter.

McLEOD, William
(1906)
Centre-forward: 13 app., 8 goals
1906: 5-8½, 11-10
Born: Hebburn, Co. Durham, June 1887
Career: Hebburn Argyle; CITY June 1906 (£25); Leeds City Nov. 1906 (£350 plus proceeds from a match); Notts County Oct. 1919 (£1,250); Doncaster Rovers cs 1921.

Big, strong, centre-forward reckoned to have a powerful shot in both feet and to be a fine header of the ball. Billy was a prolific scorer in League football throughout his career. At Leeds he finished the club's leading scorer nine seasons in a row and totalled 177 goals in 301 FL and FA Cup matches. Unfortunate to miss representative honours although he was on one occasion reserve for England.

McMAHON, Francis G.
(1971-1973)
Midfield: 54 app. + 1 sub, 2 goals
1972: 5-10, 11-7
Born: Belfast, 4 Jan. 1950
Career: Distillery; Coventry City late 1969; Waterford early 1971; CITY July 1971; Darlington Mar. 1973 (in part exchange for Alan Harding) (Hartlepool on loan Oct. 1973); Yeovil Town July 1974; Bath City during 1977/78 season; Taunton Town manager June 1980.

Frank was a red-haired midfield player who impressed with his energy and skill despite a rather slight build. A regular under David Herd but was transferred by Graham Taylor shortly after he took over as manager.

McMANUS, C(harles) Eric
(1979-1980)
Goalkeeper; 21 app.
1979: 6-0, 11-2
Born: Limavady, Co. Derry, 14 Nov. 1950
Career: Coleraine 1966; Coventry City Aug. 1968 (£8,000); Notts County May 1972 (£3,000); Stoke City Oct. 1979 (£35,000) (CITY on loan Dec. 1979 to Apr. 1980); Bradford City Aug. 1982 (£15,000); (Middlesbrough on loan Jan. 1986; Peterborough United on loan Mar. to May 1986); Tranmere Rovers Aug. 1986; Boston United Sep. 1986 to 1987. Walsall youth development officer/coach c.1990.

Honours: Northern Ireland amateur international (Bradford City) FL Div.3 champions 1985

Experienced 'keeper who had an extended loan period at Sincil Bank, arriving as a replacement for Peter Grotier when the latter moved to Cardiff. Totalled 396 FL outings, most of which were with Notts County and Bradford City.

McMILLAN, S.
(1893)
Half-back: 3 app.
Career: Leith Athletic; Millwall Athletic; CITY Aug. 1893.

Scottish defender who made occasional appearances as deputy for Mettam and Richardson in City's half-back line in the early part of the 1893/94 season.

McMILLAN, William
(1898-1904, 1904-1907)
Right-back: 178 app., 1 goal
1898: 5-8, 11-6
Born: in Scotland, c.1876
Died: Feb. 1958
Career: Lanark Athletic; CITY July 1898; Newark Town cs 1904; CITY later in 1904; Newark Town cs 1907; Castleford Town cs 1909 -1910. Subsequently appeared in Lincoln League football for South End, RAMC (Wednesday League) and, after the Great War, Waddington and Boston Town.

Dependable Scot who was a regular in City's defence for six seasons, switching from full-back to centre-half in 1903/04. At the end of that season he was not resigned and played a few games for Newark Town in the Midland League before returning to Sincil Bank where he gave three more years service to the reserves (he made only one further FL appearance for the club). Continued to turn out in local football until in his 40's when he became involved in coaching junior teams. Served with the RAMC during the Great War.

McNEIL, Richard ("Dixie")
(1972-1974)
Centre-forward: 96 app. + 1 sub, 53 goals
1973: 5-10, 11-12
Born: Melton Mowbray, 16 Jan. 1947
Career: Holwell Works; Leicester City Nov. 1964; Exeter City June 1966; Corby Town July 1967; Northampton Town May 1969 (£3,000); CITY Jan. 1972 (£9,500); Hereford United Aug. 1974 (£20,000); Wrexham Sep. 1977 (£60,000); Hereford United Sep. 1982; retired Jan. 1983. Wrexham manager Apr. 1985 to Nov. 1989; Coventry City asst. manager Jan. to Nov. 1990.

Honours: (Hereford United) Welsh Cup finalist 1976
FL Div. 3 champions 1976
(Wrexham) FL Div. 3 champions 1978
Welsh Cup finalist 1979 (2nd leg only)

One of City's most prolific goalscorers of the post-war period and a more than adequate replacement for Phil Hubbard who was sold to Norwich shortly before Christmas 1971 when he was the club's leading scorer. McNeil was surprisingly sold by Graham Taylor after two and a half seasons at Sincil Bank, but continued to score regularly, finishing with a career record of 518 FL appearances plus 4 as substitute, 239 goals.

McNEIL, Robert M.
(1985)
Full-back: 4 app.
1985: 5-9, 10-12
Born: Bellshill, Lanarkshire, 1 Nov. 1962
Career: Hull City (appr.) July 1979; (prof.) Nov 1980; Blackpool on trial late 1985; CITY non-contract Oct. 1985; Preston North End Dec. 1985; Carlisle United Aug. 1987; Bridlington Town 1988; Goole Town 1993.

Experienced full-back who came to Sincil Bank after rejecting terms with Hull. He spent a month at Lincoln but did not play after appearing in a 7-0 defeat at Derby. Turned out for Bridlington at Wembley in the 1990 FA Vase final when they finished runners-up to Yeading. Became a police officer on leaving full-time football.

McPARLAND, Ian J.
(1992)
Forward: 3 app. + 1 sub,
1991: 5-8, 10-8
Born: Edinburgh, 4 Oct. 1961
Career: Ormiston Primrose; Notts County Dec. 1980; Hull City Mar. 1989 (£155,000); (Walsall on loan Mar. to May 1991); Dunfermline Athletic cs 1991; Falkirk on trial cs 1992; CITY non-contract Aug. 1992; Sliema Wanderers (Malta) Sep. 1992; Northampton Town extended trial Oct. 1992; Instant Dict (Hong Kong) Feb. 1993 to Mar. 1994.

Experienced Scot who failed to impress in a short spell at Sincil Bank. Had earlier spent nine years at Meadow Lane, making 190 FL appearances plus 31 substitutions, scoring 69 goals.

McPHAIL, Daniel
(1931-1939)
Goalkeeper: 309 app,
1936: 5-11, 12-0
Born: Campbeltown, Argyll, 9 Feb. 1903
Died: Oct. 1987
Career: Falkirk; Portsmouth Jan. 1922; CITY May 1931 (for Tom Maidment and a fee); retired cs 1939.

Honour: (City) FL Div.3 (North) champions 1932

Highly consistent goalkeeper and the first City player to make 300 Football League appearances for the club. Won much praise during his time at Sincil Bank for example: *"Never showy, but clean and workmanlike in all that he does"*, and, *"Alert with shots from all angles and reliable in an emergency"*. Earlier made 128 FL appearances for Portsmouth before losing his place due to a broken wrist. A fine golfer too. Settled in Lincoln and ran a bookmaking firm for many years.

McQUAKER, Thomas
(1897)
Born: Glasgow, 25 Dec. 1867
Career: Glasgow junior football; CITY on trial Feb. 1897.

Scottish triallist whose solitary FL outing came in a 4-0 away defeat at Burton Swifts in Feb. 1897. A report of the match noted that he was *"so complete a failure amongst the half-backs that he was brought forward"*.

MACRILL, F.
(1896-1897)
Outside-right: 3 app.
Career: Grantham Rovers; CITY Nov. 1896; St. Marys (Lincoln) cs 1897.

Local lad who apparently signed for the City Swifts (reserves) because he was tired of travelling to and from Grantham every week. His three FL outings came as deputy for Jimmy Lynes, all resulting in defeats.

McVAY, David Reid
(1981)
Defender: 13 app.
1981: 6-1, 12-11
Born: Workington, 5 Mar. 1955
Career: Notts County (amat.), (prof.) July 1973 (Torquay United on loan Sep. 1977); Peterborough United July 1979; CITY Aug. 1981; Grantham Town Nov. 1981; Boston United later in Nov. 1981; retired Jan. 1983.

Defender who made his Notts County debut at 18 and went on to make a total of 101 appearances, plus 12 as sub, while at Meadow Lane. Joined the Imps on a three month trial but failed to win a contract and was released. Later employed as a sports journalist with the Nottingham Evening Post.

MAIDMENT, James Harry C.
(1930-1931)
Goalkeeper: 41 app.
1930: 5-10, 12-0
Born: Monkwearmouth, Sunderland, 28 Sep. 1901
Died: 12 Feb. 1977
Career: Robert Thompson's (Sunderland); Southend United (amat.) May 1923, (prof.) Sep. 1923; Newport County Aug. 1924; CITY May 1930; Notts County May 1931; Accrington Stanley July 1933 to June 1934.

Sound, consistent goalkeeper who missed only one match in his season with the Imps, the club losing out to Chesterfield in the title race after leading the table for much of the campaign. Jim finished with a FL record of 354 appearances, 3 goals - the goals coming from his occasional role as Newport's penalty taker. Brother of Tom (see below) and nephew of Billy Charlton (Newport and Tranmere). Died at Edwalton, Notts.

MAIDMENT, Thomas
(1926-1931)
Inside-right: 126 app., 43 goals
1926: 5-10½, 12-0
Born: Monkwearmouth, Sunderland, 4 Nov. 1905
Died: 14 Jan. 1971
Career: St. Columbas Institute; Robert Thompson's (Sunderland); Sunderland May 1925; CITY Jan. 1926; Portsmouth May 1931 (in part exchange for Dan McPhail); Workington Aug. 1932; Cardiff City Jan. 1933; Blyth Spartans Sep. 1934.

"A football enigma" according to one contemporary observer - international class at his best, but such performances were few and far between. His strong points included clever ball control, a tremendous volley and powerful headwork. Brother of Jim Maidment.

MAIR, Gordon
(1984-1986)
Outside-left: 57 app., 3 goals
1985: 5-9, 10-6
Born: Coatbridge, 18 Dec. 1958
Career: Notts County (appr.), (prof.) Dec. 1976; CITY Aug. 1984 (£25,000); Motherwell cs 1986; Clydebank Apr. 1991; Ayr United cs 1992 to May 1994.

Scottish winger, one of the most skilful players on the club's books on his day although did not live up to early promise. Had earlier spent eight seasons at Meadow Lane where he totalled 123 FL appearances plus 8 as substitute, scoring 19 goals.

MANN, J. John
(1895)
Goalkeeper: 8 app.
Career: Glasgow junior football; CITY Aug. to Nov. 1895.

Mann signed from the same Scottish junior club as Archibald McFarlane and was a regular choice in the early part of the 1895/96 season. He was considered a fine 'keeper but too easily put off when encountering robust forwards. Lost his place after a particularly nervous performance against Grimsby Town in the FA Cup and did not appear in the first team again.

MANNING, John Tom ("Cracker")
(1911-1919)
Outside-right: 90 app., 9 goals
1912: 5-9½, 13-1
Born: Boston, Lincs, 1886
Died: Mar. 1946
Career: Boston Lindum; Boston Swifts; Boston Town; Hull City Apr. 1905; Bradford City Aug. 1907; Rochdale June 1910; CITY Aug. 1911; Rotherham County Aug. 1919; Queens Park Rangers July 1920; Boston Town July 1921.

Considered one of City's best outside-rights of the pre-1914 era. Jack was known for his acceleration, trickery and shooting power, and as a critic noted in 1913 he was *"impervious to hard knocks, gets through by weight where light men would be hustled off"*. Had a further 31 outings, scoring 10 goals, in the Central League championship side of 1911/12 and also appeared regularly for the Imps throughout the Great War.

MANSLEY, Allan
(1971-1972)
Forward: 3 app.
1970: 5-7, 10-10
Born: Liverpool, 31 Aug. 1946
Career: Sheffield Wednesday (amat.); Crewe Alexandra (amat.); Guinness Exports; Skelmersdale United Nov. 1966; Blackpool June 1967; Brentford Jan. 1968 (Fulham on loan Dec. 1970); Notts County Mar. 1971 (CITY on loan Dec. 1971) to May 1972.

Honour: (Skelmersdale) FA Amateur Cup finalist 1967

Winger who joined the Imps on loan from Notts County along with Terry Cooper at the end of 1971. Returned to Meadow Lane when his month's loan period was over.

MASON, David Garrioch
(1896)
Inside-right: 4 app.
1895: 5-8
Born: Glasgow, 20 Sep. 1876
Career: Glasgow junior football; Rotherham Town cs 1894; Leicester Fosse Apr. 1895; CITY Oct. 1896; Warmley cs 1897; Gravesend United Feb. 1899.

A regular performer in the Second Division with Rother-ham and Leicester but had the misfortune to appear for the Imps in the middle of a run of 12 consecutive defeats and was not selected for the first team again.

MARCH, Harold James
(1930-1932)

Inside-left: 10 app., 5 goal
Born: Gamston, Notts., 30 Jan. 1904
Died: 22 July 1977
Career: Army football; Hull City Nov. 1929; CITY Sep. 1930; Grantham Aug. 1932 to cs 1934.

Deputised with some success for Harry Kitching in the 1930/31 campaign but played only reserve football the following season. Had earlier represented the British Army before joining his brother on Hull City's books.

MARDENBOROUGH, Stephen A.
(1993-)

Midfield/forward: 14 app. + 7 sub, 2 goals
1993: 5-7, 11-9
Born: Selly Oak, Birmingham, 11 Sep. 1964
Career: Coventry City (appr.), (prof.) Aug. 1982; Wolverhampton Wanderers Sep. 1983 (Cambridge United on loan Feb. 1984); Swansea City July 1984; Newport County July 1985; Cardiff City Mar. 1987; Hereford United July 1988; IFK Ostersund (Sweden) July 1989; Cheltenham Town Nov. 1989; Darlington July 1990; CITY July 1993 (£10,000)

Honours: (Darlington) FL Div.4 champions 1991

Speedy right-sided player who never showed his best form at Lincoln and was listed as being available on a free transfer at the end of his first season with the club despite being still under contract. Signed after finishing top scorer for Darlington in the 1992/93 campaign - the fee being settled by a tribunal. A career aggregate of 200 plus appearances to date.

MARKLEW, Herbert
(1933-1935)

Centre-forward: 7 app., 3 goals
1934: 5-11, 11-7
Born: Dinnington, nr. Sheffield, 4 Apr. 1910
Died: Mar. 1987
Career: Dinnington Main; CITY Nov. 1933; Dinnington Main cs 1935.

Went straight in the League side for a couple of games but found the transition from his colliery side too great. Made a brief return at the end of the season after a grounding with the reserves but was unable to dislodge either Johnny Campbell or Chick Reed as a first team regular.

MARLOW, Geoffrey Arthur
(1937-1939, 1940-1949)

Outside-left: 80 app., 26 goals
1949: 5-10½, 12-0
Born: Worksop, 13 Dec. 1914
Died: 8 Nov. 1978
Career: Dinnington Main; CITY cs 1937; Newark Town cs 1939; CITY Nov. 1940 (guest for Mansfield Town 1942-1945); Grantham Aug. 1949; Stalybridge Celtic Sep. 1950; Skegness Town cs 1951; Lincoln Claytons cs 1955.

Honour: (City) FL Div.3 (North) champions 1948

"Has real dash, initiative, and shooting power", noted a 1938 critic. Geoff returned after the war to become a regular in the 1946/47 and 1947/48 seasons. Equally well-known as a local cricketer with Ruston Bucyrus and Lincolnshire (58 appearances between 1946 and 1957), representing the Minor Counties on one occasion.

MARRIOTT, Frank
(1924-1925)

Full-back: 3 app.,
1924: 5-7, 11-7
Born: Sutton-in-Ashfield, Notts., 26 Oct. 1893
Career: Sutton Junction; Notts County Aug. 1919; Swansea Town Aug. 1923; CITY Sep. 1924; Grantham cs 1925.

Full-back who appeared mostly in City's reserve side. Had earlier spent four years at Meadow Lane, appearing regularly in the first team and earning good reviews. For example (1922) *"... a dashing and capable back. Knows no fear, places the ball with nice judgment, and is a keen and resourceful player"*. In the Great War saw service in the Dardanelles, Egypt, France and Belgium during four years in the Army.

MARSHALL, James Hind
(1924-1925)

Inside-left: 3 app., 1 goal
1924: 5-11, 12-0

Born: Glenguie, Peterhead, 9 June 1890
Died: 8 July 1958
Career: Vale of Grange; Partick Thistle 1911; Bradford City June 1914; Oldham Athletic Sep. 1920 (£2,250); Southport Jan. 1924; Rotherham County June 1924; CITY Dec. 1924 as player-coach; Queen of the South June 1925. Later spent time in Holland as a trainer and coach before returning to become Newport County trainer July 1946 to May 1948.

Well-travelled Scot whose main role at Sincil Bank was as a coach although he made a handful of first team appearances, scoring on his debut in a 3-0 home win over Durham City. Despite being at the end of his career he had lost none of his speed - on joining Queen of the South it was said, *"He is a sprinter of some note, and is still able to do the 'hundred' in a little over 'even' time"*.

MARSHALL, Lester
(1925-1927)

Right-back/centre-forward: 19 app., 6 goals
1926: 5-10, 12-0
Born: Castleford, Yorks., 4 Feb. 1902
Career: York City; CITY Jan. 1925 (£100); Scarborough June 1927; York City cs 1928.

Full-back who was converted to centre-forward by the then non-League York City and responded by scoring freely (5 in an FA Cup-tie, 5 in a Midland League match and 6 in a North Riding Senior Cup-tie). The Imps were attracted by such form and he had an extended first team run after signing but later returned to the defensive role for which he was thought to be better suited.

MARTIN, Albert Ogden
(1919-1920)

Half-back: 3 app.,
1919: 5-7½, 10-0
Born: Lincoln, 1896
Died: 17 Feb. 1975
Career: Rustons Staff (Lincoln); CITY May 1919; Rustons Staff 1920; Retford Town (Central Alliance) in season 1921/22.

Local lad who occasionally deputised in City's League team during the first season after the Great War, although he mainly turned out for the reserves in the Midland League.

MARTIN, John
(1904-1906)

Centre-forward: 65 app., 30 goals
1904: 5-11½, 12-0
Born: South Shields, 1882
Career: Tyne Dock; Kingston Villa; CITY May 1904; Blackburn Rovers Aug. 1906; Brighton & Hove Albion May 1908; Millwall Athletic May 1909 to 1911.

Signing from north-eastern junior football who finished leading scorer in the 1905/06 season with 18 goals and was subsequently snapped up by First Division Blackburn Rovers. Scored consistently with all his clubs - 28 goals in 62 FL and FA Cup ties at Ewood Park and a further 42 in 107 Southern League outings with Brighton and Millwall.

MATHISON, George
(1933-1934)

Left-half: 37 app.
1933: 5-11, 11-0
Born: Walker, Newcastle-upon-Tyne, 24 Nov. 1909
Died: 19 Apr. 1989
Career: Walker Celtic; Newcastle United Dec. 1926; CITY Mar. 1933 (£675); Gateshead Aug. 1934; Burnley May 1937 to 1938.

Mathison was signed along with Bill Dodgin to strengthen City's half-back line at a time when they were facing relegation from Division Two. They failed to avoid the drop but his arrival was said to have *"... helped to materially stiffen Lincoln's half-way line"*. Was reported to have been the first player for whom Gateshead had paid a fee.

MATTHEWS, Barry J.
(1949-1952)

Outside-left: 2 app.
1949: 6-0
Born: Sheffield, 18 Jan. 1926
Career: Sheffield United (amat.); CITY (amat.) Oct. 1949; Corby Town cs 1952; Peterborough United cs 1953; Corby Town cs 1954; Spalding United June 1955 to cs 1956.

Amateur player who was given two first team outings in Nov. 1949. Afterwards appeared regularly with the club's reserve and Lincolnshire League teams. Matthews was a draughtsman in a local factory and a former Sheffield University student.

MATTHEWS, Neil
(1992-)

Forward: 52 app. + 8 sub, 18 goals
1993: 5-11, 12-0
Born: Humberston, nr. Cleethorpes, 19 Sep. 1966
Career: Grimsby Town (appr.) July 1983, (prof.) Sep. 1984 (Scunthorpe United on loan Nov. 1985; Halifax Town on loan Oct.-Dec. 1986; Bolton Wanderers on loan Mar. 1987); Halifax Town Aug. 1987; Stockport County July 1990 (£70,000) (Halifax Town on loan Sep. 1991); CITY on loan Dec. 1992, (perm.) Feb. 1993 (£20,000)

A capable forward, sharp and quick-moving, and one of the very few who have appeared in the Football League for all three Lincolnshire clubs. Impressed during his loan spell for City, scoring in each of his first three outings after coming on as substitute, but has not always found goals as easy to come by since.

MATTHEWSON, Trevor
(1987-1989)

Centre-half: 43 app., 2 goals
1988: 6-1, 12-5
Born: Sheffield, 12 Feb. 1963
Career: Sheffield Wednesday (appr.) June 1979, (prof.) Feb. 1981; Newport County Oct. 1983; Stockport County Sep. 1985; CITY Aug. 1987 (£13,000); Birmingham City Aug. 1989 (£30,000 plus a further £15,000 after 35 apps.); Preston North End Aug. 1993.

Gutsy, competitive central defender who skippered the Vauxhall Conference championship side after sigining from Colin Murphy's former club. Went on to make a further 167 FL outings plus 1 as substitute at Birmingham, appearing for them at Wembley when they won the 1991 Leyland Daf Cup. His transfers from Newport and St. Andrews were both set by tribunals. Nephew of Reg (Sheffield United and Fulham).

MEACOCK, W(illiam) Robert
(1935-1938)

Half-back: 106 app.
1935: 5-9, 11-10
Born: Hoole, nr. Chester, 26 July 1910
Career: Hoole FC; Blackpool May 1930; Torquay United Aug. 1931; Tranmere Rovers July 1933; CITY May 1935; Birmingham June 1938 (£3,000); Bristol City June 1939.

"A real artist with the ball ... his headwork alone has won him unstinted praise, and he knowns all the other tricks of a first grade centre-half", was a favourable 1936 comment on Bob. His Lincoln career only really took off when Con Moulson was transferred to Notts County in Sep. that year. A regular also with Tranmere (57 app., 3 goals) but considered not quite up to standard by Birmingham.

MEASHAM, Ian
(1985)

Full-back/midfield: 6 app.
1985: 5-11, 11-8
Born: Barnsley, 14 Dec. 1964
Career: Huddersfield Town (appr.), (prof.) Dec. 1982; (CITY on loan Oct. 1985; Rochdale on loan Mar. to May 1986); Cambridge United Aug. 1986; Barnet Oct. 1988; Burnley Nov. 1988; Doncaster Rovers Sep. 1993.

Honour: (Burnley) FL Div.4 champions 1992

Measham was recruited on loan by John Pickering in the early part of the 1985/86 season but City did not pursue a permanent signing and he returned to Leeds Road. Has made a total of 250 plus FL appearances to date. Suffered a broken neck in a freak accident when playing for Doncaster at Torquay in Feb. 1994.

MEATH, Trevor J.
(1969-1972)

Midfield: 42 app. + 1 sub, 5 goals
1971: 5-11½, 12-10
Born: Wednesbury, Staffs, 20 Mar. 1944

Career: Darlaston, Walsall May 1964; CITY Oct. 1969 (£4,000); retired through injury Oct. 1972; Boston United Jan. to cs 1973; Holbeach United in season 1973/74.

Powerful midfield player whose time at Sincil Bank was badly affected by the knee injury which eventually ended his career. Received a testimonial match against Crystal Palace two months after retiring. Later tried to come-back with Boston United reserves and Holbeach before giving up the game completely. Settled in the Lincoln area and found employment as an electrician.

MEESON, Arthur William
(1929-1932)

Goalkeeper: 12 app.
1931: 5-9, 11-10
Born: Headington, Oxford, 10 Apr. 1904
Died: 30 May 1971
Career: Oxford City; Arsenal May 1928; Fulham Dec. 1928 (£175); CITY Aug. 1929 to May 1932

Honour: England amateur international (1 app. vs Scotland 1928)

Reserve 'keeper given an extended run in the League team at the end of the 1929/30 season after Kendall was sold to Sheffield United. Appeared only once more in the first team before departing on a free transfer.

MERRITT, Richard
(1925-1926)

Outside-left: 22 app., 3 goals
1925: 5-8½, 11-5
Born: Shiney Row, Co. Durham, 22 July 1897
Died: 1978
Career: South Shields during season 1921/22; Durham City cs 1923; CITY May 1925; York City 1926; Notts County May 1929 to May 1930.

Shared the outside-left spot with Frank Alford in his Lincoln season, moving on to Midland League York the following summer. He had earlier made 72 Northern Section appearances with Durham City, scoring 11 goals.

METTAM, Edward ("Ned")
(1889-1896)

Half-back: 85 app.,
Born: Lincoln, 1868
Died: 31 May 1943
Career: Lincoln junior football; CITY 1889 to cs 1896

Local lad who appeared regularly in City's half-back line throughout their first four seasons of League football. His brother Alfred ("Major") had been a Lincoln stalwart of the 1880's. Ned was a capable cricketer too, appearing for the Lindum and Stamp End clubs and representing Lincolnshire on a couple of occasions.

MEUNIER, James Brown
(1912-1914)

Full-back: 23 app.
1912: 5-8½, 11-10
Born: Poynton, Stockport, 1885
Died: 30 Sep. 1957
Career: Heaton Chapel; Stockport County (amat.) 1903; Manchester City cs 1904; Southport Central cs 1906 (in Canada Sep. 1906 to 1907); Everton Oct. 1908 (£50); CITY June 1912; Coventry City July to Nov. 1914; Hyde United cs 1919; Macclesfield Dec. 1919.

Strong defender who had captained the Everton reserve side to two Lancashire Combination championships. At Lincoln he served as deputy for both Clem Jackson and Watty Wilson and occasionally played in goal for the reserves. Perhaps better known as a cricketer serving a number of clubs in different parts of the country as a professional, including Lindum CC (1913) and appearing once for Lincolnshire in the Minor Counties (1914) and twice for Warwickshire in 1920.

MIDDLEMASS, Ernest
(1948-1949)

Centre-forward: 2 app.
1949: 5-11, 11-7
Born: Newcastle-upon-Tyne, 30 Aug. 1920
Career: South Shields; CITY June 1948; Corby Town Aug. 1949; Kettering Town cs 1952.

Signed after scoring 29 goals in 29 North-Eastern League games in 1947/48, but although heading the scoring list for the Imps' reserves with 18 goals in the following campaign he received few first team opportunities. Was employed as a woodwork instructor.

MIDDLETON, Frederick T.
(1954-1963)

Right-half: 300 app., 16 goals
1955: 5-9, 12-1
Born: West Hartlepool, 2 Aug. 1930
Career: Newcastle United Apr. 1948; CITY May 1954 (£1,000); Worksop Town Aug. 1963; Skegness Town later in 1963/64 season; Gainsborough Trinity Aug. 1964; Boston FC Aug. 1966; Ruston Bucyrus (Lincoln) Oct. 1966.

Popular fair-haired wing-half known for his consistency and effort *"always in the thick of it ... never pulls back"*, as a reporter of the time noted. Made no senior appearances in six seasons at Newcastle but was a first team regular throughout his time with the Imps. Eventually returned to live in Hartlepool and worked in a local factory.

MILLER, George
(1910-1911)

Left-half: 22 app.
1910: 5-9, 11-4
Born: Riggend, Airdrie, Lanarkshire
Career: Larkhall United; CITY June 1910 to cs 1911.

Signed after winning Scottish junior international honours with Larkhall and appeared in the first 21 matches of the 1910/11 season. Lost his place after suffering a broken arm and was only selected once more.

MILLER, Walter
(1911-1914)

Centre-forward: 35 app., 8 goals
1912: 5-11, 12-2
Born: Newcastle-upon-Tyne, 1882
Career: Wallsend Park Villa; Third Lanark; Sheffield Wednesday cs 1907; West Ham United 1908; Blackpool cs 1909; CITY May 1911; Merthyr Town Jan. 1914; Dundee Aug. 1914.

"A born centre; unselfish, a dead shot and has the knack of keeping his men well together", was a complimentary assessment in 1913. Walter had earlier finished leading scorer with 20 goals from 27 appearances when City won the inaugural Central League championship. Later ran into trouble with the club's management for neglecting training and general misconduct, being suspended 'sine die' on at least two occasions before departing for Southern League Merthyr.

MILNER, John
(1963-1967)

Wing-half: 109 app., 6 goals
1965: 5-9½, 11-9
Born: Huddersfield: 14 May 1942
Career: Hundersfield Town on groundstaff, (prof.) May 1959; CITY Oct. 1963; Bradford Feb. to cs 1967; Cambridge United; Sligo Rovers to Dec. 1967; Boston Beacons (USA) 1968; Denver Dynamo (USA) 1974.

Saw regular first team action at Lincoln until dropped early in the 1966/67 season - he had missed only one FL match in the previous campaign. Left the club in Feb. 1967 when his contract was cancelled by mutual consent and spent a brief spell at Park Avenue before eventually moving to play abroad.

MITCHELL, Andrew
(1923)

Outside-right: 1 app.
1923: 5-7, 10-6
Career: Scottish junior football; CITY Aug. to Sep 1923.

Scottish trialist whose only FL appearance for the Imps was in the opening match of the 1923/24 season, a 1-1 draw at home to Halifax Town.

MITCHELL, Robert
(1986-1987)

Defender/midfield: 41 app. + 3 sub, 2 goals
1986: 5-10, 11-0
Born: South Shields, 4 Jan. 1955
Career: Hebburn Youths; Sunderland (appr.), (prof.) Jan 1972; Blackburn Rovers July 1976; Grimsby Town June 1978; Carlisle

United Aug. 1982; Rotherham United Mar. 1983 to May 1985; Hamrun Spartans (Malta) late in 1985; CITY Jan. 1986; Louth United Aug. 1987; Spalding United Sep. 1987; Boston United Jan. to cs 1988; Louth United from Aug. 1989.

Honour: (Grimsby Town) FL Div. 3 champions 1980

Midfield player whose career closely followed that of manager George Kerr, the two having been together at Grimsby, Rotherham, Lincoln and Boston United. A veteran by the time he came to Sincil Bank, his FL career totalled 289 matches, 26 as substitute, and 16 goals.

MITCHELL, Thomas
(1929-1930)

Centre-forward: 3 app.
1929: 5-10, 12-0
Born: Trimdon Grange, Co. Durham, 27 June
Career: Trimdon Grange FC; Hartlepools United cs 1922; Stockport County July 1924; Blackburn Rovers Feb. 1926 (£2,100); CITY Sep. 1929 to c.1930.

Experienced centre-forward who suffered a serious injury in the home match with Accrington Stanley shortly after signing and was reported to be still on the 'sick list' in Sep. 1930. Well thought of at Blackburn where a 1928 critic recorded, *"... dribbles well, and can kick or head a ball with force and direction"*.

MOODY, V(incent) Roy
(1946-1947)

Outside-right: 1 app.
Born: Worksop, 12 Mar. 1923
Career: Worksop Town; CITY Nov. 1946 to Mar. 1947.

Signed for Worksop, then competing in a local district League, Moody made his solitary FL appearance for the Imps on 15 Mar. 1947 in a 3-1 home victory over Carlisle. Did not appear again at first or reserve team level and was released shortly afterwards.

MOORE, Isaac
(1889-1893)

Wing-half: 22 app., 3 goals
1896: 5-6, 11-3
Born: Dundee, 8 Apr. 1867
Died: 10 Sep. 1954
Career: Our Boys (Dundee); CITY 1889 (Aston Villa on loan later in 1889); Burton Wanderers cs 1893; Swindon Town Jan.- cs 1896.

One of City's early imported professionals from Scotland, Moore was loaned to Aston Villa to cover for an injury crisis soon after signing. Returned to Lincoln and appeared as a centre-forward or inside-left in the Midland League and Football Alliance campaigns of the early 1890's, but generally turned out in the half-back line in the club's first FL season. Later settled in Burton and was employed in Bass and Co's fitting shop for 30 years.

MOORE, J(ohn) Leslie
(1965-1967)

Centre-half: 59 app.,
1966: 6-0, 12-6
Born: Sheffield, 7 July 1933
Career: Sheffield Club; Worksop Town Aug. 1957; Derby County Nov. 1957 (£1,000); Boston FC July 1965; CITY Oct. 1965; Lockheed Leamington July 1967. Buxton Aug. 1968, player-manager May to Nov. 1970; Worksop Town manager June 1972 to July 1973.

Experienced central defender signed after he had drifted into non-League soccer with Boston FC. Lost his place towards the end of the 1966/67 season and left on a free transfer. A part-time professional who was also employed by an insurance company.

MOORE, John M.
(1961-1965)

Outside-right: 30 app., 5 goals
1962: 5-7, 10-8
Born: Carlton, Nottingham, 1 Feb. 1943
Career: Arnold St. Marys 1957; CITY Nov. 1961; Arnold cs 1965.

Recruit from the Central Alliance who made his FL debut soon after joining the club and scored once in a 3-2 defeat by Reading. Never able to win a regular first team place and returned to Arnold in the summer of 1965.

MOORE, William J. ("Pal")
(1924-1925)

Outside-left: 33 app., 2 goals
1924: 5-10, 12-0
Born: Ballyclare, Co. Antrim, c.1887
Died: 17 Aug. 1932
Career: Brantwood; Glentoran 1917; Falkirk Nov. 1920; CITY May 1924; Ards July 1925; Glentoran Mar. 1926.

Honours: Northern Ireland international (1 app. vs Scotland 1923) (Glentoran) Irish Cup winner 1917; finalist 1919.

Moore was signed in time to appear in City's last fixture of 1923/24 and played a great game despie travelling all night to do so. Described around that time as *"... fast, accurate with his passes, and a blazing shot"*. A 1927 cigarette card was also complimentary, *"A strong, well built, dashing player who retains something of schoolboy zest for the game"*. Played 116 Scottish League First Division matches for Falkirk, scoring 13 goals, and won Irish international honours at both junior and senior levels.

MORGAN, Ernest
(1949-1953)

Centre-forward: 3 app.
1950: 5-9, 12-3
Born: Barnsley, 13 Jan. 1927
Career: Royston Boys Club (Barnsley); Rawmarsh; CITY Sep. 1949; Gillingham Aug 1953 (£3,000) to 1957. Chatham Town coach 1960, manager May 1962 to cs 1966; Dartford manager July

1966 to cs 1972; Maidstone United manager cs 1972; Dartford manager 1972 to Feb. 1975; Tonbridge manager c.1978 to 1980; Dartford manager 1982.

Morgan had a prolific scoring record for City's reserves but was never given an extended run in the first team. Netted 36 Midland League goals in 1952/53 and after stepping down a division to join Gillingham he went on to score 73 goals in 155 FL outings including a club record 31 in season 1954/55. Was later involved in managing several Kent non-League sides. Later settled in Rainham.

MORRIS, George R.
(1897-1900)
Left-half: 66 app., 4 goals
1900: 5-8, 11-7
Born: Manchester, 1879
Career: Manchester St. Augustines; CITY Oct. 1897; Glossop North End Feb. 1900 (a fee and a guaranteed match); Barnsley Nov. 1900; Millwall Athletic cs 1901 to 1903.

Dependable half-back who rarely missed a game for City until losing his place to Jack Cowley in Dec. 1899. Aggregated a total of 154 FL and Southern League appearances.

MORTON, Alan
(1963-1965)

Inside-forward: 58 app., 20 goals
1963: 5-9, 10-10
Born: Peterborough, 6 Mar. 1942
Career: Peterborough United (amat.); Arsenal (amat.) Feb. 1959, (prof.) Apr. 1959; Peterborough United Oct. 1961; Wisbech Town late 1962; CITY July 1963; Chesterfield July 1965; Boston FC Sep. 1966; Spalding United cs 1967; Boston FC Nov. 1967; Lincoln Claytons cs 1968.

Inside-forward who began well scoring two on his club debut and finishing leading scorer with 18 goals in his first season, including two hat-tricks. Was in and out of the side in his second campaign and moved on to Chesterfield in the summer of 1965. Continued playing in the Lincoln Sunday League for Gatehouse until the mid-1970's.

MORTON, William Henry
(1922-1923)
Inside/outside-left: 21 app., 4 goals
1922: 5-9, 10-12
Born: Ilkeston, Derbys., 16 Dec. 1896
Career: West Hallam and Ilkeston St. Johns prior to WW1 service; Ilkeston United 1919; Derby County Aug. 1920; Newcastle United Sep. 1921; CITY May 1922; Wigan Borough June 1923 to 1924.

Adaptable player who had turned out at both right-back and half-back with Derby where he made 24 FL appearances. No senior outings at Newcastle and only became a regular at Sincil Bank after several men departed during a financial crisis. Served with the Sherwood Foresters in WW1 during which he spent time as a prisoner-of-war.

MOSS, Ernest
(1983)
Centre-forward: 10 app. + 1 sub, 2 goals
183: 6-1½, 13-2
Born: Chesterfield, 19 Oct. 1949
Career: Chesterfield Tube Works; Chesterfield Oct. 1968; Peterborough United Jan .1976 (£16,000); Mansfield Town Dec. 1976 (£18,000); Chesterfield Jan. 1979 (£15,000); Port Vale June 1981 (£16,000); CITY Mar. 1983; Doncaster Rovers June 1983; Chesterfield July 1984; Stockport County Dec. 1986; Scarborough Aug. 1987; Rochdale Mar. 1988; Kettering Town Aug. 1988; Matlock Town as player-coach cs 1990; Kettering Town player-coach Jan. 1991; Boston United asst.manager June 1992.

Big, powerful striker signed on a short term contract by Colin Murphy to boost City's flagging promotion hopes. Ernie travelled widely in a FL career spanning 20 years, making almost 750 appearances and scoring 244 goals. His aggregate of 161 for Chesterfield remains a club record. Runs sports shops in Chesterfield and Matlock in partnership with Geoff Miller the former Derbyshire and England cricketer.

MOULSON, Cornelius ("Con")
(1932-1936)
Centre-half: 88 app.
1936: 5-11½, 11-10
Born: Clogheer, Tipperary, 3 Sep. 1906
Died: 27 Oct. 1989
Career: Cleethorpes Town; Grimsby Town (amat.), (prof.) during season 1929/30; Bristol City May 1931; CITY June 1932; Notts County Sep. 1936 (£2,000); retired during WW2. Subsequently City's trainer-coach Jan. to Mar 1965 and trainer for a short time afterwards.
Honour: Eire international (5 app.)

"Marvellous is not too great a word to apply to the judgment of his head work. A remarkable 'stopper' but is constructive also, and a pivot of all-round ability", was a glowing description around the time of his transfer

to Meadow Lane. Became only the second player in the club's history to receive international honours whilst on the Imps' books. Returned as a wartime guest making 97 appearances and scoring twice. Later worked as a machinist in a local engineering factory, before returning to Sincil Bank again at the age of 58 as coach in charge of training and tactics. It proved a disastrous spell with the Imps losing all eight matches. Bother of George Moulson (see below).

MOULSON, George Bernard
(1947-1949)

Goalkeeper: 60 app.
Born: Clogheen, Tipperary, 6 Aug. 1914
Career: Army football; Grimsby Town cs 1936; CITY June 1947; Peterborough United Aug. 1949 to 1954.

Honours: Eire international (3 app. vs Spain, Portugal & Switzerland 1949)
(City) DL Div.3 (North) champions 1948

Con's younger brother and a member of an Irish family that migrated to the Grimsby area in the 1920's. Made his senior debut for the Mariners in the 1939 FA Cup semi-final during which he was stretchered off with concussion. Appeared regularly as a guest for the Imps during WW2 (102 app.) and was an ever-present in the 1947/48 promotion campaign, eventually losing his place when Arthur Jepson was signed. On leaving football worked for and later ran his father-in-laws fish merchant's business in Grimsby.

MOWATT, Archibald
(1899-1900)

Outside-right: 8 app., 1 goal
Born: South Shields, 1870
Career: Wallsend Park Villa, Newcastle East End 1891; Newcastle United Dec. 1892; CITY June 1899; Newcastle United cs 1900.

Only appeared once in Newcastle's League team but was considered a popular reserve in his long spell with them.

Scored on his Lincoln debut, a 3-0 home win over Middlesbrough in the opening match of the season, but soon lost his place and did not appear in the first team again until the last few weeks of the campaign.

MOWATT, Magnus James
(1938-1939)

Outside-right: 6 app., 1 goal
1938: 5-7, 10-9
Born: Glasgow, c.1915
Career: Dalreen Amateurs; St. Francis (Glasgow); Morton Juniors (Greenock); Clyde 1935: Dumbarton; Brentford June 1937; CITY June 1938; Clyde cs 1939.

Mowatt was first choice to begin with but the Imps had a terrible start to the season (they did not record a win until Oct.) and he was one of several men who lost their places. Returned to Scotland on a free transfer the following May.

MOYSES, Christopher Raymond
(1983-1984)

Full-back: 2 app., + 2 sub
1984: 5-9½, 11-7
Born: Lincoln, 1 Nov. 1965
Career: CITY schoolboy, YTS Oct. 1982, non-contract Nov. 1983; Halifax Town July 1984; Boston United Aug. 1985; (Shepshed Charterhouse on loan); Grantham; Spalding United cs 1987; Kings Lynn cs 1989; Boston FC cs 1990; Bourne Town Jan 1991; Lincoln United Nov. 1991; Sleaford Town (Lincs. League) cs 1992.

Defender who played in the last four matches of the 1983/84 season before moving on to Halifax where he made 21 appearances plus 4 as substitute. Has since spent several seasons touring round the south Lincolnshire non-League scene.

MUNRO, James F.
(1953-1958)

Outside-right: 161 app., 24 goals
1957: 5-6, 10-2
Born: Garmouth, Morayshire, 25 Mar. 1926
Career: West End (Elgin); Waterford July 1947; Manchester City Nov. 1947; Oldham Athletic Mar. 1950 (approx. £6,000); CITY Feb. 1953 (in exchange for Bill McGlen); Bury Jan. 1958 (£2,000) to cs 1959; Weymouth; appeared for Poole Town in 1960/61 and later had a spell as player-coach of Ely City.

Small and skilful wingman who was a regular in the Imps first team until losing his place to Ron Smillie towards the end of the 1956/57 season. Appeared as a wartime guest with Abredeen and Dunfermline Athletic and later made 119 FL appearances for Oldham, scoring 21 goals. On leaving football worked for a brewery and then spent 17 years with the Post Office.

MURPHY, Aidan J.
(1986)
Midfield: 2 app.
1986: 5-10, 10-10
Born: Manchester, 17 Sep. 1967
Career: Manchester United (appr.), (prof.) Sep. 1984 (CITY on loan Oct. 1986; Oldham Athletic on loan Feb. 1987); Crewe Alexandra July 1987; Scarborough Aug. 1992; Woking Oct. 1992; Mossley later in 1992; Witton Albion Feb. 1993.

Honours: England schools international (4 app., 1983)
England youth international (8 app., 1985, 1986)

Skilful but light-weight midfielder who had his introduction to League football at Sincil Bank. Appeared regularly with Crewe (93 app. plus 14 as sub) but was released by Scarborough after a trial and has since dropped into non-League football.

MURRAY, John
(1966)
Left-back: 4 app.
Born: Glasgow, 9 Mar. 1945
Career: Kirkintilloch Rob Roy, Stirling Albion Jan. 1964; CITY on trial Nov. to Dec. 1966.

Scottish full-back who was Ron Gray's first signing for the club. Returned north of the Border when his month's trial period was completed.

MURRAY, Joseph
(1931-1932)
Right-half: 1 app.
1929: 5-7½, 10-6
Born: Hull, 28 Aug. 1908
Died: Apr. 1988
Career: Dairycoates (Hull); Hull City (amat.) 1925/26 season, (prof.) Apr. 1926; CITY Aug. 1931; retired through injury cs 1932.

Former Hull City reserve whose solitary FL appearance for the Imps was in the home match with Stockport

County on 17 Oct. 1931. After leaving football he worked in his native city at a waterworks, as a coal trimmer on the docks and for a firm of timber importers, before retiring.

MUSSON, Ian S.
(1973-1974)
Forward: 11 app.
1974: 5-7½, 11-0
Born: Lincoln, 13 Dec. 1953
Career: Sheffield Wednesday (appr.), (prof.) Feb. 1971; CITY July 1973; Lincoln United July 1974; Buxton; Lincoln United Feb. 1976; Rustons Sports (Lincoln) Dec. 1979; Boston FC 1980 to cs 1983. Later played in Lincoln Sunday League football. Appointed asst.-manager Nettleham July 1993, manager Jan. 1994.

Local-born player signed by Graham Taylor after failing to break through to the first team with Wednesday. Always a fringe player at Lincoln and was released on a free transfer at the end of the season.

MUTCH, Adam
(1925)
Inside-left: 8 app., 2 goals
1925: 5-8, 11-0
Born: Aberdeen, 7 Mar 1901
Career: Aberdeen; Accrington Stanley July 1924; CITY Aug. to Nov. 1925; Forfar Athletic Dec. 1925; Arbroath Jan. 1926; Walsall Mar. 1926; Montrose later in 1926.

Smart scheming inside-man who appeared in eight of the first nine fixtures in 1925/26. His brief stay at Lincoln was terminated when the club cancelled his contract.

NAYLOR, Stuart William
(1980-1986)
Goalkeeper: 49 app.,
1984: 6-4, 12-10
Born: Wetherby, West Yorks, 6 Dec. 1962
Career: Yorkshire Amateurs; CITY schoolboy Feb. 1979, (prof.) June 1980 (Kettering Town on loan Jan. 1983; Peterborough United on loan Feb. to Apr. 1983; Crewe Alexandra on loan Oct. 1983 to May 1984 and again Aug. to Nov. 1984); West Bromwich Albion Feb. 1986 (£100,000)

Honours: England youth international (1 app. vs Austria 1980)
England 'B' international (3 app. vs Switzerland, Iceland, Norway 1989)

Tall, well-built 'keeper who won England youth honours while on City's books. His first team opportunities were restricted by the form of David Felgate and he spent lengthy periods out on loan. However, when given an extended run he performed well and was soon snapped up by West Bromwich Albion. Played at centre-forward for the Imps in an emergency at Newport in Oct. 1982.

NEAL, Richard Marshall
(1954-1957, 1963-1964)

Left-half: 156 app., 15 goals
1958: 6-1, 12-9
Born: Dinnington, nr. Sheffield, 1 Oct. 1933
Career: Dinnington MW; Wolverhampton Wanderers Mar. 1951 (£25); CITY July 1954 (£1,000); Birmingham City Apr. 1957 (£18,500 plus Bert Linnecor); Middlesbrough Oct. 1961 (£23,000); CITY Aug. 1963 (£3,000); Rugby Town Oct. 1964; Hednesford Town as player-manager May 1965 to cs 1967; Brierley Hill player-manager cs to Dec. 1967; Blakenall player-manager Feb. 1968.

Honours: England Under-23 international (4 app. vs Denmark, France 1956, Scotland, Bulgaria 1957).
(Birmingham City) Inter-Cities Fairs Cup finalist 1960

Tall powerfully built player reckoned to be strong in all areas of the game. Perhaps the best Lincoln development of the 1950's, winning three England Under-23 caps before his transfer to Birmingham. Returned for a second spell at Sincil Bank before dropping down to non-League football. Later worked as a licensee in the West Midlands. Son of Richard Neal, snr., a prominent player in the inter-war period.

NEALE, Keith I.
(1957-1959)

Inside-right: 8 app., 1 goal
1958: 5-8½, 11-3
Born: Birmingham, 19 Jan. 1935
Career: Metropolitan (Birmingham Works League), (Wolverhampton Wanderers amat.); Birmingham City (amat.) Aug. 1953, (prof.) Feb. 1954; CITY Nov. 1957; Kettering Town July 1959; Boston United Sep. 1960; Gainsborough Trinity Aug. 1963.

Inside-forward who went straight in the first team after signing but soon lost his place and spent most of his time at Sincil Bank in the reserves. Later settled in the Worcestershire village of Chaddesley Corbett.

NEALE, Philip Anthony
(1974-1985)

Defender/midfield: 327 app. + 8 sub, 22 goals
1983: 5-10, 11-5
Born: Scunthorpe, 5 June 1954
Career: Scunthorpe United (amat.); Lincoln United cs 1973 to cs 1975; CITY (amat.) Oct. 1974, (prof.) July 1975 to cs 1985; Worcester City; Gloucester City.

Honour: (City) FL Div.4 champions 1976

Versatile player who first appeared as an amateur while studying Russian at Leeds University. Initially used as a striker or in midfield but later switched to the back four playing mostly at full-back with an occasional game in the centre of the defence. Gave the club 10 years of excellent service spanning the eras of both Graham Taylor and Colin Murphy and appearing in two promotion sides. Even better known as a cricketer with Lincolnshire as a teenager, then Worcestershire (1975-1992) captaining the side from 1982 and leading them to the County Championship title in 1988 and 1989. Appointed Director of Cricket to Northamptonshire CCC in 1993.

NEAVE, George D. ("Geordie")
(1895-1896)

Centre-half: 29 app.
Career: CITY July 1895 to Apr. 1896; Dundee Sep. 1896.

Scottish half-back who gave almost a year's valued service, missing only the final match of the season. Returned north of the border to run a business.

NEILL, Quentin Durward
(1888-1895)

Full-back: 59 app.
Born: Glasgow, c.1866
Died: 9 Aug. 1901

Career: Queens Park; CITY Dec. 1888 to Jan 1895.

One of City's best known players of the late 19th century. Neill was one of four Scottish professionals signed when the club committee decided that improvements were necessary following an early exit from the FA Cup in the 1888/89 season. Captained the side for many years, rarely missing a game and winning great respect. On his retirement it was recorded "... *at his best there were few forwards that could beat him ... Always a fair opponent and a gentlemanly player".* Left the club after a dispute with the committee, returning briefly to Glasgow before emigrating for South Africa. Killed in action during the Boer War after enlisting with Driscoll's Scouts.

NELSON, George
(1946-1948)
Inside-forward: 1 app.
Born: Mexborough, Yorks., 5 Feb. 1925
Career: Sheffield Wednesday (amat.) 1942; Denaby Rovers; Sheffield United Aug. 1943; CITY Sep. 1946 to cs 1948.

Nelson's single FL appearance for the Imps was at New Brighton in Nov 1936. He had previously guested with Dundee for a whole season but rejected their offer of a professional contract. Served in the Royal Navy on a submarine during the war.

NEVIN, George William
(1937-1939)
Full-back: 8 app.,
1938: 5-10, 12-7
Born: Lintz, nr. Gateshead, 16 Dec. 1907
Died: 1973
Career: Lintz Colliery; Dipton United; Newcastle United Aug. 1925, later developed with White-le-Head Rangers, returning to Newcastle Dec. 1928 (£100); Sheffield Wednesday May 1930; Manchester United Dec. 1933; Sheffield Wednesday Mar. 1934; Burnley May 1935; CITY May 1937; Rochdale cs 1939.

A reliable reserve with all his clubs - he aggregated only 46 appearances in over a decade as a League player, 26 of these being for Burnley. At Lincoln he occasionally stood in for the regular full-back Hartshorne and Corbett. A former miner and nephew of John Nevin who played for Crewe Alexandra and York City between the wars.

NICHOLSON, Shane Michael
(1986-1992)
Defender/midfield: 122 app. + 11 sub, 7 goals
1990: 5-10, 11-6
Born: Newark, 3 June 1970
Career: CITY schoolboy July 1984, YTS July 1986, (prof.) Sep. 1987; Derby County Apr. 1992 (£80,000 rising by a further £20,000 after 25 appearances).

Became the Imps' youngest post-war League debutant when he appeared against Burnley in Nov. 1986 at the age of 16 years and 172 days. A first team regular at 17, developing into a strong left-footed player and was still in his early 20's when sold to Derby County. Just beginning to establish himself in the first team at the Baseball Ground.

NIDD, G(eorge) Frederick
(1897-1898)
Full-back: 9 app.
1903: 5-9, 11-2
Born: Boston, Lincs., 1869
Died: 1956
Career: Preston North End 1893; Everton 1893; Southport Central; Stalybridge Rovers 1896; Halliwell Rovers Mar. 1897; CITY Sep. 1897; Grimsby Town 1898; Watford cs 1900; Brentford cs 1902; Fulham cs 1903; Grays United Aug. 1904; Clapton Orient Mar. 1905; Watford Sep. 1907.

Experienced defender who suffered a bad knee injury in an FA Cup-tie at Gainsborough shortly after signing and did not recover fitness until towards the end of the season. Appeared for Lincoln under the pseudonym "Sydney", possibly because he had already been reinstated as an amateur on one occasion and did not wish his re-entry into the professional ranks to be widely known. Later worked as a schools attendance officer in the south of England.

NIGHTINGALE, Samson
(1936-1938)
Inside-right: 2 app.
1936: 5-6, 10-7
Born: Rotherham, 5 Nov. 1916
Died: 6 Dec. 1982
Career: United Steelworks (Rotherham); Woodhouse (Sheffield); CITY July 1936; Scunthorpe United Aug. 1938; Doncaster Rovers cs 1940 -1942 (guested for Grimsby Town in 1941/42).

Only given an opportunity in City's League team in Apr. 1938, shortly before being released. Did well for Scunthorpe, starring in their Midland League championship side of 1938/39 and scoring 41 goals during the first wartime season. One of five Rotherham brothers who were active in South Yorkshire football in the 1940's.

NISBET, George
(1906-1909)

Half-back: 62 app., 1 goal
1909: 5-9, 11-4
Career: Maxwelltown Volunteers; CITY May 1906 to around Oct. 1909.

Reliable half-back and a regular in City's team for three seasons until losing his place at the start of the 1909/10 campaign. Later became a prominent Labour Party official in the Ayrshire town of New Cumnock.

NORTH, Marc Victor
(1985)
Defender: 4 app.
1985: 5-10, 11-0
Born: Ware, Herts., 25 Sep. 1966
Career: Luton Town (appr.), (prof.) Mar. 1984 (CITY on loan Mar. -May 1985; Scunthorpe United on loan Jan. 1987; Birmingham City on loan Mar. 1987); Grimsby Town Aug. 1987 (£40,000); Leicester City Mar. 1989 (£100,000); Luton Town trial, July 1991; Grimsby Town trial, Sep. 1991; Leicester United Oct. 1991; Walsall trial, Jan. 1992; Shepshed Albion Jan. 1992; Boston United Mar. 1992; Kettering Town Mar. 1992; St. Andrews (Leics. Senior League) 1993/94 season.

Defender who came on loan from Luton for the last few months of the 1984/85 season. He had been signed by the Hatters as a schoolboy goalkeeper but was then converted to a defender and later switched to striker. Finished leading scorer for Grimsby in 1987/88 with 11 goals prompting Leicester to pay a large fee for him. Brother of Stacey who appeared for Luton, West Bromwich and Fulham.

NORTHCOTT, Thomas Theodore
(1955-1957)
Centre-forward: 94 app., 34 goals
1956: 5-9, 12-0
Born: Torquay, 5 Dec. 1931
Career: Hele Spurs (Torquay); Torquay United (amat.) 1948, (prof.) Nov. 1951; Cardiff City Oct. 1952 (a fee and two players); CITY July 1955 (£3,000); Torquay United Nov. 1957 (approx. £5,000); Bridgwater Town cs 1966; Newton Abbot Spurs.

Honour: England youth international (1949)

Won representative honours as a teenager with England youths and the Devon county team before going on to make 572 FL appearances plus 2 as substitute, scoring 182 goals. The vast majority of his career was spent at Plainmoor where he totalled over 400 outings. At Lincoln he took over the centre-forward position when Andy Graver was sold to Stoke and finished leading scorer in 1955/56 with 20 goals. His younger brother George was also a Torquay United stalwart for a decade.

O'CONNOR, Philip Kelvin
(1975)
Winger: 4 app., 1 goal
1975: 5-10, 12-0
Born: Romford, Essex, 10 Oct. 1953
Died: 1985
Career: Southend United (appr.); Bexley United; Luton Town Dec. 1972 (CITY on loan Jan. 1975); Balgownie (Australia) Apr. 1975; subsequently appeared with a number of Australian clubs; St. Georges 1977-1979; Leichhardt 1980-1982; Wollongong City 1982.

Honour: Australia international (20 app.)

Winger who spent a month on loan at Sincil Bank as cover for Dick Krzywicki, scoring on his debut in a 3-1 win at Torquay. Migrated to Australia shortly afterwards where he won international honours. Died in a car crash toward the end of 1985.

O'DONNELL, Dennis
(1901-1905)

Forward: 118 app., 31 goals
1904: 5-10½, 10-12
Born: Willington Quay, Northumberland, 1880
Career: Willington Athletic; CITY Sep. 1901 (£47); Sunderland
May 1905 (£370); Queens Park Rangers May 1906; Notts County
cs 1907; Bradford June 1908.

An excellent City development of the Edwardian period
capable of taking all five front positions although principally appearing as an inside-forward. Finished leading
scorer in the 1904/05 season with 13 goals before being
sold to First Division Sunderland for a club record fee.
Brother of Magnus O'Donnell (see below).

O'DONNELL, Magnus
(1904-1906)

Inside-left: 45 app., 11 goals
1904: 5-11½, 11-2
Born: Willington Quay, Northumberland, 1882
Career: Wallsend Park Villa; CITY May 1904; Barnsley cs 1906;
Newark cs 1907; Grantham Avenue cs 1908; Castleford Town
1909/10 season.

Younger brother of Dennis, above and it was said "... his
play greatly resembled that of his brother - resourceful
and accurate in passing but needed some pace". A
regular first teamer at Sincil Bank until Jan. 1906 when
he lost his place to Martin Kelly. Later made 21 Fl
appearances for Barnsley before switching to Midland
League football.

ORMISTON, Andrew Paisley
(1907-1909, 1919-1920)

Centre-half: 44 app., 2 goals
1909; 5-11½, 12-8
Born: Peebles, 1 Mar. 1884
Died: 1952
Career: Hebburn Argyle; CITY Nov. 1907; Chelsea cs 1909
(guested for Grimsby Town and CITY during WW1); CITY July
1919 to cs 1920. Peebles Rovers manager from Aug. 1924.

Took over the centre-half berth shortly after signing and
held his place for the rest of that season and throughout
the 1908/09 Midland League championship campaign
(28 app., 4 goals) before David Calderhead signed him
from Chelsea. He grossed 102 FL and FA Cup appearances at Stamford Bridge where he was later described
as "... a commanding centre-half and especially fine
header of the ball". Returned to Lincolnshire on the
outbreak of war and eventually rejoined City for the first
season of peace time football. His son, a Peebles
Rovers amateur, was on the Imps' books in 1937/38.

O'ROURKE, Peter
(1899-1900)

Right-half: 32 app.
Born: Newmilns, Ayrshire, 22 Sep. 1873
Died: 10 Jan. 1956
Career: Mossend Celtic; Celtic Feb. 1895; Burnley May 1897;
CITY July 1899; Third Lanark cs 1900; Chesterfield Town 1901;
Bradford City June 1903 to 1906, appointed reserve team manager

1904, coach Mar. 1905, manager Nov. 1905 to June 1921;
Pontypridd secretary-manager July 1922; Dundee Hibernians
manager Dec. 1922; Bradford manager Apr. 1924 to Feb. 1925;
Bradford City manager May 1928 to May 1930; Walsall manager
Oct. 1930 to Dec. 1931; Llanelli coach 1932 to July 1933.

Honour: (Burnley) FL Div.2 champions 1898

Solid half-back who missed only two matches in his
season at Sincil Bank. O'Rourke was a former Scottish
junior international and went on to become a prominent
figure in the football world for half a century. He
achieved considerable success as a manager at Bradford
City steering the club into the First Division in 1908 and
winning the FA Cup (1911) and the Northern Section
title (1928/29). Two of his sons, including Peter junior,
played the game professionally.

OSBORNE, Charles H.
(1894-1895)

Left-half: 6 app.
Born: Lincoln, 1873
Career: Adelaide (Lincoln); CITY Sep. 1894; Sheppey United cs
1895 to c.1900.

Local lad whose six FL appearances for City all ended
in defeat, and included an outing in the club record 11-3
loss at Manchester City. Proved a versatile performer
for Southern League Sheppey where he also appeared at
full-back and occasionally in goal.

OWEN, Robert G.
(1947-1955)

Left-half: 246 app., 5 goals
1951: 5-9, 11-7
Born: Sunderland, 5 May 1924
Career: Huddersfield Town during WW2; Murton Colliery Welfare;
CITY Jan. 1947; South Shields cs 1955; Whitley Bay coach Oct.
1963 to 1977.

Honours: (City) FL Div.3 (North) champions 1948,1952

Wing-half who went straight into City's FL team after signing forms as a part-timer and remained a first choice for the next seven seasons. Firm and assured in tackling with a constructive approach. On leaving Sincil Bank he returned to his native north-east, finding employment as a fitter with the National Coal Board. Later scouted for Watford when Graham Taylor was manager at Vicarage Road.

PAGE, George
(1924-1926)

Left-back: 64 app., 3 goals
1924: 5-10, 12-7
Born: Darlington, 30 Nov. 1898
Career: Rise Carr FC (Darlington); Doncaster Rovers; Barnsley May 1921; Accrington Stanley May 1922; Ashington July 1923; CITY July 1924; Crewe Alexandra June 1926; York City Sep.1927

A shrewd signing, Page proved a consistent and dependable partner firstly for Tom Sisson and later Walter Webster in his two seasons at Sincil Bank. His career aggregate was 150 FL appearances and 6 goals.

PALLISTER, William
(1902-1905)

Left-back: 59 app.,
1904: 5-9½, 12-2
Born: Gateshead, 1884
Career: Sunderland; CITY May 1902 to cs 1905

North-eastern recruit who succeeded the weighty but popular Will Gibson as City's left-back. He remained a first team regular until Oct. 1904 when Billy Simpson was switched from centre-half to replace him. Following this he was restricted to Midland League football apart from a single FL outing in Mar. 1905.

PANTHER, Frederick, George
(1923-1925)

Centre-forward: 15 app., 3 goals
1924: 5-8, 10-0
Born: Manchester, 4 Apr. 1903
Died: 1971
Career: Celtic FC (Lincoln); CITY (amat.) Mar. 1923, (prof.) Apr. 1924 (also assisted Lincoln Claytons in season 1923/24); Newark Town July 1925; Peterborough & Fletton United c.1926; Luton Town Dec. 1926; Brighton & Hove Albion Sep. to Oct. 1928; Folkestone later in 1928/29; Raith Rovers June 1929.

Panther was one of a number of local players recruited to fill the ranks of City's Midland League side early in 1923 to cover for the professionals who departed when asked to accept a wages cut. He impressed sufficiently to win a contract the following year, but did not appear regularly in senior football until moving north of the Border. John Litster in his Raith Rovers centenary history remarks, *"Fred Panther, a bullet-headed character at centre-forward, was signed from Folkestone in the*

[1929] close season. His 'up and at 'em style won him 64 goals in 86 appearances". Panther later ran a confectionary shop close to Raith's Stark's Park ground.

PARKER, Graham Sydney
(1968-1969)

Wing-half: 4 app. + 1 sub
1969: 5-7, 10-5
Born: Coventry, 23 May 1946
Career: Coventry Schools; Aston Villa (appr.) July 1961, (prof.) May 1963; Rotherham United Dec. 1967 (approx. £6,000); CITY July 1968 (£7,000); Exeter City Mar. 1969; Torquay United May 1974 to cs 1977.

Honours: England Schools international (6 app., 1961)

Graham was given his FL debut by Villa in Apr. 1964, shortly before his 18th birthday, but only played a handful more first team games before moving on. He was a reserve at Sincil Bank, mainly turning out for the North Midlands League side but saw regular first team action after moving to the south-west. A career aggregate of 244 appearances plus 7 as substitute to the majority of which were during his spell at Exeter.

PARKER, Harry
(1903-1904)

Outside-left: 30 app., 3 goals
1903: 5-6, 10-10
Career: Glossop cs 1901; Whitwick White Cross cs 1902; CITY June 1903 to cs 1904.

Useful outside man who partnered Freddy Simpson on City's left flank in his season at Sincil Bank. He was recruited from the same Midland League side as Thomas Price.

PARKINSON, Steven
(1991-)

Midfield: 1 app. + 4 sub
1993: 5-11, 12-0
Born: Lincoln, 27 Aug. 1974
Career: Horncastle Town Juniors; CITY on YTS July 1991, (prof.) May 1993 (Witton Albion on loan, Oct. 1993; Kings Lynn on loan, Mar. 1994).

Horncastle youngster who signed terms after captaining the junior side whilst on YTS forms. A competitive midfield player, he made his full FL debut at Gillingham in the final match of the 1993/94 season as a replacement for David Ridings.

PARR, Henry ("Harry")
(1946-1956)

Wing-half/inside-forward: 112 app., 13 goals
1949: 5-9, 11-7
Born: Newark, 23 Oct. 1915

Career: Ransomes & Marles and City (amat.) pre-WW2; asst. Ransomes, Notts County, Newark Town, Peterborough United and Clapton Orient during WW2; Ransomes & Marles 1945; CITY (amat.) Aug. 1946 to around 1956

Honours: England amateur international (1 app. vs Ireland 1947) (City) FL Div.3 (North) champions 1948

Amateur wing-half who first appeared for the Imps' reserves in 1939/40. Returned to the club after the war and played regularly in the first three seasons of peace time football during which he also represented the Lincolnshire county side. Made his last FL appearance in Sep. 1950 but remained on the books at Sincil Bank until the mid-1950's playing for the reserve and Lincolnshire League sides. Harry is the only City player to win England amateur honours whilst with the club. Worked as a civil servant for the Lincoln Telephone Manager's Department. A cousin of Jack Parr who appeared for the Imps during WW2.

PARSONS, David
(1920)
Inside-right: 12 app., 4 goals
1919: 5-7½, 11-0
Career: Eston United; CITY Feb. to cs 1920; Eston United; Ashington early in 1921; Hartlepools United Aug. 1921.

Recruit from Teesside who was one of several amateurs to appear for City in the first season after the Great War. Scored on his FL debut in a 2-2 draw at Grimsby and played regularly in the first team until the end of the campaign.

PATERSON, William
(1936-1937)
Centre-half: 2 app.
1937: 5-11, 12-10
Career: Distillery; Greenock Morton; Arbroath; Stenhousemuir 1935; CITY Sep. 1936; Mansfield Town May 1937 to 1939.

Scot who was restricted to just two FL outings for the Imps as deputy for regular centre-half Bob Meacock.

He had more success at Field Mill where he gave fine service until war broke out, making 63 FL appearances. A 1938 comment was "... very speedy to tackle and recover and, although primarily a defensive pivot, likes to exploit the long pass to the wings. Keen and enthusiastic".

PATTISON, Frank
(1914-1916)
Outside-right: 11 app., 2 goals
1914: 5-8, 11-7
Born: South Bank, Middlesbrough, Mar. 1889
Died: 8 Mar. 1950
Career: Sunderland; Clapton Orient cs 1913; CITY June 1914; Rustons Aircraftmen (Lincoln) cs 1916; Mid-Rhondda June 1919; Boston Town July 1921, retired cs 1923.

Fast, sharp-shooting winger who shared the outside-right position with Jack Manning during his only season of peacetime football at Sincil Bank. After leaving football was employed as a licensee for 29 years until his death at the age of 61.

PAYNE, Frank Ernest
(1949-1950)
Goalkeeper: 5 app.
1950: 5-10, 11-12
Born: Ipswich, 18 Mar. 1926
Career: Nottingham Forest during WW2; Ollerton Colliery cs 1946 -cs 1947; Derby County Dec. 1947; Hull City Aug. 1948; CITY Aug. 1949; Kippax Legionaires Sep. 1950; Swillington Welfare July 1951; Farsley Celtic Oct. 1956.

Reserve to Arthur Jepson, Payne appeared in the first four FL fixtures of the 1949/50 campaign and also the final match of the season. His only other senior experience was in a fifth round FA Cup tie for Derby at Middlesbrough in Feb. 1948. Later turned out for several West Yorkshire non-League sides.

PEAKE, Trevor
(1979-1983)
Centre-half: 171 app., 7 goals
1981: 6-0, 12-9
Born: Nuneaton, 10 Feb. 1957
Career: Nuneaton Borough; CITY June 1979 (£15,000); Coventry City June 1983 (£100,000); Luton Town Aug. 1991 (£100,000).

Honour: (Coventry FA Cup winner 1987)

Calm and dependable central defender who was one of Colin Murphy's first signings. First appeared at Sincil Bank with the Nuneaton Borough team beaten 6-0 by the Imps in the 1976 FA Cup-tie and went on to win England semi-professional honours before arriving at Sincil Bank. Was a virtual ever-present in his four seasons with the club, establishing a strong partnership with Steve Thompson at the heart of City's defence at a time when they were one of the best teams in the lower divisions. Spent eight years in top flight football at Highfield Road and came close to an England 'B' cap, being selected for the squad only to drop out through injury. Appeared for Luton against Chelsea in the 1994 FA Cup semi-final.

PEARMAN, James
(1899-1900)
Goalkeeper: 1 app.
Born: Lincoln, 1877
Career: Casuals (Lincoln); St. Marys (Lincoln); CITY Aug. 1899 to cs 1900.

Local youngster whose opportunities for first team action were restricted by the presence of Cullen and Webb. His solitary FL outing came in a 3-1 defeat at Walsall on 23 Dec. 1899.

PEDEN, George Wright Watson
(1967-1974)
Left-back: 223 app. + 2 sub, 14 goals
1970: 5-8, 11-3
Born: Rosewell, Midlothian, 12 Apr. 1943
Career: Arniston Rangers; Heart of Midlothian cs 1964; CITY Apr. 1967; Worksop Town cs 1974; Lincoln United cs 1978 to Sep. 1978; Skegness Town. Retired cs 1980.

Scottish-born full-back who developed into one of the club's most loyal and effective defenders since the war. Went straight in the first team after signing and established a run of over 100 consecutive appearances before he lost his place. Stayed at Sincil Bank several years, suffering a badly broken leg at Scunthorpe in Mar. 1971 which put him out of action for some time. Best remembered for his powerful tackling and thundering penalty kicks. Voted supporters' Player of the Season in 1972/73 and shared a testimonial against Chelsea with John Kennedy in his final season. Later returned to Scotland where he was employed by a double glazing firm and had a spell as manager of the Bonnyrigg club.

PEGG, Frank Edward
(1926-1931)

FRANK PEGG Lincoln City
GARTH DYKES

Outside-left: 115 app., 51 goals
1926: 5-8, 11-0
Born: Beeston, Notts, 2 Aug. 1902
Career: Sawley United (Long Eaton & District League); Blackpool (on trial); Nelson (on trial) Dec. 1924; Loughborough Corinthians later in 1924/25; Sunderland May 1925; CITY May 1926; Bradford City May 1931; Norwich City June 1932; New Brighton Aug. 1933; Great Yarmouth Town Sep. 1934 to 1936.

On signing for the Imps it was said he "... *can travel and get in a fast centre while on the run. Also has a reputation with a scoring shot*". Although he had a reputation for missing chances by shooting wildly his goals tally shows that when he did connect his shots were often unstoppable. Suffered a bad injury in the final match of the 1928/29 season and made only a handful more FL appearances before moving on. Maintained his goalscoring touch even at the end of his career - he netted six for Yarmouth during an away game in November 1934.

PHILLIPS, Henry George
(1899-1900)
Centre-forward: 2 app., 1 goal
Career: Sandford Hill (Staffs.); CITY May 1899 to Feb. 1900.

Recruit from the Potteries who scored on his debut against Middlesbrough in the opening match of the 1899/1900 campaign but only appeared once more for the first team and was released before the end of the season.

PHIPPS, W.
(1893)
Outside-left: 2 app.
Career: CITY Sep. to c.Oct. 1893.

Winger who appeared a couple of times in place of first choice William Graham in the early part of the 1893/94 season. Did not impress and was released shortly afterwards.

PICK, William Edward
(1926)
Outside-left: 2 app.
1925: 5-8, 10-7
Born: Clay Cross, Derbys., 5 June 1903
Died: 27 Aug. 1981
Career: Danesmoor Rovers (Chesterfield); Bury Feb. 1925 (after a month's trial); CITY Apr. 1926; Portsmouth Aug. 1926; Newport County July 1927; Coventry City Nov. 1928; Watford Dec. 1930; Barrow July 1932; Stockport County 1933.

Only at Sincil Bank for a brief period, his two FL appearances coming at the very end of the 1925/26 season. Later developed a reputation as a goalscoring winger with a powerful shot - he scored 40 for Newport's first and reserve teams in 1927/28 and won representative honours for the Welsh League against the Irish Free State League. Also had success at Coventry were he netted 25 goals in 74 FL outings.

PILGRIM, J(ohn) Alan
(1966-1971)

Defender: 20 app. + 3 sub, 1 goal
1970: 5-9, 11-5
Born: Billingborough, Lincs., 20 July 1947
Career: Billingborough; CITY Mar. 1966; Boston United Dec. 1971; Skegness Town cs 1973 appointed player-coach Aug. 1975, player-manager Mar. 1976 to Mar. 1978; Ruston Bucyrus (Lincoln) Mar. 1978.

Versatile reserve who appeared in both defence and midfield for the Imps. Made his debut as a substitute in the 7-0 defeat at Crewe in Mar. 1966, remaining a part-time professional during his spell with the club. His best season was 1967/68 when he made 15 appearances plus 1 as substitute, taking over the left-half position when Jim Grummett was moved up to the forward line.

PLATNAUER, Nicholas R.
(1994-)

Full-back: 13 app.
1993: 5-11, 12-10
Born: Leicester, 10 June 1961
Career: Bedford Town; Bristol Rovers Aug. 1982; Coventry City July 1983 (£50,000); Birmingham City Dec. 1984 (£55,000); (Reading on loan, Jan 1986); Cardiff City Sep. 1986; Notts County Aug. 1989 (£50,000); (Port Vale on loan, Jan. to Apr. 1991); Leicester City July 1991; Scunthorpe United Mar. 1993; Kettering Town cs 1993; Mansfield Town Aug. 1993; CITY Feb. 1994.

Honour: (Cardiff) Welsh Cup winner 1988

Determined and enthusiastic full-back signed after David Clarke was sold to Doncaster. At the very beginning of his career he had made his FL debut for Bristol Rovers against the Imps having given up a job as a bank clerk to sign for the Eastville club. Has made over 300 League appearances to date.

PLATTS, Albert John
(1910-1914)

Outside-left: 29 app., 4 goals
1912: 5-9, 11-7
Born: Worksop, 1885
Career: Anston Juniors (Sheffield) 1903; Denaby United cs 1906; Worksop Town 1908; CITY May 1910; Scunthorpe United cs 1914; Rotherham Town cs 1919.

Shared the left-wing position with Tommy Yule in his first season with the Imps but was then restricted to a handful of outings as deputy to Horace Brindley for the rest of his time at Sincil Bank. In 1913 reckoned to be *"... an outside-left of speed and skill, quick to seize his chances and make the most of them"*.

POLLITT, Michael
(1992-1994)

Goalkeeper: 57 app.
1993: 6-3, 14-11
Born: Bolton, 29 Feb. 1972

Career: Manchester United YTS, (prof.) July 1990 (Oldham Athletic on loan, Oct. 1990; Macclesfield Town on loan, Jan. 1991); Bury July 1991 (CITY on loan, Mar. to cs 1992; Altrincham on loan, Aug. 1992); CITY on loan Sep. to Oct. 1992, permanently Dec. 1992 (Altrincham on loan Dec. 1992); Darlington Aug. 1994.

Young 'keeper who spent two spells on loan at Sincil Bank as cover for Ian Bowling and Matt Dickins before signing permanently. Remained first choice until Mar. 1994 when he lost his place to Andy Leaning.

PONTING, Walter Thomas
(1938-1939)

Centre-forward: 26 app., 18 goals
1938: 5-10½, 13-0
Born: Grimsby, 23 Apr. 1913
Died: 17 Aug. 1960
Career: Humber United (Grimsby); Grimsby Town May 1930; Chesterfield May 1936; CITY Nov. 1938 to 1939.

Weighty centre-forward denied a place with his home town club by the presence of Welsh international Patsy Glover. Walter won Midland League championship medals while at Blundell Park before moving on to success with newly promoted Chesterfield (38 goals in 80 Second Division matches). His Lincoln career got off to a fine start with 9 goals in his first 5 games including a hat-trick against non-League Bromley in the FA Cup, but was terminated prematurely by the war. Known for his hard right-foot shot cleverly delivered on the half-turn, and considered a difficult man to contain. Joined the Auxiliary Fire Service on the outbreak of war and, in Nov. 1939, the Grimsby Borough Police Force.

POPPITT, James
(1907-1908)

Inside-forward: 23 app., 3 goals
1907: 5-7½, 11-7
Born: c.1882
Career: Wellington (Birmingham League); Wolverhampton Wanderers cs 1900; Swindon Town cs 1902; Reading May 1903; Swindon Town May 1904; Notts County cs 1905; CITY June 1907 to cs 1908.

Experienced forward who shared the inside-right position with Billy Langham in his season at Sincil Bank. Before joining the Imps it was reported he *"... has scarcely realised expectations so far but showed great skill in passing whenever in the League team. Wants more speed and greater accuracy in shooting"*.

POSKETT, Thomas William
(1932-1934)

Goalkeeper: 10 app.
1933: 5-11, 12-0
Born: Esh Winning, Co. Durham, 26 Dec. 1909
Died: 19 Dec. 1972
Career: Chopwell; Crook Town; Grimsby Town Dec. 1928; CITY May 1932; Notts County May 1934; Tranmere Rovers Aug. 1935; Crewe Alexandra July 1937 to 1947.

Efficient 'keeper who was reserve to the even more capable Dan McPhail in his two seasons with the club. All his first team outings came in the early part of 1934 after McPhail was suspended for being sent off. Remained an understudy until joining Crewe where he made a total of 101 FL appearances and stayed until after the war.

POSNETT, Arthur
(1906-1907)

Outside-right: 3 app., 1 goal
Born: Leicester, 1882
Career: Liberal Club (Lincoln); CITY Oct. 1906; Gainsborough Trinity cs 1907; later assisted Liberal Club in 1909/10; Grantham Avenue from cs 1911; South End (Lincoln) in 1913/14; Newland Athletic c.1916 to cs 1920; Horncastle Town in 1920/21.

Recruit from Lincoln League football who was principally a reserve at Sincil Bank. Scored in his second match - a 4-0 victory over Gainsborough - and later signed for the Northolme Club although he did not appear in the League for them.

POWELL, Gary
(1990)

Forward: 11 app.
1990: 5-10, 10-2
Born: Hoylake, Cheshire, 2 Apr. 1969
Career: Everton YTS, (prof.) July 1987 (CITY on loan, Sep. to Nov. 1990; Scunthorpe United on loan Nov. 1990; Wigan Athletic on loan Mar 1991, permanent July 1991; Altrincham late 1993; Macclesfield Town early in 1994.

Striker signed by Allan Clarke for an extended loan period. Although he showed considerable promise he was unable to find the net but later had limited success with Wigan (57 app. + 27 as sub, 17 goals) before moving down to the Vauxhall Conference.

POWELL, William H.
1932-1934)

Left-back: 4 app.
1933: 5-10, 11-7
Career: Merthyr Town; CITY Aug. 1932 to cs 1934.

One of four men signed from Southern League Merthyr in the summer of 1932 although only two (Powell and Iorwerth Williams) made City's League side. Proved a useful reserve back appearing in four consecutive first team fixtures during Dec. 1932 and Jan. 1933 as cover for James Smith.

POYNTON, William
(1966)

Defender: 0 app. + 1 sub
1965: 5-5½, 10-13½
Born: Shiremoor, Newcastle-upon-Tyne, 30 June 1944
Career: Burnley July 1961; Mansfield Town July 1964; Lockheed Leamington July 1966; Oldham Athletic (on trial) Sep. 1966; CITY (on trial) Oct. to Dec. 1966.

Defender who spent most of his time at Sincil Bank in the reserves. Came on as substitute for Jim Grummett for the final six minutes of the fixture at Bradford City in Oct. 1966. Had earlier made 20 FL appearances for Mansfield.

PRICE, Thomas
(1903)

Centre-forward: 11 app., 3 goals
Career: Whitwick White Cross; CITY Feb. to cs 1903.

Price went straight into the first team after signing from Midland League Whitwick and performed well enough to keep his place ahead of Peter Proudfoot who was switched to a defensive role. However, City failed to score in their final four games of the season and he was not retained for the following campaign.

PRINGLE, Charles Ross
(1931-1933)

Right-half: 58 app., 1 goal
1930: 5-7, 11-0
Born: Barrhead, Renfrewshire, 18 Oct. 1894
Career: Maryhill; St. Mirren during WW1; Manchester City June 1922; Manchester Central June 1928; Bradford cs 1929; CITY May 1931; Stockport County Feb. to May 1933; Zurich Club (Switzerland), coach summer of 1933; Hurst Oct. 1933; Waterford trainer-coach early 1934/35 season; St. Mirren coach later 1934/35.

Honours: Scotland international (1 app. vs Wales 1921)
Scottish League (1 app. vs Irish League 1921)
(Manchester City) FL Div.2 champions 1928
FA Cup finalist 1926
(City) FL Div.3 (North) champions 1932

Wing-half who brought the experience of more than 300 appearances at St. Mirren and Manchester City with him to Sincil Bank. Captained the Imps' 1932 championship side and in addition to his leadership skills was known for his energetic displays and hard tackling. Son-in-law of the famous Billy Meredith.

PRINGLE, Henry ("Harry")
(1922-1934)

Forward: 292 app., 60 goals
1928: 5-7, 11-0
Born: Perkinsville, Co. Durham, 8 Apr. 1900
Died: 8 Jan. 1965
Career: Craghead United; Arsenal; Chester-le-Street 1921; CITY May 1922; Grantham player-manager June 1934, manager cs 1935, trainer cs 1936 to cs 1949; Aveling-Barford (Grantham) trainer cs 1949.

One of the Imps' greatest servants of the inter-war period. Summed up in late career as *"... an enthusiastic team man, a hard working forager and provider for others, but never a great shot. His best displays have been given on heavy grounds, as apparently he experiences some difficulty in controlling a light ball"*. Established a new club record for FL appearances and became the first player to exceed 300 League and Cup games for City. Popular man who married a director's daughter.

PROUDFOOT, Peter
(1900-1903)

Forward: 79 app., 20 goals
1900: 5-10½, 11-2
Born: Wishaw, Lanarks, Nov. 1880
Died: 4 Mar. 1941
Career: Wishaw FC; Wishaw United cs 1900; CITY Dec. 1900; St. Mirren cs 1903; Millwall Oct. 1904; Clapton Orient cs 1905; Chelsea Apr. 1906; Stockport County cs 1908; Greenock Morton cs 1909; Stockport County 1910. Clapton Orient manager Apr. 1922 to Apr. 1929, Apr. 1930 to Apr. 1931, and Jan. 1935 to Jan. 1939.

Versatile Scottish forward who occasionally turned out at wing-half and full-back towards the end of his spell at Sincil Bank. A well-known character in the football world, famed for his unpredictable behaviour - a story is told of how he beat man after man in one match, his superb skills leaving him only the goalkeeper to beat,

however, he proceeded to ignore the ball and instead laid out the 'keeper with a flying leap! Appeared as a defender in later career.

PUGH, David Henry
(1898-1902, 1905-1908)

Outside-right: 91 app., 11 goals
Born: Wrexham, 1875
Died: 26 May 1945
Career: Wrexham Grosvenor; Wrexham 1895; Stoke May 1897; CITY Mar. 1898 to 1902 and Feb. 1905 to 1908.

Honours: Wales international (7 app.)
(Wrexham) Welsh Cup winner 1897; finalist 1896

One of the Imps' most popular players at the turn of the century and the first man to win international honours when on the club's books - he was 'capped' three times during his spell at Sincil Bank. A traditional winger known for his speed, trickery and an ability to cross the ball accurately. City kept his FL registration when he was released in the summer of 1902 and he eventually returned to give three more years service with the Midland League side (he did not appear in the first team after the end of the 1900/01 season). Settled in the Lincoln area and remained prominent in local sport for some time playing cricket for the St. Andrews club and making one appearance for Lincolnshire in the Minor Counties competition (1909).

PUNTER, Brian
(1959-1964)

Centre-forward: 75 app., 21 goals
1962: 5-10, 11-5
Born: Bromsgrove, Worcs., 16 Aug. 1935
Career: Wolverhampton Wanderers Sep. 1953; Kidderminster Harriers cs 1954; Bromsgrove Rovers cs 1956; Leicester City May 1958; CITY Nov. 1959; Hereford United July 1964; Arcadia FC (Pretoria, South Africa) 1966; Hereford United Sep. 1967; Nuneaton Borough cs 1970.

Honours: England youth international (1953)
(Hereford) Welsh Cup finalist 1968 (both legs)

Centre-forward who had won international youth honours whilst with Wolves but had to wait until he arrived at Sincil Bank before making his FL debut. In five seasons with the club he was only a regular in the 1961/62 and 1962/63 campaigns and on both occasions finished leading scorer. Moved on to Southern League Hereford after being placed on the 'open to transfer' list in May 1964.

PUTTNAM, David Paul
(1990-)

Midfield: 148 app. + 7 sub, 16 goals
1993: 5-10, 11-9
Born: Leicester, 3 Feb. 1967
Career: Kirkby Muxloe; Leicester United; Leicester City Feb. 1989 (£8,000); CITY on loan Jan. 1990, signing permanently Mar. 1990 (£35,000).

Highly rated wingman - fast and tricky with an ability to cross the ball accurately. Popular with the supporters who voted him Player of the Season in 1992/93 but missed a large part of the following campaign through injury.

PYLE, Tom
(1895-1900)
Outside-left: 27 app., 3 goals
Born: Lincoln, 1875
Died: 20 Dec. 1958
Career: Princess (Lincoln); CITY Mar. 1895 to cs 1900; Adelaide (Lincoln) cs 1901 to c.1905.

Local player who appeared mostly with the Swifts (reserve) side during a five year spell at Sincil Bank. Was considered to be not quite up to the standard of Second Division football. Died in the nearby village of Washingborough.

RABY, William ("Joe")
(1891-1894, 1897)
Forward: 26 app., 7 goals
1902: 5-6, 10-6
Born: Heighington nr. Lincoln, 3 Jul. 1873
Died: 18 Dec. 1954
Career: St. Catherines (Lincoln); CITY Sep. 1891; Gainsborough Trinity cs 1894; CITY Apr. to cs 1897; Gainsborough Trinity later in 1897; Tottenham Hotspur cs 1899; Wellingborough cs 1900; Gainsborough Trinity later in 1900; Stockport County cs 1902; Doncaster Rovers cs 1904.

Recruit from local junior football who was mostly a reserve with City. Did well later in his career with both Gainsborough and Stockport where he was a regular first- teamer. Settled in Lincoln and worked as an engine fitter. Father of Walter Raby who appeared for City in 1920/21 and later Grimsby Town plus Clapton Orient.

RAMSAY, Craig J.
(1978-1982)
Forward: 3 app. + sub, 2 goals
1981: 5-7, 11-13½
Born: Dunfermline, 19 Sep. 1962
Career: Gibraltar Red Imps; CITY schoolboy Nov. 1978, (appr.) Sep. 1979, (prof.) Sep. 1980; Yaro (Finland) Apr. 1982; remained in Finland throughout the 1980's and was with Kokkolan PV in Feb. 1987 (occasionally returned for brief spells in English non-League football eg: Grantham Nov. 1986 to Jan. 1987).

Small Scottish-born striker who scored for the Imps on his FL debut (against Newport County in Feb. 1980) when still a teenage apprentice. Found his first team opportunities very limited and later moved to Finland where he was still playing in the early 1990's.

RANSHAW, John W.
(1946-1947)
Outside-left: 3 app.
Born: Nettleham, Lincs., 19 Dec. 1916
Career: Lincoln Corinthians; Gainsborough Trinity 1937 (Sheffield United on trial Aug. 1938); Newark Town (Grimsby Town, Chesterfield, Mansfield Town and CITY during WW2); Grantham cs 1945; CITY Feb. 1946 (Ernest Hoyland and £150); Peterborough United July 1947; Boston United June 1948; March Town 1949; Nettleham cs 1950.

Local player who had assisted Grimsby Town for three wartime seasons, totalling 27 goals from 89 appearances. Played six matches for the Imps in 1945/46 but served as understudy to Geoff Marlow in his only season of peacetime football at Sincil Bank. Later ran a newsagents business in Nettleham and held the post of groundsman for City during the late 1950's until Jan. 1965.

RANSHAW, Richard W.G.
(1986-1988)
Forward: 0 app. + 1 sub
Born: Sleaford, Lincs., 17 Apr. 1970
Career: CITY YTS July 1986; Gainsborough Trinity Sep. 1988; (Skegness Town in Feb. 1989); Louth United Aug. 1989 (Peterborough United on trial in 1989/90); Skegness Town cs 1990; Nettleham Oct. 1990; Harrowby United early in 1991; Bridlington Town early in 1992; Lincoln United cs 1992; Grantham Town cs 1993; Lincoln United Aug. 1993.

Youngster who appeared as a substitute for the injured Bob Cumming during the final two minutes of City's home match against Hartlepool on 27 Aug. 1988. Has since established a reputation as a strong bustling striker in local non-League football and been a prominent figure in Lincoln United's rise to the Premier Division of the Northern Counties East League.

RANSON, John George
(1935-1936)
Centre-forward: 5 app., 1 goal
1935: 5-10, 11-12
Born: Norwich, 1 Apr. 1909
Career: Norwich City trial Oct. 1927, (amat.) Aug. 1928, (prof.) later in 1928/29 season; Swansea Town June 1929; Chester July 1931; Gateshead June 1932; Millwall May 1933; Burton Town June 1934; Carlisle United Nov. 1934; CITY June 1935; Blyth Spartans June 1936; Spennymoor United Sep. 1936; Durham City Oct. 1936; Horden Colliery Welfare; Durham City 1939.

Reserve centre-forward who finished leading scorer for the Midland League side with 21 goals but found his first team opportunities very much restricted by the presence of Johnny Campbell. Described as having a "... facile use of either boot and difficult to hold because of his tenacity". A schoolmaster by profession, he gave up teaching in 1933 and was later in the hotel trade. Father of the England RU international, J.M. Ranson.

RAW, Henry
(1936-1938)

Right-half/inside-right: 66 app., 7 goals
1936: 5-10, 11-0
Born: Tow Law, Co. Durham, 6 July 1903
Died: 1965
Career: Tow Law Town; Huddersfield Town (amat.) Mar. 1923, (prof.) cs 1925; West Bromwich Albion Mar. 1931; CITY July 1936; retired cs 1938.

Honours: (Huddersfield) FA Cup finalist 1930

After representing County Durham when with Tow Law, Harry graduated to the great Huddersfield Town side of the 1920's, making 70 FL and FA Cup appearances (11 goals). Mainly a reserve at West Bromwich where he won three Central League championship medals. Successfully captained the Imps, his experience being an asset in the development of young players.

RAWCLIFFE, Peter
(1990)

Midfield: 0 app. + 1 sub
1987: 5-6, 10-2
Born: Grimsby, 8 Dec. 1963
Career: Grimsby Amateurs; Louth United; Grimsby Town Sep. 1986 to cs 1988; Boston United Dec. 1988 to Oct. 1989; Scunthorpe United on trial; Holbeach United; CITY July 1990; Lincoln United Oct. 1990; Kings Lynn Mar. 1991; Boston FC Mar. 1992; Brigg Town Aug. 1992; Boston FC Sep. 1992.

Diminutive non-contract player whose only FL experience for City came when he replaced the injured John Schofield after 11 minutes of the home match with Chesterfield in Sep. 1990. Also saw League action at Grimsby: 9 app., plus 13 as substitute, 1 goal.

RAYSEN, Leonard
(1926-1927)

Outside-left: 1 app.
Born: c.1908
Career: Sheffield junior football; CITY Nov. 1926; Grantham Feb. to cs 1927.

Trialist winger whose solitary League outings came in a 2-2 draw at home to Wrexham on 20 Nov. 1926. Later appeared for Grantham in the Midland League scoring 2 goals in 12 appearances.

READ, Arthur
(1924-1925)

Left-half: 8 app.
1924: 5-8, 11-0
Born: Saxilby, Lincs
Career: Saxilby; Bargoed United; Aberdare Athletic 1921; Gillingham 1922; CITY May 1924 to cs 1925.

Local lad who eventually arrived at Sincil Bank after a three year spell in Division Three South with Aberdare (31 app.) and Gillingham (61 app.). Began his Lincoln season as first choice but soon lost his place to Richard Rushton and departed on a free transfer the following summer.

REDDISH, John
(1933-1935)

Left-back: 53 app.,
1935: 5-8½, 11-12
Born: Nottingham, 22 Dec. 1904
Died: 18 Oct. 1989
Career: Boots Athletic (Nottingham); Tottenham Hotspur Mar. 1927; CITY July 1933; Notts County Sep. 1935; Dundee Aug. 1936.

Reddish had been mostly a reserve at White Hart Lane, making only 6 FL appearances in just over six seasons, but was City's first choice left-back from signing, until Jan. 1935, when he lost his place to James Smith. He was a reliable defender who also played cricket professionally (1 appearance for Notts. in 1930). When his football career was over he spent time coaching in the Channel Islands, only leaving when WW2 broke out.

He returned after the war becoming games master of Elizabeth College, Guernsey - a post he held until his mid-60's.

REDFEARN, Neil David
(1984-1986)

Midfield: 96 app. + 4 sub, 13 goals
1985: 5-10, 12-4
Born: Dewsbury, Yorks., 20 June 1965
Career: Nottingham Forest (appr.); Bolton Wanderers June 1982; CITY on loan Mar. 1984, permanently Aug. 1984 (£8,250 plus share of future fee); Doncaster Rovers Aug. 1986 (£17,500); Crystal Palace July 1987 (£100,000); Watford Nov. 1988 (£150,000); Oldham Athletic Jan. 1990 (£150,000); Barnsley on loan Sep. 1991, permanently Oct. 1991 (£150,000).

Honour: (Oldham Athletic) FL Div.2 champions 1991

Powerful and competitive midfield man who played an important role in Colin Murphy's side of the mid-1980's. Sold to Doncaster Rovers for a disappointingly low fee (the amount was fixed by a tribunal) and has since gone on to aggregate more than 400 FL appearances, mostly in the higher divisions.

REED, Charles William ("Chick")
(1932-1935)

Centre-forward/inside-right: 55 app., 24 goals
1934: 5-8, 11-0
Born: Holbeach, Lincs., 21 Mar. 1912
Died: 28 July 1964
Career: Spalding Institute; Spalding United cs 1929; Sheffield United Nov. 1930 (£50); CITY Aug. 1932 (£125); Southport Mar. 1935; Chesterfield Feb. 1936; Spalding United cs 1937; Mansfield Town Dec. 1937; Notts County May 1938 to WW2. Assisted Spalding United again after the war and served on the club committee in the early 1950's.

Enthusiastic and vigorous forward possessing a powerful shot. Had a good scoring record when called on for first team duties but was even more prolific with the Midland League side scoring 5 goals in a match on two separate occasions and netting 44 times in the 1932/33 season. Successfully switched to left-half on joining Notts County. His name also appeared as 'Read' in the contemporary press.

REID, James Greig
(1910-1912)

Inside-right/centre-forward: 36 app., 3 goals
1910: 5-8½., 10-7
Born: Peebles, 1 May 1890
Died: 22 Apr. 1938
Career: Peebles Rovers (trials with Chelsea and Partick Thistle); CITY Mar. 1910; Airdrieonians cs 1912; Clydebank Oct. 1927; retired cs 1928.

Honours: Scotland international (3 app., vs Wales 1914, 1920; Ireland 1924)
Scottish League (3 app.)
(Airdrie) Scottish Cup winner 1924

"Exceptionally promising", wrote a 1910 commentator - a perceptive comment as Jimmy won the first of his Scotland caps soon after returning north of the Border. While with Lincoln his clever footwork and subtle play won praise although he was criticised for his lack of goals and only appeared twice in the first team in the 1911/12 Central League championship campaign. Headed the Scottish League scoring list on two occasions, switching to outside-right towards the end of his career. Later became proprietor of an Airdie tobacconists shop.

RICHARDS, Gary Vivian
(1985-1986)

Defender: 2 app. + 5 sub
1984: 5-8½, 11-1
Born: Swansea, 2 Aug. 1963
Career: Swansea City (appr.), (prof.) Aug. 1981 to May 1985; spent the summer of 1985 playing in Swedish football before joining CITY on a non-contract basis Nov. 1985; Cambridge United Mar. 1986; Torquay United July 1986; Newport County Nov. 1988 to Feb. 1989; Saltash; Stroud; Barnstaple; Barry Town Oct. 1990; Ton Pentre; Haverfordwest season 1991/92.

Honour: Welsh youth international (7 app.)
(Swansea) Welsh Cup winner 1983

Defender signed on non-contract terms by John Pickering shortly before he lost the manager's position. Richards fell out of favour with new boss George Kerr and soon moved on to Cambridge. Has since appeared with a succession of clubs in the south-west of England and south Wales.

RICHARDS, Stephen C.
(1985-1986)

Centre-half: 21 app.
1986: 6-0, 12-0
Born: Dundee, 24 Oct. 1961
Career: Hull City (appr.) July 1978, (prof.) Oct. 1979 to May 1983; Bridlington Trinity; Lierse SK (Belgium); Grantham; York City on non-contract basis Dec. 1984; Goole Town; Gainsborough Trinity

July 1985; CITY Aug. 1985 on trial, signing terms Sep. 1985; Cambridge United on non-contract basis Mar. 1986; Scarborough cs 1986; Halifax Town cs 1991; Doncaster Rovers May 1992; Guiseley cs 1993.

Began his career promisingly with Hull but was then badly affected by injuries and drifted around until arriving at Sincil Bank. Proved a solid central defender but, like his namesake Gary, fell out of favour when George Kerr arrived and departed for Cambridge. Has since totalled over 300 FL appearances, including a club record 164 for Scarborough.

RICHARDSON, George William Richard
(1920-1921)
Left-half: 12 app.
1921: 5-9½, 10-7
Born: Gainsborough, 1899
Died: Nov. 1963
Career: Gainsborough Wednesday; CITY Feb. 1920; Sheffield United Dec. 1921 (£1,225); Bournemouth & Boscombe Athletic July 1924 (£200); Boston Town June 1925, remaining for several seasons.

Lincolnshire-born wing-half who established himself as a first-teamer early in 1921 going on to make 22 appearances in the Midland League championship season and quickly attracting a big fee from First Division Sheffield United. Saw little FL action at either Bramall Lane or Bournemouth and eventually moved back into non-League football with Boston.

RICHARDSON, John Mettam ("Mick")
(1892-1896)
Centre-half: 64 app., 6 goals
Born: Lincoln, 1874
Died: 10 July 1920
Career: St. Catherines (Lincoln); CITY cs 1892; Gainsborough Trinity cs 1896; Constitutional Club (Lincoln).

A stalwart of City's early days in the Football League, Richardson appeared regularly in the first team until losing his place following a 4-2 FA Cup defeat by Grimsby Town in Nov. 1895. Moved on to local rivals Gainsborough, appearing for them in their final season of non-League football before their election to Division Two.

RIDINGS, David
(1994-)
Midfield: 10 app.
1994: 6-1, 12-8
Born: Farnworth, Lancs., 27 Feb. 1970
Career: Bolton junior football; Curzon Aston; Macclesfield Town Apr. 1991; Curzon Aston later in 1991; Halifax Town Jan. 1993; CITY Feb. 1992 (£10,000).

Had his introduction to League football in the season Halifax were relegated to the Vauxhall Conference - scoring twice on his debut in a 3-0 win at Darlington. Made 21 FL appearances in all for the Yorkshire club

scoring 4 goals. A competitive midfield player signed by Keith Alexander to provide penetration and goal-scoring power.

RILEY, Harold
(1931-1933)
Inside-forward: 57 app., 25 goals
1932: 5-8, 11-0
Born: Oldham, 2 Nov. 1909
Died: 8 Apr. 1982
Career: Altrincham; Hurst; Birmingham (amat.) Dec. 1928; Ashton National 1929/30; Accrington Stanley June 1930; CITY June 1931; Notts County June 1933 (in exchange for Tom Feeney); Cardiff City June 1934; Northampton Town June 1936; Exeter City Nov. 1938 to WW2; Ruston Bucyrus (Lincoln) in 1945/46.

Honour: (City) FL Div.3 (North) champions 1932

Signed from Accrington along with George Whyte, having scored 18 goals in 32 matches during the 1930/31 season. A contemporary described him as "... *of diminutive build and extremely fast and clever with the ball ... He is remarkable with his head for so small a player ...*". Riley was also a noted cricketer with Ruston Bucyrus and Lincolnshire (9 Minor Counties appearances 1948-49), once scoring 164 - the county's fourth highest individual total.

RILEY, John Leonard
(1913-1914)
Outside-right: 6 app.
1913: 5-9, 11-4
Born: Riddings, Derbys., 1888
Career: Sutton Town; CITY May 1913 to 1914.

Recruited from Central Alliance soccer along with a team-mate G.W. Bellamy, who did not make City's senior side. Riley was described on signing as "... *fast, pushful, has the makings of a player*", and appeared in the first five games of the 1913/14 season before being replaced by the more experienced Jack Manning.

RIPPON, Thomas ("Pip")
(1920-1922)

Inside-/centre-forward: 33 app., 10 goals
1921: 5-7, 10-7
Born: Beighton, nr. Sheffield, 4 Feb. 1888
Died: 29 May 1950
Career: Derbyshire junior football; Grimsby Town during the 1910/11 season; CITY cs 1920; Worksop Town May 1922; York City in 1923/24; Wath Athletic in 1924/25.

Speedy, opportunist forward: *"excels in distributive work, but is also a crack shot, as his scoring record testifies"*. Rippon scored 38 goals in 123 League and FA Cup games for the Mariners and hit 23 in 35 Midland League outings for the Imps in their 1920/21 championship side. Younger brother of Willis Rippon (Grimsby and Rotherham Town).

RITCHIE, Robert
(1899)
Outside-left: 1 app.
1899: 5-8½, 11-0
Career: Victoria United (Aberdeen); CITY May to c.Nov. 1899.

It was reported in Aug. 1899 that Ritchie had been *"... Victoria United's outside-left for a number of years"*, but he failed to win a regular place at Lincoln and soon departed. (Victoria United were one of three side who merged to form Aberdeen FC in 1903). His solitary FL appearance for the Imps came when he deputised for Tom Pyle in a 5-0 defeat at Small Heath on 2 Oct. 1899.

RIX, John
(1939)
Right-half: 3 app.
1939: 5-8½, 11-6
Born: Lintz, Bursopfield, Co. Durham, 12 July 1908
Died: 1979
Career: Lintz Colliery; West Bromwich Albion Nov. 1927; CITY June 1939; retired during WW2.

Solid half-back who skippered the Imps in the three fixtures played at the start of the 1939/40 season before war intervened. He had been mostly a reserve at The Hawthorns appearing in only 68 League and FA Cup matches in over a decade, but had won junior international honours for the Birmingham FA and three Central League championship medals.

ROBERTS, Alan
(1989-1990)
Forward: 10 app.
1990: 5-9, 10-0
Born: Newcastle-upon-Tyne, 8 Dec. 1964
Career: Middlesbrough (appr.), (prof.) Dec. 1982; Darlington Sep. 1985; Sheffield United July 1988 (£16,000); CITY Oct. 1989 (£60,000); retired through injury Nov. 1990.

Highly skilled wingman signed from the Blades for a club record fee. Roberts was injured in an FA Cup tie against Billingham Synthonia a month later and although he returned to first team action after a short break the knee gave way again and he was eventually forced into early retirement. Received a testimonial against Sheffield United in Apr. 1991.

ROBERTS, Evan Evans
(1894-1895)
Goalkeeper: 23 app.
1892: 5-11½, 12-0
Born: Bolton, 1870
Career: Bolton Wanderers; Kettering Sep. 1892 to cs 1893; CITY Sep. 1894; Rotherham Town Apr. to cs 1895.

Former Bolton Wanderers reserve who signed amateur form for Kettering in time for their introduction to Midland League soccer. Joined Lincoln as a replacement for the injured Broadbent and remained first choice until a disastrous spell in Mar. (consecutive defeats at Burslem, 7-1, and Manchester City, a record 11-3), led to his release. His brief association with Rotherham came when he appeared for them in a friendly against the Imps in one of the last ever games played on the old John O'Gaunts ground.

ROBERTS, Henry
(1928-1930)
Inside-/centre-forward: 33 app., 23 goals
1928: 5-8, 11-0
Born: Barrow-in-Furness, 1 Sep. 1907
Died: Oct. 1984
Career: Barrow Wireworks 1922; Barrow Dec. 1925; Chesterfield June 1926; CITY Aug. 1928; Port Vale June 1930; Millwall Apr. 1931; Sheffield Wednesday (on trial) Oct. 1933; Peterborough United Nov. 1935; Spalding United cs 1938.

Honour: England international (1 app. vs Belgium 1931)

Young forward who did not particularly impress in his first season with the club and was initially given a free transfer in the summer of 1929. The directors changed their minds however, and he went on to score 21 times in 23 FL outings during the following season, winning full England international honours 12 months later. Said to be a *"clever footballer, very adept in the skilful manner in which he beats opponents"*.

ROBERTS, Robert
(1892-1893)
Half-back: 16 app., 2 goals
c.1890: 5-11, 10-0
Born: Penycae, nr. Wrexham, July 1864
Died: 15 Mar. 1932
Career: Druids (Ruabon) 1882; Bolton Wanderers Apr. 1884; Preston North End Mar. 1892; CITY Nov. 1892 as player-coach to cs 1893. Subsequently had a brief spell as Leicester Fosse's trainer-coach.

Honours: Wales international (10 app.)
(Druids) Welsh Cup finalist 1883, 1884

Veteran international defender signed as captain and player-coach in a bid to strengthen the side after the Imps got off to a poor start in their first ever Football League campaign. Played well for the first few matches but, as a local newspaper put it *"... there was ONE FAILING ABOUT BOB, he gave way to drink ..."*, and was afterwards suspended twice by the club committee. He escaped more serious punishment because it was felt the team could not do without him.

ROBERTSON, Hugh
(1897-1899)

Centre-forward: 64 app., 34 goals
Career: Scottish football; Millwall Athletic cs 1894; Burnley June 1895; CITY June 1897; Millwall Athletic May 1899; Woolwich Arsenal Mar. 1900; Dundee cs 1900; Leicester Fosse, trial Nov. 1900, but not offered a contract.

Described shortly after signing for Lincoln as *"a fine, well-built player, with plenty of devil and dash, holds his wings well together and* [is] *a clever shot at goal"*. Robertson gave City two years of exellent service, being an ever-present and leading scorer in both campaigns.

ROBERTSON, Thomas Henry
(1910-1911)

Centre-forward: 8 app., 1 goal
1910: 5-9, 11-0
Born: Gateshead, 1889
Career: Wallsend Park Villa; CITY May 1910 to cs 1911; retired through injury but subsequently recovered fitness; Ashington early 1920's until 1926.

Scored on his debut in a 2-2 draw with Glossop and appeared in a handful of first team matches before suffering a fractured kneecap in a reserve match against Notts County in Dec. 1910. The injury necessitated a long spell in hospital and in Oct. 1912 he took legal action against Lincoln City FC. Although medical evidence considered his knee was sound, he was unable either to play football or resume his former occupation as a brass finisher and was therefore forced to work as a labourer at a lower wage; the judge found in favour of the club. He recovered fitness and starred with Ashington in their first five FL seasons, scoring 61 goals in 151 League appearances.

ROBINSON, Ernest George
(1935-1939)

Right-back: 64 app.,
1936: 5-9½, 11-8
Born: Shiney Row, Co. Durham, 1908
Died: 1991
Career: York City; Notts County 1929; Nelson June 1930; Northampton Town Mar. 1931; Tunbridge Wells Rangers later in 1931; Barnsley Aug. 1932; Sheffield United May 1933 (£500); Carlisle United Aug. 1934 (£175); CITY Aug. 1935 to cs 1939.

Dependable and enthusiastic defender summed up after his Carlisle season as *"sturdy, good tackler with strong kick aided by real direction"*. Lost his first team place

through injury in Dec. 1936 and thereafter remained deputy to Jack Hartshorne. Ernie worked as a trainer/coach in Holland post-war, finishing with the Enschede club. Emigrated to Canada in 1985 where he died six years later in Vancouver.

ROBINSON, John ("Jackie")
(1949-1950)

Inside-right: 8 app., 5 goals
1950: 5-9, 12-0
Born: Shiremoor, Newcastle-upon-Tyne, 10 Aug. 1917
Died: 1979
Career: Shiremoor; Sheffield Wednesday 1935; Sunderland Oct. 1946 (£5,000); CITY Oct. 1949 to 1950; retired through injury.

Honours: England international (4 app.)
Football League (1 app. vs Irish League 1939)

Regarded as a young prodigy in his Wednesday days, winning his first cap at 19. Jackie's grace, confidence and mastery of ball control captivated the critics until war intervened. Scored after only six minutes on his debut for City against Darlington but his career was tragically ended soon afterwards when he suffered a fractured left leg in a home game with Wrexham on Christmas Eve, 1949.

ROBINSON, Thomas Edward
(1934-1935)

Inside-left: 33 app., 14 goals
1934: 5-9, 11-2
Born: Coalville, Leics., 11 Feb. 1909
Died: Mar. 1982
Career: Coalville YMCA; Gresley Rovers; Birmingham Jan. 1929 (£100 including another player); Blackpool May 1933; Chesterfield Oct. 1933; CITY June 1934; Northampton Town 1935; Gillingham July 1936; Walsall May 1937; Tunbridge Wells Rangers cs 1938; Nuneaton Borough.

Inside-forward who received few opportunities in higher grade football but did well when dropping down to the Third Division. A career record of 121 FL appearances, 36 goals. Robinson worked as a miner.

ROBINSON, William Atkin
(1929-1930)

Centre-forward/inside-left: 17 app., 7 goals
1929: 5-8½, 11-0
Born: Pegswood Colliery, Northumberland, 20 Dec. 1898
Died: 1975
Career: Hartlepools United during season 1924/25; Bradford July 1928; CITY June 1929; Gainsborough Trinity Aug. 1930; Ashington cs 1932.

Billy had done well in his final season at Hartlepools, scoring 28 goals in 34 FL outings, but was unable to get regular Second Division football at Bradford. He began his Lincoln season as first choice but spent most of the second half of the campaign in the reserves, for whom he finished leading scorer with 25 goals.

ROBSON, James
(1923-1924)
Outside-left: 10 app.
1922: 5-8, 11-7
Born: Durham
Career: Blackburn Rovers cs 1922; CITY Oct. 1923 to cs 1924.

Robson had impressed in pre-season trial matches with Blackburn, his performances being praised as *"skilful, if as yet unpolished"*, but he only saw reserve team action at Ewood Park. Received his Lincoln debut against Rotherham in Dec. but the remainder of his first team outings came towards the end of the campaign when he deputised for Harry Sillito.

ROBSON, Joseph William
(1925-1928)
Half-back: 60 app., 1 goal
1927: 5-11, 11-7
Born: Ryhope, Co. Durham, 26 Oct. 1899
Career: Sunderland Schools pre-WW1; Durham City during season 1923/24; Rochdale June 1925; CITY Oct. 1925 to cs 1928; Durham City Dec. 1928.

Honour: England schools international (2 app., vs Scotland, Wales 1913)

Strong centre-half: *"... Joe at his best has a way with him that opposing centre-forwards find difficult to deal with"*. And a later comment said that he was a *"tireless feeder and tackler"*. He had earlier made 57 FL appearances for Durham. Brother of Fred, a Durham City colleague and, before that, a Swansea Town stalwart.

ROBSON, Matthew Henry
(1909-1915)
Half-back: 121 app., 3 goals
1913: 5-10½, 11-2
Born: Springwell, nr. Gateshead, 1891
Career: Gateshead junior football; Washington United; Wallsend Park Villa; CITY May 1909 to cs 1915 (assisted Rustons Aircraftmen and Notts County during the Great War); Scunthorpe United July 1919; Boston Town 1920, appointed reserve team player-coach cs 1924.

Versatile half-back regarded as fast with fine distribution and heading skills and a good shot. Matt went straight in the first team after signing from the North Eastern League but only won a regular place (at right-half) at the start of the 1911/12 season. A firm favourite with the Imps' supporters in the years leading up to WW1.

RODGERS, David Michael
(1982)
Centre-half: 3 app.
1981: 6-1¼, 13-2
Born: Bristol, 28 Feb. 1952
Career: Bristol City July 1969; Torquay United Feb. 1982; CITY Mar.- May 1982; Forest Green Rovers cs 1982.

Honours: England schools international (1 app. vs Northern Ireland 1967)

Experienced central defender who had played amost 200 games for Bristol City before joining Torquay on non-contract forms. Came to Sincil Bank on a short term contract at a time when the Imps were pushing hard for promotion to Division Two, only to be foiled in the last game of the season at Fulham.

ROE, Archibald
(1923-1924)
Centre-forward: 27 app., 12 goals
1923: 5-8, 11-2
Born: Hull, 9 Dec. 1893
Died: 1947
Career: South Shields 1918; Birmingham 1919; Gillingham cs 1920; Castleford Town July 1921; Arsenal Aug. 1922; CITY Nov. 1923; Rotherham County Dec. 1924 to 1925.

"... a hard as nails centre-forward... only of moderate height, but he feared no foe, and his duels with defenders apparently about twice his size often caused the fur to fly". Roe had done well with Arsenal's reserves, scoring 23 goals in 37 London Combination outings and headed City's scoring list in 1923/24. Later became a publican in Sheffield.

ROGERS, William
(1897)
Centre-forward: 1 app.
Career: Abercorn; CITY Feb. 1897.

A Scot who was given a brief trial in one of the club's worst ever seasons. His single FL appearances came in a 4-0 defeat at Burton Swifts on 6 Feb. 1897.

ROONEY, Robert M.
(1963-1964)
Inside/outside-left: 28 app., 3 goals
1962: 5-8, 11-7
Born: Cowie, Stirlingshire, 8 July 1938
Career: Clydebank; Sheffield United June 1958 (£300); Doncaster Rovers Oct. 1962 (£5,000); CITY Jan. 1963 (in exchange for Albert Broadbent); Cambridge City cs 1964; Gainsborough Trinity cs 1965; Spalding United Dec. 1967.

Rooney turned out regularly for the Imps from signing until Oct. 1963, after which he only appeared twice more before being placed on the open to transfer list. Despite six years as a professional his total League experience amounted to just 48 appearances, 7 goals.

ROSS, William
(1897-1898)
Outside-left: 22 app., 3 goals
1902: 5-11, 11-7
Born: Kiveton Park , Sheffield, 1874

Career: Chesterfield Town cs 1894; Sheffield United cs 1895; CITY Nov. 1897; Gravesend United cs 1898; Reading 1899; Notts County May 1900; Grimsby Town June 1904; Glossop May 1905 to 1908.

Consistent wingman possessing speed and a fair shot who was signed to replace the departed Robert Downie. Had earlier been on the verge of joining local rivals Gainsborough Trinity, according to a Sheffield newspaper the clubs had agreed a £50 fee but the deal fell through because of a dispute and City benefitted. After retiring Ross worked in the hotel trade. In 1914 he tried to join the Glossop FC board but fell foul of the FA's then ban on former professionals becoming club directors. He was also a useful cricketer and in 1902 was on the Notts CCC groundstaff.

ROUND, Kenneth, Arthur
(1938-1939)

Left-half: 3 app.,
1938: 5-10, 11-8
Born: Dudley, Worcs., 13 Oct. 1917
Died: Oct. 1988
Career: Round Oak Works; Brierley Hill Alliance 1936; Dudley Town 1937; CITY May 1938 to cs 1939.

"Reported tricky with the ball, a good supporter of the attack, and a reliable defender", said a pre-season publication. Round was principally a reserve in his season at Lincoln, deputising for the regular left-half, George Whyte, on three occasions in Sep. 1938. He had earlier won junior international honours for the Birmingham FA against Scotland.

ROWE, Douglas Heath
(1933-1934)

Outside-left: 11 app., 5 goals
1934: 5-9, 11-10
Born: Nottingham, 9 July 1909
Died: 6 May 1978
Career: Sneinton FC (Nottingham); Luton Town Mar. 1932 (initially on amateur forms); CITY Aug. 1933; Southampton Aug. 1934; Union Sportif Tourcoing (France) Oct. 1934.

Rowe proved a useful stand-in for Jacky Wilkinson in a season that saw City lose their Second Division status. At Luton he had made 22 FL appearances scoring 8 times. Had a brother who represented Great Britain as a wrestler in the Olympic Games. Died in Grimsby.

RUDKIN, Thomas William
(1938-1939)

Outside-left: 2 app., 1 goal
1938: 5-7, 10-6
Born: Peterborough, 17 June 1919
Career: Creswell; Wolverhampton Wanderers (amat.) Feb. 1938, (prof.) shortly afterwards; CITY May 1938; Peterborough United June 1939 (guested for Grimsby Town, Middlesbrough, Southampton, Darlington, Hartlepools United and CITY in WW2); Arsenal Jan. 1947 (£1,800); Southampton Aug. 1947; Bristol City May 1949; Hastings United cs 1951; Weston-super-Mare as player-

manager May 1942 to Feb. 1953 when he joined Peterborough United's staff.

Youngster given his City debut at Chester on 31 Dec. 1938 and scored on his only other FL appearance for the club (a 4-2 defeat at Hull the following month). The bulk of his wartime experience came at Grimsby (23 app., 14 goals) and Darlington (37 app., 9 goals) whilst in peacetime he aggregated only 49 League outings, mostly with Bristol City.

RUSHTON, Richard
(1924-1925)

Left-half: 44 app., 1 goal
1924: 5-10½, 11-7
Born: Willenhall, Staffs., 18 Sep. 1902
Died: 1981
Career: Bloxwich Strollers; Willenhall Swifts 1923; CITY July 1924; Sheffield Wednesday Oct. 1925; Barnsley May 1926; Wombwell Aug. 1927; Connah's Quay Aug. 1928; Bury June 1929; Swindon Town July 1930;. Wellington Town July 1931.

Honours: (Connah's Quay) Welsh Cup winner 1929

Recruited from Birmingham League football, and was a regular in City's line-up throughout his time with the club. Saw little FL action elsewhere but enjoyed success with Connah's Quay in the 1928/29 season when besides the Welsh Cup, the Welsh National League (North) was won.

RYAN, Michael Joseph
(1952-1953)

Outside-right: 7 app.
1950: 5-7, 10-0
Born: Welwyn Garden City, Herts., 14 Oct. 1930
Career: Chase of Chertsey; Arsenal July 1948; CITY June 1952; York City Jan. to cs 1953.

Promising wingman who had represented the British Army while on National Service (called up Mar. 1949 and served with the RASC). Ryan made no senior appearances with Arsenal and only four for York who were reported to have paid a 'four-figure fee' for him.

SAMUELS, Robert William Lewis
(1967-1968)

Inside-forward: 3 app. + 1 sub
1967: 5-10, 11-12
Born: Aberdeen, 18 May 1946
Career: Sunnybank (Aberdeen); Dundee United 1964; CITY July 1967; Stevenage Athletic Aug. 1968; Keith July 1969 to Sep. 1970.

Samuels arrived with little senior experience gained north of the Border and spent most of his Lincoln year in the reserves, helping them to win the North Midlands League Cup. On joining Highland League Keith he was described as, *"a nippy team man, quick to make and seize chances"*.

SAUNDERS, James E.
(1906-1909)

Goalkeeper: 65 app.
1909: 5-9, 11-7
Born: Birmingham
Career: Glossop; Middlesbrough; Manchester United Aug. 1906; CITY Oct. 1906; Chelsea May 1909; Watford May 1910 (£50); Liberal Club (Lincoln).

A capable 'keeper for the Imps, although always a reserve with his other senior clubs, making only spasmodic first team appearances. An ever-present in the 1908/09 season when he collected Lincolnshire Senior Cup and Midland League championship medals. Made a surprise return to Sincil Bank as a guest player in Jan. 1918 when on leave from military service in France.

SAUNDERS, John George
(1979-1980)

Centre-half: 25 app. + 1 sub, 1 goal
1979: 6-1, 12-6
Born: Worksop, 1 Dec. 1950
Career: Mansfield Town (appr.), (prof.) Mar. 1969; Huddersfield Town Oct. 1972 (£20,000); Barnsley on trial Dec. 1975, permanent Mar. 1976 (£5,000); CITY June 1979; Doncaster Rovers Aug. 1980; Worksop Town cs 1981 to Nov. 1983, later became manager to Nov. 1983.

Central defender signed by Colin Murphy to partner the inexperienced Trevor Peake at the heart of City's back four. Saunders was initially first choice but lost his place later in the season when Steve Thompson emerged as Peake's regular partner. Aggregated 411 FL appearances plus 2 as subsititute in a lengthy professional career before beginning a long association with Worksop where he later served as social club manager and, in the later 1980's club chairman.

SAVAGE, R(obert) Edward
(1928-1931)

Right-half: 96 app., 3 goals
1929: 5-10, 11-8
Born: Louth, Lincs., 1912
Died: 30 Jan. 1964
Career: Stewton (Lincs.); CITY late 1928; Liverpool May 1931; Manchester United Dec. 1937; Wrexham 1938; retired during WW2.

Former Louth Grammar School boy given his introduction to League football when only 17 and becoming a first team regular in his second season. Regarded as one of City's best discoveries of the inter-war period and summed up as *"fast, resourceful, and a good judge in defence or attack"*. His form soon attracted the attention of bigger clubs and he was snapped up by Liverpool for whom he went on to make over 100 FL appearances. Ted also excelled at swimming and was a noted runner with the Grimsby Harriers AC. Worked in the licensing trade after giving up football.

SAXBY, Michael William
(1983-1984)

Centre-half: 10 app., 1 goal
1983: 6-2, 13-10
Born: Mansfield, 12 Aug. 1957
Career: Mansfield Town (appr.), (prof.) Jan .1975; Luton Town July 1979 (£200,000) (Grimsby Town on loan, Mar. to May 1983; CITY on loan, Nov. 1983 to Feb. 1984); Newport County on trial, July 1984; Middledsbrough Oct. 1984 to Apr. 1986; Oakham United; Nuneaton Borough Nov. 1986; Alfreton Town Nov. 1988 as asst.-manager.

Well-built central defender signed for an extended loan period to cover for injuries. Spent ten years in the game and despite being badly affected by knee problems he totalled 193 FL outings plus 3 as substitute. Had been apprenticed as a newspaper composite before becoming a professional footballer. Older brother of Gary (Mansfield and Northampton).

SAYER, Stanley Charles
(1926-1927)

Inside/centre-forward: 32 app., 6 goals
1926: 5-8, 12-0
Born: Chatham, 2 Feb. 1895
Died: 3 Apr. 1982
Career: Army football; Ramsgate; Millwall Athletic Jan. 1921 (£25); Northfleet United Aug. 1922; Tranmere Rovers Mar. 1923; New Brighton July 1925; Wigan Borough Nov. 1925; CITY Mar. 1926; Southend United July 1927; Dartford 1929; Ramsgate Town.

Sayer was known for his clever constructive approach play and was said to have been a mentor for Dixie Dean in his Tranmere days. At Lincoln he was credited with the emergence of Harold Andrews as a goalscoring force. Totalled 50 goals in a career aggregate of 201 games.

SCANLON, Albert Joseph
(1962-1963)
Outside-left: 47 app., 11 goals
1962: 5-9, 11-3
Born: Manchester, 10 Oct. 1935
Career: Manchester United (amat.) 1951, (prof.) Dec. 1952; Newcastle United Nov. 1960 (£17,500); CITY Feb. 1962 (£2,000); Mansfield Town Apr. 1963; Belper Town Aug. to Oct. 1966.

Honours: England under-23 international (5 app.)
Football League (1 app. vs Irish League 1959)

One of the original Busby Babes, Albert spent eight years at Old Trafford where he made 127 League and Cup appearances and survived the 1958 Munich air disaster. Arrived at Sincil Bank in late career but rarely missed a game in his year with the Imps which saw the club relegated to Division Four for the first time, and on their way to a bottom four position by the time he departed. Nephew of Charlie Mitten who signed him when manager of Newcastle.

SCANLON, Edward A.
(1909-1911)
Inside-right/wing-half: 29 app., 3 goals
1909: 5-8, 11-7
Born: Hebburn, Co. Durham, c.1888
Career: Wallsend; North Shields Athletic; CITY Aug. 1909; South Shields cs 1911; Jarrow 1912; Swindon Town May 1914 to cs 1915.

Appeared at inside-right in his first season with the club, switching to half-back in 1910/11 when the competition for forward places was stronger. On joining Southern League Swindon he was said to be *"a forward who knows the way to goal and what to do when he arrives there"*. Worked in South Shields after the Great War.

SCHOFIELD, Harry
(1898-1900)
Left-back: 17 app.
Career: Manchester St. Augustines; CITY Mar. 1898 to Feb. 1900.

Full-back signed from the same club as George Morris, being a replacement for Tommy Eyres after the latter had been given his release. City recruited Will Gibson the following summer however, and Schofield remained a reserve for the rest of his time at Sincil Bank.

SCHOFIELD, John David
(1988-)
Midfield: 209 app. + 10 sub, 10 goals
1993: 5-11, 11-3
Born: Barnsley, 16 May 1965
Career: Huddersfield Town; Woolley MW; Shepshed Charterhouse; Matlock Town cs 1987; Gainsborough Trinity Mar 1988; CITY Nov. 1988 (£10,000)

Hard-working and aggressive midfield player who has occasionally turned out in the back four when required. John never made Huddersfield's FL team, but was given his debut by Colin Murphy shortly after joining the Imps from non-League football. Club captain during the 1993/94 campaign when he was also voted Player of the Season by the supporters.

SCOTT, Christopher
(1987-1989)
Defender: 4 app.
1989: 6-1, 13-0
Born: Wallsend, 11 Sep. 1963
Career: Cramlingham; Whitley Bay; North Shields; Blyth Spartans; Northampton Town c.1987 (Darlington on loan, Nov. 1987, British Timken Duston on loan, 1987/88); CITY Dec. 1987 (£6,000); Whitley Bay 1989.

Central defender signed to boost City's challenge for the Vauxhall Conference championship but spent long periods on the injury list. Stayed with the Imps for their first season back in Leauge football and was then released on a free transfer. No FL appearances at Darlington or Northampton.

SCOTT, Frank
(1897-1901)
Inside-/outside-right: 45 app., 8 goals
1902: 5-8, 11-0
Born: Boultham, Lincoln, c.1876
Died: 3 July 1937
Career: Adelaide (Lincoln); CITY Oct. 1897; New Brompton cs 1901; Brighton & Hove Albion Aug. 1902 to cs 1904.

Local foundry worker who proved a useful addition to City's forward strength at the turn of the century. Later spent three years in Southern League football eventually returning to find employment in a Lincoln engineering works. Subsequently became a licensee from 1932 until his death at nearby Saxilby, aged 61.

SCOTT, Keith
(1990-1991)

Centre-forward: 7 app. + 9 sub, 2 goals
1990: 6-3, 12-0
Born: Westminster, London, 10 June 1967
Career: Hinckley Athletic; Bedworth United in 1987/88; Hinckley Athletic cs 1988; Leicester United cs 1989 (trial with Leicester City later in 1989); CITY Mar. 1990 (£22,500) (Gateshead on loan, Oct. 1990; Boston United on loan Feb. 1991); Wycombe Wanderers on loan Mar. 1991, permanent later in the same month (£30,000 plus share of a future fee); Swindon Town Nov. 1993 (£300,000)

Former bank clerk who was signed by City after scoring prolifically in non-League soccer. Seemed to find it difficult to adjust to the faster pace of the Football League and was allowed to depart after receiving few opportunities. Helped Wycombe to success in the Vauxhall Conference and FA Trophy in 1992/93 before earning a big-money transfer to then Premiership Swindon Town.

SCOTT, Kevin A.
(1973-1976)

Centre-half: 1 app.
Born: Lincoln, 12 Nov. 1954
Career: CITY (amat.) Feb. 1973 to cs 1976; Rustons Sports (Lincoln) cs 1976.

Amateur central defender who appeared mainly with the Imps' reserve and junior sides, receiving his only FL outing as a replacement for Terry Cooper in the 3-3 home draw with Doncaster Rovers in Apr. 1974. Scott was a student at Sheffield Polytechnic for much of his time that he was on the club's books. Won representative honours with the British Polytechnics XI and the Lincolnshire FA county team.

SCOTT, Richard Sydney Arthur
(1966-1967)

Wing-half: 9 app. + 1 sub, 1 goal
1966: 5-10, 10-7
Career: Thetford; Norwich City (amat.), (prof.) Nov. 1958; Cardiff City July 1963 (£4,000); Scunthorpe United Sep 1964 (in part exchange for Keith Ellis); CITY July 1966; Kings Lynn Mar. 1967; Lowestoft Town in 1968/69; Later assisted Thetford until 1983.

Honours: (Norwich City) League Cup winner 1962
(Cardiff City) Welsh Cup winner 1964

Experienced free transfer signing who was unable to win a regular first team place during the nine months he spent at Sincil Bank. Only 28 FL outings during his Norwich years but was a regular at Cardiff and Scunthorpe.

SELLARS, Peter
(1974-1977)

Midfield: 0 app. + 1 sub
Born: Market Rasen, Lincs., 15 Mar. 1958
Career: Market Rasen Town; CITY schoolboy Feb. 1974, (appr.) Aug. 1974, (prof.) Mar. 1976; Market Rasen Town cs 1977.

Diminutive midfield player whose only FL experience came whilst still an apprentice, when he came on for the final 16 minutes of the home match with Workington on 21 Feb. 1976. He suffered a broken nose in that game but shortly afterwards was awarded a full-time contract and stayed a further season with the Imps before returning to Lincolnshire League football.

SELLARS, William
(1935-1936)

Outside-right: 33 app., 2 goals
1932: 5-5½, 10-8
Born: Sheffield, 7 Oct. 1907
Died: 7 Nov. 1987
Career: Park Labour (Sheffield); Rotherham United during season 1927/28; Southport May 1932; Burnley July 1933; Bradford June 1934; CITY July 1935 to May 1936.

Small tricky wingman who had begun his career playing alongside Allan Hall in Sheffield junior football. Sellars was a regular first team choice in his Lincoln season, and altogether aggregated 256 FL appearances, scoring 52 goals.

SERTORI, Mark A.
(1987-1990)

Forward: 43 app. + 7 sub, 9 goals
1990: 6-3, 12-0
Born: Manchester, 1 Sep. 1967
Career: Stockport County Feb. 1987; CITY Aug. 1987; Wrexham Feb. 1990 (£30,000); Bury cs 1994.

Honours: (Wrexham) Welsh Cup finalist 1990, 1991

One of several players signed from Colin Murphy's former club Stockport at the start of the Vauxhall Conference season. Sertori made his debut at Barnet playing in midfield but was generally used as a striker, scoring some vital goals. He made regular reserve appearances in the back four before a permanent switch to defence on joining Wrexham.

SHARMAN, Richard
(1897-1899)

Goalkeeper: 6 app.
Born: Lincoln, 1874
Career: Nondescripts (Lincoln); Gainsborough Trinity 1896; CITY early in 1897 to cs 1899; Adelaide (Lincoln) from around Sep. 1900.

Well-known local 'keeper who proved a useful stand-in during his two seasons on the club's books. Returned to Lincoln League football after being re-instated as an amateur by the FA in Aug. 1900 and was a prominent figure with Adelaide for several years. A contemporary noted of him "... although his diminutive stature is against him, he holds an excellent record in League circles".

SHARP, Brittain Cooper
(1904-1906, 1907-1908)
Forward: 14 app., 1 goal
Born: Lincoln, 1883
Career: St. Catherines (Lincoln); CITY Aug. 1904; Newark Town cs 1906; CITY cs 1907; Worksop Town cs 1908.

One of many local players recruited by the Working Mens Committee at the turn of the century to fill the ranks of City's reserve side. Sharp was given his FL debut along with Thomas Asnip in an away match at Manchester United in Oct. 1904. Summed up (1906) as, *" on the small side, but what he lacks in height he makes up in trickiness"*. Netted 34 goals for the Reserves in 1907/08.

SHAW, Bernard
(1953-1955)
Inside-forward/wing-half: 9 app., 1 goal
1953: 5-8½, 11-7
Born: Selby, Yorks., 4 Sep. 1929
Career: Buckley Juniors, Hull City May 1948 to 1949; Goole Town; CITY Oct. 1953; Peterborough United cs 1955 to c.1959; assisted Ely City from cs 1963.

Shaw had signed for Hull as a teenager but never made their FL side. However, he quickly got into City's Second Division team but then failed to win a regular place and after being made available for transfer joined crack Midland League side Peterborough, helping them to four consecutive titles prior to their election to Division Four.

SHAW, George ("Slotch")
(1886-1896)
Half-back/forward: 13 app.,
Born: Lincoln, 1865
Died: 15 Dec. 1928
Career: Lincoln Ramblers; CITY in season 1886/87 to cs 1896.

A stalwart of the Imps' sides of the late 1880's and early 1890's. Shaw had begun his career as a free scoring forward and once netted six times for City in a 7-1 friendly victory over Mexborough in Sep. 1887. By the time the club won League status he was past his prime and had moved back into the half-back line. He missed most of the 1892/93 season after suffering a bad injury in one of the opening matches and deputised only occasionally thereafter. Employed for many years in Rustons engineering works.

SHAW, Richardson
(1895)
Goalkeeper: 7 app.
Born: Halifax, 1876
Career: Peterborough GN Loco, CITY Apr. to Nov. 1895. Peterborough GN Loco later in 1895.

Youngster given a brief run in the first team after Evan Roberts was released following a disastrous spell. Had a few more chances in the early part of the 1895/96 campaign, until Boullemier was signed and immediately became first choice. Apperaed for Peterborough GN Loco when they won the Peterborough Senior Cup in 1896.

SHAW, Wainwright
(1897)
Goalkeeper: 8 app.
1894: 10-0
Born: Sheffield, 1870
Career: Basford Wanderers; Mansfield; Bulwell 1893; Grantham Rovers cs 1894; CITY May 1897 to around Oct. 1897.

Signed from Midland League Grantham Rovers where he had been regarded as their star player: *"... practically the man of the team and it was he who kept the players together ... had a tremendous lot of work to do but invariably pleased the critics"*. He had received an offer from First Division Bolton Wanderers but turned them down because he wished to continue working in Grantham. Shaw was City's first choice 'keeper at the beginning of the 1897/98 season but the team got off to a bad start winning just one point from their first eight FL fixtures and the committee brought in William Wilkinson from South Shore as a replacement.

SHEARMAN, Frederick P.
(1895-1896, 1897)
Outside-right: 17 app., 3 goals
Career: Wainfleet FC (Lincs.); CITY Oct. 1895 to cs 1896 and again briefly from Jan. 1897; Skegness c.1899.

Shearman was a well-known figure in east Lincs. junior football with a reputation for scoring goals - he hit four for the City Swifts team against Hull Albany shortly after signing. Shared the right-wing position with Frank Smallman in 1895/96 returning briefly to assist in the following season's troubled campaign.

SHELTON, William
(1911)
Outside-left: 2 app.
Career: Arnold St. Marys; CITY Mar. to cs 1911; Netherfield Rangers (Notts Alliance) in 1911/12.

Short-stay winger who appeared twice for the Imps in Apr. 1911 - the away fixture at Huddersfield and the home match with Fulham. At the end of the season the club were voted out of the League and Shelton departed.

SHIPLEY, George Michael
(1980-1985, 1989)
Midfield: 229 app. + 1 sub, 42 goals
1985: 5-8, 10-8
Born: Newcastle-upon-Tyne, 7 Mar. 1959
Career: Southampton (schoolboy) Sep. 1974, (appr.) Aug. 1975, (prof.) Mar. 1977 (Reading on loan Mar. to May 1979; Blackpool on loan, Oct. 1979); CITY Jan. 1980 (£45,000); Charlton Athletic July 1985 (£15,000); Gillingham July 1987 (£40,000); CITY on

trial Aug. 1989; retired Sep. 1989. Scouted for Maidstone United and coached part-time with Southampton then appointed Gillingham youth team manager July 1991; Middlesbrough youth coach Sep. 1991; Bradford City coach June 1994.

Left-sided midfield player signed by Colin Murphy for a then club record fee. Shipley was one of the most influential men in City's successful side of the early 1980's, providing tenacity, skill and goalscoring power to he twice finished leading scorer for the club. He was also consistent, missing only eight matches in his first five seasons at Sincil Bank. He returned for a trial in the summer of 1989 but aggravated an old injury when playing in a pre-season match with Huddersfield and announced his retirement shortly afterwards.

SHORT, David ("Joey")
(1958-1960)
Outside-left: 4 app.
1959: 5-4, 10-0
Born: St. Neots, Hunts., 14 Apr. 1941
Career: St. Neots Town; CITY Nov. 1958; Bedford Town July 1960.

Tiny winger who received few first team opportunites at Sincil Bank and was released on a free transfer at the end of his second season. Short was a part-time professional who worked as a printer.

SILLITO, Henry ("Harry")
(1922-1924)
Outside-left: 48 app., 2 goals
1922: 5-8½, 11-0
Born: Chester-le-Street, Co. Durham, 10 July 1901
Died: 17 Dec. 1993
Career: Washington Colliery; Chelsea Jan. 1921; CITY Aug. 1922; Merthyr Town Oct. 1924 to 1925; assisted Grantham from cs 1928.

Harry did not make the Chelsea first team but appeared regularly for the Imps in his two seasons with the club. Summed up (1923) as "... fast, accurate shot, and smart in middling the ball". Later had 21 FL outings with Merthyr in Division Three (South).

SIMMONITE, Gordon
(1982-1985, 1987-1988)
Defender: 71 app. + 1 sub
1983: 5-10, 11-4
Born: Sheffield, 25 Apr. 1957
Career: Rotherham United (appr.); Sheffield Wednesday Aug. 1975; Boston United Aug. 1978; Blackpool Sep. 1980 (£15,000); CITY Nov. 1982 (£5,000); retired through injury Oct. 1985; Grimsby Town youth team coach; Stockport County asst.-manager Nov. 1986; CITY asst.-manager July 1987; Gainsborough Trinity as a player Nov. 1987; CITY Dec. 1987; Gainsborough Trinity cs 1988; Matlock Town cs 1990; Buxton Oct. 1992.

Solid back four player who was a regular in the Imp's line-up until suffering a fractured ankle at Bournemouth in Mar. 1985 which led to his retirement. Returned to Sincil Bank with Colin Murphy at the start of the Vauxhall Conference campaign only to leave the following Oct. to join the South Yorkshire Police. Made a surprise comeback to his playing career when he appeared for City at Boston on Boxing Day 1987 and his experience was to prove an asset to the side as they went on to clinch the Conference title. Had earlier won England semi-professional honours with Boston.

SIMMONS, Anthony John
(1986-1988)
Forward: 14 app. + 5 sub, 5 goals
1987: 5-11, 10-8
Born: Stocksbridge, Yorkshire, 9 Feb. 1965
Career: Sheffield Wednesday (appr.), (prof.) Feb. 1983; Queens Park Rangers Nov. 1983; Rotherham United on loan Mar. 1984, permanent from Aug. 1984; CITY Sep. 1986 (in part exchange for John McGinley) (Cardiff City on loan Feb. 1987); Gainsborough Trinity Oct. 1988; Spalding United Mar. 1990; Holbeach United in season 1990/91; Lincoln United Sep. 1991.

Honours: England youth international (1983)

As a youngster Simmons attracted a large fee from QPR after making just one FL appearance for Wednesday. Suffered a knee injury early on at Loftus Road and when he recovered he moved back to south Yorkshire without appearing in the League for the London club. Struggled to win a senior place at Sincil Bank and was eventually released on a free transfer in the summer of 1988. Has since remained in the Lincoln area, working for European Gas Turbines and performing a significant role for Lincoln United in their rise up the non-League pyramid.

SIMPSON, C(harles) Fred
(1902-1908)
Inside-/outside-left: 124 app., 37 goals
1904: 5-7, 10-3
Career: Midland Athletic (Lincoln); CITY Apr. 1902; Newark Town cs 1908; Worksop Town 1909.

Freddy was one of the best of the local players discovered by the Working Mens Committee at the turn of the century. Although prone to injury, he appeared regularly for the Imps in his six years at Sincil Bank, departing when the club lost their Second Division status in the summer of 1908.

SIMPSON, Herbert
(1884-1893)
Defender: 3 app.
Born: Sleaford, Lincs., 1863
Died: 29 Dec. 1929
Career: St. Peter-in-Eastgate (Lincoln); Lincoln Albion; Brittania (Lincoln); Lincoln Rovers; CITY 1884; retired late 1893.

One of the first players to join the club after it was formed, Herbert developed into one of City's finest local players of their pre-League days. Remained a fixture in the side until the early 1890's, appearing in 24 FA Cup matches between 1884 and 1891, including the very first tie against Hull Town in Nov. 1884. He began his career as a half-back but switched to right-back soon after joining the Imps. Said to be *"full of vigour"* and brave too - he once played half a match with a dislocated collar-bone. Simpson was also prominent in local cricket, he was appointed groundsboy with the Lindum CC at the age of 14 and later turned down a post as the club professional because he preferred to complete his apprenticeship. Subsequently lost a finger in an accident at work which ended his chances of playing the game at a higher level.

SIMPSON, John Lyles
(1957)

Goalkeeper; 5 app.
1957: 6-1, 12-8
Born: Appleby, Westmoreland, 5 Oct. 1933
Died: 7 Dec. 1993
Career: Penrith (Penicuik Athletic while on National Service); Netherfield (Lancashire Combination); CITY Mar. 1957; Gillingham June 1957 (£750); (Margate on loan early 1972); Maidstone United cs 1972; retired cs 1973.

Honour: (Gillingham) FL Div.4 champions 1964

Promising youngster who replaced Mitchell Downie towards the end of the 1956/57 season but then refused the terms offered to him by the club. A bargain buy for Gillingham to whom he gave 15 years service, setting a club record of 571 FL appearances. Later ran a newsagents shop near the Gills ground and operated as a part-time bookmaker from the Crayford dog track.

SIMPSON, John W. ("Baggy")
(1919-1920)

Inside-left: 4 app.,
1919: 5-7, 11-7
Career: Lincoln Rovers; Army football; CITY Aug. 1919; Scunthorpe United cs 1920; later assisted Grantham Sep. 1922 to cs 1923 and, from Aug. 1924, Horncastle Town.

A short but sturdy inside-forward who joined the Imps after declining offers from other clubs. All his FL outings came in the first half of the 1919/20 season and at the end of the campaign he moved on to Scunthorpe United - then members of the Midland League.

SIMPSON, Joseph W.
(1894-1895, 1896-1898. 1899-1901)

Defender: 70 app.
Career: Lincoln junior football; CITY Sep. 1894 to Oct. 1895; Newark later in 1895; Kettering Feb. 1896; CITY Nov. 1896 to cs 1898; St. Marys (Lincoln) in 1898/1899; CITY cs 1899 to cs 1901.

A stalwart of City's first and reserve teams of the 1890's: *"his greatest characteristic is dash and fearlessness, and he can always be relied upon to do his utmost"*. Joe left the club in Oct. 1895, reportedly going on 'strike' after the reserve players had not been paid their wages for some weeks, but returned 12 months later and spent most of the next two seasons as a regular in the Imps' Second Division side. He was signed for a third time to captain the club's reserves on their entry to Midland League football. Brother of Walter, see below.

SIMPSON, Walter
(1897-1898)

Full-back: 2 app.
Career: Lincoln junior football; CITY Feb. 1897 to cs 1898.

Local lad who partnered his brother Joe at full-back on two occasions in the 1897/98 season - the away match at Newcastle and the home fixture with Walsall.

SIMPSON, William
(1902-1908)

Centre-half/left-back: 140 app.
1904: 5-9, 11-10
Born: Sunderland, c.1878
Died: Mar. 1962
Career: Selbourne; Sunderland c.1898; CITY June 1902; retired 1908.

Sturdy defender and club captain who began as a centre-half but took over the left-back position from William Pallister late in 1904. He later recalled how he had been reluctant to move south, eventually agreeing to come "for a holiday" for one season only but stayed in Lincoln for the rest of his life. His playing career was ended by a serious knee injury suffered in a reserve match and he was later employed in a local engineering works before becoming landlord of the Roebuck Hotel in High Street, a position he held from 1921 - 1947.

SIMS, Frank
(1950-1958)

Centre-half: 3 app
1957: 5-11, 12-4
Born: Lincoln, 12 Sep. 1931
Career: Ruston Bucyrus (Lincoln); CITY (amat.) May 1950, (prof.) Aug. 1951; Boston United July 1958; Lincoln Claytons cs 1961

Part-time professional who was restricted to just three FL outings in a seven year spell at Sincil Bank by the outstandingly consistent Tony Emery. Father of Steve, see below.

SIMS, Steven Frank
(1990)

Centre-half: 5 app
1989: 6-1½, 13-9
Born: Lincoln, 2 July 1957
Career: Lincoln United; Leicester City (appr.) Aug. 1973, (prof.) July 1974; Watford Dec. 1978 (£175,000); Notts County Sep. 1984 (£50,000); Watford Oct. 1986 (£50,000); Aston Villa June 1987 (£50,000); Burton Albion June 1990; CITY Sep. to Nov. 1990; Boston FC asst/manager cs 1991; Stafford Rangers in 1991/92; Shepshed Albion Jan. 1992.

Honours: England 'B' international (1 app.)
England under 21-international (10 app.)

Former Lincoln Schools player who went on to a lengthy career in top flight football winning international honours. Came to Sincil Bank on a non-contract basis at the age of 33 but had the misfortune to suffer a fractured jaw in his fifth outing, at home to Rochdale, and never played in the League again. A career record of 378 FL appearances plus 3 as substitute, 13 goals. Son of Frank.

SISSON, Thomas
(1923-1926)

Defender: 75 app., 1 goal
1924: 5-10, 12-0
Born: Basford, Nottingham, 19 Oct. 1894
Died: 11 Aug. 1976
Career: Players Athletic (Nottm.); Notts County cs 1914; Hucknall Byron; Gillingham cs 1920; CITY Dec. 1923 (initially on a month's trial); Peterborough & Fletton United cs 1926; Sutton Town July 1927.

Solid all-round defender - resolute, quick, a sure tackler and expert in anticipating opponents' moves. Arrived having played 73 Southern Section matches with the Gills and showed his versatility at Lincoln taking both full-back postions, left-half (in the 1925/26 season) and appearing on one occasion at centre-forward. Tom was also an able cricketer and spent the 1925 season as a professional with the Lindum CC.

SISSONS, William Stanley
(1924-1926)

Goalkeeper: 74 app.
1924: 5-10, 11-2
Born: Kiveton Park, Sheffield, 1 Feb. 1901

Died: 28 June 1988
Career: Kiveton Park, CITY Mar. 1924 to 1926; retired through injury.

First choice 'keeper for the 1924/25 and 1925/26 seasons winning a reputation for his good anticipation and for an ability to deal with low shots. Broke a forearm in the reserve match against Scunthorpe in Sep. 1926, the injury necessitating several operations and eventually bringing his football career to an end. Reported to be still receiving 'sick compensation' from the club in Sep. 1930. Continued to live in the Lincoln area and ran the post office in the village of Langworth for 17 years.

SIVELL, Laurence
(1979)

Goalkeeper: 2 app
1979: 5-8, 11-0
Born: Lowestoft, 8 Feb. 1951
Career: Ipswich Town (appr.), (prof.) Feb. 1969; (CITY on loan Jan. to Mar. 1979); retired Mar. 1984.

Laurie became Colin Murphy's first signing for the Imps when he arrived early in 1979, but he made few first team appearances because bad weather meant that City did not play at all in February of that year. Had 141 FL outings in a 15 year spell at Portman Road where he spent much of the time as understudy to Paul Cooper. Later won wider fame as one of the players in the film 'Escape to Victory'.

SLADE, Donald
(1912-1913)

Centre-forward: 23 app., 9 goals
1913: 5-8, 12-0
Born: Southampton, 26 Nov. 1888
Died: 24 Mar. 1980
Career: Southampton Ramblers (Blackpool on trial Mar. 1909); Southampton 1910; CITY Aug. 1912; Woolwich Arsenal Dec. 1913 (£1,000); Fulham May 1914; Dundee 1919; Ayr United 1920 to 1924.

Signed on a free transfer from Southern League Southampton where he had failed to win a regular first team place. Succeeded Walter Miller as City's centre-forward at the start of the 1913/14 season but the club then found themselves in financial difficulties and Slade was sold to Arsenal. His departure was soon followed by that of Tommy Fern to Everton, the pair raising a total sum of £2,500. Later spent five seasons in the Scottish League making 124 appearances and scoring 46 goals. Originally employed as a bricklayer but after leaving football worked as a licensee, first in Scotland and then in the south of England.

SMALLMAN, Francis Joseph Bruce
(1888-1893, 1894-1896)
Outside-right: 58 app., 23 goals
Born: Gainborough, 1869
Career: St. Johns (Lincoln); CITY 1888; Burton Wanderers cs 1893; CITY Oct. 1894 to cs 1896.

Speedy right-winger who was a prominent player for the Imps in the early 1890's. Frank finished leading scoring for the Midland League championship side of 1889/90 (14 goals of which 5 came in a 10-2 victory over Leek) and also in the club's first FL season - his 17 goals from 22 games including 4 in the home match with Burton Swifts on 11 Feb. 1893, the first hat-trick recorded by a City player in the new competition. Later helped Burton Wanderers to the Midland League title in 1893/94 before returning to give Lincoln two more years service. Worked as a licensee during his football career.

SMEDLEY, Lawrence
(1945-1949)
Inside-forward: 11 app., 7 goals
1949: 6-2½, 13-0
Born: Sheffield, 7 May 1922
Career: Sheffield junior football; CITY May 1945 (amat.) Aug. 1945, (prof.); Frickley Colliery Aug. 1949.

Reserve inside-forward who had an excellent scoring record when called up for first team duty. Laurie scored three times in nine appearances in the 1945/46 season and netted on his FL debut against Halifax but never won a regular place and departed for Midland League Frickley.

SMILLIE, Ronald Drummond
(1956-1960)
Outside-right: 91 app., 15 goals
1958: 5-5½, 10-3
Born: Grimethorpe, nr. Barnsley, 27 Sep. 1933
Career: Barnsley Oct. 1950, (prof.) Dec. 1950; CITY June 1956 (£2,000); Barnsley June 1960 (£1,500); Chelmsford City cs 1962.

Winger recruited from Barnsley where he had spent most of his six year spell in the reserves. Smillie was a part-time professional who also worked as a miner at Grimethorpe Colliery. A career total of 202 FL appear-ances and 32 goals; Ron is the father of Neil Smillie whose clubs include Crystal Palace, Brighton and Reading.

SMITH, Alexander
(1895-1897)

Wing-half/inside-forward: 45 app., 9 goals
1899: 5-8½, 12-0
Born: Old Kilpatrick, Dumbartonshire, 7 Nov. 1873
Died: Jan. 1908
Career: St. Mirren; CITY Aug. 1895; Third Lanark cs 1897; Swindon Town May 1898 to cs 1900.

"Plays a good and effective game, places well", was one critic's view whilst another noted *"he can always be depended upon to play a plodding and fair game"*. Alec was club captain in 1896/97 but returned to Scotland to follow his trade as a patternmaker for the following campaign. City tried to sign him again in the summer of 1898 but he chose to join Southern League Swindon. Returned to Scotland for a second time to take over his father's business and died at the early age of 34 leaving three small children.

SMITH, David
(1968-1978)
Outside-left/midfield: 358 app. + 13 sub, 52 goals
1972: 5-7, 10-7
Born: Thornaby-on-Tees, Yorks., 8 Dec. 1947
Career: Stockton-on-Tees Schools; Middlesbrough (appr.), (prof.) Dec. 1964; CITY July 1968; Rotherham United July 1978 to cs 1980. Later appeared for several seasons in Lincoln Sunday League football before joining Stamford Town Dec. 1993 to Apr. 1994 as player/asst.manager.

Honours: England schools international (1 app. vs Ireland 1963)
(City) FL Div.4 champions 1976

Skilful winger and one of the club's most loyal and consistent performers of the post-war era, his total of appearances being second only to that of Tony Emery. Dave was a regular in City's first team, apart from injuries for a decade, and played an important role in the 1975/76 championship campaign during which he scored the 100th goal of the season in the victory at Stockport. He was surprisingly released in the summer of 1978 but was then given a testimonial at Sincil Bank against Watford the following year. Later appeared in local Sunday football for several seasons and at the age of 44 he was on the subs bench for St. Hugh's in the Lincs. Sunday Cup final.

SMITH, Henry
(1908)

Outside-right: 2 app.
Career: Whitchurch; Chirk; Neston; CITY Apr. to cs 1908.

Short term signing who played in a couple of fixtures towards the end of the 1907/08 campaign - a season which saw the Imps finish bottom of the table and voted out of the League for the first time.

SMITH, James
(1931-1936)

Left-back: 116 app., 3 goals
1933: 5-10½, 12-0
Born: Thurnscoe, nr. Rotherham, 6 May 1908
Died: July 1956
Career: Brodsworth; Doncaster Rovers (amat.) 1924, (prof.) 1926/27; CITY Aug. 1931; Bradford City Aug. 1936; Peterborough United Aug. 1937, appointed trainer Nov. 1946.

Honours: (City) FL Div.3 (North) champions 1932

"... has improved by leaps and bounds. Robust, without fear and a strong kicker", was a 1932 verdict. Smith proved a sound defender during five seasons with the Imps and also had a reputation as an amateur boxer. Was later a licensee in Peterborough.

SMITH, James Michael
(1968-1969)

Wing-half: 54 app.
1967: 5-9, 11-4
Born: Sheffield, 17 Oct. 1940
Career: Sheffield United groundstaff 1957, (prof.) Jan. 1959; Aldershot July 1961; Halifax Town July 1965; CITY Mar. 1968 (£1,000); Boston United player-manager June 1969; Colchester United player-manager Oct 1972 (retired as a player 1973); Blackburn Rovers manager June 1975; Birmingham City manager Mar. 1978; Oxford United manager Mar. 1982; Queens Park Rangers manager June 1985; Newcastle United manager Dec. 1988; Middlesbrough coach Mar. 1991; Portsmouth manager May 1991.

Influential wing-half signed on the Mar. 1968 transfer deadline when he had been on the point of joining Cork Celtic. Almost an ever-present in his time at Sincil Bank and extremely popular with the fans but was surprisingly given a free transfer in May 1968. The decision sparked protests from City fans but for Smith it proved the start of a long and successful managerial career during which he has taken teams to promotion on four occasions and QPR to the League Cup final in 1985.

SMITH, Jeffrey Edward
(1958-1967)

Left-back: 315 app., 2 goals
1962: 5-9, 11-6
Born: Warren, Sheffield, 8 Dec. 1935
Career: Sheffield United (prof.) June 1953; CITY Feb. 1958 (£2,500); released May 1967.

Quietly efficient defender who showed skill and a high degree of consistency in a nine year spell at Sincil Bank. Jeff was one of the few players to remain throughout the early 1960's when the Imps dropped from the Second Division to the bottom of the Fourth. Eventually released on a free transfer by Ron Gray in the summer of 1967. He had made just one FL appearance whilst at Bramall Lane.

SMITH, Lindsay James
(1981)

Centre-half: 5 app.
1981: 5-11, 12-0
Born: Enfield, Middlesex, 18 Sep. 1954
Career: Colchester United (appr.) turned prof. Mar. 1972 (Charlton Athletic on loan Aug. 1977, Millwall on loan Sep. 1977); Cambridge United Oct. 1977 (£12,000) (CITY on loan Sep. 1981); Plymouth Argyle Nov. 1982 (£20,000); Millwall July 1984; Cambridge United Aug. 1986 (£5,000); Bury Town (Suffolk) on loan Jan. 1989, later signed permanently.

Loan signing who deputised for Trevor Peake in the early part of the 1981/82 campaign. In all he spent nearly 20 years as a professional, totalling 600 app., principally with Colchester and Cambridge United.

SMITH, Mark C.
(1993-)

Centre-half: 20 app., 1 goal
1993: 6-1, 12-2
Born: Sheffield, 21 Mar. 1960
Career: Sheffield Wednesday (appr.), (prof.) Mar. 1978; Plymouth Argyle July 1987 (£170,000); Barnsley Nov. 1989 (£145,000); Notts County Oct. 1992 (£70,000); (Port Vale on loan Jan. 1993; Huddersfield Town on loan Feb. 1993; Chesterfield on loan Mar. 1993); CITY July 1993, appointed player-coach Mar. 1994 and youth team coach cs 1994.

Honours: England under-21 international (5 app.)

Experienced central defender recruited on a free transfer towards the end of his career. Although he missed much of the 1993/94 season through injury he proved a steadying influence with an ability to organise City's back four.

SMITH, Michael
(1977-1979)

Centre-half: 20 app. + 5 sub
1978: 6-0½, 12-0
Born: Sunderland, 28 Oct. 1958
Career: Lambton Street Boys Club (Sunderland); CITY July 1977; Wimbledon Dec. 1979 (£12,500) (Aldershot on loan Oct. 1984); retired through injury during 1987/88 and assisted Vaux Ryhope; Gateshead; Bath City and Seaham Red Star before joining Hartlepool United Oct. 1989 following a trial cs 1989, to 1992.

Honour: (Wimbledon) FL Div.4 champions 1983

Mick Smith signed as a youngster as part of what ranks as one of the most successful post-war transfer deals made by the Imps: four teenagers recruited form the same Sunderland boys' club appeared in the League within months of joining the club and two - Smith and Mick Harford - went on to lengthy careers in higher grade football. Smith made 203 appearances plus 2 as sub at Plough Lane, participating in the Dons rise to the First Division. He then retired through injury only to make a brief comeback two years later and assisted Hartlepool in their 1990/91 promotion campaign.

SMITH, Neil
(1990-1992)

Midfield: 13 app. + 4 sub
1991: 5-10, 10-12
Born: Warley, West Midlands, 10 Feb. 1970
Career: Shrewsbury Town YTS 1986, (prof.) July 1988; Redditch United cs 1989; CITY Mar. 1990 (£7,000) (Bromsgrove Rovers on loan Feb. 1991); Cheltenham Town on loan Nov. 1991, permanently Jan. 1992.

Youngster whose Football League experience amounted to just one appearance as a substitute before joining the Imps. Always on the fringe of the first team at Sincil Bank playing both in midfield and as a sweeper but was never able to win a regular place and was allowed to leave on a free transfer midway through the 1991/92 season.

SMITH, Paul M.
(1987-)

Forward/full-back: 204 app. + 11 sub, 27 goals
1993: 5-10, 11-10
Born: Rotherham, 9 Nov. 1964
Career: Sheffield United (appr.), (prof.) Nov. 1982 (Stockport County on loan Aug. 1985); Port Vale July 1986; CITY Sep. 1987 (£48,000).

Paul was signed as a striker for a then club record fee to boost City's challenge for the Vauxhall Conference title. He first appeared at full-back towards the end of the 1989/90 campaign before switching permanently during the following season. A consistent performer in both postions, his pace proving a valuable asset to the Imps' defence.

SMITH, Thomas
(1911)

Outside-right: 1 app
Career: Manchester junior football; CITY Mar. to Apr. 1991.

Promoted to City's Division Two team after a single reserve outing when it was said he played "a fairly good game". Appeared in the home match with Blackpool on 18 March 1911 and two further Midland League games before departing.

SMITH, Walter Alfred
(1900-1903)

Inside-left: 90 app., 21 goals
Born: Lincoln 1874
Died: 14 Nov. 1958
Career: Blue Star (Lincoln); Grantham Avenue Dec. 1899; CITY Jan. 1900; Small Heath May 1903; Newark cs 1904; Brighton & Hove Albion July 1906; Norwich City May 1907; Southend United cs 1908; Liberal Club (Lincoln) in 1909/10.

Talented youth who almost escaped the attentions of the Working Mens Committee who ran City's reserve side and were responsible for the recruitment of local players. Wally had apparently been overlooked and was attracting the scouts from bigger clubs at Grantham when he was finally signed. A clever forward who was said to be *"... one of the smallest footballers playing in League games"*. He suffered a bad injury on joining Small Heath and never appeared in their first team, but later experienced Southern League football with Brighton, Norwich and Southend totalling 68 matches, 15 goals. At the time of his death at Leigh-on-Sea he was described as a retired journeyman brickmaker.

SMITH, William ("Tich")
(1898-1899)

Right-half: 33 app.
5-6½, 12-4
Born: Sawley, nr. Long Eaton, Derbys., 10 Nov. 1871
Died: Sep. 1907
Career: Long Eaton Rangers in 1887; Notts County cs 1889; Nottingham Forest cs 1890; Long Eaton Rangers 1894; Notts County cs 1896; Loughborough cs 1897; CITY July 1898 to cs 1899. He also assisted Burton Swifts.

Honours: Played for England in an unofficial international vs. Canada 1892
Football Alliance (1 app. vs Football League 1891)

Sturdy wing-half who was something of a celebrity by the time he arrived at Sincil Bank. Experienced top class football from the late 1880's being particularly successful at Forest where he won representative honours and helped them to the Football Alliance championship in 1890/91.

SNAREY, Charles
(1903-1904)

Right-back: 3 app.
1903: 5-8, 11-2
Born: Oakham, Rutland, 1881
Career: Reading junior football; CITY Feb. 1903 (initially on trial) to cs 1904.

Defender who was given three first team outings in Nov. 1903 as deputy for Albert Groves. Spent the remainder of his spell at Sincil Bank in the reserve side playing Midland League football.

SOULSBY, Thomas
(1905)

Outside-right: 3 app., 1 goal
1905: 5-6, 10-10
Born: Mickley, Northumberland, 24 Oct. 1876
Career: Mickley; Liverpool 1899; Tottenham Hotspur cs 1901 to cs 1902; later assisted Mickley before joining CITY, May to Nov. 1905.

Winger whose previous senior experience amounted to two years in Liverpool's reserve side and a season at Tottenham when he had appeared in one London League

fixture and one friendly match. *"Very fast and plays outside-right principally"*, was one contemporary verdict. His three FL outings for the Imps all came in the early part of the 1905/06 campaign. He then suffered a recurrence of an old knee injury playing for the reserves and never appeared for the Imps again.

SPEARS, Alan Frederick
(1963-1964)

Outside-left: 2 app.
1963: 5-7, 10-8
Born: Amble, Northumberland, 27 Dec. 1938
Career: Amble Schools; Newcastle United Feb. 1956; Millwall May 1960; CITY July 1963; Cambridge City Feb. 1964.

Honours: England schools international (5 app. 1954)

Free transfer signing from Millwall where he played 31 FL matches scoring 5 goals in a three year stay. He appeared in the opening two fixtures of the 1963/64 season but then lost his place and moved on to Southern League Cambridge City the following Feb.

SPENCER, Thomas William
(1936-1937)

Outside-left: 4 app., 1 goal
1936: 5-8, 11-5
Born: Deptford, London, 22 Mar. 1914
Career: Hastings (Southern Amateur League); Bexhill cs 1933; Hastings Nov. 1933; Tunbridge Wells Rangers Jan. 1934; Fulham July 1936; CITY Nov. 1936; Ashford cs 1937; later signed for Watford Nov. 1943.

Winger who could take both flanks but only turned out on the left side for the Imps. He had earlier spent two and a half seasons at Tunbridge Wells having been signed by former City player George Beel. Played four sports professionally - football, cricket, boxing and table tennis but was best known as a cricketer with Kent CCC (76 matches, 1935 - 1946). Later became a first-class umpire, standing in 17 Tests and has since been awarded the OBE. Has lived in Seaton Delaval, Northumberland since the early 1950's.

SPENCER, Tom Hannah
(1972-1974)

Centre-half: 67 app. + 7 sub, 10 goals
1973: 5-11, 12-9½
Born: Glasgow, 28 Nov. 1945
Career: Neilston; Celtic cs 1963; Southampton July 1965; York City June 1966; Workington Mar. 1968 (in exchange for another player); CITY Jan. 1972 (£10,000); Rotherham United July 1974 to cs 1978. Bristol Rovers coach Dec. 1980 to cs 1981; Worksop Town asst/manager May 1981, manager Nov. 1983 to 1987.

Powerful central defender who occasionally appeared in midfield and had actually been a centre-forward in the early part of his career. Tom was signed at the same time as Dixie McNeil as part of the Imps bid to win promotion from Division Four in the 1971/72 season and both scored on their debuts in a 4-1 home win over

Brentford. He proved a solid performer although prone to injury totalling 428 FL appearances plus 11 as sub., 50 goals with his four teams. After retiring from the game he spent two years as manager of a Worksop sports centre before joining the coaching staff at Bristol Rovers.

STAINTON, Bryan Edward
(1959-1965)

Full-back/centre-half: 25 app.
1962: 5-8, 11-0
Born: Scampton, Lincs., 8 Jan. 1942
Career: Lincoln Schools; Ingham FC; CITY (amat.) Aug. 1959, (prof.) Mar. 1962; Gainsborough Trinity July 1965; Lincoln Claytons cs 1973; Rustons Sports (Lincoln); Lincoln United 1983 to 1985.

Local lad who signed for City after writing off for a trial. He appeared regularly with the reserve and 'A' teams before being given an extended run in the first team at centre-half at the beginning of 1964/65. Lost his place after a change in management and later spent eight seasons at Gainsborough Trinity, making a total of 382 appearances. Still lives in Lincoln.

STANT, Philip R.
(1990)

Forward: 4 app
1991: 6-1, 12-7
Born: Bolton, 13 Oct. 1962
Career: Army football to Reading Aug. 1982; returned to the Army before joining Hereford United Nov. 1986; Notts County July 1989 (£175,000); (Blackpool on loan Sep. to Nov. 1990; CITY on loan Nov. 1990; Huddersfield Town on loan Jan. 1991); Fulham Feb. 1991 (£60,000); Mansfield Town Aug. 1991 (£50,000); Cardiff City Dec. 1992 (£100,000); (Mansfield Town on loan Aug. 1993).

Honours: (Cardiff) FL Div.3 champions 1993
Welsh Cup winner 1993, finalist 1994

Strong and direct striker whose professional career took off after he was bought out of the Army by Hereford. Did not impress in a short loan spell at Sincil Bank which coincided with the departure of Allan Clarke as manager, but has done well elsewhere netting 100 plus goals in over 200 FL appearances.

STEVENSON, George Henry
(1925-1927)

Centre-forward: 11 app., 6 goals
1926: 5-9½, 10-4
Born: Nottingham, 1905
Career: Lenton (Nottm.); Stamford Town; CITY on trial early in 1925, full terms May 1925; Shirebrook June 1927.

Stevenson had an excellent scoring record with City's reserves (19 goals in 1925/26) and this was maintained in his occasional first team outings. However the Imps had a surplus of goalscorers on their books and he was allowed to drift into Midland League football. Summed up as "... lightweight but has speed and accuracy of shooting".

STILLYARDS, George William Edward
(1942-1951)

Defender: 100 app., 2 goals
1949: 5-8½, 11-0
Born: Whisby, nr. Lincoln, 29 Dec. 1918
Career: St. Botolphs (Lincoln); Lincoln Rovers; CITY (amat.) Sep. 1942, (prof.) Nov. 1942 (Stalybridge Celtic on loan Aug. 1950 - cs 1951); Skegness Town cs 1951; Grantham July 1953; Brigg Town cs 1954.

Honour: (City) FL Div.3 (North) champions 1948

Solid defender who made occasional wartime appearances before earning a first team place (at left-half) at the start of 1946/47. Was a regular for the next two and a half years, settling at right-back, before losing his place when Horace Green was signed. A fine club cricketer with Rustons CC, appearing twice for Lincolnshire in 1950.

STIMPSON, Reginald Redvers
(1920-1922)

Defender/forward: 1 app.
1921: 5-11, 12-0
Born: Lincoln, 25 Aug. 1900
Died: 1977
Careeer: St. Andrews (Lincoln); Robeys (Lincoln); CITY on trial Apr. 1920, signing terms Aug. 1920; Worksop Town June 1922; St. Swithins Athletic (Lincoln) in 1923/24.

"A local player with a big future before him. Excellent in defence and attack, and not afraid to use his weight", was a 1921 verdict. However, he received just two first team opportunities at Sincil Bank - a Midland League game against Denaby in Dec. 1920 (when he played right-back) and a Northern Section visit to Accrington 12 months later when he appeared at centre-forward.

STOREY, Luke Dawson
(1947-1949)

Outside-right: 11 app., 2 goals
1949: 5-9½, 11-7
Born: Dawdon, Sunderland, 17 Dec. 1920
Career: Blackhall Colliery; CITY (amat.) July 1947, (prof.) Sep. 1947; Grantham Sep. 1949; Stalybridge Celtic cs 1950; Corby Town Sep. 1951 to cs 1952.

Speedy winger from the north-east who appeared mostly for City's Midland League team. Luke was a part-time professional who was employed in a local engineering works.

STOTHERT, James
(1893-1894)

Left-back: 18 app.
Born: Blackburn
Career: Braeside; Bohemians 1888; Blackburn Rovers Oct. 1891; Darwen Dimmocks 1891; Knuzden Rovers Feb. 1892; Brierfield; CITY Dec. 1893 (£7) to cs 1894; Notts County Nov. 1894 to cs 1896; Bacup cs 1896; Barnsley cs 1897; Crewe Alexandra cs 1898.

Stothert had been involved in controversy in the early 1890's, appearing for other clubs at a time when his playing registration was held by Blackburn, and in Apr. 1892 he was banned 'sine die' by the FA for his third such offence. The ban was subsequently lifted and after appearing for Brierfield he joined the Imps in preference to the Lancashire League side Fairfield as the former offered higher wages (30 shillings a week). Proved a consistent performer and was an ever-present in his short stay with the club. Later made 24 FL appearances with Notts County.

STOUTT, Stephen P.
(1989-1991)

Midfield: 36 app. + 10 sub, 1 goal
1990: 5-8, 11-6
Born: Halifax, 5 Apr. 1964

Career: Bradley Rangers; Huddersfield Town from June 1980, signing non-contract forms Jan. 1984; Wolverhampton Wanderers Apr. 1985; Grimsby Town July 1988 (Boston United on loan, Nov. 1989); CITY Dec. 1989 (£9,000); Boston United cs 1991; CITY youth team manager July 1993 to cs 1994.

Midfield man who gave up full-time status with Huddersfield to join the fire service but resumed it on joining the Wolves. Spent much of his time at Blundell Park out of action with an injured knee but eventually recovered fitness and signed for the Imps. Later succeeded Keith Alexander as manager of the club's junior side.

STRODDER, Gary J.
(1981-1987)

Centre-half: 122 app. + 10 sub, 6 goals
1984: 6-1, 11-3½
Born: Cleckheaton, Yorks., 1 Apr. 1965
Career: Yorkshire Amateurs; CITY schoolboy Jan. 1980, (appr.) July 1981, (prof.) Apr. 1983; West Ham United Mar. 1987 (£100,000); West Bromwich Albion Aug. 1990 (£190,000).

Gary was given his FL debut whilst still an apprentice, in the opening match of the 1982/83 season and developed into a fast and hard tackling defender. Spent four seasons as a regular first teamer before being sold to West Ham shortly before the Imps were relegated to the Vauxhall Conference. Later moved on to the Hawthorns where he linked up with former City colleagues Stuart Naylor and Simeon Hodson. Son of Colin Strodder (Huddersfield, Halifax and Boston United).

STRONG, Thomas Philips
(1912-1915)

Full-back: 8 app.
1912: 5-9, 11-0
Born: Newcastle-upon-Tyne, 1890
Died: July 1917
Career: Tyneside junior football; CITY Aug. 1912 to cs 1915 (Aug. -Sep. 1914 playing in Scotland).

Tommy was mostly a reserve at Sincil Bank. He was given his FL debut at left-half against Blackpool in Feb. 1914 but made the remainder of his first team appearances as a full-back in the 1914/15 season. Killed in action during the Great War.

SUNLEY, David
(1978-1980)

Forward: 36 app. + 5 sub, 6 goals
1979: 5-8, 11-6
Born: Skelton, North Yorkshire, 6 Feb. 1952
Career: Preston North End and Middlesbrough on trial; Sheffield Wednesday (appr.) cs 1968, (prof.) Jan. 1970 (Nottingham Forest on loan, Oct. 1975); Hull City Jan. 1976 (£7,500); CITY July 1978; Stockport County Mar. 1980 to cs 1982; Tsuen Wan (Hong Kong); Stafford Rangers; Burton Albion; Stocksbridge Works; Sheffield Club.

Experienced centre-forward who scored on his City debut against Tranmere but had the misfortune to appear in one of City's worst post-war teams. Fell out of favour when Colin Murphy arrived as manager and eventually left on a free transfer. A career record of 295 FL appearances plus 29 as substitute, 45 goals.

SVARC, Robert Louis
(1968-1971)

Forward: 40 app. + 5 sub, 16 goals
1970: 5-7, 11-2
Born: Leicester, 8 Feb. 1946
Career: Leicester City (appr.) Oct. 1961, (prof.) Mar. 1963; CITY Dec. 1968 (£6,000) (Barrow on loan, Sep. to Nov. 1970); Boston United on loan, Oct. 1971, permanent Dec. 1971 (£1,750); Colchester United Dec. 1972 (£6,000); Blackburn Rovers Oct. 1975 (£25,000) (Watford on loan Sep. 1977); retired through injury Oct. 1977.

Stocky striker of Czech descent who received limited first team opportunities at Sincil Bank. Scored regularly for the reserves, including 20 in the 1969/70 season when the North Midlands League championship was won. Departed for non-League Boston where he became a Jehovah's Witness, and began to realise his true football potential under Jim Smith. Followed Smith to Colchester and Blackburn making a further 158 FL appearances (plus 8 as sub) scoring 75 goals before injury ended his career. Remained in the Blackburn area and went into business installing burglar alarms.

SWAN, Andrew ("Harry")
(1898-1899)

Centre-forward: 13 app., 10 goals
1902: 5-8, 11-12
Born: Dalbeattie, Kirkcudbright, 1878
Career: Dalbeattie; CITY Nov. 1898; New Brompton cs 1899; Barnsley cs 1900; Woolwich Arsenal May 1901; Gainsborough Trinity; Stockport County Dec. 1901; Mexborough cs 1902; Tottenham Hotspur May 1904 to cs 1905; Plymouth Argyle cs 1906 to 1907.

Early recruit from an area of Scotland which was to provide City with many players around the turn of the century. Swan had won representative honours for the Southern Counties of Scotland XI and made his debut for the Imps at outside-left. However, when switched to centre-forward he proved a revelation, scoring 9 goals in 11 games. Later embarked on a lengthy career around the Football and Southern Leagues.

SWINBURNE, Trevor
(1986-1897)

Goalkeeper: 34 app.
1986: 6-0, 14-7
Born: East Rainton, Co. Durham, 20 June 1953
Career: East Rainton Youths; Sunderland (appr.), (prof.) June 1970 (Sheffield United on loan); Carlisle United May 1977; Brentford

Aug. 1983; Leeds United June 1985 (Doncaster Rovers on loan Sep. 1985); CITY Feb. 1986; retired May 1987.

Burly 'keeper who spent 17 years as a professional although only really a regular with Carlisle for whom he made 248 FL appearances. Came to Lincoln late in his career, his spell coinciding with the club's descent from the Third Division to the Vauxhall Conference in successive seasons. Joined the prison service after leaving football. Both his father Tom (Newcastle Utd) and his brother Alan (Oldham Ath) appeared in League football as goalkeepers.

"SYDNEY"
(1897-1898)

See entry under NIDD, George Frederick

SYKES, E. Albert A.
(1928-1931)

Left-half: 42 app., 1 goal
1928: 5-8, 11-5
Born: Maltby, nr. Rotherham, 1900
Career: Maltby Victoria, Maltby Main CW; Birmingham Nov. 1924; Brighton & Hove Albion May 1926; CITY June 1928; Peterborough & Fletton United cs 1931; Luton Town; Grantham in 1932/33 season.

Steady and reliable wing-half who had previously worked as a miner. Saw little FL action at Birmingham (1 app) and Brighton (16 app) but received a couple of extended runs with Lincoln when Alf Hale was temporarily switched to centre-half.

SYMM, Colin
(1972-1975)

Midfield: 60 app. + 9 sub, 7 goals
1973: 5-10, 11-10
Born: Dunstan-on-Tyne, 26 Nov. 1946
Career: Redheugh Boys Club (Gateshead); Gateshead; Sheffield Wednesday May 1965; Sunderland June 1969; CITY June 1972; Boston United July 1975 to cs 1978.

Neat, stylish midfield player who arrived on a frees transfer from Sunderland. He had earlier sampled top flight football at Hillsborough and Roker Park (a total of 25 app. plus 9 as sub.) but was in and out of the Imps' side in a three year stay.

TAYLOR, Albert
(1936-1937)

Outside-left: 4 app
1936: 5-10, 11-12
Born: Ashington, Northumberland, c.1910
Career: Bedlington United; Gateshead Oct 1929; Chelsea Apr. 1931; Bristol Rovers May 1933; CITY Aug. 1936; Gillingham June 1937.

Given all his first team appearances in the left wing position, although he could also play centre-forward and finished top scorer for the Midland League side with 19 goals in his Sincil Bank season. Released on a free transfer, he joined Gillingham and was with them in the season they lost their FL status.

TAYLOR, Arthur
(1900-1901, 1902-1909)
Centre-half: 6 app
Career: Midland Athletic (Lincoln); CITY Mar. 1900; Midland Athletic cs 1901; Grantham Avenue Nov. 1901; CITY Sep. 1902 to 1909.

Local lad who was a stalwart of the Imps' Midland League side for several years in the early 1900's. All his FL outings came in the 1905/06 season as a replacement for Dick Hood.

TAYLOR, Frank
(1905-1908)
Forward: 36 app., 10 goals
Born: c.1887
Died: Jan. 1928
Career: Liberal Club (Lincoln); CITY June 1905; Worksop Town cs 1908; Merthyr Town 1909.

One of several players recruited from the Liberal Club side at the turn of the century. Frank scored on his tdebut in a 3-1 victory over Clapton Orient winning praise as *"a game little trier"* who *"certainly knows where the goal lies"*. Proved a useful reserve without ever breaking through to win a regular first team place.

TAYLOR, Geoffrey A.
(1947-1948)
Outside-left: 1 app
1947: 5-8, 11-0
Born: Henstead, Suffolk, 22 Jan. 1923
Career: RAF football; CNSOBU (Norwich); Norwich City (amat.) Aug. 1946, (prof.) Sep. 1946; Reading Mar. 1947; CITY Aug. 1947; Boston United Mar. to Apr. 1948; Stade Rennais (France); Brighton & Hove Albion Aug. 1948; Stade Rennais Dec. 1949 as player-coach; Bristol Rovers Sep. 1951; Queens Park Rangers Nov. 1953.

Geoff was signed after a successful trial with City's reserves in the 1946/47 season, but made only one FL appearance to at Chester on 15 Nov. 1947. Despite an impressive list of six different clubs he managed a career total of only 10 FL outings.

TAYLOR, Graham
(1968-1973)
Full-back: 150 app. + 1 sub, 1 goal
1972: 5-8, 11-4
Born: Worksop, 15 Sep. 1944
Career: Scunthorpe United (amat.); Grimsby Town (amat.) Aug. 1961, (prof.) July 1962; CITY July 1968 (£4,000), appointed player-coach July 1972, manager Dec. 1972 (retired from playing cs 1973); Watford manager June 1977; Aston Villa manager May 1987; England manager July 1990 to Nov. 1993; Wolverhampton Wanderers manager Mar. 1994.

Solid if unspectacular defender signed after making 189 FL appearances with the Mariners. Served as club captain although he had several spells out injured and scored his only goal on his debut in a 5-0 home win over Notts County. As a schoolboy he had won representative honours with the England Grammar Schools XI (at inside-forward) and he began his coaching career at a very early age, qualifying as the youngest ever FA Staff coach when only 21. He coached the Lincolnshire League team, City School Old Boys, from Jan. 1970 before becoming the Imps' coach and manager from Dec. 1972. He went on to build City's record breaking team which won the Fourth Division title in 1975/76, moving to Watford where he spent 10 years and took the Hornets from the Fourth Division to the First and into Europe. After further success at Villa Park he commenced a troubled spell as England manager which ended with the failure to qualify for the 1994 World Cup finals.

TAYLOR, James
(1923)
Centre-foward: 1 app
Career: Adelaide (Lincoln) and Lincoln Butchers (Lincoln Wednesday League); Coventry City on trial Feb. - Mar. 1923; CITY Aug. 1923 to Nov. 1923.

Local lad given his chance at Grimsby on the 29 Sep. 1923 after James Mackey dropped out through illness at the last moment. Said to be *"a robust player ... of the bustling type"*.

TAYLOR, William
(1969-1971)
Inside-forward: 74 app. + 5 sub, 6 goals
1970: 5-9, 11-11
Born: Edinburgh, 31 July 1939
Died: 30 Nov. 1981

Career: Bonnyrigg Rose; Leyton Orient Aug. 1959; Nottingham Forest Oct. 1963 (£4,000); CITY May 1969; retired May 1971; Fulham coach cs 1971; Manchester City coach May 1976; Oldham Athletic coach July 1979 until his death. Also served as England coach from Oct. 1974.

Slightly built but skilful player who was a regular in City's team until surprisingly released in the summer of 1971. Like his namesake and Sincil Bank contemporary Graham, he developed a talent for coaching which extended to international level. At the time of his sudden death he had been an England coach for seven years.

TENNANT, David
(1966-1969, 1974-1975)

Goalkeeper: 39 app
1964: 5-11, 11-0
Born: Walsall, 13 June 1945
Career: Aston Villa (amat.) cs 1961; Walsall (amat.) cs 1962, (prof.) Aug. 1963; Worcester City July 1965; Grimsby Town Aug. 1966; CITY Sep. 1966 (initially on trial); Rochdale Aug. 1969; Corby Town cs 1971 to cs 1973; CITY Aug. 1974 to cs 1975 (Lincoln United Mar. to cs 1975); Skegness Town cs 1975; Ruston Bucyrus (Lincoln) in 1977/78.

Tennant shared the goalkeeper's jersey with Colin Treharne in 1966/67 but then spent two seasons as a reserve to John Kennedy. Drifted into non-League football only to rejoin City in the summer of 1974, appearing in several pre-season fixtures before Peter Grotier was signed. No FL outings in his second spell at Sincil Bank.

THACKER, Jack
(1939)

Goalkeeper: 1 app
Born: c.1919
Career: Morris-Motors FC (Coventry); CITY Feb. 1939; Morris-Motors FC (Coventry); Coventry City during WW2.

A recruit from Central Amateur League football, Thacker deputised for Dan McPhail in a 4-0 defeat at Rochdale on 1 Apr. 1939 after City's regular 'keeper fell ill. He was also selected for the following match but missed his rail connection and never appeared again.

THOM, Lewis M.
(1967-1969)

Outside-left: 45 app. + 2 sub, 4 goals
1967: 5-7, 11-2
Born: Stornoway, Isle of Lewis, 10 Apr. 1944
Career: Banks o'Dee; Aberdeen 1961; Dundee United May 1964; Shrewsbury Town Sep. 1965; CITY May 1967; Bradford June 1969; Altrincham cs 1970; Elgin City Oct. 1970; Inverness Clachnacuddin cs 1971; Huntly in 1972/73.

Began his senior career in top flight Scottish football, making 48 appearances with Aberdeen and Dundee United before moving south. A clever orthodox winger who was a regular for the Imps in 1967/68, scoring the

equaliser at Derby in the FL Cup round 4 tie, to set up a replay which attracted a record crowd to Sincil Bank. Later returned to Scotland and finished his playing career in the Highland League.

THOMAS, John William
(1983-1985)

Forward: 56 app. + 11 sub, 18 goals
1984: 5-8, 11-3
Born: Wednesbury, Staffs., 5 Aug. 1958
Career: Everton July 1977 (Tranmere Rovers on loan, Mar. to May 1979, Halifax Town on loan, Oct. 1979); Bolton Wanderers June 1980; Chester City Aug. 1982; CITY Aug. 1983 (£12,500); Preston North End June 1985 (£15,000); Bolton Wanderers May 1987 (£30,000); West Bromwich Albion July 1989 (£30,000); Preston North End Feb. 1990 (£50,000); Hartlepool United Mar. 1992; Halifax Town July 1992 to 1993.

Striker pursued for several months by Colin Murphy before he was eventually signed up and responded by netting 13 goals to finish top scorer in his first season. Although frequently changing clubs he has maintained a good scoring record throughout his career and up to the end of the 1992/93 season had scored 125 goals in 320 FL outings plus 37 as substitute.

THOMPSON, Alexander
(1939-1948)

Right-back: 34 app., 1 goal
1949: 5-9½, 11-8
Born: Sheffield, 8 Dec. 1917
Career: Woodhouse Alliance (Sheffield); Sheffield Wednesday June 1937; CITY June 1939; Tranmere Rovers June 1948; Boston United Aug. 1949 to cs 1951.

Full-back who waited seven years for his League debut for the Imps due to the outbreak of war. A regular in 1946/47 but was then replaced by George Stillyards at the beginning of the following campaign. One of the first City players to sign up for military service during WW2, he made a further 27 wartime appearances for the club.

THOMPSON, Christopher David
(1983)

Midfield: 5 app. + 1 sub
1984: 5-11, 12-2
Born: Walsall, 24 Jan. 1960
Career: Bolton Wanderers (appr.), (prof.) July 1977 (CITY on loan, Mar. to May 1983); Blackburn Rovers Aug. 1983; Wigan Athletic July 1986; Blackpool July 1988; Cardiff City Mar. to cs 1990; Walsall on non-contract form Feb. to Apr. 1991; Fleetwood in 1991/92.

Honour: England youth international (1978)

Chris was signed on loan to cover for the injured Glenn Cockerill at a time when the Imps were anxious to revive a flagging chase for promotion. He stayed at Sincil Bank to the end of the season but the team fell away to finish in sixth position. Made well over 200 FL appearances in a professional career lasting 14 years.

THOMPSON, David
(1964-1965)

Centre-forward: 3 app., 1 goal
1964: 6-1, -
Born: Middlesbrough, 26 Feb. 1945
Career: Whitby Town (trials with Derby County and Wolverhampton Wanderers); CITY (amat.) May 1964, (prof.) June 1964; Kettering Town July 1965.

Young centre-foward signed after a successful season with Whitby in which he helped them to win the Northern League Cup and finished leading scorer with 26 goals. Netted on his debut for the Imps at Barrow in Aug. 1964 but did not retain his place and was only given a couple more games towards the end of the campaign before receiving a free transfer.

THOMPSON, John Henry
(1957-1960)

Goalkeeper: 42 app
1958: 5-9½, 10-9
Born: Newcastle-upon-Tyne, 4 July 1932
Career: Newcastle United Sep. 1950; CITY May 1957 (£2,500); Horden Colliery cs 1960; later assisted Annfield Plain before retiring during season 1963/64.

Capable 'keeper who had understudied the famous Ron Simpson at his local club and been restricted to just eight First Division appearances. He was first choice at Sincil Bank in 1957/58 but then lost his place and spent two years as a reserve before returning to the north-east. Later worked in the Civil Service.

THOMPSON, J(ohn) Trevor
(1979-1982)

Full-back: 80 app., 1 goal
1980: 5-9, 12-0
Born: North Shields, 21 May 1955
Career: West Bromwich Albion schoolboy, (appr.) 1970, (prof.) Jan. 1974; Washington Diplomats (USA) 1976; Newport County July 1978 (£7,500); CITY Dec. 1979 (£10,000); Gainsborough Trinity June 1982; Worksop Town; Boston FC player-manager Feb. to Dec. 1987; retired through ill health. Lincoln Moorlands player-manager cs 1990 to 1993.

Tough-tackling full-back who missed just three games in the 1980/81 promotion campaign, but appeared only 12 times the following season and was released in May 1982. Has since remained in Lincoln, working as a postman, and continued to play with the Moorlands club into his late 30's.

THOMPSON, Steven Paul
(1980-1985, 1989-1990)

Centre-half: 180 app. + 1 sub, 8 goals
1988: 6-1, 14-4
Born: Sheffield, 28 July 1955
Career: Frecheville; Worksop Town; Boston United cs 1975; CITY Apr. 1980 (£15,000); Charlton Athletic Aug. 1985 (£15,000); Leicester City July 1988 (£15,000); Sheffield United Nov. 1988

(£20,000); CITY Aug. 1989, manager Nov. 1990 to May 1993; assisted with managerial duties at Doncaster Rovers Jan. 1994.

Commanding central defender, quick to win a first team place and soon developed a strong partnership with Trevor Peake in the middle of City's back four which proved a key feature of Colin Murphy's early 1980's side. Later spent four years in higher grade football before returning to Sincil Bank as club captain but suffered a series of injuries which restricted his appearances. Succeeded Allan Clarke as manager and retired from playing. Remained in the post for two and a half years, leaving when the Imps failed to reach the play-offs in 1992/93 and his contract was not renewed. A fine all-round sportsman in his schooldays, representing Yorkshire at football, cricket and basketball.

THOMPSON, Thomas
(1903-1904)

Inside-right/centre-forward: 6 app.
1903: 5-8½, 10-9
Career: Southwick (Sunderland); CITY May 1903; Southwick cs 1904.

Recruited from Wearside League football, Thompson mostly took the inside position with City. All his first team games came in the early part of the season and he spent the rest of the campaign with the reserves.

THOMSON, Gavin
(1895)

Centre-forward: 5 app., 3 goals
Career: Glasgow junior football; CITY Aug. to Oct. 1895

Signed along with another Glasgow junior player, Edward Docherty, and scored twice on his debut at Grimsby. Failed to settle in Lincoln and returned north of the Border after just a few weeks at Sincil Bank.

THORPE, Edwin
(1919-1921)

Full-back/outside-right: 12 app
1919: 5-9, 10-7
Born: Kiveton Park, nr. Sheffield, c.1898
Career: Sheffield Wednesday during WW1; CITY June 1919; Doncaster Rovers July 1921; York City cs 1922; Reading Aug. 1923.

Versatile player - "... *kicks well with either foot*" - who had made occasional appearances as a guest player for City during the Great War. Failed to establish himself in the first team in two seasons with the club (14 Midland League outings in 1920/21) and later spent two years in non-League football before making a further three FL appearances with Reading.

THORPE, Levy
(1922-1924)

Left-half: 69 app., 9 goals
1923: 5-6½, 10-7
Born: Seaham Harbour, Co. Durham, 18 Nov. 1889
Died: 26 Feb. 1935
Career: Seaham Harbour; Blackpool 1911 (Bradford City on trial Sep. 1913); Burnley Nov. 1913 (£750); Blackburn Rovers 1920 (£3,000); CITY Sep. 1922; Rochdale June 1924.

Club captain and considered to be one of the classiest players to appear for City in the inter-war period. His experience proved invaluable in bringing on the club's youngsters and he was knowledgeable in all aspects of the game. Unlucky not to win representative honours - he was selected for the Football League against the Scottish League in 1914/15 but withdrew through illness and was then reserve for a wartime England versus Wales international which was cancelled due to a rail strike. Later suffered a long illness and was given a benefit match at Bloomfield Road in 1934.

THURSBY, R(obert) Stanley
(1929-1932)

Outside-right: 21 app., 6 goals
1930: 5-10, 10-10
Born: Lincoln, 5 Mar. 1909
Career: Burton Road (Lincoln); CITY (amat.) 1929; City School Old Boys (Lincoln) in 1932/33; Spalding United 1933.

Lincoln-born amateur who had played with the Burton Road side from a very early age. Shared the right-wing spot with Evan Jenkins in the 1929/30 season when he made the majority of his FL appearances (17). Well known as a local sprinter.

TICE, W.
(1893-1894)

Goalkeeper: 10 app
Career: Army football; CITY Sep. 1893 to Jan. 1894.

Tice was a soldier based at Lincoln Barracks who became City's regular 'keeper in the early part of the 1893/94 season. He performed well until consecutive defeats at Small Heath (0-6) and Newcastle United (1-5) at the turn of the year led the committee to recall James Gresham.

TIERNEY, Herbert
(1912-1913)

Right-half: 2 app
1912: 5-9½, 11-7
Born: Rochdale, 1888
Career: Heaton Park (Manchester Amateur League); Bolton Wanderers 1907; Exeter City 1908; Darlington cs 1911; CITY Aug. 1912; Castleford Town cs 1913; Goole Town cs 1914; assisted Rochdale in 1916/17 and again Dec. 1918 to cs 1920.

"*Comes with excellent credentials*", noted a 1912 football annual. At Lincoln he appeared regularly with the reserves, for whom he also turned out at right-back, but deputised just twice for Matt Robson in the first team. Had earlier made a solitary Division One appearance with Bolton and 32 in the Southern League with Exeter.

TIMMIS, Samuel
(1896-1897)

Centre-half: 18 app., 2 goals
Born: Audley, Staffs., c.1872
Career: Audley (North Staffs and District League); CITY May 1896 -cs 1897.

On signing he was described as "... *a resourceful, untiring worker from first to last ... puts in some vigorous shots at goal, and altogether is a player from whom much will be expected*". Timmis held the centre-half position for the first 15 matches of the season but lost his place after a disastrous run of 12 consecutive FL defeats in what was one of the worst-ever teams to represent the club.

TOMAN, J(ames) Andrew
(1985-1986)

Midfield: 21 app. + 3 sub, 4 goals
1985: 5-9, 11-2
Born: Northallerton, Yorks., 7 Mar. 1962
Career: Shildon; Northallerton Town; Bishop Auckland; CITY Aug. 1985 (£6,000); Bishop Auckland 1986; Hartlepool United Jan. 1987 (£6,000); Darlington Aug. 1989 (£40,000); (Scarborough on loan, Feb. 1993); Scunthorpe United Aug. 1993; Scarborough Dec. 1993.

Honour: (Darlington) FL Div.4 champions 1991

Skilful midfield man given a contract after impressing in a Lincs. Cup match at Gainsborough when on trial. One of several players who fell out of favour when George Kerr replaced John Pickering as manager and after drifting into non-League football made a successful comeback with Hartlepool. Subsequently became Darlington's record signing and was an influential figure as the Quakers won successive Vauxhall Conference and Fourth Division titles.

TOWLER, Bernard Edward
(1932-1938)

Inside/outside-left: 68 app., 32 goals
1936: 5-6½, 10-4
Born: Ipswich, 13 Mar. 1912
Died: 19 May 1992
Career: Lincoln Corinthians; CITY (amat.) Aug. 1932, (prof.) Sep. 1932; Notts County Aug. 1938; (CITY as a guest during WW2); Ruston Bucyrus (Lincoln) in 1945/46; Boston United Oct. 1946.

Scored freely in City's reserve side but did not appear regularly in the first team until the 1935/36 season. Had his best years at Sincil Bank when he returned to assist the Imps in wartime, scoring 71 goals in 88 matches, including seven hat-tricks. Bernard was a part-time professional who was employed in a local engineering works and was later a partner in a plant hire firm. Died in the nearby village of Bassingham.

TRACEY, Michael George
(1961-1962)

Forward: 12 app., 5 goals
1960: 5-11, 11-9
Born: Durham, 14 Feb. 1935
Career: Oxford University; Corinthian Casuals; Accrington Stanley, (amat.) in 1957/58; Crook Town cs 1958; Luton Town Nov. 1959; CITY July 1961; Worksop Town July 1962; Matlock Town cs 1965.

Honours: England amateur international (3 app.)
(Crook Town) FA Amateur Cup winner 1959

Former top-class amateur who came to Sincil Bank on a free transfer. Showed his versatility by appearing in all five forward postions but never won a permanent first team place. Worked as a solicitor and later became a partner in a Lincoln firm before retiring in 1980 to a farm in Ireland.

TREHARNE, Colin
(1966-1967)

Goalkeeper: 20 app
1965: 5-10, 13-0
Born: Bridgend, Glamorgan, 30 July 1937
Career: Army football (RAOC); Mansfield Town (amat.) 1959, (prof.) Dec. 1960; CITY July 1966; Ilkeston Town cs 1967; Heanor Town cs 1970; Boston FC cs 1971; Worksop Town in 1972/73 season. Manager of Ashby Institute in mid-1970's and later Hykeham United (Lincs. League).

Sound and reliable 'keeper who had represented his battalion in the Notts. Thursday League, turning professional on leaving the Army. Treharne shared the goalkeeper's position with Dave Tennant in his Sincil Bank season before leaving on a free transfer. Settled in nearby North Hykeham and worked in the frozen food business.

TREVIS, Derek A.
(1970-1973)

Forward/defender: 100 app. + 8 sub, 18 goals
1972: 5-11, 11-0
Born: Sheldon, Birmingham, 9 Sep. 1942
Career: Aston Villa June 1962; Colchester United Mar. 1964; Walsall Sep. 1968 (£11,000); CITY July 1970 (£6,000); Philadelphia Atoms (USA) May 1973; Stockport County Sep. 1973; Philadelphia Atoms 1974 to 1975; San Diego Jaws as player-coach 1976; Las Vegas Quicksilver as player-coach 1977; Philadelphia Fury 1978.

Useful player who began his City career as a partner to Percy Freeman in the Imps' forward line, scoring on his debut in a 1-1 draw against League newcomers Cambridge United, but later switched to central defence and often appeared as a sweeper. Aggregated 392 FL appearances plus 12 substitutions, 39 goals in a decade of League football before spending several years in the United States. At one point he was tipped to return to Sincil Bank as manager but did not get the job.

TROOPS, Harold
(1949-1958)

Outside-right/left-back: 295 app., 32 goals
1949: 5-9, 11-2
Born: Sheffield, 10 Feb. 1926
Died: 5 Mar. 1963
Career: Hadfield Sports (Sheffield); Barnsley Dec. 1946; CITY Aug. 1949; Carlisle United June 1958 (£2,000); retired May 1960.

Honour: (City) FL Div.3 (North) champions 1952

Harry began as a centre-forward with Barnsley, appearing in his early days at Sincil Bank as a goalscoring winger before switching to full-back early in 1954. A 1950 critic noted "... showed remarkable speed on the right wing [but] was not always consistent". On retiring from football was employed in a Sheffield steelworks before his tragic death in a road accident at the age of 37.

TURNBULL, Roy
(1969-1970)

Inside-forward: 0 app. + 2 sub
Born: Edinburgh, 22 Oct. 1948
Career: Gorgie Hearts; Heart of Midlothian 1965; CITY Sep. 1969 to May 1970.

Honours: Scotland schools international
Scotland youth international

A reserve with both his senior clubs, Roy received two brief outings towards the end of his stay at Sincil Bank. Proved a valued member of the side which won the North Midlands League championship in 1969/70.

TURNER, Brian
(1947-1948)

Centre-forward: 5 app
1947: 5-11½, 11-0
Born: Whittlesey, Cambs., 27 Aug. 1925
Career: March Town (CITY, amat. Nov. 1947 to Feb. 1948); Walthamstow Avenue Mar. 1949.

Amateur who made an immediate impact when he scored four goals on his reserve team debut in a 7-0 thrashing of Grimsby Town's second string. A club brochure of the time described him as "... a very modest player, Turner was not happy about his inclusion in the first team. City were forced to play him". Appeared for Cambridge University against Oxford in their 1947/48 match and later continued his studies at London University. Despite scoring prolifically at all levels of non-League football he failed to find the net in his Northern Section appearances. A schoolteacher by profession.

TURNER, Christopher Robert
(1978)

Goalkeeper: 5 app
1978: 5-11, 11-0
Born: Sheffield, 15 Sep. 1958
Career: Sheffield Wednesday (appr.) Mar. 1975, (prof.) Aug. 1976 (CITY on loan Oct. 1978); Sunderland July 1979 (£75,000); Manchester United July 1985 (£250,000); Sheffield Wednesday Sep. 1988 (£175,000) (Leeds United on loan, Nov. 1989); Leyton Orient on loan, Oct. 1991, signing permanently Nov. 1991 (£75,000).

Honours: England youth international (5 app. 1977)
(Wednesday) FL Cup winner 1991
(Sunderland) FL Cup finalist 1985.

Young 'keeper who deputised for Peter Grotier during a month on loan at Sincil Bank. Subsequently played in top flight football for over a decade appearing in more than 450 FL matches.

TURNER, Ian
(1978)

Goalkeeper: 7 app.
1978: 6-0, 12-5
Born: Middlesbrough, 17 Jan. 1953
Career: South Bank; Huddersfield Town Oct. 1970; Grimsby Town Feb. 1972 (Walsall on loan Feb. 1973); Southampton Mar. 1974 (£25,000 including another player) (Newport County on loan Mar, 1978; Fort Lauderdale Strikers, USA June to Aug. 1978; CITY on loan, Oct. to Dec. 1978); Walsall Jan. 1979 (£25,000) (Halifax Town on loan Jan. 1981) to Mar.1982; Witney Town July 1981; Salisbury; RS Southampton; Waterlooville; Romsey player-manager 1986; Brockenhurst player-manager 1987; AFC Totton player-manager 1988.

Honour: (Southampton) FA Cup winner 1976

Ian succeeded his namesake Chris as Peter Grotier's deputy during the transition period between Willie Bell's departure and the arrival of Colin Murphy. After leaving full-time football he worked for an oil company.

TURNER, Philip
(1980-1986)

Midfield: 239 app. + 2 sub, 19 goals
1985: 5-8, 10-3
Born: Sheffield, 12 Feb. 1962
Career: Sheffield Rangers; CITY schoolboy Oct. 1976, (appr.) July 1978, (prof.) Feb. 1980; Grimsby Town Aug. 1986 (in exchange for Gary Lund); Leicester City Feb. 1988 (£42,000); Notts County Mar. 1989 (in part exchange for another player).

One of a series of talented youngsters developed in City's Sheffield nursery side in the late 1970's. Phil was a first team regular soon after signing professional forms, becoming a cultured midfield player with neat ball skills. A career total of 453 FL appearances plus 21 as substitute, 41 goals to the start of the 1993/94 season.

TURNER, Wayne Leslie
(1981-1982)

Midfield: 16 app.
1982: 5-9, 11-5
Born: Luton, 9 Mar. 1961
Career: Luton Town schoolboy, (appr.) 1977, (prof.) Apr. 1978 (CITY on loan Oct. 1981 to Mar. 1982); Coventry City July 1985 (£75,000); Brentford Sep. 1986 (£35,000); Barnet Sep. 1988 to c.1990; later Luton Town reserve team coach.

Midfield player who spent six months on loan at Sincil Bank, helping transform the side into promotion candidates, after arriving when they were in a lowly position in the Third Division. Later captained both Coventry and Brentford, before joining then non-League Barnet after a dispute over terms.

TYNAN, Thomas Edward
(1978-1979)
Forward: 9 app., 1 goal
1978: 5-10½, 11-11
Born: Liverpool, 17 Nov. 1955
Career: Liverpool (appr.) 1971, (prof.) Nov. 1972 (Swansea City on loan Oct. 1975; Dallas Tornado, USA, Apr. to Aug. 1976); Sheffield Wednesday Sep. 1976 (£10,000); CITY Oct. 1978 (£33,000); Newport County Feb. 1979 (£25,000); Plymouth Argyle Aug. 1983 (£55,000); Rotherham United July 1985 (£25,000); Plymouth Argyle on loan Mar. to May 1986, signing permanently Sep. 1986 (£25,000); Torquay United May 1990 as player-coach; Doncaster Rovers July 1991; Goole Town player-manager Oct. 1992 to Feb. 1993.

Honour: (Newport) Welsh Cup winner 1980

Striker brought by Willie Bell for a club record fee only to prove a spectacular failure both on and off the field at Lincoln. Bell departed a few weeks after signing him and he was soon sold by new manager Colin Murphy. Best remembered at Sincil Bank for his record of scoring in virtually every game he played against the Imps after leaving. A major success elsewhere, netting a total of 254 FL goals and finishing leading scorer in all competitions in the 1982/83 season.

URWIN, Joseph Sydney
(1933-1934)
Outside-right: 8 app., 1 goal
1934: 5-7½, 11-11
Born: High Spen, Co. Durham, c.1912
Career: Tanfield Lea Institute; Bradford City Sep. 1930; Chesterfield May 1931; Throckley Welfare 1932; CITY Dec. 1933; Stockport County July 1934.

Stocky winger given an extended run on City's right flank towards the end of the 1933/34 campaign. Saw little first team action elsewhere: Bradford City 1 app., Stockport County 6 app., 2 goals.

VARNEY, John Francis
(1951-1953)
Left-back: 20 app., 4 goals
1951: 5-11, 12-10
Born: Oxford, 27 Nov. 1929
Career: Oxford City; RAF football; Hull City (amat.) during 1948/49, (prof.) Dec. 1949; CITY May 1951 to cs 1953; Headington United Sep. 1954.

Honour: (City) FL Div.3 (North) champions 1952

A member of the Imps' 1951/52 promotion side until suffering a bad injury at Wrexham on Christmas Day which put him out for some time. Refused the terms offered to him in the summer of 1953 and returned to live in Oxford. Took a 12 month break from the game before making a comeback as a centre-forward with Southern League Headington (later to win League status after changing their name to Oxford United).

VICKERS, T(homas) Hedley
(1895-1898)
Half-back: 12 app.
Born: Lincoln 1877
Died: 4 Mar. 1955
Career: London Hospitals; CITY (amat.) Dec. 1895 to 1898; later assisted Lincoln Lindum.

Former Lincoln Grammar School boy who was a medical student at St. Mary's Hospital, London when he first appeared in the League for City. A contemporary noted of him "... his style is purely amateur ... without appearing to exert himself, he is always there when wanted, and his judgement in placing the ball is 'par excellent'". Died at Nuffield House, Guy's Hospital.

WADSLEY, Harold
(1909-1910)
Inside-left: 2 app., 1 goal
Career: Netherfield Rangers (Notts Alliance); CITY Feb. 1909; Sutton Junction cs 1910; Peterborough GN Loco; Grantham Avenue cs 1913.

Wadsley did well during the run-in to the Midland League title in 1908/09 scoring five goals in seven games, but Ronald Mackenzie took over the inside-left position when the Imps returned to Division Two and he spent most of his time in the reserves. Later appeared with several Central Alliance teams.

WAITES, Sydney Hastings
(1920-1924)
Outside-right: 3 app
1922: 5-9½, 10-0
Born: Gateshead, 20 Sep. 1901
Career: Technical School Old Boys (Lincoln); CITY cs 1920; Newark Town July 1924; Halifax Town Sep. 1925; Stockport County May 1928; Boston Town cs 1929; New Brighton Aug. 1930 to cs 1931; Tunbridge Wells Rangers cs 1932.

Showed promise in his early days at Lincoln but experienced little senior action until joining Halifax Town (96 FL app., 13 goals). Developed into a fast winger with good ball control skills. Also a regular in his New Brighton season: 37 app., 6 goals.

WAITT, Michael H.
(1987-1989)
Centre-forward: 7 app. + 1 sub, 1 goal
1988: 6-4, 12-0
Born: Hexham, Northumberland, 25 June 1960
Career: Arnold Kingswell; Keyworth United; Notts County Dec. 1984; CITY July 1987 (£17,500); Boston United Dec. 1989; Lai Sun (Hong Kong) Dec. 1989; Spalding United Dec. 1990; Nuneaton Borough Jan. 1991; Grantham Mar. 1991; Gedling Town; Ilkeston Town; Napier City (New Zealand) player-coach Jan. 1992.

Giant striker who was one of the players signed by Colin Murphy as he built the team which was to take the Vauxhall Conference title at the first attempt. Did well in his first few games, scoring regularly, but then suffered a badly broken leg in the home match with Cheltenham Town in Oct. 1987. The injury put him out of the game for two years and although he made a brief come back he could not win a regular first team place and was released.

WAKEHAM, Peter Francis
(1965-1966)

Goalkeeper: 44 app.
1965: 6-0, 11-13
Born: Kingsbridge, Devon, 14 Mar. 1936
Career: Torquay United juniors 1952, (prof.) Sep. 1953; Sunderland Sep. 1958 (£7,000); Charlton Athletic June 1962 (approx. £4,000); CITY May 1965; Poole Town July 1966.

Experienced 'keeper who was City's first choice throughout the 1965/66 campaign before being allowed to leave on a free transfer. Earlier in his career he had been considered for representative honours and went on tour in 1959 with the England under-23 squad but did not play.

WALKER, Alan
(1983-1985)

Centre-half: 74 app. + 1 sub, 4 goals
1984: 6-1, 12-7
Born: Mossley, 17 Dec. 1959
Career: Mossley; Stockport County (amat.) July 1978; Bangor City Aug. 1978; Telford United Feb. 1980; CITY Oct. 1983 (£21,500); Millwall July 1985 (£32,500); Gillingham Mar. 1988 (£50,000); Plymouth Argyle Sep. 1992; Mansfield Town Sep. 1992; Barnet Aug. 1993.

Honour: (Millwall) FL Div.2 champions 1988

Highly effective central defender who had captained Telford to victory in the 1983 FA Trophy final. Made the transition from top class non-League football with ease, earning a transfer to Second Division Millwall after two seasons at Sincil Bank.

WALKER, Harold
(1934-1936)

Outside-right: 18 app., 2 goals
1935: 5-8, 10-10
Born:
Career: Throckley Welfare; CITY Sep. 1934 (initially on trial); Gateshead May 1936 to 1938.

Capable wingman. After reaching peak form early in 1935 he sustained an injury which put him out of action for several weeks. Understudied Billy Sellars in the 1935/36 season. Made 39 Northern Section appearances for Gateshead, scoring 12 goals.

WALKER, John
(1899-1900)

Outside-left: 6 app.,
Died: 1 Aug. 1900
Career: Leith Athletic; Heart of Midlothian; CITY June 1899 to Jan. 1900.

The first black player to play for City and one of the very few to appear in pre-WW1 League football - a circumstance which drew much comment at the time and undoubtedly created extra pressures for Walker. A skilful winger: *"... is repeatedly doing pretty work and centres accurately"*, noted one observer in the early part of the season. Returned to Scotland where he died shortly afterwards.

WALKER, William
(1921-1922, 1924)

Outside-left: 36 app., 5 goals
1921: 5-8½, 11-0
Born: Durham, c.1891
Career: Darlington Albion (Darlington FC on trial); Darlington St. Augustines; Fulham Sep. 1909; CITY Aug. 1921 to May 1922, returning for a brief trial in Jan. 1924.

A regular for Fulham in their early days as a FL club, playing a total of 176 League and FA Cup matches for them and scoring 26 goals. He made 33 appearances for Lincoln in 1921/22 before being given a free transfer. Subsequently had severe appendix problems which kept him out of the game for 18 months, returning to Sincil Bank for a brief trial in Jan. 1924 but was unable to win a contract.

WALLINGTON, F(rancis) Mark
(1988-1991)

Goalkeeper: 87 app
1990: 6-1, 14-11
Born: Sleaford, Lincs., 17 Sep. 1952
Career: CITY schoolboy Nov. 1969; Heckington United (Grantham League); Walsall (amat.) cs 1971, (prof.) Oct. 1971; Leicester City

Mar. 1972 (£30,000); Derby County July 1985 (£25,000); CITY Aug. 1988; retired May 1991.

Honours: England under-18 schools international (2 app. 1970)
England amateur youth international
England under-23 international (2 app. 1976)
(Leicester) FL Div.2 champions 1980
(Derby Co.) FL Div.2 champions 1987

Quickly snapped up by Leicester after only a handful of games with Walsall and took over the 'keeper's jersey when Peter Shilton was sold to Stoke. Established a club record of over 300 consecutive appearances at Filbert Street before moving on to Derby where he played a major role in two promotion campaigns. Finally made his debut in City's first team at the age of 35 - 19 years after being on the club's books as a schoolboy. A career aggregate of 577 FL games. Subsequently engaged in coaching on a self-employed basis.

WALLS, David
(1971-1973)
Winger: 9 app
1971: 5-6, 9-6
Born: Leeds, 16 June 1953
Career: Leeds United schoolboy, (appr.) May 1969; CITY July 1971; Golden Cross (Lincoln Sunday League) in season 1973/74.

Lightweight but skilful winger signed on a free transfer by David Herd. Given several opportunities by new manager Graham Taylor towards the end of the 1972/73 campaign but was released shortly afterwards.

WALSHAW, Kenneth
(1947)
Inside-left: 17 app., 6 goals
1947: 5-9, 11-7
Born: Tynemouth, 28 Aug. 1918
Career: Sunderland Aug. 1944; CITY Aug. 1947; Carlisle United Dec. 1947; Bradford City Aug. 1950 to 1951; later with North Shields in early 1950's.

Inside-forward signed as a part-time professional for a four-figure fee from First Division Sunderland where he had failed to make the League team. Had a good scoring record in his brief spell at Lincoln before returning to the north of England. Also appeared as a left-winger with his other clubs.

WARD, Fred ("Yaffer")
(1914-1923, 1925-1926, 1928-1931)
Left-back: 108 app., 10 goals
1921: 5-8½, 13-0
Born: Lincoln, 30 June 1894
Died: Sep. 1953
Career: Lincoln junior football: Stamp End, South Bar, West End; CITY Nov.1914 (Grimsby Town as a guest during WW1); Wigan Borough Feb. 1923; CITY Sep. 1925; Rochdale Sep. 1926; CITY Aug. 1928 to 1931.

Hugely popular full-back who was the mainstay of City's defence in the years after the Great War. *"His vigorous methods and famous sliding tackle were known and feared by all opponents, while his hefty kicking, though not always tempered by discretion, invariably aimed to propelling the ball as far away from his own goal as possible".* Transferred to Wigan Borough along with James McGrahan at a time when the club were in serious financial difficulties and on the verge of collapse. Later spent two further spells with the Imps when he was mainly used as a reserve. Afterwards became licensee of the Golden Eagle public house on High Street, just a few minutes walk from the ground.

WARD, James ("Tim")
(1896-1897)
Inside-forward: 4 app
Career: Nondescripts (Lincoln); CITY cs 1896 to cs 1897.

One of several local players who made a brief contribution for the Imps in the troubled 1896/97 season. Ward's FL debut on 16 Jan. against Darwen coincided with City's first win since Sep. - breaking a club record sequence of 12 consecutive defeats.

WARD, John Peter
(1969-1979, 1982)

Centre-forward: 224 app. + 17 sub, 91 goals
1975: 5-8, 10-10
Born: Lincoln, 7 Apr. 1951
Career: CITY (amat.) July 1969 (also with Adelaide Park, Lincoln Sunday League), (prof.) Mar. 1971 (Workington on loan Sep. to Nov. 1972); Watford July 1979 (£15,000); Grimsby Town June 1981; CITY Mar. to cs 1982. Watford coach May 1982, becoming asst.-manager in 1985; Southend United coach Sep. 1987; Reading scout; Aston Villa asst.-manager Jan. 1988 to Jan. 1991; York City manager Nov. 1991; Bristol Rovers manager Mar. 1993.

Honour: (City) FL Div.4 champions 1976

Local centre-forward who was appearing with City's reserve and 'A' teams and with top Sunday side Adelaide Park when he signed professional forms. Took a couple of seasons to establish a regular first team place for himself but then developed into an extremely effective goalscorer. Most of his efforts were from inside the six yard box but he became one of the most successful scorers of his time in the lower divisions. Netted 29 League and cup goals in 1975/76 when City won the Fourth Division championship. Early in 1977/78 suffered a bad injury but came back and later moved on to Watford where he was re-united with Graham Taylor and other former Imps including Sam Ellis and Dennis Booth. Returned for a very brief spell at Sincil Bank under Colin Murphy before going into coaching and management.

WARD, Paul Terence
(1991-1994)
Midfield: 38 app. + 1 sub
1991: 5-11, 12-5
Born: Sedgefield, Co. Durham, 15 Sep. 1963
Career: Chelsea (appr.), (prof.) Aug. 1981; Middlesbrough Sep. 1982; Darlington Sep. 1985; Leyton Orient July 1988 (£10,000); Scunthorpe United Oct. 1989 (£45,000); CITY Mar. 1991 (£30,000); Gainsborough Trinity cs 1994.

Hard tackling midfield player signed by Steve Thompson on the transfer deadline in 1991. Suffered a severe knee injury during the Coca Cola Cup-tie at Doncaster in Aug. 1992 which put him out of action for nearly two years and he did not play again for the Imps. A career record of 312 FL appearances, 11 as sub., 17 goals.

WARD, Stephen
(1977-1981)
Full-back: 2 app.
1980: 5-10, 10-13
Born: Chapeltown, Sheffield, 27 Dec. 1960
Career: CITY schoolboy Nov. 1975, (appr.) July 1977, (prof.) May 1979 to Aug. 1981; Matlock Town Jan. to Mar. 1982.

One of the many talented youngsters from the Sheffield area developed by City in the late 1970's. Ward had two FL outings in the early part of the 1980 deputising for Trevor Thompson.

WARD, Warren
(1985-1986)
Forward: 15 app. + 6 sub, 8 goals
1985: 6-0, 13-0
Born: Plympton, Devon, 25 May 1962
Career: Yorkshire Amateurs; Guiseley; York City non-contract basis Mar. to May 1985; CITY July 1985 (Exeter City on loan, Feb. to Apr. 1986); Crewe Alexandra on trial Aug. 1986; Boston United Sep. 1986; Kings Lynn cs 1989; Spalding United in 1990/91; Lincoln United cs 1991; Wisbech Town Dec. 1992; Grantham cs 1993, appointed manager cs 1994.

Scored on his Lincoln debut and remained a first team regular until George Kerr took over as manager. He then spent several months on loan at Exeter, returning to Sincil Bank shortly before the end of the campaign. Despite a modest total of appearances he finished joint leading scorer in what proved to be his only season with the club. Later became a development officer with the Lincs. FA.

WARDLE, Geoffrey
(1961-1962)
Wing-half: 1 app
1961: 6-1, 12-7
Born: Trimdon, Co. Durham, 7 Jan. 1940
Career: Houghton Juniors (West Bromwich Albion amat.); Sunderland Jan. 1958; CITY June 1961; Kings Lynn July 1962; Matlock Town cs 1963; Spalding United cs 1967.

Geoff came to Sincil Bank after three years on the books at Roker Park without making the first team. His solitary League outing came when he deputised for Ray Barnard in the Division Three match at home to Coventry on 14 Oct. 1961.

WARREN, Lee A.
(1990)
Midfield: 2 app. + 1 sub, 1 goal
1990: 6-0, 11-3
Born: Manchester, 28 Feb. 1969
Career: Leeds United YTS, (prof.) July 1987; Rochdale Oct. 1987; Hull City Aug. 1988 (£40,000) (CITY on loan, Sep. 1990); Doncaster Rovers cs 1994.

Neat midfield player signed on loan by Allan Clarke at the start of the 1990/91 season. Scored after 15 minutes of his debut against Scunthorpe but returned to Boothferry Park the following month. Went on to establish himself as a regular in the Tigers' line-up.

WARRINGTON, Anthony
(1953-1957)
Goalkeeper: 2 app
1954: 5-10, 11-4
Born: Ecclesfield, Sheffield, 12 Feb. 1934
Career: Thorncliffe Juniors (Sheffield); CITY (amat.) Aug. 1953, (prof.) Mar. 1954; Grantham July 1957.

Reserve 'keeper who was given just two first team outings at Sincil Bank: at home to Fulham in Apr. 1954 and away at West Ham two years later. Coincidentally both games were won 4-2.

WATFORD, Albert
(1946-1947)
Right-back: 14 app
Born: Chesterfield, 12 Feb. 1917
Career: Chesterfield Feb. 1944 (CITY as a guest player in 1944/45); CITY Sep. 1946; Scunthorpe United Sep. 1947; Boston United cs 1949 to cs 1951.

Albert Watford was nearly 30 when he finally made his debut in peacetime football - he had appeared in 29 wartime games for Chesterfield and the Imps. Although he played a couple of games at centre-half most of his outings came at full-back when he deputised for Alex Thompson towards the end of his Lincoln campaign.

WATSON, Albert
(1924-1925)
Outside-right: 1 app
1924: 5-8, 11-7
Born: c.1904
Career: Leeds Amateurs; Yorkshire Amateurs; CITY Aug. 1924 to cs 1925.

Reserve winger given a solitary League appearance in the home match against Chesterfield on 18 Apr. 1925. This proved his only first team opportunity at Sincil Bank and he was released shortly afterwards.

WATSON, Arthur E.
(1934-1936)
Full-back: 37 app
1934: 5-11, 11-0
Born: South Hiendley, nr. Barnsley, 12 July 1913
Career: Monckton Colliery; CITY Nov. 1934; Chesterfield June 1936; Hull City June 1939 (£250); retired May 1947.

Youngster who impressed on taking over from the injured Jack Buckley with his powerful kicking, timely tackling and ability to anticipate a game's developments. A reserve at Chesterfield but a firm favourite at Boothferry Park in the first post-war season. Brother of William Watson, see below.

WATSON, Donald
(1956-1957)
Inside-forward: 14 app., 2 goals
1957: 5-8, 11-8
Born: Barnsley, 27 Aug. 1932
Career: Worsborough Bridge; Sheffield Wednesday Sep. 1954; CITY Nov. 1956; Bury Nov. 1957; Barnsley Jan. 1962 (approx. £2,500); Rochdale July 1962; Barrow July 1964 to 1965; Buxton from Oct. 1966.

Honour: (Bury) FL Div.3 champions 1961

Useful inside-forward who had a brief run in the first team straight after signing but subsequently appeared rarely. Also played at centre-forward for his other clubs, notably Bury for whom he was an ever-present in their 1960/61 championship side, scoring 23 goals. A career total of 278 FL appearances, 85 goals.

WATSON, Graham Sidney
(1978-1980)
Midfield: 43 app., 2 goals
1979: 5-10, 11-6
Born: Doncaster, 3 Aug. 1949
Career: Doncaster Rovers (appr.), (prof.) Nov. 1966; Rotherham

United Feb. 1968 (a deal in which Watson, Dennis Leigh and approx. £8,000 were exchanged for three Rotherham players); Doncaster Rovers Jan. 1969 (£8,000); Cambridge United Sep. 1972 (£5,000); CITY Sep. 1978 (£15,000); Cambridge United Mar. 1980 to 1983.

Honours: (Doncaster Rovers) FL Div.4 champions 1969 (Cambridge United) FL Div.4 champions 1977

Solid and reliable midfielder signed by Willie Bell shortly before his departure for the USA. Watson was one of the few players to remain a first team regular under new manager Colin Murphy, staying until Mar. 1980, when he returned to Cambridge on a free transfer. Totalled over 400 FL outings in a career lasting 17 years.

WATSON, William
(1903-1907, 1908-1909)
Outside-right/inside-forward: 120 app., 28 goals
1904: 5-7½, 11-4
Career: South Bank; CITY July 1903; Newark cs 1907; CITY cs 1908 to cs 1909; Castleford Town in 1909/10.

A regular in City's Second Division team for four seasons, heading the scoring list in 1906/07 when he appeared at inside-forward. Returning after a year with Newark to participate in the Midland League championship campaign of 1908/09 when he made a further 33 appearances, scoring 15 goals.

WATSON, William
(1935-1936)
Full-back: 9 app
1934: 5-10, 10-10
Born: South Hiendley, nr. Barnsley, 29 May 1916
Career: Monckton Colliery; CITY Feb. 1935 (initially on trial); Chesterfield June 1936; Rochdale June 1948 to 1954.

Signed as a teenager and given his FL debut shortly afterwards. William was described in his Chesterfield days as showing "... excellent mobility and execution" and "a gentleman both on and off the field". Had a lengthy post-war spell with Rochdale where he made a total of 200 League appearances. Brother of Arthur Watson, see above.

WEBB, Alan Richard
(1984)
Defender: 11 app
1984: 5-10, 12-0
Born: Wrockwardine Wood, Salop, 1 Jan. 1963
Career: West Bromwich Albion (appr.) 1979, (prof.) Jan. 1980 (CITY on loan, Mar. to May 1984); Port Vale Aug. 1984 to 1992.

Solid, reliable central defender who also appeared at full-back. Webb was signed for an extended loan period to cover for injuries which had depleted City's back four in the early part of 1984. A regular first team choice for most of his eight years at Vale Park where he made 187 FL outings plus 3 as substitute.

WEBB, Alfred
(1899-1904)

Goalkeeper: 131 app
1903: 6-0, 13-2
Born: c.1878
Died: 25 Aug. 1932
Career: Mansfield Mechanics; CITY on trial Apr. 1899, permanent May 1899 to cs 1904; Mansfield Mechanics cs 1905.

Alfred Webb was first choice 'keeper almost from his senior debut in Sep. 1899 until Dec. 1903 when he lost his place to Ernest Boast. He was an ever-present in 1901/02 when the Imps registered their best ever performances in both the League (5th in Division Two) and FA Cup (last 16). Previously worked as a miner in a Mansfield colliery.

WEBSTER, Walter George
(1925)

Right-back: 12 app
1925: 5-10, 12-0
Born: West Bromwich, 22 May 1895
Died: 15 Sep. 1980
Career: Kingsbury Colliery; Walsall 1921; CITY June 1925; Sheffield United Oct. 1925 (£1,650); Scunthorpe United Aug. 1930; Torquay United Aug. 1931; Rochdale July 1933; Stalybridge Celtic Aug. 1934.

Webster had won junior international honours for the Birmingham FA against Scotland in Apr. 1922 and was immediately made captain on joining the Imps. Won considerable praise from contemporaries *"... one of the finest backs in the Northern Section"*, and *"a very classy type of full-back"*. His form in the opening matches of the season persuaded FA Cup holders Sheffield United to pay City a club record fee for his services. Mostly a reserve at Bramall Lane before moving into the Midland League with Scunthorpe. Returned to Sheffield after his playing career was over and continued to live there until his death.

WEST, Dean
(1989-1993, 1993-)

Midfield: 45 app. + 25 sub, 13 goals
1993: 5-10, 11-7
Born: Wakefield, 15 Dec. 1972
Career: Leeds United schoolboy; CITY YTS forms July 1989, (prof.) July 1991; Boston United July-Aug. 1993; CITY Aug. 1993 (Boston United on loan Aug. to Sep 1993).

Dean was given his FL debut in the final match of the 1990/91 season whilst still on YTS forms and scored once in a 6-2 victory over Carlisle. Released in the summer of 1993 but was quickly re-signed, going on to win a regular place as a wide midfield player with goalscoring potential before he suffered an injury which put him out of action for several weeks.

WEST, Gary
(1985-1987, 1991, 1991-1993)

Centre-defender: 100 app. + 4 sub, 5 goals
1992: 6-2, 13-2
Born: Scunthorpe, 25 Aug. 1964
Career: Sheffield United (appr.), (prof.) Aug. 1982; CITY Aug. 1985 (£35,000); Gillingham June 1987 (£50,000); Port Vale Feb. 1989 (£70,000) (Gillingham on loan Nov. 1990; CITY on loan Jan. 1991); CITY Aug. 1991 (£25,000) (Walsall on loan Sep. to Nov. 1992); Boston United Mar. to cs 1993; Kings Lynn in 1993/94; Gainsborough Trinity Aug. 1994.

Honour: England youth international (1983)

Tall and stylish central defender. A regular in his first spell with the club which coincided with the team's descent from the Third Division to the Vauxhall Conference in successive seasons. West was voted Player of the Season by the supporters in 1986/87 and moved on to Gillingham when the Imps went out of the League. A first choice at the start of his second permanent spell but rarely made the starting line-up after Dec. 1991.

WEST, G.
(1896-1897)

Inside-forward: 1 app
Career: CITY cs 1896 to cs 1897

West was a youngster who played mainly with the City Swifts (reserve) side. His single FL appearance came on 2 Jan. 1897 in a 2-1 defeat at Newcastle United.

WESTBROOK, Henry Alfred
(1921-1922)

Goalkeeper: 2 app
Born: Chertsey, Surrey, 24 May 1896
Died: 4 Nov. 1977
Career: Woking junior football; CITY Oct. 1921 to May 1922.

Reserve 'keeper who deputised twice for Bob Bainbridge in Feb. 1922. However, City resolved the problem of finding a successor to Bainbridge shortly afterwards when they signed teenager Jack Kendall, and Westbrook - having become surplus to requirements - was given a free transfer at the end of the season.

WHALLEY, Robert
(1930-1931)

Inside-right/centre-forward: 9 app., 4 goals
1930: 5-8, 10-7
Born: Flimby, Cumberland, c.1905
Career: Workington; Nottingham Forest May 1928 to 1929; Peterborough & Fletton United; CITY July 1930; Peterborough & Fletton United cs 1931; Luton Town cs 1932 to 1933.

When City's 1930/31 promotion challenge was faltering the club's management sprung a surprise by replacing the three regular inside-forwards with three youngsters from the reserves - Whalley, Jack Halliday and Harold March. The move proved an initial success but the lack of experience soon showed, vital matches were lost and despite leading the table for most of the campaign the Imps finished runners-up to Chesterfield. Whalley saw little first team action elsewhere - no senior appearances at Forest and only four (one goal) at Southern Section Luton.

WHITE, Devon W.
(1984-1986)
Centre-forward: 21 app. + 8 sub, 4 goals
1985: 6-3, 14-0
Born: Nottingham, 2 Mar. 1964
Career: Radford Olympic; Arnold; CITY Dec. 1984 (£2,000) (Boston United on loan Oct. 1985; Naxxar Lions, Malta, on loan Dec. 1985); Boston United July 1986; Shepshed Charterhouse; Grantham Aug. 1987; Bristol Rovers Aug. 1987; Cambridge United Sep. 1992 (£100,000 and a player); Queens Park Rangers Mar. 1993 (£100,000).

Honour: (Bristol Rovers) FL Div.3 champions 1990

Tall gangly centre-forward who proved a handful for opposition defences despite his inexperience. Rejected the terms offered to him in June 1986 and resumed his career as an electrician with the Electricity Board, but was tempted back into the full-time game 12 months later by Bristol Rovers. Netted 54 goals in 190 FL appearances plus 12 as sub for the West Country club before big money transfers took him to Loftus Road and Premiership football.

WHITE, Frederick
(1950-1951)
Goalkeeper: 42 app
1949: 6-1½, 12-7
Born: Wolverhampton, 5 Dec. 1916
Career: Wolverhampton junior football; Everton May 1935; Sheffield United May 1937; CITY May 1950 (£200); Gainsborough Trinity Aug. 1951; retired through injury cs 1952. Subsequently spent 20 years on Sheffield United's staff, working as reserve team manager, coach and scout; Leeds United scout and then scouting for Jim Smith's various clubs.

The intervention of war meant that Fred had to wait until Oct. 1947 for his League debut - a dozen years after becoming a professional. However, he had figured in many of the Blades' fixtures during WW2 and in the 1945/46 FA Cup competition. First choice at Sincil Bank in the 1950/51 campaign, only prevented from being an ever-present by injury. After his involvement with the full time game ceased he worked as a salesman in the building trade, latterly scouting for several clubs managed by the former City player Jim Smith.

WHITE, Malcolm
(1964-1965)
Goalkeeper: 25 app
1964: 6-2½, 13-10
Born: Sunderland, 24 Apr. 1941
Career: Coseley Amat. (Wolverhampton) (Wolverhampton

Wanderers amat.); Grimsby Town Aug. 1958; Walsall Aug. 1963; CITY July 1964 (in exchange for Terry Carling); Bradford City July 1965; Halifax Town Nov. 1965; Los Angeles Wolves (USA) Mar. 1968 (£1,000); Boston United June 1969 to 1974.

Shared the goalkeeping spot with Bob Graves during his season at Sincil Bank. A critic noted of him during his Lincoln spell "... agile, alert, with a keen sense of anticipation". Enjoyed a fair amount of League action - 229 appearances in all - before finishing his career in the Northern Premier League with Boston United.

WHITE, Stephen J.
(1983)
Forward: 2 app. + 1 sub
1983: 5-11, 11-10
Born: Chipping Sodbury, Glos., 2 Jan. 1959
Career: Mangotsfield United; Bristol Rovers July 1977; Luton Town Dec. 1979 (£175,000); Charlton Athletic July 1982 (valued at £100,000 in part exchange for Paul Walsh in a £350,000 deal) (CITY on loan, Jan. 1983; Luton Town on loan, Feb. 1983); Bristol Rovers Aug. 1983 (£35,000); Swindon Town July 1986.

Honours: England schoolboy international (1 app vs Wales 1977) (Luton Town) FL Div.2 champions 1982

Striker who was signed on loan as a stand-in for the injured Derek Bell. Has since had a lengthy career in the game and up to the end of the 1992/93 season had scored 164 goals in 431 games plus a further 66 as substitute.

WHITE, William W.
(1936-1938)
Inside-right: 46 app., 11 goals
1937: 5-8½, 11-6
Born: Kirkcaldy, Fife
Career: Musselburgh Bruntonians; Reading cs 1927; Bristol Rovers cs 1928; Charlton Athletic July 1930; Gillingham Dec. 1930; Aldershot June 1932; Carlisle United June 1934; Newport County Nov. 1934; Bristol City May 1935; CITY Dec. 1936; Hull City June 1938 to 1939.

Well-travelled Scot signed as a replacement for Alf Horne when the latter moved on to Mansfield. Known for his persistence and enthusiasm: at Lincoln it was said "... has won his way into prominent place in goalscoring list by dint of sheer dash". White was also a skilled banjo player being a member of a family group that toured Fife.

WHITFIELD, Frank
(1924-1925)
Centre-half: 23 app., 1 goal
1924: 5-10, 11-10
Born: Anston, Sheffield, 15 Dec. 1900
Career: Huddersfield Town during 1920/21; Wigan Borough cs 1922; CITY Sep. 1924; Southend United May 1925; Doncaster Rovers cs 1926.

Centre-half signed from Wigan Borough where he had appeared in 67 Northern Section outings over two seasons. Frank was first choice at Sincil Bank until Bob Fenwick returned from Meadow Lane, but rarely played in City's League team after this.

WHITTLE, Ernest
(1950-1954)

Inside-left: 145 app., 62 goals
1950: 5-6, 11-0
Born: Lanchester, Co. Durham, 25 Nov. 1925
Career: South Moor Juniors; Newcastle United; West Stanley; CITY Jan. 1950 (£300); Workington Mar. 1954; Chesterfield Nov. 1956; Bradford Aug. 1957; Scarborough June 1958; Ruston Bucyrus (Lincoln) cs 1961; Lincoln Claytons Mar. to cs 1966; appointed trainer/coach for CITY's 'A' team June 1966.

Honour: (City) FL Div.3 (North) champions 1952

Stocky inside-forward and a regular in the Imps' first team during his four years at Sincil Bank. Maintained a good scoring record, shining in the 1951/52 promotion campaign when he was an ever-present, netting 19 goals including a hat-trick in a 7-0 win over Workington. Both his son, Ken (an apprentice in the mid-1960's), and grandson Simon (on YTS forms in the early 1990's) were later on City's books.

WHYTE, George
(1931-1939)

Outside-left/left-half: 299 app., 34 goals
1931: 5-8½, 11-4
Born: Cowdenbeath, 24 Mar. 1909
Died: 23 Oct. 1992
Career: Dunfermline Athletic (amat.); Rhyl Athletic 1928; Accrington Stanley July 1929; CITY June 1931; Gainsborough Trinity cs 1939.

Honour: (City) FL Div.3 (North) champions 1932

Recruited from Accrington with Harold Riley, George went on to become one of the great City stalwarts of the 1930's. His appearance total includes a run of four seasons when he was an ever-present, his total of consecutive League games between Aug. 1934 and Sep. 1938 amounting to a club record of 171. Well known as a dead-ball specialist - both from free-kicks and penalties. Originally a left-winger but was felt to have *"a tendency to take the ball back to beat a defender"* and he switched to the half-back position in the 1932/33 season. Remained in the area when his playing career was over and later worked for the Lincoln Co-operative Society.

WIELD, Thomas William
(1904-1908, 1909-1919)

Half-back: 131 app., 5 goals
1905: 5-10½, 10-10
Born: Lincoln 1886
Died: 1963
Career: St. Catherines (Lincoln); CITY Aug. 1904; Grantham Avenue cs 1908; CITY May 1909; Scunthorpe United Oct. 1919; Gainsborough Trinity cs 1920; Grantham FC Sep. to Oct. 1922; later assisted Horncastle Town and, from Nov. 1925, Lincoln Claytons.

Local lad, given his introduction to Second Division football as a teenager. Spent 18 months on the injury list before having a season at Grantham. Later became a regular in City's first team in the years up to WW1. Appeared throughout the war, often playing at full-back, and then moved into Lincs. non-League football. A fearless defender, fine spoiler and quick in intervention.

WIGGETT, David J.
(1974-1976)

Centre-half: 4 app. + 2 sub
1975: 6-0, 11-12
Born: Sheffield, 25 May 1957
Died: 23 Mar. 1978
Career: CITY (appr.) Jan. 1974, (prof.) June 1975; Hartlepool on loan, Oct. 1976, permanent Dec. 1976 (£3,000)

Promising youngster given his League debut at 16, but found first team opportunities at Sincil Bank limited by the presence of Sam Ellis and Terry Cooper. Did well with Hartlepool (54 FL app., 1 goal) until tragically losing his life in a car accident.

WIGGINTON, Clive Anthony
(1977-1979)

Centre-left: 60 app., 6 goals
1978: 6-0, 12-7
Born: Sheffield, 18 Oct. 1950
Career: Grimsby Town (appr.) cs 1968, (prof.) Oct. 1968; Scunthorpe United July 1975; CITY Sep. 1977 (£5,000); Grimsby Town Mar. 1979 (£10,000) (Doncaster Rovers on loan, Mar. to May 1982); Torquay United July 1982; Doncaster Rovers Oct. 1982; retired May 1983; Skegness Town player-manager Dec. 1983.

Honour: (Grimsby) FL Div.3 champions 1980

Solid and experienced defender, a little on the slow side by the time he joined the Imps, but still proved a useful performer in his 18 months at Sincil Bank. Spent 15 years in the professional game, aggregating 474 FL appearances plus a further 8 as substitute. Later played for AFC Ferryboat in the Lincoln Sunday League.

WILKINSON, Barry J.
(1961-1964)

Centre-forward: 6 app., 3 goals
Born: Lincoln, 19 July 1942
Career: Bracebridge Community Centre (Lincoln); CITY (amat.) Aug. 1961, (prof.) Dec. 1963; Ruston Bucyrus (Lincoln) Aug. 1964; retired cs 1972.

Local lad who netted regularly for City's reserves and junor sides, heading the scoring list with 14 goals for the North Regional League team in 1963/64. Still an amateur when he made his first League appearances, but only spent a short time on the club's books as a professional before receiving a free transfer and dropping into Lincs. League football.

WILKINSON, Herbert ("Bert")
(1945-1952)

Full-back: 39 app
1949: 5-8, 10-10
Born: Sunderland, 2 Aug. 1922
Career: Murton Colliery (Charlton Athletic amat. in 1944/45 season); CITY Aug. 1945; Frickley Colliery cs 1952; Grantham Aug. 1953 to cs 1955.

Useful part-time professional who could play at outside-right as well as in defence. Generally appeared with the reserves in the Midland League, only seeing regular first team action in 1948/49 when he had 17 outings in Division Two. Bert also made 6 appearances for the Imps in 1945/46, the final season of wartime football.

WILKINSON, Jack
(1932-1935)

Outside-left: 93 app., 19 goals
1935: 5-6½, 10-7
Born: Wath-on-Dearne, Yorks., c.1908
Died: Apr. 1979
Career: Dearne Valley Old Boys; Wath Athletic Feb. 1925; Sheffield Wednesday Oct. 1925 (£250); Newcastle United May 1930 (£3,000); CITY Sep .1932 (£600); Sunderland Jan. 1935; Hull City Oct. 1936; Scunthorpe United Aug. 1937 to WW2. Appointed manager of Ransomes & Marles (Newark) Dec. 1947.

Scored over a century of goals in five seasons with Dearne Valley OB, which proved the start of a lengthy career in which he experienced top flight football early on at Hillsborough and Newcastle. Joined City after their promotion to Division Two and was rarely absent in his spell at Sincil Bank. Jack was known to contemporaries as a small and crafty wingman.

WILKINSON, William
(1897-1898)

Goalkeeper: 20 app
Career: Rotherham Town; South Shore (Blackpool) cs 1896; CITY Nov. 1897; Chatham cs 1898; Gravesend United Sep. 1898.

Recruited from South Shore, a Lancashire League side later to amalgamate with Blackpool. Described as "... *tall and slim. He has an exceedingly long reach, and is able to use his feet equally as well as his hands"*. Went straight into City's first team on signing and missed only two FL games while on the club's books.

WILLIAMS, Darren
(1989,1990)

Midfield: 7 app. + 2 sub
1990: 5-10, 10-5
Born: Birmingham, 15 Dec. 1968
Career: Leicester City (appr.) July 1985, (prof.) Dec. 1986 (CITY on loan Nov. 1989 and again Mar. to May 1990; Chesterfield on loan, Sep. 1990); Worcester City Nov 1990; Tamworth Mar. 1992; Brierley Hill cs 1993; Hinckley Athletic later in 1993; Redditch United Oct. 1993.

"Neat and tidy" midfield man who had two separate spells on loan at Sincil Bank during the 1989/90 campaign. Saw little F.L. action to an aggregate of 16 app. plus 6 as sub., 3 goals - before moving on to Southern League football.

WILLIAMS, Iorwerth
(1932-1936)

Wing-half: 2 app
1935: 5-7, 11-0
Born: in Wales, c.1914
Career: Merthyr Town; CITY June 1932; Crittall's Athletic (Braintree) 1936.

One of four Merthyr player signed up by the Imps in the summer of 1932 although only two - Williams and William Powell - actually appeared in League football. Both of his FL outings came in the 1934/35 season; at right-back against Crewe in Nov. and at right-half against Accrington the following March.

WILLIAMS, Paul Darren
(1989)

Full-back: 3 app
1990: 5-11, 12-0
Born: Burton-on-Trent, 26 Mar. 1971
Career: Derby County YTS, (prof.) July 1989 (CITY on loan, Nov. 1989)

Honours: England under-21 international (6 app.)

Defender who came on loan when just 18 years old, but did enough to show that he was likely to develop into a very talented player. Has become an accomplished midfield player at the Baseball Ground, finishing leading scorer in the 1991/92 season and winning representative honours with England under-21's and for a Division Two side against the Italian Serie B in Mar. 1992.

WILLIAMS, Steven Robert
(1992-)
Centre-forward: 4 app. + 4 sub, 1 goal
1993: 6-1, 11-7
Born: Sheffield, 3 Nov. 1975
Career: CITY schoolboy 1991; YTS July 1992, (prof.) June 1994.

Former Horncastle schoolboy who recovered from serious leg injuries to break into City's first team during the 1993/94 campaign. Scored within 15 minutes of coming on for his senior debut in the Autoglass Trophy tie against Darlington and has already shown he has the potential to develop into a powerful, hustling striker.

WILLIAMSON, Charles Harold
(1984)
Full-back: 5 app
1984: 5-8, 11-5
Born: Sheffield, 16 Mar. 1962
Career: Sheffield Wednesday (appr.), (prof.) Feb. 1980 (CITY on loan Feb. 1984; Southend United on loan Mar. 1985); Chesterfield July 1985; Stafford Rangers cs 1987; Goole Town Oct. 1988; Gainsborough Trinity Jan. 1990; Maltby MW cs 1991.

One of several defenders signed on loan during the 1983/84 season as cover for a small squad depleted by injuries. Charlie was a regular for Wednesday only in the 1981/82 campaign, but made 47 FL appearances plus 8 substitutions in a two year spell at Chesterfield.

WILMOT, James
(1910-1911)
Right-back: 2 app
1910: 5-8½, 11-7
Career: Dunston (Northern Combination); Shildon Athletic; CITY May 1910 to cs 1911.

Recruit from North-Eastern League football who was mainly a reserve in his season at Sincil Bank. Deputised twice for Clem Jackson but otherwise appeared only in Midland League football.

WILSON, Archibald
(1951-1952)
Goalkeeper: 4 app
1952: 6-0½, 14-4
Born: South Shields, 4 Dec. 1924
Career: South Shields United; Tyne Dock Engineers; Gateshead Aug. 1945; South Shields cs 1947; CITY Apr. 1951; North Shields June 1952.

Archie was described in a 1951 regional football annual as *"a big lad, he shaped well ..."*. Made a couple of appearances at the end of the 1950/51 campaign when Fred White was injured and started the following season

as first choice, only to be replaced almost immediately by Jimmy Jones. Occasionally turned out as an inside-forward with City's 'A' team in the Lincs. League.

WILSON, David G.
(1990)
Midfield: 3 app
1990: 5-9, 10-10
Born: Todmorden, West Yorks., 20 Mar. 1969
Career: Manchester United (appr.), (prof.) Mar. 1987 (CITY on loan, Nov. 1990; Charlton Athletic on loan, Mar. 1991); Bristol Rovers July 1991 to cs 1993.

Slightly built midfield player who arrived on loan during the last days of Allan Clarke's spell as manager of the Imps. Generally a reserve with all his clubs, aggregating just 20 FL appearances plus 5 as substitute to the end of the 1992/93 season.

WILSON, Jack ("Jock")
(1896-1897)
Right-back: 35 app
1896: 5-10½, 12-3
Born: Ayrshire, c.1870
Career: Edinburgh St. Bernards; New Brompton cs 1895; CITY May 1896; Manchester City Dec. 1897 to cs 1898; Small Heath in 1898/99; Swindon Town May 1899 to cs 1900.

A City regular in his first season but then fell into trouble with the management after getting out of condition. He was released and shortly afterwards linked up with Manchester City. An 1897 observer noted of him *"He is a powerful back, displays great judgement - the result of varied experience - and his sterling play has made him a great favourite with the football public"*.

WILSON, James
(1937-1939)
Inside-right: 36 app., 8 goals
1937: 5-8, 10-10
Born: Seaham Harbour, Co. Durham, c.1916
Career: Seaham Colliery; CITY July 1937; Derby County June 1939; Linfield during WW2.

Youngster who was a regular in the Imps side in the 1938/39 campaign, his performances quickly attracting the attention of First Division Derby. War intervened to put a brake on his career and he later moved to Northern Ireland where he was reported to be still living in 1991.

WILSON, Thomas
(1895)
Outside-left: 2 app
1896: -, 10-10
Born: c.1875
Career: Army football; CITY Aug. to Sep. 1895; Oldham County cs 1896.

Wilson appeared in two of the first three fixtures of the 1895/96 season but was then recognised as an Army deserter and arrested. Involved in further controversy when with Lancashire League Oldham County, the club's professionals staging a brief strike in an attempt to persuade the directors to pay them extra money for midweek matches and to fulfil a promise to find them work in the town.

___

WILSON, Walter ("Wattie")
(1907-1915)

Left-back: 171 app., 6 goals
1909: 5-9, 12-0
Born: Armadale, West Lothian, 4 Nov. 1879
Died: 23 Feb. 1926
Career Dykehead; Queens Park; Celtic; Clyde; Dykehead; Albion Rovers; Bathgate; Peebles Rovers; CITY (amat.) Oct. 1907, (prof.) Nov. 1907 to cs 1915; Fosdyke Watermen (Lincoln) in 1915/16; Newland Athletic (Lincoln) in 1916/17.

A major figure in Lincoln football from joining City until his death. Summed up as a *"... fearless tackler and strong kicker* [who] *only requires more certainty in headwork to make a first-class left-back"*, and, *"probably the most dependable man in the team"*. Appeared in a run of 204 consecutive first team matches from signing until Dec. 1912, comprising Division Two, Midland League, Central League and FA Cup fixtures. The run was nearly broken when he was suspended for 14 days after being sent off against Glossop in Nov. 1909, but the Imps only played once during the period and that match was abandoned. Retained an interest in the game after retirement and in 1921 he established the Lincoln Hospital Cup (known locally as the 'Wilson Cup'), a charity fixture played annually by City against top class opposition. Was for many years licensee of the Crown and Anchor public house in Newland, Lincoln.

___

WILTSHIRE, Herbert Henry
(1893-1894)

Left-half: 27 app.
Born: Worcester, 1871
Career: Bristol junior football, CITY cs 1893 to cs 1894.

Wiltshire was signed on the recommendation of Mr Jope of Wednesbury, an acquaintance of City's management committee, and on arriving it was said *"he is going to make a half-back of the very top of the tree"*. Appeared in all but one of City's Division Two fixtures in the 1893/94 season before moving on.

WINDLE, William H.
(1948-1951)

Outside-left: 91 app., 22 goals
1949: 5-4½, 10-0
Born: Maltby, nr. Rotherham, 9 July 1920
Career: Denaby United; Leeds United Oct. 1947; CITY Feb. 1948; Chester Oct. 1951 (£2,000); New Brighton Nov. 1955.

Honours: (Chester) Welsh Cup finalist 1953, 1954

Tiny winger whose early Lincoln period was dogged by cartilage trouble. Recovered well after an operation to give two more years valued service to the Imps and a further four years to Chester where he made 126 FL appearances, scoring 20 goals.

___

WINDSOR, Robert
(1949-1950)

Outside-right: 11 app., 1 goal
1949: 5-7, 10-7
Born: Stoke-on-Trent, 31 Jan. 1926
Career: Stoke City Dec. 1943; CITY Feb. 1949; Wellington Town Aug. 1950.

Bobby Windsor was one of a number of players recruited by the Imps in the early part of 1949 in a vain attempt to avoid relegation from Division Two. Lost his place to Harry Troops the following season and appeared only twice more before joining Cheshire League Wellington Town (later to change their name to Telford United).

___

WINFIELD, Philip
(1957-1959)

Right-half: 1 app
1958: 5-9½, 11-7
Born: Denaby, Yorks., 16 Feb. 1937
Career: Denaby United; CITY Oct. 1957; Ramsgate cs 1959; Gravesend & Northfleet cs 1965.

Part-time professional who made rapid progress in the 1957/58 season, signing for the Imps after just five Midland League games for Denaby and quickly receiving his FL debut at home against Liverpool. It proved his only senior game for the club before he departed for a lengthy spell in Southern League football.

___

WITHERS, Alan
(1955-1959)

Outside-left: 97 app., 18 goals
1957: 5-6½, 10-7
Born: Bulwell, Nottingham, 20 Oct. 1930
Career: Aspley Boys Club; Blackpool July 1949; CITY Feb. 1955; Notts County Jan. 1959 (£1,500); Wisbech Town cs 1963; Boston FC cs 1966; Lockhead Leamington Aug. 1967; Loughborough United Nov. 1967.

Began his FL career in dramatic fashion scoring a hat-trick on his debut for Blackpool against Huddersfield in Nov. 1950, but received few further opportunities at Bloomfield Road where he was understudy to the great Stanley Matthews. Did not become a first choice for the Imps until the 1956/57 season when he succeeded Roy Finch on City's left-wing, remaining a regular for the rest of his time at Sincil Bank. At Meadow Lane he made 121 FL appearances, scoring 22 goals.

WITHERS, Colin Charles
(1969-1970)

Goalkeeper: 1 app
1965: 6-3, 14-4
Born: Erdington, Birmingham, 21 Mar. 1940
Career: West Bromwich Albion (amat.) in 1956/57; Birmingham City May 1957; Aston Villa Nov. 1964 (£18,000); CITY June 1969; Go Ahead Club (Deventer, Holland) June 1970; Atherstone Town Aug. 1971 to cs 1973.

Honour: England schoolboy international (1 app. vs Northern Ireland 1954)

Experienced 'keeper who had seen plenty of top flight action with Blues and the Villa. He began his Lincoln season as first choice but soon lost his place to John Kennedy and spent the rest of the campaign assisting the reserves to the North Midlands League championship. On retirement he ran a Blackpool guest house and was later a licensee in Bridgnorth, Shropshire.

WOLSTENHOLME, Arthur
(1914-1915)

Inside-right: 30 app., 7 goals
1914: 5-8½, 12-4
Born: Bolton, 14 May 1889
Career: Tonge; Oldham Athletic Mar. 1908; Blackpool Dec. 1909; Gillingham Aug. 1912; Norwich City Aug. 1913; CITY July 1914 to cs 1915; Oldham Athletic May 1919 (£75); Newport County June 1920; Darlington June 1921; Nelson May 1922, appointed to training staff during 1923/24; retired from playing c.1925.

Honour: (Nelson) FL Div.3 (North) champions 1923

"He has a peculiar style ... indeed sometimes he does not appear to be in the running until a goal has been scored from his apparently indifferent play" was one contemporary's verdict on this much travelled player. Wolstenholme was leading scorer for Norwich in the 1913/14 season and altogether made well over 300 appearances in the Football and Southern Leagues in a career lasting nearly two decades.

WOODCOCK, Anthony Stewart
(1976)

Forward: 2 app. + 2 sub, 1 goal
1976: 5-10, 11-0
Born: Eastwood, Notts., 6 Dec. 1955
Career: Nottingham Forest (appr.) 1972, (prof.) Jan. 1974 (CITY on loan, Feb. 1976; Doncaster Rovers on loan, Sep. 1976); FC Koln (West Germany) Nov. 1979 (£650,000); Arsenal June 1982 (£500,000); FC Koln July 1986 (£200,000); Fortuna Koln as a player, becoming sporting director on his retirement in Apr. 1990; SC Brueck (West Germany) coach from around Dec. 1991.

Honour: England international (42 app)
England 'B' international
England under-21 international (2 app)
(Forest) European Cup winner 1979
FL champions 1978
FL Cup winner 1978, 1979

One of the most distinguished players to turn out for the Imps in the post-war period, albeit before his career really took-off. Came on loan together with another Forest youngster, Bert Bowery, and scored on his debut in a 6-0 win over Southport. Soon gained a place in the Forest team, going on to win a first cap against Northern Ireland in May 1978 and became a regular in the England team of the early 1980's.

WOODFIELD, John
(1897)

Outside-right: 1 app
1897: 5-9, 11-0
Career: South Wales junior football; CITY June to Sep. 1897; Kettering Nov. 1897.

Woodfield had been playing in Cardiff the previous season when a local newspaper described him as *"fast, clever and quite unselfish"*. Earlier, in Jan. 1894, he had appeared in an international trial for South Wales against North Wales. Spent the summer of 1897 as groundsman for the Lindum CC, but after appearing in the opening match of the 1897/98 season (a 5-0 defeat at Newton Heath) he was released due to lack of fitness.

WORSDALE, M(ichael) John
(1971-1974)

Outside-right: 55 app. + 12 sub, 9 goals
1972: 5-7, 10-9
Born: Stoke-on-Trent, 29 Oct. 1948
Career: Stoke City (appr.), (prof.) Nov. 1965; CITY May 1971; Worksop Town cs 1974; Gainsborough Trinity July 1976; Skegness Town June 1977.

Appeared only four times in a six year spell at Stoke before arriving at Sincil Bank on a free transfer. Played regularly under David Herd (himself a former Stoke player) in the 1971/72 campaign when the Imps came close to winning promotion. Later worked at a local sports centre.

WORTHY, Albert
(1927-1933)

Right-back: 198 app., 5 goals
1928: 5-8, 11-7
Born: Pilsley, Derbys., 1 Nov. 1905
Died: 1 Feb. 1978
Career: Danesmoor (Derbyshire Senior League); Chesterfield Nov. 1925; CITY June 1927; Southend United June 1933; Rochdale Aug. 1934; Gainsborough Trinity cs 1937; Shrewsbury Town cs 1938.

Honour: (City) FL Div.3 (North) champions 1932

Considered one of the best Northern Section full-backs of his time and a fine servant to the club. Renowned for his powerful kicking. As a 1928 local football annual put it: *"... has unwaveringly played a fine standard of aggressive and defensive football. Has shrewd calculation and measurement of an opponent's intention, and admirable resource and recovery. Though only 5ft.8in., he is a handy man in a scrimmage, and his weight, 11st.7lbs., serves him well in a jostle, while he is not handicapped in a race".*

WRIGHT, Albert
(1946-1947)

Goalkeeper: 1 app
Career: Nottingham Forest (amat.) during 1945/46; Ollerton Colliery; CITY (amat.) Aug. 1946, (prof.) Jan. 1947.

Reserve 'keeper whose only FL outing came in a 3-0 home defeat by Hull City on 28 Dec. 1946. Turned professional shortly afterwards but was one of several goalkeepers on the club's books and found himself released before the end of the season.

WRIGHT, Brian R.
(1959-1961)

Inside-forward: 22 app., 3 goals
1960: 5-7, 10-8
Born: Leicester, 9 Jan. 1937
Career: Leicester City Feb. 1954; CITY Jan. 1959; Bedford Town July 1961.

Honour: England youth international (1955)

Mostly a reserve at Lincoln although he suffered a number of injuries. One of several players released in May 1961 when the Imps were relegated from Division Two. Made just two FL appearances in a five year spell at Filbert Street.

WRIGHT, J(ohn) Douglas
(1948-1954)

Wing-half: 233 app., 2 goals
1950: 6-0, 11-9
Born: Southend-on-Sea, 29 Apr. 1917
Died: Dec. 1992

Career: Chelmsford City; Southend United Aug. 1936; Newcastle United May 1938 (£3,250); CITY Dec. 1948 (£600); Blyth Spartans as player/coach Dec. 1954, player/manager cs 1955, secretary May 1957 to Nov. 1960.

Honours: England international (1 app. vs Norway 1939)
(City) FL Div.3 (North) champions 1952

Doug Wright had been wounded in the leg during WW2 and it was felt that his career in top class football was over. An inspirational signing by Bill Anderson, he proved to be perhaps the classiest of all City's players in the post-war period. A real football artist with immaculate ball control, superb timing in the tackle and an excellent reader of the game. Captained the side from his second game until his departure in Dec. 1954 - a six year stint when the Imps fielded one of the strongest teams in their history. In the mid-1960's he was reported to be working on Tyneside docks and was later employed by the CEGB at Blyth Power Station.

WRIGHT, William S.
(1978-1979)

Defender: 3 app
1979: 5-9, 12-4
Born: Wordsley, Staffs., 26 Apr. 1959
Career: Birmingham City (appr.), (prof.) Apr. 1977; CITY July 1978 (Nuneaton Borough on loan Feb. 1979); Runcorn Aug. 1979; Manager of Congleton Town season 1992/93.

Defender signed by Willie Bell on a free transfer. Began the season as first choice but quickly lost his place and fell out of favour when Colin Murphy became manager. Afterwards had a long association with the game with non-League clubs in the north-west of England.

WRIGLEY, Bernard
(1923-1925)
Goalkeeper: 9 app
1925: 5-9, 12-0
Born: Clitheroe, Lancs., 1894
Career: Clitheroe Royal Blues; Clitheroe Amateurs; Great Harwood; Blackburn Rovers Aug. 1921 (approx. £25); CITY Nov. 1923 to Jan. 1925; Grantham Nov. 1925 to cs 1926; Great Harwood; Grantham Feb. to cs 1927.

Signed from Blackburn on the recommendation of Ronald Sewell - a top class 'keeper with strong connections with the Lincoln area. Wrigley was kept out of City's team by the brilliant form of Jack Kendall, but when the latter was sold to Everton, he was given his chance. Remained first choice at the start of the 1924/25 campaign, but then lost his place to Bill Sissons after consecutive 4-0 defeats at Wigan and Southport.

YATES, Mark Jason
(1993)
Midfield: 10 app., + 4 sub
1993: 5-11, 11-9
Born: Birmingham, 8 July 1970
Career: Birmingham City YTS July 1986, (prof.) July 1988 (Colchester United on loan Aug. 1990 to Feb. 1991); Burnley Aug. 1991 (£40,000) (Kidderminster Harriers on loan Nov. 1992; CITY on loan Feb. to Apr. 1993); Doncaster Rovers July 1993; Kidderminster Harriers Aug. 1994.

Hard working midfield player signed to cover for the injured Graham Bressington. Yates had been considered a promising youngster in his early career at St. Andrews but was allowed to leave after appearing in the Leyland Daf Cup winning team of 1991.

YORKE, Andrew E.
(1927-1930)
Left-back: 106 app., 6 goals
1929: 5-11, 10-7
Born: Blyth, Northumberland, 14 June 1894
Career: Sleekburn Albion (Ashington & District League); Bedlington United; Blyth Spartans; Sunderland May 1921; Coventry City May 1913; Northampton Town cs 1925; CITY Aug. 1927; Newark Town Sep. 1930; Scarborough Aug. 1934.

A contemporary summing up was: *"... has risen to displays of distinct cleverness and dash. Gives little away, and is a powerful defender with head as well as feet"* Formed one of the best full-back partnerships in the Northern Section of the late 1920's with Albert Worthy. During his time at Sincil Bank he ran a confectionary shop in the Bracebridge area of Lincoln and in July 1939 was appointed the first ever landlord of the newly opened Roaring Meg public house.

YOUNG, Alfred
(1929-1935)

Centre-half: 148 app., 5 goals
1929: 5-10, 12-0
Born: Wingate, Co. Durham, 27 Nov. 1900
Died: 31 July 1975
Career: Wingate Albion, Trimdon Grange; Hartlepools United (amat.) cs 1921, (prof.) during season 1923/24; Gillingham May 1928; Workington Sep. 1929; CITY Oct. 1929, appointed asst.trainer and coach in May 1934, and trainer in July 1938, remained on the backroom staff at Sincil Bank until July 1957 when he was made Chief Scout before retiring in 1963.

Honour: (City) FL Div.3 (North) champions 1932

"A tireless worker and a fine defensive half-back ... clever with his head ... always endeavours to place his passes when parting with the ball" was one favourable opinion of Alf. Captained the Imps for two season, leading the side to the Northern Section championship in 1932. A loyal servant to the club for over 30 years before eventually retiring.

YOUNG, Edward
(1937-1938)
Outside-right: 5 app., 1 goal
1937: 5-9, 11-0
Career: West Wylam CW; CITY Apr. 1937 to cs 1938

Reserve winger recruited from a Northern Alliance club. Given a brief run in City's first team towards the end of the 1937/38 campaign in place of Jack Callender, his goal coming in a 3-2 victory over Crewe Alexandra on Easter Monday.

YOUNG, J.
(1919)
Left-half: 1 app
Career: CITY Aug. to Oct. 1919

Signed after impressing in a pre-season trial match. Received his solitary FL outing at White Hart Lane on 27 Sep. 1919 in rather unusual circumstances - a rail strike meant the team had to travel down to London a day early and as a result two of the selected players had to withdraw. City lost 6-1 and, because Young was not registered on time, they were subsequently fined two guineas by the Football League. Had risen to the rank of lieutenant in the Army during WW1.

YOUNG, Richard H.
(1949-1954)

Left-back: 100 app., 2 goals
1950: 6-0, 12-7
Born: Gateshead, 17 Apr. 1918
Died: 31 Jan. 1989
Career: Wardley Colliery; Reyrolle's FC (Hebburn); Hebburn St. Cuthberts; Wardley Colliery; Sheffield United Nov. 1935; CITY Mar. 1949 (£2,000); appointed player/coach during season 1951/52 and club trainer on retiring cs 1954; Carlisle United as trainer July 1956 for 19 years, becoming manager Nov. 1975 to Nov. 1976, asst.-manager 1976-1977, manager again 1980 to 1982 when he retired.

Partnered Horace Green at full-back for two and a half seasons before losing his place to John Varney. Dick continued to appear for City's reserve and 'A' teams until leaving for Carlisle in 1956. Spent over a quarter of a century at Brunton Park in various backroom and managerial roles.

YOUNGER, William
(1961)
Inside-left: 4 app
1961: 5-10, 11-0
Born: Whitley Bay, Northumberland, 22 Mar. 1940
Career: Seaton Delaval; Nottingham Forest May 1957 (CITY on loan, Feb. 1961); Walsall June 1961; Doncaster Rovers Dec. 1961; Hartlepools United Aug. 1962; Ramsgate July 1963.

Loan signing who came at a time when City were struggling to avoid relegation from Division Two. Younger was unable to change the club's fortunes - all four games he played in were lost - and he returned to the City Ground. In his early days at Forest it was said he "... impressed as a useful schemer, but needs more finishing power".

YULE, Thomas
(1909-1911)
Outside-left: 63 app., 8 goals
21910: 5-6½, 11-0
Born: Douglas Water, Lanarks., 4 Feb. 1888
Career: Portobello (Edinburgh); CITY Aug. 1909; Wolverhampton Wanderers May 1911; Burslem Port Vale May 1913.

Clever winger, short but sturdy, who quickly made the transition from junior to Second Division football. Moved on to Molineux when the Imps were voted out of the League in 1911 and made a further 33 FL appearances, scoring 7 goals.

APPENDIX ONE

The players in this section qualify for entry on one of four grounds: an appearance in an abandoned Football League game; an appearance as an unused substitute in a FL game; an appearance in a senior cup competition during a season when the club were members of the FL (for these purpose 'senior' is defined as FA Cup, Football League Cup, Associate Members Cup, Division Three North Cup and Football League Trophy, or equivalent competition under a sponsor's name); a spell on the club's books without appearing in the FL where the player went on to become famous in another area of his life.

AINSWORTH, Walter
(1937-1938)
Centre-half
1937: 5-11, 11-6
Born: c.1916
Career: South Bank; Sheffield Wednesday; CITY May 1937; Cheltenham Town cs 1938; Plymouth Argyle Feb. 1939.

Appeared in the Northern Section Cup round 1 match against Doncaster Rovers on 28 Oct. 1937. City fielded a weakened team and lost 7-2.

AUBREY, Alan William
(1973)
Goalkeeper
1973: 6-4, 15-0
Born: Leeds, 18 April 1948
Career: Leeds United, Burnley and Chesterfield (amat.); Bradford 1970; Gainsborough Trinity cs 1972; CITY Jan. 1973 (£1,500); Gainsborough Trinity cs 1973; Mossley cs to Nov. 1974.

Although a goalkeeper, Aubrey was selected as a substitute against Northampton Town on 3 Feb. 1973 due to an injury crisis but did not come on the field.

BLOOMER, Brian Mc.
(1974)
Forward
Born: Cleethorpes, 3 May 1952
Career: Grimsby Town (appr.); Barton Town; Grimsby Amateurs; Lincoln United 1973 (CITY as permit player Jan. 1974); Grantham Town cs 1974; Lincoln United Dec. 1974; later with Brigg Town and Scunthorpe United Aug. 1978 to 1979.

Appeared as an unused substitute in the home match against Workington on 12 Jan. 1974. Later made 3 app. plus 4 as substitute for Scunthorpe, scoring one goal.

BOLDRA, Francis Robert
(early 1890's)
Outside-right
Born: c.1871
Died: 12 Apr. 1952
Career: Rustons Apprentices in 1893/94 season; CITY (in Swifts team).

No senior appearances for the Imps. Boldra became famous in 1937 as the winner of a national magazine competition to find 'the average man of Britain'.

BROWN, Paul
(1981-1983)
Full-back
Born: Lincoln, 10 Dec. 1964
Career: CITY (appr.) Aug.1981; Lincoln United 1983 to 1989.

Brown came on as a substitute for Chris Moyses in a Football League Trophy match against Scunthorpe United on 14 Aug. 1982.

BURLISON, Thomas H.
(1953-1957)
Wing-half
1953 5-8½, 10-7
Born: Edmondsley, Co. Durham, 23 May 1936
Career: CITY (amat.) Oct. 1953, becoming a part-time prof. Dec. 1953; Hartlepools United July 1957; Darlington Aug. 1964.

No FL experience at Lincoln but saw considerable action at Hartlepools (148 app.) and Darlington (24 app.). Later became a prominent politician and trade union official, serving the GMB Union as Deputy General Secretary, and the Labour party as an NEC member and national treasurer.

BUXTON, George
(1891-1893)
Defender
Career: CITY 1891 to cs 1893.

A regular in City's team in the Football Alliane during the second half of 1891/92, turning out at full-back. Appeared at right-half in the FA Cup second qualifying round tie against Mansfield Greenhalgh's in Oct. 1892.

DIXON, Andrew
(1990)
Full-back
1990: 6-1, 10-11
Born: Louth, Lincs., 19 Apr.1968
Career: Grimsby Town (appr.), (prof.) May 1986; Southend United cs 1989; CITY on non-contract basis July to Sep. 1990; later with Southend Manor during season 1991/92, joining Chelmsford City Aug. 1992 on non-contract forms.

Made a total of 59 FL appearances plus 3 as substitute before coming to Sincil Bank. Came on as a sub. in the Rumbelows Cup first round, first leg tie at Halifax in Aug. 1990 and was also selected once as an unused sub. for a League match.

EYRE, Frederick
(1963-1964)
Wing-half
Born: Manchester, 3 Feb. 1944
Career: Manchester City (appr.), (prof.) July 1961; CITY July 1963 -1964; Huddersfield Town (trial); Crewe Alexandra Aug. 1964 before a spell in non-League football, then Bradford Dec. 1969.

No senior experience with the Imps and only one FL appearance in total (with Bradford). Eyre later became well known as the author of a series of humorous books on football such as 'Kicked into Touch' (1981).

HALL, Stuart
(1981-1985)
Forward
Career: CITY schoolboy May 1981, (appr.) Apr. 1983, non-contract forms Oct. 1984.

Hall appeared several times as an unused sub. during the 1982/83 season, including for a Milk Cup tie against West Ham. He came on as sub. for Gordon Hobson in the Football League Trophy quarter-final tie against Norwich City in Dec. 1982. A pupil of Valley School, Worksop - City needed the permission of his headmaster so that he could appear in their line-up.

HARVEY, Allan
(1960-1961)
Outside-left
1960: 5-9½, 11-0
Born: Barnsley, 11 Apr. 1942
Career: Leeds United Apr. 1959; CITY May 1960; Toronto City (Canada) May 1961; Barnsley Oct. 1961; Gainsborough Trinity Dec. 1961; Toronto City May 1961; Toronto Inter Roma; Later appeared for Toronto Falcons in the NASL in 1968.

No FL outings with any of his clubs, but played for the Imps in their first-ever League Cup match against Bradford in Oct. 1960. Later settled in Canada.

HAYDEN, Percy
(1907)
Centre-half
Career: Manchester junior football; CITY Nov. 1907.

One of three Manchester-based amateurs who made their debuts for City in the Second Division game at Glossop on 23 Nov. 1907. The match was abandoned when heavy rain and dark clouds made visibility difficult. Never played for the club again.

HOLMES, Stephen P.
(1988-1990)
Defender/midfield
Born: c.1972
Career: CITY YTS Nov. 1988 (Boston FC on loan, in 1988/89); Gainsborough Trinity; Guisborough; Frickley Athletic 1991.

Appeared as an unused sub. on three occasions in the 1988/89 season and was given a full outing in the Vauxhall Conference Shield match against Enfield in Oct. 1988.

HULME, James
(1895)
Outside-left
Career: Strathclyde; CITY Oct. 1895.

Signed along with his team mate William Gillespie, Hulme scored two goals in his only game for the Imps - a record 13-0 away win at Peterborough on 12 Oct. in an FA Cup first qualifying round tie. Did not settle in Lincoln and returned to Glasgow the following week.

KELLEHER, Joseph
(1964-1974)
Full-back
Born: c.1951
Career: CITY juniors 1964, (amat.) July 1967; Ruston Bucyrus (Lincoln) cs 1974 to early 1980's; Ruston Sports (Lincoln) to cs 1989.

Amateur player who had appeared with City's junior and reserve sides from the mid-1960's. His only senior game came in a first round FA Cup tie against Barrow in Nov. 1970. Well known in local non-League and Sunday football.

LINIGHAN, Brian
(1953-1959)
Centre-half
1953: 5-10, 11-7
Born: West Hartlepool, 17 Mar. 1936
Career: CITY (amat.) Oct. 1953, part-time prof. Dec. 1953 (Oswestry Town on loan during 1956/57; Darlington on loan Oct. 1958); Ashington Feb. 1959.

Played out of postion (at centre-forward) in the abandoned Division Two match against Cardiff in Mar. 1958, his only other FL experience was at Darlington where he made one appearance during his loan period. Father of David (Ipswich), Andy (Norwich and Arsenal), Mark (Hartlepool) and Brian & John (Sheffield Wednesday).

MORGAN, James
(1992-1994)
Goalkeeper
Born: Lincoln, 11 Sep. 1975
Career: CITY schoolboy, YTS July 1992; Corby Town (trial) Aug 1994; Boston Town Aug. 1994.

Junior team member who appeared as substitute goalkeeper on several occasions during the 1993/94 season without being called upon for duty.

PARKIN, David
(1986-1988)
Midfield
Career: CITY schoolboy June 1984, YTS July 1986; Grantham Aug. 1988; Lincoln United Oct. 1988; Nettleham in 1989/90; Lincoln United 1990.

Came on as a sub. in the Freight Rover Trophy match at Hartlepool in Dec. 1986 and was also used as a sub. on one occasion in the Vauxhall Conference campaign.

ROTHWELL, Herbert
(1907)
Full-back
Career: Glossop from 1890's to 1902; Manchester junior football; CITY Nov. 1907; Chorlton 1908.

Well known amateur player who had earlier made 69 FL appearances for Glossop between 1898 and 1902. Played for City in the abandoned match at Glossop on 23 Nov. 1907 and was selected for the following game against Leicester but failed to arrive.

TRUEMAN, Frederick S.
(1952)
Forward
Born: Scotch Springs, South Yorkshire, 6 Feb. 1931

Career: Maltby; CITY (amat.) Nov. 1952.

Famous as a Yorkshire and England cricketer, appearing in 67 Tests between 1952 and 1965 and taking 307 wickets. Freddie Trueman was in the RAF based at nearby Hemswell when he played for City's Lincolnshire League team, scoring four goals on his debut. He was promoted to the Midland League side the following week and appeared in a 0-0 draw with Peterborough United which attracted a record reserve crowd of 7,328 to Sincil Bank. However, after one further appearance in the Midland League he ceased his connection with the club.

WHITTLE, Kenneth
(1964-1967)
Forward
Born: Sedgefield, Co. Durham, 25 Sep. 1948
Career: CITY (appr.) June 1964; Rugby Town Aug. 1967; Boston FC cs 1968; Lincoln Claytons cs 1969.

Appeared an an unused substitute during the 1966/67 campaign. Later spent a season in Southern League football under the management of former City player Bill Hails before returning to Lincolnshire. Son of Ernie Whittle.

APPENDIX TWO

A number of players appear either on published lists (such as those produced by the Association of Football Statisticians) or in the contemporary press who it has now been established did not play in League football for the Imps. These are as follows:-

G.Baxton is shown as playing vs Darwen on 12 Nov. 1892, in fact Kelly appeared at right-half; it seems some newspapers reprinted the City team from the previous FA Cup game against Greenhalgh's in error (George Buxton had played).

Davey (1894/95 season) is an error for **Harry D'Arcey**.

C.Taylor was shown in some Manchester newspapers as playing left-back for City vs Newton Heath on 16 Nov. 1895. The Lincoln press show Eyres as playing and make special mention of the fact that Taylor was the away linesman.

Mumford and **Sutton** appear in newspaper reports for the game at Woolwich Arsenal on 25 Dec. 1896 when the FL registers show two established men - **Brailsford** and **Alec Smith**.

The appearances made by **Jock Wilson** for 1897/98 are incorrectly allocated to **Thomas Wood Wilson** (who left before the start of the season) in the FL registers.

Similarly the appearances for **Joseph W. Simpson** for 1899/1900 were wrongly allocated to **A.E.Simpson**.

W.Laughlan (1909/10 season) is an error which has appeared for **Billy Langham**.

Winter (1923/24) is another error: **Ted Wynter** was the club trainer for a while but did not appear in the FL for City.

Finally **William ('Bill') Marriott** is incorrectly shown in the FL registers as playing vs Bournemouth on 19 Aug. 1961 when the appearance should be allocated to **John McClelland**.

APPENDIX THREE

This section contains brief details of players who appeared for City in one of their four seasons since 1892 as a non-League club and of those whose only games were in the 1945/46 FA Cup.

1908/09 (MIDLAND LEAGUE)

Robert Aitken Right-back; 1907: 5-11, 11-0; Born: c.1885;
Career - Maxwelltown Volunteers; CITY May 1907 to cs 1909.

Walter Jones Outside-left;
Career - Manchester City; CITY cs 1908; Accrington Stanley, May 1909.

"Sammy" Keetley Centre-half;
Career - Netherfield Rangers; CITY Apr. 1909 on trial.

William Morris Centre-forward;
Career - Bulwell White Star; Stanton Hill Victoria Nov. 1908; CITY (amat.) Nov. 1908, (pro) Jan. 1909; Liverpool May 1909.

William Robinson Winger;
Career - Walsall; CITY May 1908; Walsall Dec. 1908; Derby County May 1909; Walsall 1910 -1913.

1911-12 (CENTRAL LEAGUE)

William ("Billy") Batty Inside-left; Born: Killamarsh, nr. Sheffield, 13 July 1886.
Career - Thorncliffe; Mortomley; High Green Swifts; Sheffield United May 1907; Bristol City Mar. 1910; CITY cs 1911; Swindon Town cs 1912; Barnsley 1922 as player-coach.

William Cooper Half-back; Born: Mexborough
Career - Denaby; Barnsley; Portsmouth 1907; Dundee 1908; Rochdale; CITY cs 1911.

1920-21 (MIDLAND LEAGUE)

Alcock Goalkeeper
Career - Clowne; CITY cs 1920 to 1921.

Charles ("Oscar") Brentnall Centre-forward; 1920: 5-8½, 11-0; Born: Chesterfield 1897;
Career - Wadsley Bridge; Rotherham County; Sheffield Wednesday cs 1919; CITY cs 1920; Worksop Town cs 1921; Denaby United 1922; Rotherham County cs 1923.

Harris Right-back
Career - Cranwell Works (Sleaford & District League); CITY May to cs 1921.

Henry Stanley Hatsell Right-back; 1920: 5-10, 12-0; Born: c.1896;
Career - Bradford; CITY Dec. 1920 to 1921.

Matthew Hopper Outside-right; 1921: 5-6, 11-0; Born: Co. Durham c.1900
Career - Ashington; CITY July 1920; Millwall Athletic Apr. 1921; Sittingbourne cs 1923; junior football; Coventry City Aug. 1926; Ashington Aug. 1927; Annfield Plain Nov. 1928.

Lincoln Centre-forward
Career - CITY on trial May 1921.

Walter Leslie Raby Inside-left; 1921: 5-8½, 11-0; Born: Lincoln 23 Sep. 1902; Died: 9 Mar. 1973
Career - St.Andrews (Lincoln); Robeys (Lincoln); CITY 1920; Grimsby Town May 1921; Clapton Orient June 1922; Scunthorpe United Aug. 1923; later with Gainsborough Trinity. Son of "Joe" Raby.

Riley Right-half
Career - CITY on trial May 1921.

1945-46 (FA CUP)

George Cartwright Right-back
Career - Sheffield junior football; CITY on amateur forms Oct. 1945 to c.1947.

Frederick W. ("Reg") Parkin Goalkeeper
Career - CITY Aug. 1945; Scarborough cs 1946.

Edward Wroe Right-half. Born c. 1922.
Career - Barnsley junior football; CITY Feb. 1945 to cs 1946; Boston United Apr. 1947.

1987-88 (GM VAUXHALL CONFERENCE)

Nigel Batch Goalkeeper; 1987: 5-10, 12-7; Born: Huddersfield 9 Nov. 1957.
Career - Derby County (appr.), (prof.) 1975; Grimsby Town July 1976; CITY Aug. 1987; Darlington on loan Sep. 1988, signing permanently Dec. 1988 (Stockport County on loan Mar. 1989).

Allen Crombie Midfield; 1987: 6-1, 12-4; Born: Lincoln 16 Oct. 1961.
Career: CITY schoolboy Oct. 1976; Lincoln United 1978; CITY Feb. 1988; Boston United (on loan) Mar. 1988, signing permanently July 1988 (£2,500); Lincoln United player-manager cs 1990; Grantham player-manager cs 1993 to cs 1994. Brother of Dean Crombie.

Leslie ("Les") Hunter Midfield; 1987: 6-2, 12-6; Born: Middlesbrough 15 Jan. 1958.
Career - Chesterfield (appr.), (prof.) Aug. 1975; Scunthorpe United July 1982; Chesterfield Jan. 1984; Scunthorpe United Mar. 1986; CITY July 1987 (£8,000); Chesterfield Dec. 1987; Matlock Town Feb. 1989; Buxton cs 1991.

Andrew R. Moore Defender; 1987: 6-0, 12-0; Born: Cleethorpes 14 Nov. 1965.
Career: Grimsby Town (appr.), (prof.) Nov. 1983; (Wigan Athletic on loan Sep. 1986); CITY Aug. 1987 (£34,000); Blackpool on trial July - Aug. 1988; Shamrock Rovers Sep. 1988; a spell in Hong Kong; Western Suburbs (Australia); Boston United cs 1991; Grantham Sep. 1992; Gainsborough Trinity Jan. 1993.

David J. Mossman Midfield; 1987: 6-1, 12-2; Born: Sheffield 27 July 1964.
Career: Sheffield Wednesday Aug. 1982 (Bradford City on loan Mar. to May 1985; Stockport County on loan Oct. to Dec. 1985); Rochdale Jan. 1986; Stockport County Mar. 1986; CITY Aug. 1987; Boston United July 1988; Gainsborough Trinity Oct. 1989; Stafford Rangers Nov. 1989; Boston United; Matlock Town cs 1991.

Richard Wilson Goalkeeper;
Career: Chesterfield; Grantham Sep. 1987; CITY on non-contract basis Oct. 1987; Eastwood Town Oct. 1988. Nephew of Bob Wilson (Arsenal and England).

APPENDIX FOUR

This section contains details of the individuals who have looked after the club's team affairs under the various titles of honorary secretary, secretary-manager and, from 1947 when team selection was included in the duties, manager.

STRAWSON, John Henry
Hon. secretary July 1884 - Feb. 1896; secretary-manager cs 1907 - May 1919

Born: East Firsby, nr. Spridlington, Lincs, 3 Nov. 1858
Died: 4 Mar. 1949
Position: Centre-forward
Career: Lincoln Rovers and City as a player retiring c.1885; Lincoln Rovers committee member 1880 becoming secretary shortly afterwards; CITY hon. secretary July 1884 - Feb. 1896; director from Feb. 1896 and chairman from Mar. 1899 - Sep. 1908; secretary-manager cs 1907 to May 1919.

Jack Strawson was without any doubt the most important individual in the history of Lincoln City. As a player he had been a competent centre-forward with the Rovers team, good enough to win representative honours for the Lincolnshire FA, and he turned out a few times for City in their first season, including an appearance in their first ever FA Cup tie against Hull Town in Nov. 1884. However, he was best known in his capacity as an administrator, being centrally involved in the day-to-day affairs of the club for 35 years. His principal achievement was to keep City in the Football League for all but two seasons in the pre-World War One period despite numerous applications for re-election. On these occasions he planned his tactics well, judging whether to send out a circular to other clubs in advance of their decision and usually making the speech at the League's annual general meeting. His style was summed up by an Athletic News reporter in 1898 : *"Who can stand a Strawsonian argument, composed, as it is, of sound common sense (from the point of the pleader) with an embroidery in equal proportion of soap and honey?"* Strawson also served the Football League as a referee from 1888 to 1905, as a Management Committee member in 1894-1895 and as auditor between 1895 and 1919. In 1918 he was presented with the League's long-service award. Outside of football he was an accountant and on retiring in 1919 he moved to Spalding where he was landlord of the Red Lion Hotel until June 1929. His brother Dick was also a City director for 20 years and for a short time the family restaurant ('Strawson's Dining Rooms') served as the Imps' headquarters.

MARTIN, Alfred
Secretary-manager Feb. 1896 - Mar. 1897

Born: Grantham, 27 May 1865
Died: 22 July 1922
Career: Grantham Rovers committee member; CITY secretary-manager Feb. 1896 - Mar. 1897

Alf Martin was the Imps' first ever paid official. He had been a referee and served as a committee member for Grantham Rovers, a professional club competing in the Midland League, in addition to his interest in the game as a journalist. He introduced many innovative ideas for publicising the club and raising funds and also established the Working Men's Committee. This was originally intended as a means of allowing ordinary supporters to become shareholders in the new limited company, but developed into a voluntary workforce for the club, lasting through to the 1930's. Despite this, Martin's spell at Sincil Bank was disastrous. The players signed were poor quality, by early 1897 the team were bottom of the League with just 6 points from 20 games, and there was talk of the club folding. The accounts he produced to the AGM were said to be inaccurate and he made a very hasty departure from Lincoln. He remained active in football administration afterwards, being appointed a member of the Lincolnshire FA Council in 1899 and later helping form the Sheffield Referees Association. However, Martin was much better known in his role as a sports journalist. In Grantham he had been proprietor of the Herald Press whose titles included the Lincolnshire Herald, the Football Chronicle and The Referee's Journal. On leaving the City he had a brief spell as the Lincolnshire Echo's Grimsby correspondent before joining the Eastern Daily Telegraph, fore-runner of the Grimsby Evening Telegraph. He soon became editor and established the 'Saturday Telegraph' football paper before moving on to Sheffield where he was the first editor of the 'Green 'Un' (then known as 'The Sports Special') and after this he had a spell as editor of the Nottingham Football News. He was also an active trade unionist and in 1917/18 held the post of President of the National Union of Journalists.

WEST, James
Hon. secretary Mar. 1897 - Sep 1900

Career: Lincoln Rovers as a player and later committee member; CITY as honorary secretary and director Mar. 1897 - Sep 1900; Newton Heath secretary-manager Sep. 1900 - July 1903.

James West was active in Lincoln football from the time he moved to the city from Lancashire in the early 1880's. He briefly played for the Rovers and was associated with City from their formation. Although not holding office he worked closely with the committee and was responsible for bringing the first professional 'imports' from Lancashire in the mid-1880's. He also served the club as an umpire and later as a referee, like Jack Strawson he was a League referee during the 1890's.

His period as honorary secretary was characterised by sound financial management and a policy of recruiting star players such as Will Gibson and 'Tich' Smith who were coming to the end of their careers. Following his spell at Newton Heath he was found guilty of making illegal payments to players and not keeping proper accounts and in Dec. 1904 he was banned from football management until 1 May 1907. By this time he had left the game and was running a Manchester public house.

CALDERHEAD, David snr.
Secretary-manager Sep. 1900 - May 1907
Personal details - see players section.

David Calderhead senior was in many ways the most successful manager in the club's history. During his seven year reign the team achieved a position in the top half of the Second Division on three occasions and in 1901/02 recorded best ever performances in both the League (5th, Div.2) and FA Cup (last 16 of the competition). His success was gained in a climate of financial restraint, there being a constant need to unearth talent from non-League football and to sell the better players to balance the books. He retained strong links with the Dumfries area, recruiting several men from Maxwelltown Volunteers, one of the town's senior clubs. He was said to have an intense dislike of publicity, later earning the nickname 'The Sphinx of Stamford Bridge', but he was one of the managers credited with starting the spiral of excessive transfer fees to obtain the players they wanted. In 26 years at Chelsea he twice gained promotion from the Second Division and took them to the 1915 FA Cup Final. In 1922 he was awarded the Football League's long-service medal. Father of David jnr. who also served the Imps as secretary-manager.

FRASER, George
Secretary July 1919 - Sep. 1919, Secretary-manager Sep. 1919 - Apr. 1921
Personal details - see players section

George Fraser's qualifications for the post of secretary-manager seem to have been twofold - he was the holder of the club's Football League appearance record and he was related to his predecessor Jack Strawson by marriage (their wives were sisters). He was not first choice for the position - local journalist Herbert Green had earlier been offered the job - and he inherited an extremely difficult situation. The training and recruitment of players had been in the hands of full-back Clem Jackson and a couple of directors, and preparations for the first season of post-war football were clearly inadequate. Not surprisingly the Imps had to seek re-election and were voted out of the League. Many of the older players departed in the close season and City were well on their way to the Midland League championship when Fraser moved on to Blundell Park.

He took Grimsby to third position in Division Three North in his first season but left when he felt the board were interfering too much in team selection and the recruitment of players.

CALDERHEAD, David jnr.
Secretary-manager Apr. 1921 - May 1924

Born: Dumfries, c.1891
Position: Centre-half
Career: Lincoln Schools; junior football; Chelsea Sep. 1907; Motherwell Apr. 1914 (Leicester Fosse as a guest during WW1); Clapton Orient 1919; CITY secretary-manager Apr. 1921 - May 1924.

Calderhead had played for the Lincoln Boys team in 1906 when he was a pupil of St. Peters School but then followed his father David snr. to Stamford Bridge where he waited several years for his FL debut. He made a total of just 43 League and FA Cup appearances for Chelsea before signing for Motherwell along with ex-City player Norrie Fairgray. On joining the Imps he was actually registered as a player but never turned out for the club. Lincoln had already been accepted into the newly formed Northern Section when he was appointed and he guided the club through the first three years of the new competition. It was a time of financial difficulties and a severe crisis in February 1923 was only overcome by the sale of a number of players and the co-operation of others in accepting free transfers. On leaving in May 1924 he became licensee of the Newmarket Hotel in Sincil Street.

HENSHALL, Horace Vincent
Secretary-manager May 1924 - June 1927
Born: Hednesford, Staffs., 14 June 1889
Died: 7 Dec. 1951
Position: Inside-forward

Career: Bridgetown Amateurs (Walsall League); Aston Villa (amat.) 1905, (prof.) May 1906; Notts County Nov. 1912 (guest for Barnsley during WW1); Sheffield Wednesday as player/reserve team coach June 1922; Chesterfield June 1923; CITY as secretary-manager May 1924 - June 1927; Notts County secretary-manager June 1927 - May 1934, secretary May 1934 - Apr. 1935.

Honour: Football League (1 app. vs Scottish League 1911)
(Notts County) FL Div.2 champions 1914

Horace Henshall was an experienced inside-forward who had just retired from playing when he came to Sincil Bank. His spell as secretary-manager proved unspectacular on the field, the Imps finishing no higher than eighth position in Division Three North. However, the club's finances improved slowly, although this was partly achieved by selling off the most promising players to bigger clubs. Henshall later returned to one of his former clubs, Notts County, and took them to the Division Three South title in 1930/31 before retiring to become a licensee in Nottingham.

PARKES, Harry Arnold
Secretary-manager June 1927 - May 1936

Born: Halesowen, Sep. 1888
Died: 11 Mar. 1947
Position: Outside-right
Career: Coombes Wood; Halesowen; West Bromwich Albion Feb. 1906; Coventry City Dec. 1908; West Bromwich Albion May 1914, becoming asst.-manager during WW1; Newport County secretary-manager June 1919 - May 1922; Chesterfield secretary-manager Aug. 1922 - Apr. 1927; CITY secretary-manager June 1927 - May 1936; Mansfield Town secretary-manager May 1936 - Jan. 1938; Notts County secretary-manager Jan. 1938 - July 1939.

Harry Parkes appeared in an FA Cup semi-final for West Bromwich Albion at the age of 17, but this was to prove his greatest achievement as a player for he soon moved on to Coventry City who were then members of the Southern League. His period as secretary-manager at Sincil Bank was a successful one - the Northern

Section title was won in 1931/32 and although the team competed in the Third Division for seven of his nine seasons they never finished lower than sixth. He showed considerable expertise at using the transfer market to the best advantage and in bringing in changes when they were needed. He continued in management almost until the outbreak of war before retiring to become landlord of the Station Hotel in Hucknall, Notts.

McCLELLAND, Joseph Bentley
Secretary-manager June 1936 - July 1947

Born: c.1884
Died: 3 July 1964
Career: Halifax and District FA secretary; Halifax Town secretary-manager May 1911 - July 1930; Sheffield Wednesday asst. manager 1930 - 1934; CITY secretary-manager June 1936 - July 1947, secretary July 1947 to cs 1949.

Joe McClelland became secretary-manager in rather unusual circumstances. On 17 June 1936 City had announced that Charlie Spencer, the former England international and currently Wigan Athletic secretary-manager, had been appointed but two days later they were forced to rethink their decision when the Lancashire club refused to release Spencer from his five year contract. McClelland who had been on the original short-list of four was then given the job the following week. He had been involved in football administration from around the age of 14 and was a central figure in the early days of Halifax Town before moving on to a position at Hillsborough which he eventually left due to ill-health. In his first season at Sincil Bank the Imps finished second in the Northern Section table, only missing out on the title when they were defeated at Stockport in the final match of the campaign. However the team went downhill after this, finishing 7th in 1937/38 and 17th the following season. He held the club together during the war years and in 1941/42 the team finished second on goal difference to Blackpool in the Football League North Championship. Joe remained in football until reaching the age of 65 when he went to work in the offices of Ruston & Hornsby, a local engineering firm. In 1945 he received the Football League's long-service award and in Sep. 1949 a crowd of 13,000 attended his benefit match between Lincoln City XI and 'Mac's All Star XI'. He died in St. George's Hospital, Lincoln at the age of 79.

ANDERSON, William
Manager July 1947 - Jan 1965

FL Record:
P 742 W 269(36.25%) D 167(22.50%) L 306 (41.23%)
Best performances: FL - 8th Div.2 1955/56; FA Cup - Round 4 1953/54 & 1960/61; FL Cup- Round 3 1963/64
Born: High Westwood, nr. Newcastle-upon-Tyne, 12 Jan. 1913
Died: 19 Feb. 1986
Position: left-back

Career: Medomsley Juniors; Chopwell Institute; Nottingham Forest Aug. 1931; Sheffield United Feb. 1932; Barnsley May 1935; retired through injury Nov. 1935; CITY trainer Aug. 1945, asst. manager Jan. 1947, trainer-manager July 1947, manager July 1948 - Sep. 1964, general manager - Oct. 1966; Nottingham Forest asst. manager Oct. 1966 - Jan. 1975; Arsenal scout from Feb. 1975; later Ipswich Town scout.

Bill Anderson's playing career was cut short when he fractured an ankle playing for Barnsley against Nottingham Forest. He returned to the north-east and worked for the Vickers Armstrong factory in Newcastle during the war before joining City where he was groomed as successor to Joe McClelland. In the summer of 1947 be became the first administrator to be given full control over team selection and signings and he was to go on to become the longest serving manager in the club's history.

His first season as manager was a tremendous one, with the club winning the Northern Section championship in style. Although they were relegated after just one year in Division Two the failure was mostly attributed to the directors' policy of operating with part-time players for much of the campaign. The side was rebuilt over the next couple of years and in 1951/52 the Division Three North title was won again - the team scored 121 League goals and set a new club record when they beat Crewe Alexandra 11-1 at Sincil Bank. Over the next nine seasons he worked wonders on a shoe-string budget to keep the Imps in the Second Division with the side often escaping relegation in desperate circumstances; in 1957/58 they recovered from a seemingly impossible position and stayed up by winning their final six matches. Relegation eventually came in 1960/61, the club then dropped straight through the Third Division and at the end of the 1962/63 season were required to seek re-election having finished in the bottom four of the Fourth.

There was a brief revival the following season but changes in the board of directors meant that team selection was taken out of Anderson's control in September 1964. He retained responsibility for tactics for a short while but even this was taken from him in January 1965 when he became 'general manager'. Although he was never associated with a particular style of play he brought a number of top class performers to Sincil Bank including George Hannah, Doug Wright, Jock Dodds and George Eastham. He was held in high regard throughout football, receiving a long-service award from the Football League in 1968, but sadly the way he was treated in his final few years at Sincil Bank seems to have left a lot to be desired. Outside of football he appeared for Lincolnshire at cricket in the Minor Counties and on one occasion stood un-successfully as an Independent candidate for the City Council in Park Ward which includes the Sincil Bank ground.

MOULSON, Cornelius ("Con")
Coach Jan. - Mar. 1965
FL Record: P8 W0(0%) D0(0%) L8(100%)
Personal details - see players section

Con Moulson was a strange choice by City's directors to succeed Bill Anderson in charge of the first team. He had been helping out with the youth side but was working full-time as a machinist for Rustons and was 58 years old at the time of his appointment. He resigned his factory job and took over the responsibility for the team's training and tactics. His first game saw City go down 2-0 at home to Bradford City - a side made up of 10 free transfers plus a player signed from Bourne Town - and things never improved. The Imps lost every match while he was in charge and he departed following the 2-0 home defeat by Doncaster Rovers on 27 Feb.

CHAPMAN, Roy Clifford
Player-coach Mar. 1965 - Oct. 1966

FL Record:
P 68 W16(23.52%) D 17(25%) L35(51.47%)
Best performances: FL - 22nd Div.4 1965/66; FA Cup -
Round 1 1965/66; FL Cup - Round 3 1966/67
Personal details - see players section

Roy Chapman succeeded Moulson at the start of Mar. 1965 by which time the Imps had lost 10 consecutive League matches. He produced a marginal improvement in fortunes - two of the remaining 10 games were won - but the club still had to apply for re-election. Despite a clear-out of players things were no better in the 1965/66 campaign. The team struggled early on despite the presence of Barry Hutchinson who was scoring almost a goal a game and after he was sold results got worse, with City again finishing in the bottom four. Chapman was replaced by Ron Gray soon after the start of the 1966/67 season but continued as a player until the following summer. He later returned to management with Stafford Rangers where he achieved some success - winning two FA Trophy finals and the 1971/72 Northern Premier League title. However, a brief spell in charge of Stockport County ended with the club having to seek re-election.

GRAY, Roland ("Ron")
Manager Oct. 1966 - May 1970

FL Record:
P 172 W 59(34.3%) D 51(29.65%) L 62(36.04%)
Best performances: FL - 8th Div.4 1968/69 and 1969/70;
FA Cup - Round 3 1968/69; FL Cup - Round 4 1967/68
Born: North Shields, 25 June 1920
Position: Half-back
Career: Tyne Dock; Sheffield United May 1938; CITY May - Sep. 1939; Watford Sep. 1942 (Dundee, Grimsby Town and Notts County as a guest during WW2) appointed trainer 1947 and manager June 1950 - Aug. 1951; Millwall trainer Oct. 1951, manager Jan. 1956 - Jan. 1958, manager again Jan. 1961 - Nov. 1963; CITY manager Oct. 1966 - May 1970; Ipswich Town chief scout Sep. 1970 - 1980's.

Ron Gray had been on City's books as a player in the late 1930's but war intervened to prevent him appearing in the first team. His professional career was ended by injury shortly after the return of peacetime football and he then commenced a lengthy spell on the backroom staff at Watford and later Millwall, briefly serving each as a manager. Immediately prior to his arrival at Sincil Bank he had been working as a freelance scout and physiotherapist.

He faced a grim task - the Imps had either been relegated or required to seek re-election in five of the previous six seasons, but he slowly began to rebuild the side. Although the club had to seek re-election yet again in 1966/67, by the start of the following campaign there had been a major transformation with new players, new team colours (red shirts and white shorts) and a new nickname ("The Red Imps"). At long last a semblance of pride had been restored to Sincil Bank and the fans were rewarded with the club's best ever performance in the League Cup. Mansfield, First Division Newcastle United and Torquay were all defeated before City went out to Derby County in a fourth round replay which attracted a ground record attendance of 23,196. The team finished in a respectable 13th place and began the 1968/69 season in tremendous form, winning the first four matches, before settling into a position on the fringe of the promotion race. They finally ended up 8th, a performance which was repeated the following season.

However, there had been changes in the board of directors with a new chairman installed, and in May 1970 Gray was sacked with 14 months of his contract still remaining. He later scouted for Ipswich Town for many years and was credited with spotting a number of the stars who were to help the Suffolk club achieve great success in the late 1970's and early '80's.

LOXLEY, Herbert
Manager July 1970 - Mar. 1971

FL Record:
P 31 W11(35.48%) D 4(12.9) L16(51.61%)
Best performances: FA Cup Round 3 1970/71; FL Cup Round 3 1970/71.
Personal details - see players section

After Gray departed the board promoted Bert Loxley, the club's trainer-coach since 1966, to the position of manager. The season began well and the team produced some impressive performances in both cup competitions. They defeated Grimsby and Sunderland in the League Cup before going out to Crystal Palace, and also reached the third round of the FA Cup where they were 3-0 up at Torquay after 31 minutes only to lose 4-3. However, the side suffered a loss of form in League matches, and after consecutive home defeats by Notts County and Bournemouth, Loxley returned to a backroom position and David Herd was appointed to replace him.

HERD, David George
Manager Mar. 1971 - Dec. 1972

FL Record:
P 82 W 30(36.58%) D 30 (36.58%) L 22(26.82%)
Best performances: FL - 5th Div.4 1971/72; FA Cup - Round 1 1971/72 & 1972/73; FL Cup-Round 3 1971/72.
Born: Hamilton, Lanarks., 15 Apr. 1934
Position: Inside/centre-forward
Career: Stockport County (amat.) Sep. 1949, (prof.) Apr. 1951; Arsenal Aug. 1954 (£10,000); Manchester United July 1961 (£37,000); Stoke City July 1968 - cs 1970; Waterford Dec. 1970; CITY manager Mar. 1971 - Dec. 1972.

Honours: Scotland international (5 app.)
Scotland under-23 international (2 app.)
(Manchester United) FL champions 1965, 1967
FA Cup winner 1963

David Herd enjoyed a glittering playing career, winning Scottish international honours and scoring over 100 FL goals for Manchester United where he had appeared in the same team of great players such as Best, Law and Charlton. His name was linked with City in Aug. 1970 but after recovering fitness he went to play in the League of Ireland. However, as the team struggled in the early spring of 1971 his name was again linked with Sincil Bank and in Mar. 1971 he was finally appointed manager after Bert Loxley returned to backroom duties.

There was no immediate change in the club's fortunes with just 2 wins from the final 15 matches, leaving them in 21st position and requiring yet another re-election bid. In the summer a number of new players were signed up and for the first time in many years the Imps mounted a serious promotion campaign. Gates were up - over 15,000 for the 'derby' games with Grimsby and Scunthorpe - and the team seemed almost invincible at home. Herd was rewarded by being named Manager of the Month for Jan., the first City boss to receive the award, but sadly it all went wrong in the final weeks of the season and the team finished in fifth place. Two of the major stars of League of Ireland football - Brendan Bradley and Jimmy McGeough - were recruited in the close season but after a bright start the team suffered a loss of confidence. There was growing talk of a crisis at the club and on 7th Dec. it was announced that Herd had quit as manager and was returning to a career looking after his business interests in the Manchester and Stoke areas. Lincoln was his only experience of football management but he is remembered for his tactical innovations. The team played a defensive formation away from home often using a sweeper as a fifth defender, but when on form they produced some sparkling football at Sincil Bank.

TAYLOR, Graham
Manager Dec. 1972 - June 1977

FL Record:
FL P 209 W 97(46.41%) D 60(28.7%) L 52(24.88%)
Best performances: FL - 9th Div.3 1976/77; FA Cup - Round 4 1975/76; FL Cup - Round 3 1975/76
Personal details - see players section

With the possible exception of David Calderhead snr., Graham Taylor ranks as the most successful manager in the history of Lincoln City. He was just 28 years old at the time of his appointment making him the youngest manager in the Football League. His early days in the post proved a real struggle and it was only after he appointed George Higgins, a member of the backroom staff at Blundell Park, as his assistant that the team began to pick up. His first League victory was not achieved until his twelfth game in charge and that only with a last minute goal, but City then lost only 3 of their remaining 14 matches and finished in 10th position.

The next season produced nothing particularly outstanding with the Imps again ending up in mid-table, but Taylor was slowly easing out the staff he had inherited and replacing them with his own players. Soon after the start of the 1974/75 campaign the team put together a fine string of results and were in the running for promotion. However, poor results towards the end of the season left them needing to win their final match at Southport. Unfortunately City were beaten 3-2 and stayed down on goal difference. This disappointment proved only a temporary set-back and the Imps swept all before them in 1975/76. Over 100 League goals were scored and Fourth Division records were set for most wins (32), least defeats (4) and most points (74). Taylor stayed one more season, taking the Imps to 9th place in Division Three, but despite signing a three year contract he left for Watford and an annual salary of £25,000 in the summer of 1977, City receiving a £26,000 "transfer fee" as compensation.

It was at Lincoln that he developed many of the ideas which he was to use later in his career - a concentration on direct ('long ball') tactics, a belief that the football club was an integral part of the local community and a recognition that a healthy club needed a sound youth policy: a team was entered in the Northern Intermediate League for the first time and a nursery side established in the Sheffield area to develop schoolboy talent. His greatest skill was, and is, man management and in particular an ability to get the best out of the resources available to him. Taylor has since gone on to great success elsewhere taking Watford from the Fourth Division to runners-up position in the First and winning promotion at Villa Park. He was much criticised for his team selection and tactics during his spell as England manager which ended with failure to qualify for the 1994 World Cup finals but has since begun to restore his reputation at club level with Wolves.

KERR, George A.M.
Manager June 1977 - Dec. 1977
and Dec. 1985 - Mar. 1987

FL Record:

P 77 W 21(27.27%) D 22(28.57%) L 34(44.15%)

Best performances: FL - 21st Div.3 1985/86; FA Cup - Round 1 1977/78 and 1986/87; FL Cup - Round 2 1977/78 and 1986/87

Born: Alexandria, Dumbartonshire, 9 Jan. 1943

Position: Inside-forward

Career: Vale of Leven; Renton Select; Barnsley May 1960; Bury Mar. 1966 (£10,000); Scunthorpe United Feb. 1968; CITY as asst. manager and coach July 1973, manager June - Dec. 1977; Grimsby Town asst. manager Aug. 1978, manager July 1979 - Jan. 1982; Rotherham United manager Mar. 1983 - May 1985; Derby County advisor; CITY manager Dec. 1985 - Mar. 1987; Derby County advisor; Boston United manager Nov. 1987 - Jan. 1990; Southampton scout.

George Kerr came to Sincil Bank as Graham Taylor's assistant having just completed a solid playing career in which he made over 300 FL appearances. He was closely involved with the club's youth policy and turned down the offer of a coaching post at Scunthorpe to become City's manager. He inherited a squad with several of the more experienced players past their prime and a number of talented youngsters who were not quite ready for regular League football. Kerr gave opportunities to several teenagers including Mick Harford and the on-loan Alan Cork but results were not as good as expected and he was dismissed after a run of only one win in nine games. He was later taken on by Grimsby Town who won promotion in his first season as coach. He was subsequently made manager and proved an instant success, taking the Mariners to the Third Division title in 1979/80. A two year spell at Millmoor followed before he returned to Sincil Bank as successor to John Pickering.

He brought in a number of his former Rotherham players including Bobby Mitchell and Kevin Kilmore but a poor run towards the end of the season saw the Imps relegated to Division Four. The 1986/87 campaign began quite brightly and City were on the fringe of the promotion race until just before Christmas but a sequence of eight defeats in nine games left them looking likely candidates for relegation out of the League and led to Kerr being sacked for a second time. Both of his spells as manager were characterised by a willingness to give chances to the club's teenagers and although many of these eventually went on to higher grade football his teams suffered from the consequent lack of experience.

BELL, William John
Manager Dec. 1977 - Oct. 1978

FL Record:

P 40 W 11(27.5%) D 13(32.5%) L 16(40%)

Best performances: FL - 16th Div.3 1977/78; FL Cup - Round 1 1978/79

Born: Johnstone, Renfrewshire, 3 Sep. 1937

Position: Full-back

Career: Neilston Juniors; Queens Park 1957; Leeds United July 1960; Leicester City Sep. 1967 (£40,000); Brighton & Hove Albion player-coach July 1969; Birmingham City coach May 1970, manager Sep. 1975 - Sep. 1977; Ipswich Town scout; CITY Manager Dec. 1977 - Oct. 1978; Campus Crusade for Christ, USA coach from Oct. 1978.

Honours: Scotland international (2 app.)
Scotland amateur international (2 app.)
(Leeds United) FL Div.2 champions 1964
FA Cup finalist 1965
Inter-Cities Fairs Cup finalist 1967

Willie Bell arrived at Sincil Bank with an impressive career in top class football behind him, having made over 200 FL appearances at Elland Road and spent two years as manager of First Division Birmingham City. He took over a team in relegation trouble but began with an eight match run without defeat and steered the Imps to the relative safety of 16th position. However, although the following season began with a victory the rest of the early games were dismal and by late October the team had lost 10 of their first 14 League fixtures. Following a 3-0 home defeat by Swindon Town Bell announced his departure for a position as football coach with the religious group Campus Crusade for Christ in Colorado, USA.

MURPHY, Colin Victor
Manager Nov. 1978 - May 1985 and May 1987 - May 1990

FL/GMVC Record:

P 440 W 181(41.13%) D 123(27.95%) L 136 (30.90%)

Best performances: FL - 4th Div.3 1981/82; FA Cup - Round 2 four occasions; FL Cup - Round 3 1981/82 and 1982/83

Born: Croydon, 21 Jan. 1944
Position: Full-back
Career: Tunbridge Wells Rangers Nov. 1965 - cs 1967; Folkestone Oct. 1968; Gravesend Dec. 1968; Hastings United June 1971, becoming coach Jan. 1972; Gravesend trainer July 1972; Nottingham Forest asst. coach Nov. 1972; Derby County reserve team coach Oct. 1973, caretaker-manager Nov. 1976, manager Jan. 1977 - Sep. 1977; Notts County asst. manager Oct. 1977; CITY manager Nov. 1978 - May 1985; Stockport County manager Aug. -Nov. 1985; Ittihad (Saudi Arabia) coach Nov. 1985; Stockport County manager Nov. 1986 - May 1987; CITY manager May 1987 - May 1990; Leicester City youth team coach Aug. 1990; Luton Town asst. manager June 1991; Southend United manager May 1992 to Apr. 1993.

Colin Murphy never played League football but won a reputation as a hard-tackling full-back in the Southern League during the late 1960's. He was given his first experience of management at Hastings, taking over team selection after the manager resigned in Mar. 1972. However, he was rejected by the directors when they made a permanent appointment the following summer - a development which proved to be an advantage to Murphy for within six months he had joined Dave Mackay and Des Anderson on the coaching staff at Forest. He followed Mackay to the Baseball Ground where he did well in developing the club's youngsters. He had a brief spell as manager but this was ended when the board brought in Tommy Docherty to replace him. A year as assistant to Jimmy Sirrel followed before he was appointed manager at Sincil Bank.

He was unable to prevent a very poor team from being relegated to Division Four but then rebuilt soundly during the close season and took the team to seventh place at the end of 1979/80. The Imps were among the leaders from the start of the following season and won promotion comfortably, losing only two of the final 24 games and setting a new Fourth Division record by conceding just 25 League goals. The next two seasons provided City's fans with some of the best performances since the 1950's. A late surge in 1981/82 saw the team rise from the fringe of the relegation zone into the middle of the promotion race, and had the last match at Fulham been won the Imps would have been back in Division Two, but a draw meant the London club went up instead.

The excellent run continued at the start of 1982/83 and City were soon well clear at the top of the table, reaching their peak with a 9-0 victory over Bournemouth just before Christmas. Then the pressures of operating with a small first team squad and demoralisation arising from the board's plans to cut the players' bonuses eventually told, and they drifted away to finish in sixth position. Murphy spent two more years with the club, selling his best players to ensure financial stability and left after the final match of the 1984/85 season when 56 supporters tragically lost their lives in the fire at Valley Parade.

He returned in the summer of 1987 after spells with Stockport and in Saudi Arabia, with the Imps now rel-

egated out of the League. The side was rebuilt completely, several of the players coming from his former Stockport team, and despite a bad start the Imps battled away to the Vauxhall Conference title - a remarkable achievement at the first attempt. He stayed two further years before leaving the club by mutual consent.

Murphy's teams were known for their high degree of organisation and their competitiveness. He was exceptionally good at developing young players recruited from non-League football and produced a string of talent later sold to higher grade clubs for large fees, notably a series of combative hustling strikers including Tony Cunningham, Mick Harford and John Fashanu. He was also famed for his programme notes which were on occasions remarkable works of literature and earned him the award of a 'Golden Bull' from the Plain English Campaign in Nov. 1989. He has since returned to coaching apart from a short period as manager of Southend which ended when the club appeared to be on their way to relegation.

PICKERING, John
Manager July 1985 - Dec. 1985
FL Record:
P 21 W 4(19.04%) D 6(28.57%) L 11(52.38%)
Best performances: FA Cup - Round 1 1985/86; FL Cup -Round 1 1985/86
Born: Thornaby-on-Tees, 7 Nov. 1944
Position: Half-back
Career: Newcastle United July 1963; Halifax Town Sep. 1965 (£1,250); Barnsley July 1974; Blackburn Rovers coach June 1975, manager Nov. 1978 - May 1979; Carlisle United coach Apr. 1980; CITY asst. manager Nov. 1981, manager July 1985 - Dec. 1985; Newcastle United reserve team coach July 1986, first team coach Sep. 1987; CITY asst. manager Nov. 1988; Middlesbrough youth coach May 1990.

John Pickering, the club's assistant manager since Nov. 1981, was the man chosen to succeed Colin Murphy as manager in the summer of 1985. He had spent most of his playing career at Halifax, where he made a club record 367 FL appearances, before entering coaching at Blackburn under Jim Smith (himself a former Halifax player). The Imps had lost several experienced players over the close season and he recruited a number of new faces including former England international Bob Latchford as replacements. The team had a fairly good start and were sixth in the table at the start of October but then suffered a series of defeats and any remaining confidence seemed to disappear after a 7-0 defeat at Derby. Pickering was finally sacked following the 4-0 home defeat by Cardiff on 14 Dec. - the team having lost 10 of their previous 11 matches. He subsequently went back to coaching and returned to Sincil Bank in Nov. 1988 for a brief spell as assistant to Murphy again.

DANIEL, Peter
Caretaker-manager Mar. 1987 - May 1987
Record: FL P 14 W 2(14.38%) D 5(35.71%) L 7(50%)
Personal details - see players section

Peter Daniel was on the club's books as a player when he succeeded George Kerr as manager in Mar. 1987, his appointment being on a caretaker basis until the end of the season. City drew his first match at Rochdale which left them in 18th position but his short spell in control proved a disaster. Only two of the remaining 14 matches were won and although they had appeared safe after beating Northampton Town 3-1, the Imps went into the final match at Swansea needing points to ensure they retained their League membership. They lost 2-0, the other results went against them and City went down to the Vauxhall Conference on goal difference - ironically this was the only occasion in the whole of the season that they were actually bottom of the table. Daniel resumed his playing career with Burnley while the board turned to Colin Murphy to rescue the club.

CLARK, Allan John
Manager June 1990 - Nov. 1990
FL Record: P 15 W 2(13.33%) D 6(40%) L 7(46.66%)
Best performances: FA Cup - Round 1 1990/91; FL Cup -Round 1 1990/91
Born: Willenhall, Staffs., 31 July 1946
Position: Centre-forward
Career: Walsall (appr.) 1961, (prof.) Aug. 1963; Fulham Mar. 1966 (£35,000); Leicester City June 1968 (£150,000); Leeds United July 1969 (£165,000); Barnsley player-manager May 1978 - Oct. 1980; Leeds United manager Oct. 1980 - June 1982; Scunthorpe United manager Feb. 1983 - Aug. 1984; Barnsley manager July 1985 - Nov. 1989; CITY manager June 1990 - Nov. 1990.

Honours: England international (19 app.)
England under-23 international (6 app.)
Football League (2 app.)
(Leeds United) FL champions 1974
(Leicester City) FA Cup finalist 1969
(Leeds United) FA Cup winner 1972; finalist 1970, 1973
European Cup finalist 1975
European Fairs Cup winner 1971

Allan Clarke had enjoyed a lengthy career in top class football, appearing in four FA Cup finals and scoring 110 goals in 270 FL games at Elland Road. His managerial career had been less successful for although he had won promotion at Barnsley and Scunthorpe, Leeds were relegated to Division Two under his control and Scunthorpe made a rapid return to Division Four after his initial success. He arrived at Sincil Bank in a blaze of publicity and immediately denounced the long-ball strategy of his predecessor Colin Murphy. The Imps adopted a passing style but proceeded to win only one of the first 11 matches. Although skilful players were brought in, most had experienced little more than Central League football and the side appeared lightweight and lacking in power up front. Clarke was

sacked after just 179 days in the job and with 18 months of his contract still to run. At the time the Imps had lost four consecutive games and were lying 23rd in the Fourth Division table.

THOMPSON, Steven Paul
Manager Nov. 1990 - May 1993

FL Record: P 114(40.35%) W 46(40.35%)
D 31(27.19%) L 37(32.45%)
Best performances: FL - 8th Div.3 1992/93 [left before final match]; FA Cup - Round 1 1991/92 and 1992/93; FL Cup - Round 2 1992/93.
Personal details - see players section

Club captain Steve Thompson was the board's choice to succeed Allan Clarke. His immediate task was to pull the team away from the bottom of the table and he achieved this comfortably, leading the Imps to a final position of 14th. The team struggled badly in the 1991/92 season and were fourth from bottom in early Feb. but then lost just once in the final 17 matches, rising to finish in 10th position. This excellent run meant that the Imps started 1992/93 as one of the bookmakers' favourites for promotion - but the challenge for Third Division status never really got off the ground due to too many crucial defeats. When it became clear that the club would not qualify for the play-offs the board announced that his contract was not to be renewed and he left before the final match of the season. It seemed a harsh decision in view of the Imps playing record under his control but he paid the penalty for the high expectations he had created and for some poor performances at Sincil Bank. Thompson's team played a version of the long-ball game and were generally sound defensively but lacked power and imagination up front. His away record was remarkable -20 wins and 21 draws from 58 matches - unfortunately the home performances were often abysmal and a low point was reached in Sep. 1991 when City crashed to a record 6-0 defeat at Sincil Bank against Barnet.

ALEXANDER, Keith
Manager May 1993 - May 1994

FL Record:
P 43 W 13(30.23%) D 11(25.58%) L 19(44.18%)
Best performances: FL - 8th Div.3 1993/94; FA Cup - Round 2 1993/94; FL Cup - Round 2 1993/94
Personal details - see players section

Keith Alexander had achieved considerable success with City's youth team and had been responsible for the development of talented youngsters such as Matt Carbon, Ben Dixon and Steve Williams.

He took charge of the first team for the final match of the 1992/93 season on a caretaker basis and was appointed permanently shortly afterwards. The Imps had a poor start to the 1993/94 campaign but then hit a run of form towards the end of the year, the high spot being two excellent performances against Everton in the Coca Cola Cup. Alexander then lost his most creative player, David Puttnam, through injury and the team seemed to lose their way with no set pattern apparent either in team selection or tactics. After finishing the season in 18th position Alexander was sacked with 12 months of his contract still to run and he later accepted a post as youth coach at Field Mill. In his short spell as manager the Imps played neat open football, characterised by a passing game - thus providing a considerable contrast to the tactics of Thompson. However, the team lacked steel and many of the performances in the second half of the season were dismal with too many home games lost.

ELLIS, Samuel
Manager from May 1994
Personal details - see players section

Like seven of the present board's eight appointments Ellis had previously been employed by Lincoln City, having been skipper of the 1975/76 Fourth Division championship side. He has considerable experience of management in the lower divisions and led Blackpool to promotion from the Fourth Division before taking Bury to the Third Division play-offs in 1989/90. He did particularly well in his seven years at Bloomfield Road operating with limited resources and often having to sell his best players to survive. His appointment as manager at Sincil Bank came after a short period assisting the club on a casual basis.

BIBLIOGRAPHY

The Football League Appearance Registers 1888 - 1993

Athletic News
Football Echo
Lincoln Daily News
The Lincoln Gazette and Lincolnshire Times

The Lincoln Leader and County Advertiser
The Lincolnshire Chronicle
Lincolnshire Echo

Lincoln City F.C. official programme

Ambrosen,A.K. Ironsides-A Lifetime in the League: Who's Who of Newport County 1912-1989(Yore Publications, 1991)

Association of Football Statisticians   The Football League Appearances and Goalscorers 1888-1984 (AFS)

Association of Football Statisticians   The Southern League First Division 1894-1920 (AFS)

Bartlett, C.J. et al   Lincolnshire Cricketers 1828-1993 (Association of Cricket Statisticians and Historians, 1993)

"Benny Dix"   Cock o' the North - An Account of Lincoln City F.C.'s Career in the Northern Section (1932)

Bluff, T. and Watson, B.   Donny : The Official History of Doncaster Rovers F.C. (Yore Publications, 1994)

Edwards, L.   The Official Centenary History of the Southern League 1894-1994 (Paper Plane, 1993)

Emms, S. and McPherson, D.   Who's Who of the Football League 1919-1939 (AFS, 1993-1994)

Goodwin, B.   The Spurs Alphabet : A Complete Who's Who of Tottenham Hotspur F.C. (ACL & Polar, 1992)

Groom,A. and Robinson,M. Peterborough United Football Club - Official History of the Posh (Yore Publications, 1992)

Hammond, M.   European Football Yearbook annually 1991-1994 (Sports Projects)

Hugman, B.J.   Football League Players' Records 1946-1988 (Arena Press, 1988)

Inglis, S.   League Football and the Men Who Made it : The Official Centenary History of the Football League 1888-1988 (Collins Willow, 1988)

Jose, C.   NASL : A Complete Record of the North American Soccer League (Breedon Books, 1989)

Lamming, D.   A Who's Who of Grimsby Town A.F.C. 1890-1985 (Hutton Press, 1985)

Lamming, D.   A Who's Who of Hull City A.F.C. 1904-1984 (Hutton Press, 1984)

Lamming, D.   Who's Who of Liverpool 1892-1989 (Breedon Books, 1989)

Lincoln City Centenary Souvenir (Lincolnshire Standard Group & Lincoln City F.C., 1983)

Mason, T.   Association Football and English Society 1863-1915 (Harvester Press, 1980)

Matthews T.   Aston Villa Who's Who 1874-1989 (Paper Plane, 1989)

Matthews T.   Who's Who of West Bromwich Albion 1879-1989 (West Bromwich Albion F.C., 1989)

Matthews T. and Allman, G.   The History of Walsall Football Club 1888 to 1992 (Sports Leisure Concepts, 1992)

Matthews, T. and Baker, R.   Who's Who of Birmingham City 1875 to 1991 (Sports Leisure Concepts, 1991)

Mortimer, G.   The Who's Who of Derby County (Breedon Books, 1992)

O'Connor,M. and O'Connor,P. Coventry City Footballers 1908-1993. Complete Who's Who (Yore Publications, 1993)

Rollin, J.   Soccer at War 1939-45 (Collins Willow, 1985)

Rothmans Football Yearbook, eds. J.Rollin, T.Williams and P.Dunk (annually 1970-1994)

Sawyer, J.J.   Down the Years with Lincoln City (1954)

Turner, D. and White, A.   The Breedon Book of Football Managers (Breedon Books, 1993)

Turner, D. and White, A.   Fulham : A Complete Record 1879-1987 (Breedon Books, 1987)

Wells R.   Who's Who of the Football League 1888-1915 (AFS, 1992-1994)

From
'YORE PUBLICATIONS'
12 The Furrows, Harefield,
Middx. UB9 6AT

(Free lists issued 3 times per year. For your first list please send a S.A.E.)

DONNY - The Official History of Doncaster Rovers *(Tony Bluff and Barry Watson)* Written by two supporters of the Club, the full statistics (from 1879) and including line-ups (from 1901). The book is well illustrated, including many line-ups, and also contains the full written history of the Club. Hardback with full coloured dustjacket and 240 pages. Price £14-95 plus £1-80 postage. packing.

COLCHESTER UNITED - The Official History of the 'U's' *(Hal Mason)*
With football involvement from the 1920's, the Author - a former journalist and Colchester programme editor - is well qualified to relate this complete history of the Club since its formation in 1937 (including complete statistics and lineups from this season). Large Hardback, 240 pages, priced £14-95 plus £2-70 postage.

AMBER IN THE BLOOD - History of Newport County: *(Tony Ambrosen).* The full written story of football in Newport from the pre-County days up to and including the recently formed Newport AFC club. The text is well illustrated, and a comprehensive statistical section provides all the results, attendances, goalscorers, etc. from 1912 to 1993 - the various Leagues and principal Cup competitions; additionally seasonal total players' appearances are included. Large hardback with 176 large pages is exceptional value at £13-95 plus £2-60 postage.

KILLIE - The Official History (125 Years of Kilmarnock F.C.) *(David Ross).* A very detailed history of Scotland's oldest professional Club. The statistics section (including line-ups) cover the period 1873 to 1994, and there are over 200 illustrations, including a team group for most seasons. A large hardback containing 256 pages, priced £15-95 plus £3-50 postage.

REJECTED F.C. VOLUME 1 (Reprint) *(By Dave Twydell)* The revised edition of this popular book - now in hardback - this volume provides the comprehensive histories of: Aberdare Athletic, Ashington, Bootle, Bradford (Park Avenue), Burton (Swifts, Wanderers and United), Gateshead/South Shields, Glossop, Loughborough, Nelson, Stalybridge Celtic and Workington. The 288 well illustrated pages also contain the basic statistical details of each club. Price £12-95 plus £1-30 postage. (Also *Rejected F.C. of Scotland:* Volume 1 covers Edinburgh and The South (Edinburgh City, Leith Athletic, St.Bernards, Armadale, Broxburn United, Bathgate, Peebles Rovers, Mid-Annandale, Nithsdale Wanderers and Solway Star - 288 pages). Volume 2 covers Glasgow and District (Abercorn, Arthurlie, Beith, Cambuslang, Clydebank, Cowlairs, Johnstone, Linthouse, Northern, Third Lanark, and Thistle - 240 pages). Each priced £12-95 plus £1-30 postage.

FOOTBALL LEAGUE - GROUNDS FOR A CHANGE (By Dave Twydell). A 424 page, A5 sized, Hardback book. A comprehensive study of all the Grounds on which the current English Football League clubs previously played. Every Club that has moved Grounds is included, with a 'Potted' history of each, plus 250 illustrations. Plenty of 'reading' material, as well as an interesting reference book. Price £13-95 Plus £1-70 Postage.

THROUGH THE TURNSTILES *(by Brian Tabner)* This incredible book which provides the average attendance of every English Football League club, for every season from 1888/89 to 1991/92. Well illustrated, and also relates the development of the game (angled towards attendances). Also details of the best supported 'away' teams, season ticket sales over the years, etc. Large format hardback and 208 packed pages. An excellent read at £13-95 plus £1-70 Postage.

COVENTRY CITY FOOTBALLERS (The Complete Who's Who)
By Martin & Paul O'Connor. One of the most detailed books of its type. Every Football (and Southern) League player has been included - around 700. Seasonal appearances of every player, brief personal details, 'pen pictures', together with very detailed information on the movements of the players to other clubs. Plus: around 100 photo's of the Club's most memorable men, and information on the principal players from the very early days. A hardback book with 224 large pages. £13-95 plus £2-60 postage.

HISTORY OF THE LANCASHIRE FOOTBALL ASSOCIATION 1878-1928. **A rare historical and fascinating** hardback reprint (first published in 1928). Contains the history of the formative days of Lancashire football. Sections within the 288 pages include the early histories of about 20 Clubs (Manchester Utd., Wigan Borough, Rochdale, etc.), Lancashire Cup competitions, Biographies, etc. For those interested in the development of the game, this is a 'must', and you will definitely not be disappointed. Price £12-95 Plus £1-30 Postage.

THE CODE WAR (Graham Williams)
A fascinating look back on football's history - from the earliest days up to the First World War. 'Football' is covered in the broadest sense, for the book delves into the splits over the period to and from Rugby Union and Rugby League, as well as Football (Soccer). Potted histories of many of the Clubs are included, as is a comprehensive index. 192 page hardback, price £10-95 plus £1-20 postage.